The Fifth Estate

Oxford Studies in Digital Politics

Series Editor: Andrew Chadwick, Professor of Political Communication
in the Centre for Research in Communication and Culture and
the Department of Social Sciences, Loughborough University

The Fifth Estate

THE POWER SHIFT OF THE DIGITAL AGE

WILLIAM H. DUTTON

OXFORD
UNIVERSITY PRESS

OXFORD
UNIVERSITY PRESS

Oxford University Press is a department of the University of Oxford. It furthers
the University's objective of excellence in research, scholarship, and education
by publishing worldwide. Oxford is a registered trade mark of Oxford University
Press in the UK and certain other countries.

Published in the United States of America by Oxford University Press
198 Madison Avenue, New York, NY 10016, United States of America.

Library of Congress Cataloging-in-Publication Data
Names: Dutton, William H., 1947– author.
Title: The fifth estate : the power shift of the digital age / William H. Dutton.
Other titles: 5th estate
Description: First Edition. | New York : Oxford University Press, [2023] |
Series: Oxford studies in digital politics | Includes bibliographical
references and index.
Identifiers: LCCN 2022054709 | ISBN 9780190688370 (Paperback) |
ISBN 9780190688363 (Hardback) | ISBN 9780190688394 (epub) | ISBN 9780190688400
Subjects: LCSH: Internet—Social aspects. | Information society. | Pluralism. | Responsibility.
Classification: LCC HM851 .D878 2023 | DDC 302.23/1—dc23/eng/20230224
LC record available at https://lccn.loc.gov/2022054709

DOI: 10.1093/oso/9780190688363.001.0001

Paperback printed by Marquis Book Printing, Canada
Hardback printed by Bridgeport National Bindery, Inc., United States of America

Preface

Networks—anchored in information and communication technologies like the internet—are used in ways that primarily follow and reinforce the existing distribution of power in societies. However, the internet and social media are enabling a new network power shift—the empowerment of networked individuals that can challenge institutions of the press, governments, business and industry, and public intellectuals and hold them more accountable to the public. This shift in the potential for networks to be used in ways that empower ordinary people is the power shift of the digital age.

This book explains the empirical basis for this claim and provides a theoretical understanding of its importance to democracy, politics, and society. Public understanding of the reality illuminated by the metaphor of a Fifth Estate is critical to its future. The empowerment of networked individuals exists by virtue of technology and policy choices across the world, but these choices are increasingly challenged by public fears, inappropriate regulatory responses, and geopolitical retreats from the vision of a free, open, and global internet.

It is in that spirit that this book seeks to convey the idea of a Fifth Estate as an empirically observable phenomenon as well as an ideal type that can be used to distinguish actors contributing to the Fifth Estate. It should be of value to those with a serious interest in the social and political dynamics of the digital age. It is relevant as well to those who place great promise in or hold deep concerns about the societal implications of the internet and related digital media.

I am optimistic about reaching well beyond academia with this book as so many people have great interest in and experience with the internet. Moreover, I have found the idea of the Fifth Estate to be relatively easy to convey to people well outside of my field. In fact, you may enjoy one very memorable instance for me when I was talking about this concept with a person I met in a jacuzzi. It was so understandable to this gentleman that it became the title of a movie!

The jacuzzi story occurred in 2011, around a talk I gave at the Alpbach Forum, in Austria, about my conception of the Fifth Estate. After my talk, sitting in a jacuzzi at my hotel in Alpbach, I met Daniel Domscheit-Berg—a key person at WikiLeaks, whom its founder, Julian Assange, had famously expelled. Like me, Domscheit-Berg was in Alpbach to speak. Daniel was lounging at the side of the pool with his partner—she had also been jettisoned from WikiLeaks. Learning who he was, I asked him about WikiLeaks and his new enterprise, OpenLeaks, explaining how central the concept of a Fifth Estate could be in helping him see the larger role of his work in shaping power shifts of the digital age.

We had a fascinating conversation about Julian Assange and WikiLeaks. It was the year before, in 2010, that WikiLeaks released some of its most notorious content, including the Afghan War Diary, the Iraq War Logs, and classified diplomatic cables of the US State Department. Having been in receipt of this material, Julian Assange and his colleagues worked with a few respected newspapers to redact this material for public distribution in order to protect individuals identified in the cables. However, an unredacted set of these files became available through a hack that might have been enabled by a failure of WikiLeaks to adequately update passwords to the protected and unredacted files—a breach that motivated Domscheit-Berg to leave and marked the beginning of the end of a dramatic chapter for WikiLeaks.

During that conversation in Alpbach, I briefed Domscheit-Berg on my idea of the Fifth Estate, arguing that WikiLeaks provided an excellent illustration of a major political transformation—one that enables individuals like Julian Assange, other whistleblowers, and many networked individuals to use the internet and related social media in ways that can hold governments and other major institutions more accountable for their activities.

Since that memorable jacuzzi, I did not cross paths with Domscheit-Berg again. However, I later saw the 2013 release of the film *The Fifth Estate*, in which Daniel was the hero—opposing Julian Assange and providing insider information about WikiLeaks to a fictional journalist of *The Guardian* newspaper. As I watched the movie, I saw our conversation from 2011 played out in the closing dialogue between Domscheit-Berg and the journalist, who concluded that what happened with WikiLeaks was heralding an entirely new information era enabled by the internet. Wikileaks was "charting a course" for changes in the dynamics of power shifts among actors across the globe.

While the script of this conversation might have captured key features of my basic argument, I have argued that leaks are only one of many strategies that networked individuals can use to enhance their networked communicative power relative to other and often more powerful actors across all sectors of society.

Of course, the Fifth Estate has been used not only as the title of a movie about WikiLeaks. It has also been used in many other ways, such as bloggers as watchdogs of the press. Some bloggers act as watchdogs, or so-called media watchdogs, even though the Fifth Estate envisions a watchdog role across all institutions, including the press. And it was used by others to refer to think tanks as independent checks on government and industry. Some think tanks use the internet to enhance their role, but they are not the Fifth Estate from my perspective. It has even been used as the title for a Canadian television show that serves as a watchdog by reporting investigations into various topics of importance to society. None of these capture the full range of actors in the Fifth Estate and the strategies they have at hand in our digital age. Even if you think you know what I mean by a Fifth Estate, please read on. You might well discover it to be a broader and more meaningful concept than you imagined and begin applying it to your own work.

As I will explain in this book, I have adapted a preindustrial age metaphor of estates of the realm to reframe discussion of the social and political role of the internet and social media in politics and everyday life in the digital age. I have been working on the development of this concept since first presenting the basic argument behind my use of this term in 2007.

Essentially, the Fifth Estate connotes a network power shift—unique to the digital age of the internet and related social media. It is composed of a moving, ever-changing collectivity of individuals who are strategically using online networks in ways that enhance their informational and communicative power vis-à-vis other actors. As a metaphor, the concept seeks to convey a new theoretical conception of how the use of the internet has fundamentally changed the dynamics of communication and power in politics and society—making politics and society more pluralistic by enabling networked individuals to exert a more independent and strategic role in shaping information and communication across all sectors of society.

In the social sciences, the Fifth Estate would be called a "sensitizing concept" as it is designed to bring you—the reader—to a set of concrete empirical observations. Once identified, the Fifth Estate is used as well as an "ideal type," providing a description of strategic behavior that fits or departs from those patterns identified with this concept. In similar ways, notions of the Fourth Estate define the characteristics of an ideal type of independent press. As with other theoretical concepts, once understood, as a sensitizing concept or as an ideal type, it tells you what to look for—what is important—to understand the politics of the Fifth Estate in the digital age.

That said, this concept captures how the new media of networking are reshaping not only political institutions and processes, such as governance, but also nearly all institutions and processes of society, from business and industry to the news and everyday life. The object of this book is to fully explain this concept, which will provide an understanding of the political and other social dynamics of empowering networked individuals of the digital age.

In describing my conception and anchoring it in empirical research, I argue that this conception should define the Fifth Estate for the field going forward. Ironically, my hope is that this ancient metaphor will help discussion of the political dynamics of the internet to break away from more traditional, institutionally centric conceptions of democratic and other social processes, which miss some of the most fundamental changes ushered in by the Fifth Estate. Drawing on decades of research, this book explains the nature and significance of these innovations and their social and political implications, illustrated by examples of the Fifth Estate in action. In such ways, this book seeks to provide fresh insights and analysis of the far-reaching social, political, and cultural changes tied to the use of social networking and other internet-related digital media and technologies.

My argument is that the framing of the concept of the Fifth Estate provides a new and empirically grounded perspective on how the internet has been used to support more pluralist democratic and social accountability. The controversies surrounding political and social upheavals over the past decade, such as in Tunisia and Egypt, or with WikiLeaks, or climate change and the extinction rebellion, have highlighted the significance of the internet in politics and governance. In such ways, this book will provide a realist's response to utopian visionaries and dystopian skeptics who dominate debate over the political implications of the internet.

To make this work more accessible, I use many examples from the short but truly incredible history of the internet, as well as from key developments that predate the rise of the internet. Too many discussions of the internet seem to lose any anchor in its historical development over the decades.

And while much of my research on the internet is based on my work in the United Kingdom and the United States, this book draws on data and examples worldwide, including global surveys of internet users and studies of internet use in many other nations across all regions of the world. The Fifth Estate developed with the rising diffusion and use of the internet across the globe—reaching beyond half of the world's population, and I hope it will be fully understood in its global significance.

Throughout this book, I use the terms internet, social media, and digital media to encompass separate but often overlapping information and communication technologies (ICTs). Some students of internet studies accept a narrow definition of the internet as a specific set of artifacts, protocols, or standards that enable heterogenous computers and digital devices to be networked, such as the Transmission Control Protocol/Internet Protocol (TCP/IP). Throughout this book, I refer to the "internet" in a broader sense to reference this network of networks and all the applications that are anchored to it, such as email, the World Wide Web (or web), and social media. Their use drives the network power shift of the Fifth Estate.

I use "social media" when I refer to applications that enable users to more easily post content and network with other users, such as YouTube, Facebook, or Instagram. Discussions about user-generated content (UGC) generally refer to much of the content on social media, even though many other internet uses, such as websites and email, have similar functions.

I use the term "digital media" to connote the broadest scope, as it would include digital information and communication that might not be networked over the internet, such as when you share photos with a person collocated with you or use earphones linked to your mobile via a blue tooth connection. Machine-to-machine communication, for example when tracking the location of a smartphone, would be subsumed by the term digital media. All these various technologies are among the assemblage of artifacts and media interrelated with one another in the hybrid media environment that enables the network power shift defined by the Fifth Estate.

The book argues that the idea of the Fifth Estate is valuable for a number of reasons. You'll see that academic research has recognized many of the patterns and trends in the use and impact of the internet and related media described in this book, but they remain largely fragmented and disjointed. The Fifth Estate provides a conceptual approach that enables many agreed-upon observations, such as about search and social media, to be more coherently connected.

Practically, the Fifth Estate has become a remarkably powerful force, even though most of the public are unaware of its existence. Public awareness of the Fifth Estate as an ideal, one that will be developed in this book, could help enhance and protect this new collectivity and its democratic role in politics and society. Networked individuals need to be more conscious of the informational and communicative power they can wield and better appreciate the civic responsibilities that accompany it—as citizens of the digital age. An individual's agency can be enhanced by their personal awareness of the Fifth Estate.

Theoretically, the Fifth Estate contributes to several prominent and emerging theoretical perspectives on politics, governance, and the role of the internet in society.

Political perspectives on pluralism and the distribution or separation of powers can be advanced by embedding the role of Fifth Estate actors. Contemporary theories of governance are broader than a more limited traditional focus on governments, political parties, and interest groups. Governance increasingly incorporates the wider social and economic context of governments and would be remiss not to include the role of ordinary networked individuals of the Fifth Estate. Likewise, theoretical perspectives on the politics of networking and the network society can be enhanced by an understanding of Fifth Estate actors, which builds on existing notions of network power, that are explained in this book.

From a policy standpoint, the Fifth Estate provides a lens for understanding and evaluating policy and regulatory initiatives. An appreciation of the role of the Fifth Estate could bring added global support for protecting freedom of expression and privacy, critical to the vitality of the Fifth Estate, along with support for internet regulation and policy that maintains the value of the internet for individuals to search, source, and network locally and across the world with increased autonomy from governmental or commercial controls that inappropriately limit or otherwise bias these outcomes. Policy research needs to focus more attention on threats to the values and affordances underpinning the Fifth Estate. Old foci on competition, for example, become more meaningful as a means for supporting choice by networked individuals in sourcing and searching the internet and related digital media.

Furthermore, as you move through the case studies of this book, you'll see that some of the most creative and colorful actors and dramatic developments around the internet are tied to the Fifth Estate. The sheer diversity of initiatives is remarkable, but they are all tied together by the role the internet plays in empowering networked individuals— virtual citizens of the digital age.

Conceptions of the social and political roles of the internet and related digital media have oscillated over the years. Initially, they were merely interesting innovations of no particular significance to politics or society. As the internet diffused more widely, utopian conceptions arose around deterministic notions of the internet democratizing the world. Later, as the internet became taken for granted as a tool of everyday life and work, it was dismissed as simply a part of our everyday life, until it became a perceived threat, such as around fake news. Dystopian conceptions arose around more deterministic views on how the internet was ushering in incivility, populist authoritarianism, and a litany of cyber harms—leading to what has been called a "tech lash." Then, in that context, the experiences of the COVID-19 pandemic brought a sobering realization that the internet was providing a lifeline for individuals and communities around the world during periods of limited travel and social interaction resulting from the pandemic. Perhaps the world has reached a point when utopian and dystopian perspectives and the determinisms behind them can be set aside for a more realistic understanding of the actual social and political dynamics of one of the most important power shifts of the digital age.

Acknowledgments

I personally regard my conception of the Fifth Estate as my most significant contribution to the study of the social and political dynamics of the internet and related media, information, and communication technologies. But my realization of what could be a new and useful idea was the outcome of decades of research in what was initially a small and very specialized field of internet studies, which has become one of the most burgeoning fields of the twenty-first century.

I studied political science in graduate school in the early 1970s at the University of Buffalo (then SUNY Buffalo). In 1974, I was then able to bring a political perspective to the study of computing in one of the first empirical studies of the role of computing in government. It was called an evaluation of urban information systems (the URBIS project) at the Public Policy Research Organization (PPRO) at UC Irvine. This project enabled me to work with the late Rob Kling, Ken Kraemer, Jim Danziger, the late Alex Mood, and John Leslie King, where one of my key foci was on the power shifts tied to computing in organizations. My interest in power shifts followed me to my work at the Annenberg School at the University of Southern California and then to Oxford University as its first Professor of Internet Studies and Director of the Oxford Internet Institute (OII).

In my early years at Oxford, my interest in power shifts helped me see the Fifth Estate emerge in the data I will describe in this book. But invaluable support was provided to my work through various funded projects that enabled me to look at different aspects of this concept. These included the Fifth Estate Project, supported by the Quello Center at Michigan State University; the OII; Oxford Internet Surveys (2003–13, 2019–22); and June Klein at Electronic Boardroom. My work on the Oxford Internet Surveys (OxIS) was complemented by involvement in the World Internet Project (WIP), coordinated at the Annenberg School's Center for the Digital Future. Additional global research of mine was enabled by work with UNESCO on freedom of expression and by grants for the Internet Values Project, which I conducted at the OII in collaboration with INSEAD, Cornell University, comScore, the World Economic Forum (WEF), and ictQATAR.

Many other projects in internet studies fed into my conceptualization of the Fifth Estate, including work when directing the UK's Programme on Information and Communication Technologies (PICT) in the late 1990s, with David Bray and others on the Performance of Distributed Problem-Solving Networks (DPSN) Project

(2007–8), which I directed with support from McKinsey and Company. I directed the Oxford e-Social Science Project (OeSS), supported by the Economic and Social Research Council (2005–12), which introduced me to networked collaboration and big data and computational analytics before the term "big data" was invented. Work on collaboration was supported as well by my involvement with a project on User-Driven Collaboration at the Technical University of Denmark (DTU) that was completed in 2014. Google funding enabled me in 2017 to direct a project on how people get information about politics, called the Quello Search Project, based at the Quello Center at MSU, which countered many deterministic views of echo chambers and filter bubbles that were dominant in the field at that time.

I wish also to acknowledge the many personal and public stories of the Fifth Estate used throughout this book as concrete illustrations of its role in politics and society. While many examples are noted and cited, many more could not be included without overwhelming readers. After reading this book, you might find it impossible to read a newspaper or listen to the news without seeing many examples of the Fifth Estate in developments around the world. I thank those who have documented these examples and apologize to all those whose experiences are just as relevant but impossible to cover in this book.

I wish to thank my editor at Oxford University Press, Angela Chnapko, who has been supportive of this book from the beginning and through the pandemic. My thanks as well to the editor of the series on digital politics, Professor Andrew Chadwick at Loughborough University. His vision for this series and support for my work was motivating. I am also grateful to two anonymous reviewers who provided insightful and constructive recommendations, which improved this book. It is an honor to be among the volumes in this series.

During the process of writing, Barbara Ball provided valuable copy-editing in preparing chapters for the publisher. My thanks to her and copy-editors at Oxford University Press. Their attention to detail and style has improved the clarity and consistency of this book.

Finally, I owe a huge debt of gratitude to all those who supported my work over the years and collaborated with me on related projects and papers. I've sought to acknowledge and cite this work throughout the book but apologize again if I have failed to give due credit to anyone. Many and various pieces of my work all added up to the Fifth Estate as a conception that I hope will repay the patience and brilliance of my colleagues in academe and at Oxford University Press.

Contents

Introduction: Reconfiguring Informational and Communicative
Power   1

Part I   THE FOUNDATIONS OF THE FIFTH ESTATE

1. The Idea and Evidence of a Fifth Estate   19

2. Fifth Estate Theories of Distributed and Network Power   33

Part II   FIFTH ESTATE STRATEGIES

3. Searching   59

4. Originating   77

5. Networking   99

6. Collaborating   119

7. Leaking   139

Part III   SHAPING THE FUTURE OF THE FIFTH ESTATE

Figures

Tables

Boxes

Abbreviations and Acronyms

ACLU   American Civil Liberties Union
ALS   Amyotrophic lateral sclerosis
ARPA   Advanced Research Projects Agency
BBS   Bulletin board system
BCC   Blind carbon copy
BGP   Border Gateway Protocol
BLM   Black Lives Matter
CB   Citizen band
CC   Carbon copy
CNO   Collaborative Network Organization
CPW   Cambridge University's Prosociality and Well-Being Lab
DWSD   Detroit Water and Sewage Department
EFF   Electronic Frontier Foundation
EMISARI   Emergency Management Information System and Reference Index
EPA   Environmental Protection Agency
FCC   Federal Communications Commission
GSR   Global Science Research
GWAP   Games with a Purpose
ICO   Information Commissioner's Office
ICT   Information and communication technology
IP   Internet protocol
IPAB   I Paid a Bribe
ISP   Internet Service Provider
IWF   Internet Watch Foundation
MOOC   Massive open online courses
NSA   National Security Agency
NTIA   National Telecommunications and Information Administration
OEP   Office of Emergency Preparedness
Ofcom   Office of Communications, UK
OII   Oxford Internet Institute
OXIS   Oxford Internet Surveys
PEN   Public Electronic Network
PGP   Pretty Good Privacy (software)

PICT	Programme on Information Communication Technologies
PMS	Picturephone Meeting Service
PPRO	Public Policy Research Organization
RMT	Rate My Teacher
RSPCA	The Royal Society for the Prevention of Cruelty to Animals
SMS	Short Message Service
TCP	Transmission Control Protocol
UGC	User-generated content
URL	Uniform Resource Locator
VPN	Virtual Private Network
WEF	World Economic Forum
WELL	Whole Earth "Lectronic Link"
WFH	Working from home
WIP	World Internet Project
WWW	World Wide Web

Introduction

Reconfiguring Informational and Communicative Power

The global diffusion and increasing centrality of the internet, social networking, blogging, texting, tweeting, and other digital media and services have enabled networked individuals to reconfigure their access to new and alternative sources of information, people, services, and related technologies of the digital age. Early in the twenty-first century, a critical mass of networked individuals had developed in most localities and nations, which can source information and network with others in ways that support distributed accountability in government, politics, business, industry, the media, and everyday life.

The rising influence of networked individuals is valued by some but feared by many as it introduces a major change that threatens the ecology of actors shaping all the traditional sectors of politics and society. The internet does not simply substitute digital media for traditional forms of information and communication, it changes how we do things and the outcomes of those activities. This book argues that the internet is playing an overwhelmingly positive role that is analogous to and as significant as the rise of the Fourth Estate, enabled by the emergence of an independent press since the eighteenth century.

This book presents the theory and empirical evidence that a network power shift has enabled a "Fifth Estate" through the networking of individuals in ways that create a new source of accountability, not only in government and politics but also in all sectors of society. It explains how the internet has become a platform for networking individuals in ways that can challenge the influence of other more established bases of institutional authority and that can be used to complement but also increase the accountability of the press, politicians, physicians, scientists, and other experts by offering networked individuals with alternative sources of information, opinion, and social support. The benefits as well as risks tied to this network power shift are addressed throughout this book.

The Power of Reconfiguring Access

Since the early days of computing, people have debated the implications of computers and telecommunications on the relative power of different actors in organizations and society. This debate was broadened with the emergence of the internet, which extended

The Fifth Estate. William H. Dutton, Oxford University Press. © Oxford University Press 2023.
DOI: 10.1093/oso/9780190688363.003.0001

computing beyond organizational and institutional boundaries and blurred them. Competing perspectives have developed around the power shifts tied to the internet, including more technologically deterministic (driven by technical change) and more socially shaped (driven by the choices of users and producers) perspectives.

Despite early optimism around the democratic potential of the internet, conventional wisdom has tied the internet to enabling a less democratic, more centralized, if not autocratic, model of control by big governmental and big tech business institutions. Since the 1980s, however, major scholars have often argued that advances in information and communication technologies like the internet and related digital media and computer-mediated communication systems are inherently more democratic than more centrally controlled one-to-many technologies, like print and broadcasting. On the one hand, Ithiel de Sola Pool (1983) called computer-mediated communication systems "technologies of freedom." Decades later, on the other hand, critics have argued that the internet can be designed and implemented in ways that support concentration, an autocracy rather than democracy (Hindman 2009; Howard 2011). Other critics worry that this communication revolution underpinned by the internet has fueled the opposite, such as populism, mobs, and vigilantism. In either case, it seems to have challenged fundamental tenets of democratic elitism, which argues that liberal democratic systems are sustained by the power of elites, who hold democratic values, to protect such democratic values as freedom of expression and privacy (Bachrach 1967).

However, social research on technology over the decades continues to demonstrate how the internet enables people to reconfigure their access to information and to people in ways that are not technologically determined. The internet and related digital media are not inherently democratic or autocratic technologies. They do not necessarily empower people or government authorities, for instance. As I argue in this book, access can be reconfigured by the many ways in which a variety of actors—including you— choose to design, implement, and use the technology. More specifically, by understanding the concept of the Fifth Estate, it is possible to gain a realistic sense of the democratic role the internet and social media are already playing while demonstrating the need to guard against changes that could undermine this new estate of the internet realm.

To understand the idea of power shifts tied to the internet, think how the internet and related online digital media have reconfigured access to information, people, services, and technology in our increasingly networked society. Table I.1 illustrates how

Table I.1 **How the Internet Is Reconfiguring Access**

Access to	Ways we do things	Outcomes of activities
Information	How you get information	What you know
People	How you communicate with people	With whom you communicate
Services	How you obtain services	Who pays what to whom from where
Technology	How you do what you do	What know-how you require

the internet changes not only the way we do things but also the outcomes of those activities—what we know; who we know; what services we receive when, where, and how; and what know-how we require.

For example, by using the internet instead of or in addition to a newspaper to get information, you might find and learn something new and different using an internet search engine or asking your friends on social media. These are different ways of getting information that can also change what you know.

Similarly, by communicating with people online, such as in business meetings, at your home, over video conferencing, or through a dating application, you might meet people you did not already know and change your network of business associates or friends. By obtaining services online, such as shopping, you might not go to a store but to an online shopping service and purchase something unavailable in your local stores or something more or less expensive than from another seller.

Finally, by using the internet to do many of the things you do, you might benefit from having particular skills and know-how, such as how to obtain, update, and safely use digital media and software. Consequently, you are using the internet in ways that can reconfigure your access to information, people, services, and technology, which can therefore influence your ability to be informed and communicate with others.

We need to understand how multiple actors are making decisions that reconfigure access to digital resources, such as information. By following the empirical consequences of prevailing patterns of use, it is possible to see that networked individuals use the internet to better source their own information and to join and create their own networks that can enhance their informational and communicative power across many sectors of society. If this capability can be understood, strategically harnessed, and protected, the internet could play an increasingly powerful role in enhancing democratic and social accountability across every sector of society.

In this sense, the concept of a Fifth Estate aims to capture a variety of empirical findings, focusing on how and why people trust and therefore use the internet, while drawing distinctions between networked individuals and networked institutions, all of which are increasingly networked in the digital age. But within the Fifth Estate that has emerged from these activities, people can span, move across, undermine, and otherwise go beyond the boundaries of existing institutions, thereby opening new avenues to increase the accountability of politicians, press, experts, and other loci of power and influence.

Yet, it has long been observed that information and communication technologies—take the telephone as an example—have "dual effects" (de Sola Pool 1977: 4). As a thought experiment of sorts, see if you can juxtapose any negative effect of a technology, like a smartphone, for example, with a positive effect. For instance, children can be spend too much time interacting with a computer—but the holding power of a computer can make it a valuable medium for learning and education, enabling children to focus on a task (Papert 1980). Throughout this book, I will address the concerns raised about how network empowerment of individuals might undermine everyday life and even democratic institutions, such as in fueling disinformation and populism. However, many of these fears are exaggerated and based on a technologically deterministic perspective; many also arise from the lack of a framework to interpret and gauge the actual impact of the rising influence of networked individuals, such as in complementing pluralistic democratic institutions.

More pluralist democratic processes have been supported in earlier periods by the rise of the press, supported by technological innovations in radio, television, and other traditional mass media, in what has been called the "Fourth Estate." The internet's broad political and social roles have similarities with traditional media, for example in the ways we virtually watch television, film, and the news online, but they also crucially differ from traditional media and the Fourth Estate in how networks help open opportunities for ordinary individuals to reconfigure their access in ways that create greater social accountability of important institutions, like the press. It can be used to shift the "communicative power" of networked individuals and institutions, which can lead to real power shifts and provide new networks of accountability through independent sources of information and collaboration that enable individuals to search, create, share, collaborate, and sometimes leak information that challenge traditional centers of authority. As one of the most seminal thinkers in the study of American politics argued, democratic theory "is concerned with processes by which ordinary citizens exert a relatively high degree of control over leaders" (Dahl 1956: 3). The empowerment of individuals is central to theories of democratic politics.

NETWORK POWER: THE VERY IDEA OF POWER IN A NETWORK SOCIETY

One of the most remarkable common observations about the study of power is that "no one can agree on how to define or measure it" (Dreztner 2022: 34), not even political scientists. Nevertheless, from Niccolò Machiavelli's *The Prince* to the present day, this has not stopped social scientists from the study of power. There is agreement on it being a relational concept—one has more or less power overtime or in relation other actors (Dahl 1957). And there is common understanding that an actor, such as a person, has power if they can force or compel another actor to do something they would not otherwise do or do something that favors "the empowered actor's will, interests, or values" (Castells 2009: 10).

Moreover, it is understood that power needs to be distinguished from similar concepts, such as authority, as someone can possess the legitimate authority to command something but be ignored. A leading scholar of the American presidency, Richard Neustadt (1960), wrote of President Harry S. Truman, who before leaving office in 1953 joked with his colleagues that the incoming president, General Dwight David Eisenhower, who had been supreme commander of the Allied forces in Europe in World War II, would be frustrated when he arrives at the White House to find that his orders were not automatically obeyed. Neustadt argued that even the president had to rely on the "power to persuade"—communication.

Clearly, ordinary people—who are the primary networked individuals of a Fifth Estate—seldom possess the authority or the institutional or legal basis, such that a state possesses, to compel others. Similarly, the Fifth Estate does not involve military power or economic power. It is their "network power" to influence others that is central to the Fifth Estate (Castells 2011; Chadwick 2013: 17). This is based on the informational and communicative power of networked individuals that can be reshaped by their access to information, people, services, and technologies via the internet and related digital technologies. In this context, Manuel Castells (1980: 10) notes that power does not necessarily require coercion. It can be exercised by "the construction of meaning on the basis of discourses through which social actors guide their actions"—through communication, what George Gerbner so clearly defined as the "interaction of messages" (Morgan 2012: 17), and access to information. Many social scientists have focused on the political implications of communication in shaping a person's or society's "sense and meaning" in social and power relations (Harste 2021: 51). This resonates well with the power of the press as a Fourth Estate as well as the network power of the Fifth Estate.

It is in this way that individuals can be empowered, as they have the ability online to network that can reconfigure their access to information, people, services, and technologies that can enhance their role relative to other actors in political and social settings. Castells (1980: 45) focuses on power in a network society as exercised through shaping networks and their connections with other networks, including information networks, with which I agree. Castells (2011) used the term "network power" to capture the variety of ways the use of networks like the internet can shape the influence of different actors. This book explicitly builds around the ability of networked individuals to be empowered by their ability to search, originate, network, collaborate, or leak information in ways that they can shape how others make sense and derive meaning in a variety of social and political contexts. This is what enhances their relative network power over time and with respect to other actors, enhancing their ability to influence others in politics and society.

Empowering Networked Individuals

There is a long line of research on the power shifts that might be tied to the use of computers and telecommunications, from the telegraph to new digital media. Edwin Parker (1970: 51) explained the potential of power shifts—when "knowledge is power"— quite clearly in the 1970s, arguing that "the actual or potential redistribution of information threatens the existing distribution of power in society."

Until the 1980s, most uses of computing were anchored in organizations, so notions of power shifts were tied to shifts across different kinds of actors in organizations. From the early 1970s, for example, my colleagues and I studied whether the use of computers in government would shift more power or control to top managers, who might know more about their organization through their control of management information systems; or to technocrats, such as the computer and information technology experts on whom the organization would be more dependent; or have more pluralistic implications, with departments and groups across the government being able to use computing in ways that supported their own work and informational power. After extensive research in American cities, we concluded that computers did not systematically have managerial, technocratic, or pluralist impacts. Instead, the technology tended to be used and implemented in ways that followed and reinforced the existing structure of power and influence—that which prevailed in each government when they adopted and implemented computer systems. We therefore concluded that computers generally reinforced power structures—what we called "reinforcement politics" (Danziger et al. 1982).

For example, throughout most of the 1960s and 1970s, it was "blue sky thinking" that individuals would have direct access to computing resources in anyway comparable to that available to most of the world in the twenty-first century. Nevertheless, scholars envisioned the creation of a public information or computing utility even in the late 1960s with the development of the ARPA computer network,[1] later called the ARPANet, and discussions of two-way interactive cable television systems (Sackman and Nie 1970). There were even futuristic visions—which today seem ridiculous—of a large mainframe computer being in the basement of a home, next to the central heating; albeit these forecasts were not taken seriously by most scientists and engineers, who were far less optimistic about households ever having even one computer. This was a time dominated by large mainframe computers and the very early days of minicomputers, still large by today's standards, but interactive and more easily accessed via a remote terminal, such as over the telephone using modems and acoustic couplers.[2]

In the 1970s, there was the early development of networks to support computer-mediated communication. For example, the Emergency Management Information System and Reference Index (EMISARI) established the potential for synchronous and asynchronous forms of networking, primarily creating and sharing text. However, these networks were so primitive by today's standards in their usability and reach that these systems remained very peripheral to any discussion of being used in mainstream politics and society (Hiltz and Turoff 1978).

Early pioneers of cyberspace—enabled by computer-mediated communication systems—would soon create wonderfully exciting visions of a public sphere for discussion of issues that would have a positive democratizing influence. Electronic computing systems were conceived to support global communication networks that would help create a virtual world. This new space anchored in online communication was called "cyberspace," as distinct from the geographical spaces of the real world. But these notions remained futuristic in the 1970s and 1980s and absorbed only a small number of academics and networking enthusiasts, but researchers today speak of a "space of flows" in contrast to a "space of places" that suggest such a future has arrived (Castells 2009).

Similarly, the personal computer was expected to be the start of a communication revolution by some in the early 1980s, as it held the potential to put computing resources into the hands of individuals and households (Williams 1982). Some saw the personal computer ushering in more democratic and egalitarian access to technology, but more powerful organizations and wealthier people had greater access to personal computers, thereby tending to reinforce existing inequalities.

In the late 1980s, Tim Berners-Lee and his colleagues at CERN began writing the code for the World Wide Web, designed to enable decentralized and globally distributed web pages that would be controlled by individuals or institutions and linked to one another, rather than controlled by a major platform, like the early and more recently evolving internet platforms of the tech giants. Berners-Lee has continued to focus on decentralizing control, such as his efforts to give individuals control of their personal data through a technology for organizing data, like applications on the web that he calls "Solid."[3]

Nevertheless, through the 1980s and even into the 1990s, the public's use of networking was too limited to be taken seriously as a tool for political and social change. What systems that did exist tended to support patterns of reinforcement politics rather than empowering networked individuals.

That said, in the aftermath of the dotcom bubble in 2001, new promise arose around the internet as a means for democratizing rather than simply reinforcing existing patterns of political communication. I first used the ARPANet, the precursor to the internet, in 1974. However, I did not become involved in longitudinal research on access to the internet in households across the United Kingdom, the United States, and other nations until 2002. At that time, as part of the World Internet Project (WIP) and the Oxford Internet Surveys (OxIS), launched in 2003, I was able to see basic trends in who used, as well as for what purposes, and did not use the internet.

Over the years, from 2002 on, as I describe in later chapters, I found that networked individuals were increasingly able to use the internet to find and create their own information and join and create their own networks, such as through social media, in ways that enhanced their "informational" and "communicative power" (Garnham 1999). However, many continued to dismiss the internet as irrelevant to mainstream political communication. For example, such a small portion of the public was connected to the internet at the turn of the century that it would have been inherently undemocratic to vote or move political debate online because it would exclude most citizens. This would advantage the connected public and disadvantage those on the wrong side of an increasingly visible digital divide. But most models of the role of the internet in politics focused on its use in existing political institutions, like voting and consultations, and failed to focus on its potential to empower a critical mass of users—not everyone—in new ways that could create a new source of informational and communicative power.

By the 2020s, with more than half of the world online via a multitude of devices accessible to many individuals, from laptops to desktop computers, to smartphones, smart watches, and connected TVs, there is no question that there is a critical mass of internet and social media users. With the design and diffusion of an array of new devices, networks, and applications, traditional conceptions of the old and new media, telecommunications, and computing have become more interwoven and interdependent. Increasingly, they are so interrelated that they have become viewed as an assemblage of human actors and technical artifacts.

Fifth Estate Actors in an Assemblage of Hybrid Media

Old and new media technologies and actors are becoming increasingly complex and blurred, such as when households watch TV programs on their computer via the internet. However, such recognitions have reinforced the need to view the many interrelationships between old and new media technologies and the people designing, producing, using, and otherwise connected with them as actors—social and technical actors alike—in a "hybrid media system" (Chadwick 2013). The idea of a hybrid media system recognizes the loss of clear distinctions among technical artifacts, such as the internet and television, and between technologies and people, such as the internet and its users. Students of technology have long defined technology as an ensemble of equipment, techniques, and people, but the technical artifacts are too commonly viewed as separate from people. For example, in referring to a network power shift, this book views the technical and social aspects of the network to be integral components, both of which contribute to the network's overall performance and implications for politics and society.

Recognition of the many interrelationships between old and new media technologies and technical artifacts and social actors are part and parcel of a "hybrid media system" (Chadwick 2013). The conceptualization of a hybrid media system incorporates what has been called an "assemblage" of people and technological artifacts and the social meanings and behaviors associated with them (Deleuze and Guattari 2004; Chadwick 2011, 2013: 14–15; Müller 2015; Briassoulis 2021). This assemblage is a hybridity perspective on the social shaping of technology that makes a more explicit recognition of the connections between social and technical aspects of a system.

These concepts of hybrid media and assemblages are closely tied to the seminal work of sociologist Bruno Latour (1987, 2005), who coined what is known as "actor network theory" (ANT) to depict the influential and inseparable roles of people and technical artifacts in shaping the use and outcomes of technical systems. I have adopted perspectives similar to ANT in using a theoretical framework of an ecology of games to describe the interrelations among networks of actors and technologies leading to a particular outcome of large technical systems, such as an innovation, event, or the news (Dutton 1992; Lin 2003; Dutton et al. 2012; Newman et al 2012).

These are not simply academic distinctions—understanding the inseparable connections between social and technical actors is critical to discussions of the role of technologies like the internet. In fact, the political and social implications of the internet and related digital media, such as network power, cannot be understood without recognizing how closely technical and social actors are interwoven, such as when internet users employ various devices to search the internet to find artifacts with the aid of search engine algorithms—all of which are designed and implemented by people.

However, in focusing on the Fifth Estate, this book zeros in on particular actors and their integral connections with specific technologies, institutions, and other actors. I am not focused on a grand theory of media or communication but on a more middle-range or even micro-oriented theory of the coming to be of the Fifth Estate within this hybrid assemblage of social and technical actors and how it interacts with various digital media technologies and actors and what difference the networks make to politics and society.

An assemblage perspective might view these interactions as too varied and complex to describe in detail, but in looking at a Fifth Estate actor involved in specific contexts, using specific technologies, working in particular institutions, and related actors, the specificities matter. Therefore, my approach is to distinguish the details of who said what to whom on what technological platforms to identify the strategies and outcomes of Fifth Estate actors. Throughout this book, you'll find me striving to specify what technology was used by whom with what effect.

You will see that a focus on the Fifth Estate moves away from many general discussions of assemblages or hybrid media; it also focuses on the institutions and estates in which a specific networked individual is the actor using the internet or related digital media. As alluded to above, this means that the same person might use the same technology, such as Twitter, sometimes as a journalist, occupying the Fourth Estate, and sometimes independently of her journalist role, as a Fifth Estate actor. A public official might post information from his home in the evening as a Fifth Estate actor rather than a governmental official. From a Fifth Estate perspective, the estate an actor represents, or their institutional role, is more important than it would be in most studies of media assemblages. You will see this unfold in the case studies of later chapters in the focus on networked individuals and how they exercised their informational or communicative network power.

A Perspective on Big Questions

What is informational and communicative power? Are such power shifts real? Do they support more democratic accountability across sectors of society? Or are they supporting autocracy or fueling mobs, the rise of populism, political instability, fake news, and disinformation across the globe? Is this simply a fetish of individualism or a practical guide to the politics of the new media of the digital age?

Born in 1997, Malala Yousafzai, the famous young Pakistani activist, was awarded a Nobel Prize in 2014 for her advocacy of human rights and education. She wrote an anonymous blog about life in Pakistan's Swat Valley under Taliban rule and voiced her views on her right to attend school before being targeted and shot at a bus stop by two members of the Taliban. She suffered major injuries. While recovering she graduated from the University of Oxford, and she spoke at the United Nations in New York on July 12, 2013, communicating her personal experience and belief: "One child, one teacher, one book, and one pen can change the world." That same year, *Time* magazine named her as one of the "100 Most Influential People in the World." In many ways, she captures the ideal of how a networked individual can make a profound difference in many sectors across society.

This book presents theoretical perspectives and concrete evidence that address such hopes as well as the fears associated with the rise of networked individuals. In doing so, it aims to convey the promise of a Fifth Estate and how to address the risks and protect its future. Before moving to this evidence, it might be useful to pause and focus on the idea of a Fifth Estate.

Related Literature and Research on the Fifth Estate

I first spoke publicly about the Fifth Estate in a 2007 lecture (Dutton 2007), entitled "Through the Network (of Networks)—the Fifth Estate," a version of which was later published (Dutton 2009). I have been refining this conception since then through a variety of research projects, talks, articles, and book chapters (all on the bibliography). Moving to a book-length treatment of this topic enabled me to more fully convey my understanding of the theory and research that underpins the idea of a Fifth Estate that demonstrates its significance.

From the beginning I have conceived of the Fifth Estate as a new power shift enabled by the technologies of the network society, where "technologies" are defined broadly as the equipment, techniques, and people involved in their design, use, and governance. It is not a new institution but a network power exercised by a collectivity of individuals who strategically use the internet and related social media to enhance their informational and communicative power vis-à-vis governments, business, industry, and other actors and institutions. By enabling a critical mass of individuals to use networking to source, share and leak information and connect with people in ways that support more distributed social accountability in business, industry, government, politics, and media, the internet has fostered the Fifth Estate.

However, other academics, researchers, and media professions have used the term in a variety of distinctly different ways. Multiple uses of this term create some ambiguity over its definition, just as in the case of other theoretical concepts, like power (Turculet et al. 2017). However, these multiple uses create a need and opportunity to explain the use of the term in the context of this book. By reviewing these, it is possible to distinguish my use of this term and clarify the meaning I attach to this concept.

Early systems that supported popular networks of communication were primarily local bulletin board systems (BBS), which individuals in households could dial up using modems connected to their telephone line. This enabled some pioneering experiments in public communication and even electronic forums, such as what was called the Public Electronic Network (PEN) system in Santa Monica, California (Dutton and Guthrie 1991)—probably the first "electronic city hall" (discussed in Chapter 8). For example, the citizens of Santa Monica networked on the forum to design facilities for this seaside city's homeless population. It was called "Shwashlock" to capture the provision of showers, washing machines, and lockers for them.[4] Despite the success of local experiments like PEN, the internet grew to enable individuals to access information and people across the world—breaking out well beyond the local community and spelling an end of this early focus on and diffusion of local networks.

The internet enabled communication to move beyond local networks to capture those interested in particular topics across a larger number of users across the world. This enabled web logs, later called blogs, to become very popular compared to other systems of computer-mediated communication. These early networks began with only a minority of the public online. There was not a sufficient number, or critical mass, of users to easily foster local political applications. Academics used them primarily for accessing information and collaborating with remote and local colleagues. Businesses began using email and the internet as a substitute for fax machines and even telegrams. Nevertheless, a few pioneering networking enthusiasts became cheerleaders for the idea of a free, open, and global internet for accessing information and people and for producing content, such as through web pages that could be easily composed by internet users and bloggers.

It was during early blogging (i.e., early twenty-first century) that conceptions of the Fifth Estate were initially focused. Bloggers were seen as the new "watchdogs," or society's whistleblowers, who could hold the Fourth Estate of the press more accountable. Stephen Cooper (2006) saw the beauty of bloggers watching the watchers (the press in turn being held more accountable), as did another Australian blogger Greg Jericho (2012). However, the Fifth Estate, as I define it, can entail a watchdog role across all institutions—not only the press—and blogging is only one of many paths networked individuals can take to hold other institutions accountable.

The concept has also been used to characterize the late Craufurd Goodwin's (1995) perspective on the role of nongovernmental, publicly oriented organizations like the Atlantic Council and the Rand Corporation. James McGann (2016) took Goodwin's (1995) perspective but focused specifically on "think tanks" playing a role in American politics as a Fifth Estate. Think tanks and related civic-minded organizations do play an important role in shaping public policy in the United States and other nations, but their independence is problematic at times, such as when allied with political parties or politicians, and their work in often funded by the public sector.

As I will explain in Chapter 2, these nongovernmental institutions are closer to the First Estate in contemporary politics, given their ties to noted public intellectuals. They also are closely tied to the Third Estate of the commons, or governments, given their staff frequently going through the revolving doors between many government agencies and think tanks. Of course, think tanks increasingly use the internet to enhance their role in policy, but the influence of the internet and new media are not a consideration in the eyes of Goodwin or McGann. It is their potential to bring expertise and independence to policy arenas that shapes their respective influence.

Those who come closer to my use of the term have chosen different labels and terminology. Eric Schmidt, the former CEO of Google, has spoken about the "internet estate" in terms close to my conception of the Fifth Estate (Schmidt and Cohen 2013).[5] And Yochai Benkler (2006, 2013), of the Harvard Berkman Center, develops a conception close to my own but focused on it being an extension of the press—what he calls the "networked Fourth Estate."

Stephen Reese (2021) also sees the institution of the press becoming increasingly hybrid, although in crisis. Focusing on the United States, Reese's wide-ranging account of what he calls the "institutional press" describes the crisis posed by an eroding trust in expertise, journalism, institutions, and democracy. He defines an institution as a "social structure formed by an interlocking network of rules and activities, roles, technologies, and collective frames of meaning, which work together to sustain its coherence, endurance, and value" (Reese 2021: 112). His account finds every aspect of his definition being challenged by factors such as the rise of a hybrid news and political information ecosystem—an assemblage of actors, organizations, and technologies that do not share the same narratives or professional values and norms. This de-institutionalization has been furthered by declining trust in the face of fake news and anti-media populism from left and right through Bernie Sanders or Donald Trump. Rather than seeking a unitary truth, journalism has been infected by hyper-partisan factions with competing narratives that are responsive to polarization of the public and media outlets. Moreover, the press continues to suffer from declining revenues based on an outdated business model in what is an inherently expensive and labor-intensive industry that is more concentrated in ways that further reinforce perceptions of an out-of-touch media elite. As you will see across the chapters of this book, the Fifth Estate relies heavily on the press and vice versa. In this respect, problems facing the press are risks to the Fifth Estate even as networked individuals become part of this political information ecosystem (Chadwick 2011).

While online media are indeed used by the press to maintain and attempt to enhance the institution of the press, just as other estates seek to exploit the value of the internet, networked individuals who are independent of the press are the core of the Fifth Estate. Journalists might originate content online independent of their role in a media institution but when acting as a networked extension of the Fourth Estate, journalists remain part of the Fourth Estate seeking to maintain and enhance the press industry as an institution—not its watchdog—even if engaging with new media and actors outside traditional boundaries of the institution.

And there are other contemporary uses of the Fifth Estate. It has been used as the title for a television news show on Canada's CBC that "brings in-depth investigations that matter to Canadians." This show may serve as a watchdog for Canadian society, but it is very different from the Fifth Estate as employed in this book. And I've noted in my hot tub story in the preface how the Fifth Estate came to be the title of a popular movie about WikiLeaks—again, leaks are only one of the strategies used by the Fifth Estate. And in 2019, Meta's CEO Mark Zuckerberg described Facebook and social media as creating a Fifth Estate "alongside the other power structures in our society" much in the way I've defined it.[6] Others have used the concept of a "Fifth Power" to refer to Meta and other new digital media or big tech platforms.[7]

Still other variants are tied to various network technologies, such as alternative media (Lievrouw 2011), inexpensive video cameras (Snowdon 2020), and the mobile phone, especially with its video capabilities (Richardson 2020). But a focus on the use of specific technologies misses the degree to which, separately and in combination, assemblages of these technologies are performing the same role in empowering individuals to independently source and distribute information.

These uses of the same and similar terms are incomplete accounts of their social and political roles. None captures the full range of actors in what I consider the Fifth Estate of our digital age. Moreover, this concept not only captures the way new media are reshaping political institutions and processes, such as governance, but also a change in the political and other social dynamics across all sectors of society, from business and industry to the news and everyday life.

Outline of the Book

The object of this book is to fully explain this concept in ways that will provide an understanding of how the political dynamics of empowering networked individuals of the digital age differ from earlier times when individuals were less capable of exploiting the internet and related network technologies. By describing my conception and anchoring it in empirical research, this book will show you how this preindustrial age metaphor helps one understand the political and related social dynamics of the internet in the twenty-first century. Ironically, this ancient metaphor helps us break away from traditional, more institutionally centric conceptions of democratic processes, such as around electronic democracy (e-democracy), electronic government (e-governments), and augmenting the press (online news) that see the internet primarily as supporting the role of traditional institutions. In doing so, traditional institutional perspectives such as e-democracy and online news miss the most significant network power shift of the digital age—that ushered in by the Fifth Estate.

This introduction has briefly outlined key themes of this book about how the internet has become a platform for networking individuals so effectively that they can challenge the influence of other more established bases of institutional authority. It has introduced the idea that real-world power shifts could be tied to the use of a variety of information and communication technologies, from the printing press to the internet.

This theme will be more fully elaborated in Chapter 1, which provides a brief overview of the nature, implications, and issues of the Fifth Estate, including the definition and explanation of key terms, concepts, and technologies, which are built on in the remaining chapters. Here and throughout the book, examples and case studies will be developed to help make the sensitizing concept of a Fifth Estate more concrete, and how it is likely to be as significant as the Fourth Estate of the press, if not more so, by enhancing pluralistic accountability in everyday life, business, and industry, and in liberal democratic states.

Chapter 2 focuses on a more in-depth presentation of the origins of the concept by building on earlier theoretical conceptions of the Fourth Estate and other established estates of the realm that preceded and provided a foundation for more contemporary pluralist theories of democracy. Similarly, the internet has enabled a new estate, the Fifth Estate, through the networking of individuals that creates a new source of accountability not only in government and politics but also in other sectors. The origins of these estates of the internet realm are indeed from the perspective of a preindustrial society, but you will see that estate theory can be transported into the digital age to offer a valuable perspective on the network power shifts tied to the internet in the information age. The fact that estates theory can help illuminate the dynamics of contemporary pluralistic systems speaks volumes about its potential value for theory and research on the internet and related digital media.

Having described the different estates of the realm, and how they connect with contemporary actors and institutions, the chapter then moves to a discussion of the critics of the Fifth Estate, which are often tied to the other four estates. This overview covers theoretical conceptions of the press as a Fourth Estate and helps identify major fears and risks—benefits and harms—tied to the Fifth Estate by different kinds of actors, from experts to mobs. Understanding the motivations for why various critics became vocal enemies of the Fifth Estate will help you gain a better sense of this new power shift and how it can be threatening to more established institutions and actors. The Fifth Estate cannot be incorporated in any of the other four estates, even though all actors across all estates often use the internet to reinforce their role in politics and society. In such ways, these two initial chapters seek to provide a clear theoretical perspective on the Fifth Estate in the context of other estates.

The next set of chapters focuses on a collection of specific examples and empirical findings on strategies of Fifth Estate actors, based on patterns of the strategic use of the internet around the world. The very idea of a Fifth Estate emerged from observing patterns of behavior discovered in surveys of how people use the internet for a wide range of activities. Survey research demonstrated how the internet enables people to source information and create networks of collective intelligence that could indeed empower them in everyday life. These chapters on strategies draw on survey research but also on case studies to provide concrete evidence of trends underpinning the rise of a Fifth Estate while focusing on the key strategies of networked individuals.

The five short chapters of Part II focus on five key strategies of Fifth Estate actors: searching, originating, networking, collaborating, and leaking. Each chapter draws on concrete examples to illustrate the significance of the Fifth Estate across a few sectors in society. Across all five chapters, examples cover a wide variety of sectors, from medical and healthcare to politics, but nevertheless remain selective and by no means comprehensive. The survey findings related to general trends are combined with case studies and more limited examples to illuminate how the strategies of networked individuals work in practice to support their network power.

Chapter 3 focuses on search, looking at findings on how people find information and check its veracity in ways that can avoid being trapped in a filter bubble (Pariser 2011) that might be created by search algorithms. By focusing on internet users, rather than the technology, you can see how risks tied to fake news, echo chambers, and filter bubbles are less likely to drive what internet users know than technologically deterministic theories suggest. Most importantly, you can see how search enables individuals to source their own information, using the same tools and infrastructures that scientists and intellectuals use. By virtue of this capability, they are less dependent on a governmental, economic, intellectual, or journalistic elite telling them what to read, hear, or believe, fostering a more diverse range of views.

Chapter 4 turns to the creation of original content by networked individuals. The origination of content—what some call user-generated content (UGC)—is perhaps the most controversial and most critical impact of the internet and social media for other estates. This chapter discusses critical perspectives on bloggers, users posting on social media platforms like Twitter, and other amateurs of the "commentariat," arguing that networked individuals are becoming an increasingly vital and credible source of original news and information, including eyewitness accounts, despite claims they are a rising source of misinformation.

Chapter 5 moves to networking, progressing from what we know, to who we know, and how this can be reshaped by social media networks. Are social media users cocooning themselves in echo chambers of like-minded individuals (Sunstein 2017)? For example, I take a critical look at arguments that social media are driving the public toward more populist beliefs and attitudes.

Chapter 6 extends this focus to collaboration, one key aspect of social networks, by describing how networked individuals can be distributed locally and globally but still collaborate and connect to create collective intelligence to serve many civic-minded roles of the Fifth Estate, such as in the development and sharing of open-source intelligence.

A final chapter on strategies, Chapter 7, focuses on leaking, one of the most controversial Fifth Estate strategies. The leaking and distribution of leaked information is developed through a discussion of WikiLeaks along with other remarkable cases. It might lead you to reconsider your views on leaking in the digital age, whether or not you support a particular leak.

In Part III, the book shifts the focus to providing a more integrated view of the Fifth Estate, dealing sequentially with its implications for theories of politics and society, the factors shaping threats to this estate, and its open future. Chapter 8 focuses on the major implications with respect to its potential contribution to democracy as well as its contribution to related democratic theories on the separation of power and pluralism. It also reminds you of a message conveyed by the many cases reviewed in this book, that is, these impacts can be relevant across other sectors of society. It can change the politics in the living room as well as in the political system.

While the Fifth Estate has been a gift to democracy and accountability across society, there are developments underway that threaten the role of the internet in supporting democratic political processes and the Fifth Estate (Miller and Vaccari 2020). Chapter 9, therefore, focuses on changes in technology, governance, policy, and practices around the internet and related digital media that could undermine the Fifth Estate. This chapter identifies and illustrates threats arising from several directions, including actions of the major tech platforms and governmental policy that might well undermine the independence of search, freedom of connection and expression online, and personal privacy.

Despite multiple threats to the future of the Fifth Estate, the final chapter makes a case that the Fifth Estate is alive and well, despite a growing chorus about the demise of democracy and social media. That said, the future differs from more conventional, albeit utopian and increasingly dystopian, perspectives that have come to dominate debate about the internet and its societal implications. In contrast, the Fifth Estate offers a more empirically realistic and grounded perspective on changes already in place that will enable institutions of democracy, governments, the press and media, and business and industry to be more pluralistic, transparent, and accountable across all sectors of society.

While the Fifth Estate can be seen as the internet's gift to democracy and society, it is not indestructible. The chapter therefore ends with a new perspective on addressing problems through initiatives around cybersecurity that can complement and possibly diminish the focus on more media-centric regulations that could undermine privacy and freedom of expression. The internet is not the Wild West, and it is not a broadcaster, and should not be governed as if it were either. The chapter concludes with a call for protecting and tracking the vitality of the Fifth Estate as one barometer of the health of liberal democratic institutions and processes in the digital age. Despite criticisms by pundits and all the other estates of the internet realm and worrisome trends in the regulation of online content, I remain optimistic about the Fifth Estate. Key arguments of the critics do not hold up to empirical evidence and analytical challenges, which suggests they will dissipate over time. With increasing awareness of the promise of the network power shift and the rise of a Fifth Estate, there should be greater support for protecting the Fifth Estate and the transparency, knowledge, and accountability it will bring to politics and society.

PART I

THE FOUNDATIONS OF THE FIFTH ESTATE

The book is divided into three parts, focusing in turn on the foundations, strategies, and future of the Fifth Estate. Part I explains and provides illustrative examples of my conception of the Fifth Estate and how it differs from others' use of this concept. I define the idea as a sensitizing concept and explain how I found the concept valuable in capturing a pattern of empirical observations. In survey research and case studies of internet use over the years, I found power shifts that were not apprehended by existing theoretical perspectives on estates, media, or distributed and network power. This led to a new concept of the Fifth Estate to capture what I view as the power shift of our digital age. In doing so, it draws on a preindustrial age conception of a Fourth Estate enabled by the printing press in the hands of journalistic institutions when they can work independently, outside of governmental or commercial control of content. In ways analogous to the press enabling journalists to reach a mass public, the internet has enabled ordinary networked individuals, as well as institutions, to access information and communicate through local and global networks. Comparisons of this preindustrial age metaphor of the Fourth Estate and a Fifth Estate of the digital age are critical to understanding this concept. Both metaphors have a foundation in technological changes of different eras, but, more important, they go beyond technology to focus attention on who uses technology under what policy and other social and institutional constraints, for what purposes, and to what effect. All internet users are not necessarily acting as a Fifth Estate—only a subset and only at specific times. However, in the digital age, you are likely to have in your hands and your household the capacity to access local and global networks in ways that can hold other individuals, groups, institutions, and bad actors more accountable for their words or actions. The internet can be strategically used to provide individuals, just like you, with relatively more informational and communicative power as explained in the chapters of Part I.

1

The Idea and Evidence of a Fifth Estate

The core idea of the Fifth Estate is the potential for individuals to be empowered by networking with other people and digital resources through the use of information and communication technologies (ICTs) like the internet and related digital media. Networked individuals can strategically use these networks of digital resources to enhance their relative informational and communicative power in relation to other individuals and institutions. The evolving collectivity of networked individuals, who use the internet strategically to enhance their informational and communicative power, enables one of the most significant power shifts of the digital age—the network power shift of the Fifth Estate.

Not all internet users are part of this evolving collectivity of networked individuals that comprises the Fifth Estate. For example, when networked individuals use digital resources in fulfilling their institutional roles, such as carrying out their job as a journalist, business executive, or political candidate, they are not part of the Fifth Estate. Nevertheless, individuals can wear multiple hats and play multiple roles. Many professional journalists, for example, also act in their individual capacity as a networked individual of the Fifth Estate. For instance, journalists might blog in ways independent of their journalistic roles, even though they draw from their journalistic skills and talent in doing so.

Similarly, malicious internet users—such as scammers, trollers, fraudsters, or pranksters—are not acting in line with a Fifth Estate role. They join a host of others who might undermine the Fifth Estate by eroding trust of other internet users and, in many respects, poison the well of digital resources. For this reason, I often refer to the "Fifth Estate" as networked citizens of the digital age—not to imply their citizenship in any nation but to acknowledge their public-spirited and civil courage in using the internet and related technologies in the public's interest. In that sense, the Fifth Estate represents an ideal type, but it has been defined by a pattern of empirical observations of actual internet users, as you will discover in the following chapters.

Fifth Estate Actors

The next chapter will clarify the Fifth Estate and identify various other estates of the internet realm, as well as their enemies, but it is useful here to gain a clear and concrete

The Fifth Estate. William H. Dutton, Oxford University Press. © Oxford University Press 2023.
DOI: 10.1093/oso/9780190688363.003.0002

sense of the potential of networked individuals and the Fifth Estate through a few real-world examples.

THE GRETA EFFECT

There are few better-known and convincing examples of networked individuals making a difference than Greta Thunberg.

Since 2018, relentlessly working on her own as an environmental activist in Sweden, she has had a singular and major impact on debates over climate change and raised awareness of the "extinction rebellion." Her impact has been so widely acknowledged that people have begun to speak of the "Greta Effect." Describing herself on her Twitter account as an "autistic climate change activist," she has warned leaders across the world of the existential threat posed by inaction on climate change.[1]

Her influence traces back to when she started spending school days protesting outside the Swedish Parliament with a simple sign that declared a strike of school children over climate change. Greta and her poster, which read *"Skolstrejk för klima-tet"* (School strike for climate), inspired students in other communities to join her school climate strike and motivated people around the world to prioritize actions to address climate change and to influence the positions of their representatives on the subject. Her personality, intellect, and personal commitment and persistence have been key, but her communicative power was greatly enhanced by Instagram posts of her strike, picturing her and her sign outside Parliament—which drew worldwide attention. By 2021 she had over 12 million followers on her Instagram account. See Box 1.1.

Greta Thunberg is a stunning example of the potential of an individual using the internet in strategic ways to enhance their communicative power in relation to other

---

Box 1.1 **Greta Thunberg: Climate Activist**

Greta was born in Sweden to Swedish parents in 2003. In 2018 at 15 years of age, she began skipping school to hold a protest vigil outside the Swedish Parliament for action on climate change. Her sign read *"Skolstrejk för klimatet"* (School strike for climate). A photo of her on strike went viral on Instagram, Twitter, and other social media, attracting other students and a worldwide following. Later that year, she spoke at the UN Climate Change Conference. In 2019, Greta toured North America for interviews and speaking engagements with her father, then she sailed across the Atlantic to avoid air travel and speak at the UN Climate Action Summit. From 2019 to 2021, she was nominated three consecutive times for the Nobel Peace Prize, and her influence has been acknowledged by being named *Time* magazine's Person of the Year in 2019.

individuals and institutions. While Greta is clearly exceptional, she is not an anomaly. You will see many examples of networked individuals identified and described in this book.

WHISTLEBLOWERS IN CHINA: FROM WUHAN TO OLYMPIC TENNIS

There are parallels between Greta's uplifting story and a sad story of one of the first doctors to die of COVID-19. When the coronavirus outbreak began in Wuhan, China, the government of China launched a concerted effort to control the narrative, including the rapid deletion of online news and social media messages. Anyone who wished to record the course of online messaging in China was forced to resort to snapping screenshots of messages before they were deleted by order of the state. In December 2019, in the early stages of the coronavirus pandemic, a 34-year-old Chinese ophthalmologist, Li Wenliang, was one of the early whistleblowers who had what Daniel Ellsberg called the "civil courage" to alert the public through social media of the serious risks of COVID-19.[2] He was later summoned by the police and reprimanded, along with several others, for "rumor-mongering."[3]

Soon after this summons, Wenliang was seen ill on social media posts and news coverage around the world. Shortly after these posts he died of the virus at Wuhan Central Hospital on February 7, 2020. His illness was apparent from his image on social media, but news of his death in light of the government's censorship was dramatic, as described by Shawn Yuan (2020):

> Within hours, his death sparked a spectacular outpouring of collective grief on Chinese social media—an outpouring that was promptly snuffed out, post by post, minute by minute. With that, grief turned to wrath, and posts demanding freedom of speech erupted across China's social media platforms.

An attempt to censor a message had the exact opposite result. Nevertheless, the government maintained a relentless effort to "eradicate" social media messages not in line with the government's narrative about the origins and severity of the virus (Yuan 2020).

A similar case of censorship in China occurred late 2021. A social media post on Weibo by Peng Shuai, a 39-year-old, three-time Olympic Chinese tennis star, alleged that she had been forced into a nonconsensual sexual encounter by a former vice premier and high-ranking member of the Chinese Communist Party, whom she named. Her post was not only removed within minutes, but she was also not seen or heard from for weeks before China's state media released a series of videos to prove she was alive and well (White and Germano 2021). Not only did these actions make the allegations even more prominent, but her censorship and disappearance sparked protests, raised concerns by the Women's Tennis Association (WTA) for her safety, and initiated moves for a diplomatic boycott of the 2022 winter Olympic Games in China as well.[4] Weeks later, in a side interview with an international reporter, Peng Shuai stressed that she had "never said or written that anyone has sexually assaulted me." The WTA continued to call for an investigation (Mitchell 2021: 8), while Peng continued to deny she was assaulted (Mitchell and Germano 2022).

JULIAN ASSANGE'S WIKILEAKS

In addition to Wenliang, many other whistleblowers come to mind as illustrative of the Fifth Estate. Arguably one of the most famous was the Australian who founded WikiLeaks in 2006: Julian Assange. As discussed in later chapters of this book, while indicted on multiple counts of the US Espionage Act, which makes it a federal offense to obtain or distribute secret classified military or diplomatic documents, he had obtained classified material that he distributed to newspapers through WikiLeaks in 2010. He did not himself hack information from the US government, but when he obtained it, he worked with respected newspapers to redact the material so that it could be safely distributed to the public. This case gets more complicated, as discussed in Chapter 7, but whatever problems have beset WikiLeaks since, the revelations in these documents and videos that were distributed were major news stories in the United States and worldwide. They challenged stated US policy and practice. Whether right or wrong ethically or legally—a question tied to each individual case—he and many other whistleblowers have been able to reach a broader public and enhance their communicative power through the strategic use of the internet.

THE NINE MINUTES DOCUMENTED IN GEORGE FLOYD'S DEATH

Another infamous but quite different example is the use of mobile video by Darnella Frazier, a networked individual, that captured the arrest and death of an unarmed black man, George Floyd, a 48-year-old, on 47th Street in Minneapolis, Minnesota, on May 25, 2020. Darnella was a local resident, a 17-year-old black woman, who later said: "If it weren't for my video, the world wouldn't have known the truth. I own that."[5] She happened to use her mobile video camera while she was walking her cousin to a convenience store. While some criticized the teenager for videoing the event rather than intervening, her video went viral in documenting the police officers, including one kneeling on Floyd's neck for what has become an infamous nine minutes during which George Floyd exclaimed that he "could not breathe." The video of his death triggered the exposure of other videos documenting analogous events and a global chain of reactions and protests, such as the Black Lives Matter (BLM) movement (Richardson 2020). *The Economist* focused on this event and its aftermath in a June 2020 issue entitled "The Power of Protest." Clearly, the mobile phone has become almost an essential component of efforts to document resistance and hold authorities more accountable, and this goes far beyond the United States.[6]

FAILURES OF THE FIFTH ESTATE

Most of these examples will be developed in later chapters along with other illustrations of the social and political dynamics of networked individuals. However, while obvious, it needs to be acknowledged early on that most efforts of networked individuals are not powerful—many are unseen or if seen are not shared or cited. For instance, George Floyd was not the first person or first black man to have died in police custody (Richardson 2020). Another sad failure of accountability was evident from the rising concerns over tainted water in Flint, Michigan, a case described in Chapter 5.

POLITICS OF EVERYDAY LIFE

Most of the examples in this chapter have focused on individuals holding major institutions more accountable, from schools and police departments to national governments. But a Fifth Estate role is evident in interpersonal and community affairs as well—networked individuals can hold other individuals accountable. This is not new in that society functions in part through social pressure and socialization by one's peers and communities, but the internet and social media can take social accountability to an entirely new level. Take two simple examples.

One was a video of a woman in Coventry, England, who in 2010 dropped a neighborhood cat, Lola, in a garbage can (called a wheelie bin in England) as she passed by the cat on a street.[7] The cat was saved and recovered, but the video went viral on social media. She regretted her "moment of madness" but was also investigated by the RSPCA (Royal Society for the Prevention of Cruelty to Animals), became a focus of press coverage, and received such social ridicule that the incident had a major impact on her life—she became the "cat bin woman."[8]

Another example was a photograph of a dentist from Minnesota, who on July 1, 2015, wounded a famous 13-year-old lion, named Cecil, with a bow and arrow when trophy hunting in Zimbabwe. He, with his guides, then tracked and killed Cecil the following morning. Cecil was being studied by researchers at the University of Oxford. The killing was thought to be legal: the dentist had a permit and killed Cecil on a private farm that was near but not inside the Hwange National Park; however, the lion was lured to the private farm with bait. The photograph went viral on social media and gained global press coverage. Legal charges followed, and it had a major impact in raising awareness of the cruelty of trophy hunting that went beyond conservationists. It led to some regulatory changes that made it more difficult for Americans to legally hunt lions.[9]

YOU AND THE FIFTH ESTATE

Perhaps you think the positive examples of social and political accountability and influence are so extreme and so out of the ordinary that the idea of a collectivity of networked individuals as a Fifth Estate is preposterous. More illustrations will be developed throughout this book to convince you otherwise. It may be even more unbelievable, but also true, that many ordinary internet users have become part of this collectivity of networked individuals that I call the Fifth Estate. Maybe without even knowing so, you might be among this collectivity. Literally.

In addition to Greta Thunberg, an earlier Time Person of the Year was "You" in 2006. This was the magazine's effort to acknowledge those who were using the internet and related digital media, such as blogs and Wikipedia, to create new information resources for the common good. In that spirit, "you" could well be part of the Fifth Estate.

Where do you turn first for information—to check a fact or understand a medical condition? Chances are you don't go to a place, consult a book, or get on the phone—you go online. And once online, you don't head for a specific destination, such as a place in your local community, instead, you take cues from your search results or your social networks. This process creates a personal source of information that you sourced that is not dependent on any particular institution such as your local government, university, newspaper, or physician. For instance, in the United States, the National Telecommunications and Information Administration (NTIA 2020) found that over half of American households used the internet for health-related activities in 2019, before the outbreak of the COVID-19 pandemic of 2020. During the pandemic, the internet became a virtual lifeline for households cut off from more traditional sources of community information. Before and during the pandemic, critics had taken issue with internet and social media sources, but even members of the UK's Royal Society argued against deleting false claims. Censorship could feed conspiracy theories, and medical evidence is the best way to counter false information (Cookson 2022). Medical professionals need to work harder to reach valid conclusions and get the evidence to the public, one of the first ports of call for households seeking information.

By virtue of this independence provided online, your communicative power can be enhanced vis-à-vis more traditional authorities. Through the internet, you can reinforce your trust in particular authorities or challenge them when necessary, ask better questions, or hold them more accountable.

If you understand this sense of empowerment in sourcing your own information, and choosing your own networks of other individuals, then welcome to the Fifth Estate. As an individual networked member of the Fifth Estate, you almost certainly use the internet, not only to find information but also to contribute by simply clicking or posting links, mailing, commenting, rating, posting photos, blogging, tweeting, crowdsourcing, or otherwise creating content that adds intelligence to the internet and furthers the Fifth Estate's independence from any single institution.

Of course, institutions, such as the press, also use the internet to maintain and enhance their communicative power. But you and other networked individuals have many of the same online tools at your fingertips, enabling you to reconfigure access to multiple sources of information and be less dependent on more traditional sources, such as particular local governments or specific news outlets. In doing so, you are opening new ways of increasing the accountability of politicians, press, experts, and other more institutionally anchored loci of power and influence.

Key Aspects of the Fifth Estate Concept

The examples provided here may seem like a fragmented set of disparate events. But they all—I argue—come together as examples of the rise of a Fifth Estate. While these actions online are encompassed by the Fifth Estate, many others are better captured as alternative kinds of events, such as protests or simple complaints or blogs. Therefore, a major aspect of this book is capturing those elements that tend to characterize actions that fit this concept of a Fifth Estate.

ENABLED BY DIGITAL MEDIA, INFORMATION, AND COMMUNICATION TECHNOLOGIES

Just as the printing press enabled the rise of a Fourth Estate, the advance of the internet and related media, information, and communication technologies have enabled the rise of the Fifth Estate. The printing press provided an opportunity for journalists to get news out quickly to large numbers of the public at a low cost. Their reporting on events and the actions of governments, business, and industry could hold major actors more accountable. Likewise, the internet and related technologies have provided the tools for individuals to potentially reach a global audience.

Examples and case studies in this book will discuss various technological advances and applications used by the Fifth Estate. It is important to note that there is no single gadget or device that is key, rather it is assemblages of many technologies—or packages of equipment, people, and know-how—that give ordinary members of the public the potential to reach large audiences (Table 1.1). They need not be technical experts nor have journalistic experience. Most of the technologies that enable the Fifth Estate are in the hands of billions of individuals across the world.

Table 1.1 **Network Digital Media, Information, and Communication Technologies**

Types	*Applications*
Searching the web	Search engines including Google Search, YouTube, Microsoft Bing, Baidu (Chinese)
Composing a website	Creating a personal web page on a web server
Blog or "weblog," website for informal notes, discussion, or information	Platforms such as Blogger, WordPress, Jekyll, Typepad
Micro-blogging	Twitter, Tumblr, Seconds (video website), Sina Weibo (Chinese)
Social Networking	Facebook, LinkedIn, Google+
Photo Sharing	Instagram, Snapchat, Pinterest
Video Sharing	YouTube, Facebook Live, Periscope, Vimeo, Twitch, Dailymotion, Veoh, Dtube
Vlogging	Video blogs or logs popular on YouTube

ENABLED, NOT DETERMINED, BY TECHNOLOGIES

The Fifth Estate is not an inherent outcome of digital media, information, and communication technologies like the internet. Decades ago, Emmanuel Mesthene (1981: 99–100) identified three "one-dimensional" views about technology as an "unalloyed blessing," an "unmitigated curse," or as "not worthy of special notice." Long since he wrote, all three views have been prominent in debates about the role of the internet in society and politics—underscoring the wisdom of his observations. The first two views are fair to characterize as technologically deterministic—in that they suggest the features of technologies are destined—or technologically wired—to have particular kinds of biases and outcomes, such as technologies of freedom or of surveillance. The last view is more focused on the use of technologies across different contexts in which we can find dual and countervailing outcomes over time.

A prominent journalist and influential academic, Evgeny Morozov (2020), seems to take this latter view in dismissing efforts to define the impacts of the internet on democracy or any other aspect of politics and society. He sees the internet as increasingly an aspect of everything, and that its role depends on how it is used in particular contexts. He calls this a "practice-based" view. I agree with his perspective to the degree that it restates what has been called a "social shaping" perspective on technology and its impacts (MacKenzie and Wajcman 1985). However, I do not conclude that the internet is of no particular importance. Even if the internet reinforces existing social and economic structures in particular settings, then that is a critical, important influence.

If you look at practice—how the internet is used across many different contexts around the world—it is true that it can be used for good or ill, for supporting or undermining democracy, and so on. However, it is inductively and empirically clear that its use is reconfiguring access to information and people in ways that enable individuals to source and network that can enhance their communicative power. As Mesthene (1981: 128–29) notes, technologies are not deterministic and their implications are often countervailing, but they are not neutral. They create "new physical possibilities and social options" that "require the emergence of new values, new forms of economic activity, and new political organizations." The Fifth Estate is not a political organization, but one of the new political power shifts enabled by the internet reconfiguring access.

SHIFTS IN COMMUNICATIVE POWER

As discussed in the introduction to this volume, power shifts are one of the most critical issues in considering the political and societal implications of the digital age. Power has been one of the most central and most avoided concepts in the scholarly study of politics. On the one hand, it has long been the essence of politics, since the times of Niccolò Machiavelli's classic *The Prince*, which advised the prince about how to wield power to rule or command his subjects. Machiavelli made politics become known as the art and science of getting and keeping power. However, for modern-day political scientists, power has also been one of the most elusive concepts to define and empirically measure. Nevertheless, it is understood not to be a thing that someone can possess, like wealth, but a relational property. A person can have power over some people, such as influencing them to do something they would not otherwise do, but not over others. It is relative to the time, place, and people involved.

Similarly, a person might have a certain ability to communicate with other people, which could be enhanced or diminished online. A one-to-many broadcast network would enhance the communicative power of the broadcaster. A one-to-one telephone call might equalize or have a "leveling effect" on the power of the two people on a call. In such ways, communication and information technologies, like the internet, do not have deterministic impacts, but they matter. Technologies make it easier or more difficult to do things. Harold Innis (1950) made this argument famous, as did his student Marshall McLuhan (1964), in saying the "medium is the message." The fact that a telegraph, for example, enabled instant communication over a long distance made a greater difference than what specifically one said over that medium. It extended the communicative power for the sender and receiver relative to not being able to communicate over a distance. In such ways, the internet can enhance the communicative power of individuals in particular situations, times, and places. In this respect, the Fifth Estate is not defined by the use of the internet or social media per se, but by its use by individuals to enhance their informational or communicative power vis-à-vis other actors (Box 1.2).

Similarly, there are multiple approaches to using the internet: from the composition of messages to the use of different platforms and social media, which could enhance one's communicative power, whether as an individual or an institution. For example, the Republic of China has begun to focus on enhancing what it calls its "discourse power" in relation to the West in the context of the rising cold war replacing e-diplomacy with

---

Box 1.2 **Informational and Communicative Power**

The catchphrase that "information is power" is almost right—but wrong in three respects. First, power is relative, over time, or in relation to others. Second, having information is less important than the ability to obtain, understand, and use that information. Many institutions, therefore, have the advantage over individuals in their ability to be informed and to communicate with whom they need to reach at the time and place they wish to do so. Third, in the age of the internet and digital media, communication or networking has become as important as information processing. Thus, institutions with a greater ability to communicate and network relative to others have relatively more communicative power compared with those that do not. In this way, informational (processing information) and communicative (networking information) power are distinguishable but without sharp boundaries between them in the digital age. For this reason, these terms are sometimes used in this book to stress the kinds of resources networked individuals use (information or communication) and other times used almost interchangeably. In that sense, the Fifth Estate is enabled by networked individuals having relatively more informational and communicative power than they had in the past and in relation to other actors who are not strategically using the internet and related media.

the United States. This is about China reshaping its communicative power vis-à-vis the West.

EMPOWERING INDIVIDUALS ACROSS INSTITUTIONAL ARENAS

The argument of this book is not that networked individuals are empowered simply by virtue of having access to the internet and related digital media, but that their strategic use of the internet has the potential to enhance their informational and communicative power. Nor do networked individuals have a monopoly over use of the internet. Institutions are using the internet in ways designed to enhance and maintain their roles in politics and society and are analogous to the strategies of networked individuals.

That said, it is possible that some individuals may be able to use the internet and related digital media more rapidly and effectively than some institutions, as well as having more convincing arguments or evidence. This is the idea that networks can move more rapidly than hierarchies in a digitally networked world. In this respect, the Fifth Estate is not defined by the use of the internet per se but by its strategic use by individuals—in contrast to institutions—in ways that enhance their communicative power vis-à-vis other actors. Too much emphasis in discussion of ICTs is placed on the implications of specific technologies, like social media, rather than the strategies and aims of particular individuals using technology, a theme developed in Chapter 2.

Across sectors of society, whether politics, health, or news, for example, there are networked institutions and networked individuals using the internet (Table 1.2). Some bloggers try to convey news to those who follow them, with some seeing themselves as citizen journalists. But in part in response to the rise of blogging, many established news organizations, such as broadcasters and newspapers, created online initiatives to reach audiences with some or more of the content they have to convey over multiple platforms. Increasingly, of course, print newspapers are diminishing as news provision has moved so predominately online.

Likewise, governmental institutions have created e-government and digital democracy initiatives, such as supporting online coverage of parliamentary or legislative proceedings, but individuals might blog about these proceedings with their own commentary on events and policies. Some scholars have seen the development of innovations in digital democracy as creating the potential for a new "fourth" branch of government in which citizens directly participate, even to the point of having "citizen legislators"—a branch they call the Fourth Estate (Trammell and Terrell 2016). These initiatives use digital media to update, reinforce, and enhance the role and legitimacy of government, but they are not acting as a new estate as they are acting as a part of government rather than independent of the government.

In education, schools and universities have innovated via multimedia classrooms, online courses, and distance education. During the coronavirus pandemic, many schools and universities moved campus-based courses online, but even before this, many educational institutions had resources online, for example through course-management platforms like Blackboard. Individual students can also use the internet and related digital media in ways not dictated by their teachers or educational institution, such as using the internet informally for learning about a topic in or outside their formal courses. The

Table 1.2 **Networked Individuals Across Institutional Arenas**

Arena	*Networked Institutions*	*Networked Individuals*
News, Press, and Media	Online journalism, BBC Online, streaming of radio and television programming, live micro-blogging, podcasting by journalists	Bloggers, online news aggregators, Wikipedia contributors, netizens, citizen journalists, whistleblowers, sources of leaks
Business and Industry	E-commerce, enterprise social media, distributed collaboration tools, online business-to-business, business-to-consumer (e.g., e-shopping, e-banking)	Using the internet to shop, compare prices and products; online information or video on how to use a device; Uber or Airbnb; peer-to-peer file sharing (e.g., music downloads)
Work and Organizations	Flatter networked structures, networking to create flexible work location and times, virtual organizations	Self-selected work collaborations, systems for co-creation and distribution (e.g., open-source software), working from home (WFH)
Government and Politics	e-government, e-democracy, digital democracy initiatives, e-consultation, e-voting, electronic surveillance, e-diplomacy	Arab Spring, social networking in campaigns, net-enabled political and social movements, online debate and consensus building, e.g., Polis (Chapter 8)
Education	Virtual universities, online learning, in-home lectures, multimedia and hybrid classrooms, massive open online courses (MOOCs)	Backchannels, informal learning via the internet, fact-checking, teacher assessment, Rate My Teacher(s), Khan Academy, YouTube
Medical and Health	NHS Direct, emailing safety alerts, texting of health and safety messages, making appointments online	Going to the internet for health and medical information, networks of patients, networks of physicians
Research	Institutional ICT services, online grant and proposal submissions, institutional infrastructures for networking, data sharing	Collaboration across disciplinary, institutional, and national boundaries, online repositories of research papers

Source: Adapted and updated from Dutton (2009: 7).

role of online access to teaching and learning during the COVID-19 pandemic was so powerful for some individuals, such as those with mobility issues, that they have wanted the choice of online or hybrid in-person and online courses to continue.

Take the example of Rate My Teachers, discussed in Chapter 6, that students began as "Rate My Teacher" to have better information about the quality of different instructors when choosing classes. Before Rate My Teacher, many universities in the United States, for example, either did not conduct systematic reviews of teaching performance or they did but failed to make their evaluations publicly accessible to their students. Some enterprising students used the internet to create their own rating system, independent of their institutions. Arguably, the rise of this application led many more universities to ask students to complete teacher evaluations and make them accessible to their students. This example has faced controversy and will be discussed in later chapters of this book, but it demonstrates how networked individuals can gain communicative power in this institutional setting.

That said, it is not always a contest of power or influence between individuals and institutions. In most cases, individual use of the internet complements and supports the work and effectiveness of institutions. Journalists use blogs and tweets as sources of information. Students networking from their homes and libraries enable universities to provide online courses. The Fifth Estate is no more a fetish of individualism than political science is a fetish of institutions. It is seen and discussed in this book as a complement and not a substitute or replacement for institutions.

STRATEGIES OF NETWORKED INDIVIDUALS

The Fifth Estate can have an effect most often because networked individuals strategically use the internet to enhance their informational–communicative power. A major focus of this book is to describe many examples of how individuals and networks have followed strategies, which I have called searching, originating, networking, collaborating, and leaking (Table 1.3). These are interrelated and not mutually exclusive, but most

Table 1.3 **Fifth Estate Strategies Enhancing Communicative Power**

Type	Illustrations
Searching	Finding information through search or social media, e.g., a patient finding information about a product or service
Originating	Individual creates information, e.g., shooting a video of an event they are attending, or writing a blog about an issue
Networking	Self-selected social networks of individuals, e.g., patients with similar problems or physicians, for sharing information
Collaborating	Distributive or open-source intelligence, crowd-sourced aggregation of information or observations, e.g., ratings
Leaking	Insiders leaking information to online networks, e.g., whistleblowers

uses of the internet and related social media can be characterized by predominantly employing one or more of these strategies. These actions can emerge from a series of activities and need not be predesigned or intentional, but they can be effective by reliance on one or more of these affordances provided by online media.

Delineating the Fifth Estate

One drawback of the concept of the Fifth Estate is that colleagues often associate it with phenomena that it should not be confused with. All internet users are not the Fifth Estate. The Fifth Estate is not one of the other estates, such as the Fourth Estate of the press, nor is it another term for electronic democracy—e-democracy. Likewise, the idea of networked individuals is distinctly different from networked individualism, malicious users, or a mob. And finally, the Fifth Estate is not the tech giants, which represent another estate of the internet realm. In Chapter 2, the Fifth Estate will be clarified in relation to related concepts, other estates of the internet realm, and other actors not to be confused with it.

The Fifth Estate is not a set of malicious users. Bad actors, such as hackers, are often focused on the financial rewards of fraud, phishing, online scams, and other cybercrimes and working for criminal organizations. They are economic enterprises, not civic organizations. Hackers working for states, such as the six Russian GRU officers charged with deployment of malware, support their respective state sponsors.[10] They are hardly independent of government.

There are good actors, in a normative sense, among the hacking community. Hackers originally referred to "compulsive programmers" who hacked together programs often forgoing sleep to complete their work (Weizenbaum 1976). The term has since been tarnished by film and news accounts of malicious hackers, but many of the heroes of the internet world and many of the Fifth Estate actors described in this book are what have been called "civic hackers," who seek to use networks for "finding creative solutions for civic problems."[11]

An Inductive Discovery Versus a Utopian Vision

Notwithstanding these constraints, as well as many counterforces, the Fifth Estate is a realistic perspective that exists in practice today. It is not a fanciful vision. It has been concretely manifested in a wide variety of contexts. It is based on how the internet has been used in a growing array of cases to effectively advance more democratic–pluralistic control in nearly every sector of society. Moreover, this role of the internet does not require some yet-to-be-invented technology, nor must it await universal access to the internet. It only requires a critical mass of networked individuals who understand its strategic potential.

However, enemies of the Fifth Estate, within the other estates, malicious users, and the mob, can undermine it, such as by imposing restrictions on freedom of expression online or reducing the autonomy of networked individuals, for example through surveillance or inappropriate regulation of content and users. Just as the Fourth Estate depends on an independent press, the Fifth depends on a significant level of independence from control by government and the other estates of the internet realm.

Rethinking Earlier Conceptions

The Fifth Estate provides an alternative conception to a phenomenon that others have sought to capture. For example, many view the internet as creating a "public sphere" as best articulated by Jürgen Habermas (1991). This offers valuable insights but is too closely tied to a romantic view of the past and therefore unable to capture the rise of an entirely new sphere of influence. That said, Habermas has been influential in focusing attention on the centrality of communication and communication systems to social and political systems (Habermas 1991; Harste 2021). In that respect, the Fifth Estate is an example of this centrality in the digital age.

The notion of an "information commons" (Kranich 2004) and its many variants are often used to characterize aspects of internet space, especially the open sharing of information for free or at low cost. However, the internet and web contain much that is trademarked, copyrighted, licensed, or otherwise owned, in addition to its enormous range of free material, such as Wikipedia, making the concept of a commons problematic.

Social science perspectives that the internet creates a new "space of flows" are supported across other disciplines (Castells 1996, 2009). For instance, a key creator of the web, Tim Berners-Lee, and his web science colleagues speak of the web as an "engineered space" creating a distributed "information space" (Berners-Lee et al. 2006). They realize this space is being shaped by an increasingly diverse set of actors, including users, and for a wide range of purposes, some of which may not be those originally sought by its designers.

It is within this information space that a Fifth Estate is being formed, but the Fifth Estate is only one component of this space. Institutional networks also occupy this information space as do other networked individuals, such as malicious users. The interplay within the Fifth Estate and its interactions with other estates of the internet realm is a key aspect of the pluralistic processes reshaping governance and social accountability in contemporary politics and society.

The Future of the Fifth Estate

We need law and policy as well as self-regulation to protect the Fifth Estate, just as we need constantly to revisit protection of freedom of expression and an independent free press. Democratic social accountability in our networked society will depend on it. The mission of this book is to provide an understanding of the Fifth Estate and its democratic potential so that networked individuals and institutions around the world can design and implement law and policy that seek to protect, maintain, and enhance its role in our digital age. The last chapters of this book, therefore, focus on some of the legal, regulatory, political, economic, and other social contexts shaping the vitality of what has been a very open future of the Fifth Estate in a digital age.

2

Fifth Estate Theories of Distributed and Network Power

A new network power—the Fifth Estate—is reshaping the dynamics of politics and society in the digital age. Major contours of political power over centuries have been captured by theories of estates and parallel theories of the distribution of powers. Each of the estates, or powers, has evolved dramatically over time, but the continuity of their influential roles in politics can be traced from preindustrial times to the emergence of an independent press in the nineteenth century—an institution that has come to be viewed as the Fourth Estate. This book provides an understanding of Fifth Estate theory: what is it, how it arises, and how it shapes politics as well as all sectors of society. The book also addresses the challenges to raising awareness of the valuable role the Fifth Estate can play in pluralist political systems. How can technology and policy defend and reinforce the empowerment of networked individuals of the Fifth Estate and its role in shaping accountability and governance in politics and society?

The democratic role of a distribution of powers, including the idea of a Fourth Estate, is reflected in more contemporary political theories of the separation of powers, pluralism, and networks. The influence of each of the four estates is anchored in different resources, ranging from authority, intellect, or money to the ability to communicate with large numbers of the public, enabling each estate to individually, and mutually, check the power of other estates and hold each more accountable in ways that counter concentrations of power in society.

However, the rising network power in the hands of ordinary individuals—networked individuals—in the digital age cannot be reduced to or well incorporated in any of the traditional estates or powers. Moreover, the collectivity of networked individuals of the Fifth Estate can hold the Fourth Estate and other centers of power more accountable in ways that do not fit into previously recognized centers of power. In such ways, the Fifth Estate can contribute to advancing theories of the estates, the separation of powers, and pluralism to better capture the dynamics of politics and society in the digital age.

I add societal changes to politics as the empowerment of networked individuals extends beyond the political system per se to reach nearly every sector of society. From the household to the dynamics of organizations, many networked individuals can gain relatively more informational and communicative power vis-à-vis other individuals and institutions through their strategic use of networks—gaining network power.

The Fifth Estate. William H. Dutton, Oxford University Press. © Oxford University Press 2023.
DOI: 10.1093/oso/9780190688363.003.0003

This book provides a theoretical explanation of how ordinary people have employed a variety of strategic approaches in their use of the internet and related digital media to be empowered and to hold others more accountable in politics and society. Just as not all news institutions are independent and reflective of a Fourth Estate, not all networked individuals are acting as a Fifth Estate. Only a subset of networked individuals approaches the idea type—following the strategies of individuals who compose this new Fifth Estate. The Fifth Estate is not determined by technological change, but it is socially shaped by technical, institutional, legal-constitutional, cultural, and other social factors that can undermine or enhance its significance overtime in different local, cross-national, or global contexts. Theory and research on the dynamics of networked individuals who take on the role of the Fifth Estate across different contexts is at the heart of this book.

Finding the Fifth Estate

Since the turn of the century, internet-enabled online social networking, the web, blogging, texting, tweeting, and other digital channels and services have provided the opportunity for networked individuals to reconfigure their access to alternative sources of information, people, services, and technologies (Dutton 1999, 2005), greatly enhanced by smartphones, like the iPhone launched in 2007, which combined with the internet to provide access to information anytime from anywhere in the world. With greater ease, networked individuals could use the internet to move across, undermine, and go beyond the boundaries of existing institutions, thereby opening new ways of increasing the accountability of politicians, press, experts, and other loci of power and influence. These capabilities allow the Fifth Estate to play a role comparable to the press—the Fourth Estate—that arose in the earlier print era. Use of the internet, like evolving uses of the printing press, augmented by the electronic mass media, is shaping new modes of governance across sectors of increasingly "networked societies" (Castells 1996). The metaphor of the Fifth Estate seeks to capture this digital age network power shift.

The idea of a Fifth Estate arose from observing empirical patterns and trends over time in how people use the internet. From this perspective, the Fifth Estate is a sensitizing concept as it helps bring you—the reader—into the multitude of observations described as this new estate. However, once identified, empirical realities vary across individuals and over time, such as with new applications and generations of users. Therefore, it becomes useful to view the Fifth Estate as an ideal type as one means for speaking about the generic pattern while acknowledging variations. That said, the concept of the Fifth Estate works as well because it is linked with other concepts of what might be called estate theory or the separation of powers. It therefore becomes possible to not only name this Fifth Estate but also to develop theoretical perspectives on its role and function in politics and society.

Throughout this book, the Fifth Estate is tied to various theoretical concepts in political science and the social sciences more generally, such as the notion of power shifts. However, this chapter turns to a more focused discussion of how this concept fits into earlier theoretical conceptions of democracy and power in the network society. I want to show how historically anchored ideal types on which the Fifth Estate builds can provide useful analogies for understanding the political and social dynamics of the digital age.

Parallels can be drawn between preindustrial age landed estates, despite being far from democratic, and twenty-first-century actors and institutions, but with the addition of a new power shift captured by the Fifth Estate. By linking this new basis of informational and communicative power to more traditional bases of power, the Fifth Estate concept suggests that the changes wrought by the internet can be seen as a more independent collectivity of networked individuals rather than simply tied to the transformation of existing institutions and power structures. Both transformations are taking place. The internet has not only transformed the roles of multiple institutions, like political parties and the press, in society, but it has also brought new forms of power into play that could enable a more democratically pluralist political and social system for the twenty-first century.

This chapter begins by anchoring the Fifth Estate to earlier conceptions of estates of the realm, focusing particular attention on the Fourth Estate, which was empowered by the rise of the press since the eighteenth century. This provides a historical perspective on Edmund Burke's discussions of the mob and the traditional landed estates of Ireland, which set the background for him to point to the press as a new Fourth Estate.

This discussion of the Fourth Estate also draws on Montesquieu's conception of a tripartite system of power in France, which provided another basis for defining a Fourth Estate, but in relation to the separation of powers designed in the US Constitution. This has been the basis for discussion of the press as a Fourth Estate in both US and Australian contexts. The chapter then explains how these preindustrial actors could be continuously transformed to adapt to the postindustrial information or network society.

The continued relevance of the Fourth Estate is evident in continuing efforts to understand the Fourth Estate in the twenty-first century and link it to the principle of the separation of powers in contemporary theoretical perspectives on the separation of powers and pluralist democracy (Cater 1959, Schultz 1998) as well as control over the internet and social media (Wu 2011). The chapter then focuses on the influence of networked individuals in the twenty-first century as analogous to the emergence of the Fourth Estate both as an empirical reality and an ideal type.

The chapter uses this framework for identifying the rationales of many unwitting critics—sometime enemies—of the Fifth Estate. Unwitting in that the Fifth Estate can be viewed as complementary rather than in opposition to the other estates as well as other actors in civil society. And unwitting in that attacks on the Fifth Estate are too often based on either a media-centric assault on social media or on a distrust of user-generated content or a monolithic view of the power of governments or economic elites than on an actor-centric view of the Fifth Estate in a pluralistic system of power. The internet and social media have enabled the rise of a Fifth Estate, but not all internet and social media users are the Fifth Estate—just as not everyone using the communication medium of the printing press or mass media, such as state-controlled media, is part of the Fourth Estate.

The Historical Origins of a Metaphor for the Digital Age

As discussed in the introduction, I use the Fifth Estate as what would be called a "sensitizing concept" in the social sciences (Blumer 1954, Bruyn 1966: 32–34), as it is used to help bring you—the reader—into a set of more concrete empirical observations. As with other theoretical concepts, once understood, it tells you what to look for—what is important. In this instance, the Fifth Estate focuses attention on the entry of networked individuals into the political dynamics of the digital age and the actors and motivations in support and in opposition to their empowerment.

THE RISE OF A FOURTH ESTATE

The concept of the Fifth Estate is most closely related to and built on contemporary use of the idea of a Fourth Estate, which evolved as a sensitizing concept to help Edmund Burke and others to alert the other estates to the growing influence of the press (Reeve 1855). The press—when playing a "watchdog" role independent of governmental or commercial control—is the Fourth Estate (Schultz 1998). In the 1950s, Cater (1959) saw the import of how the press governed through "publicity" to establish it as a virtual "fourth branch of government." In that sense, it is not only a depiction of an historical rise of the press as an influential political force but also a normative model or ideal type for how the press should function in a liberal democratic society (Cater 1959). As an ideal type, the Fourth Estate can be used to judge the actual role of the press: Is it living up to its potential as an independent source of political accountability?

The press fulfills multiple roles, but one principal role is focused on political account- ability (Curran and Seaton 1991). The power of the press as an institution has been based primarily on its ability to disclose knowledge—getting the facts and observations to a wide public.

As social and political movements and revolutions were undermining the power of other estates, such as the aristocracy and the clergy, the press was gaining influence since the eighteenth century through its ability to reach a large audience. Its influence was gained through the technology of the press in printing and distributing papers, as well as through becoming an institution that could support and protect journalists (Schultz 1998). Technical advances, from the use of shorthand to audio-recorders and cameras to the smartphone and satellite imagery, have enabled reporters to gather, process, and disclose information locally and globally with increasing levels of accuracy and authen- ticity. The growing influence and legitimacy of journalism enabled it to train profes- sional staff, become more institutionalized, and counter efforts to suppress content, such as through government censorship, taxation (stamp duties), libel and defamation actions, the jailing of editors, and outright bribery to gain favorable coverage. As Potter Stewart (1975: 634) noted: "For centuries before our [US] Revolution, the press in England had been licensed, censored, and bedeviled by prosecutions for seditious libel." As early as 1859, when John Stuart Mill wrote his famous essay *On Liberty*, he argued that necessity for freedom (liberty) of the press was self-evident in order for the press to be a check against problems such as corruption or a tyrannical government.

The idea of a Fourth Estate emerged from empirical observations that generated controversy but eventually became a more accepted depiction of the growing influence of an autonomous press as well as a conception of its potential as an ideal type—an imaginary for the press. In both ways, as a sensitizing concept and ideal type, the Fourth Estate reframed discussion of the political significance and independence of the press from formal branches of government. In contrast, some proponents of Fourth Estate theory saw the press as virtually a new branch of government (Cater 1959), while others saw the Fourth Estate as the "people" in some form of a more plebiscitary democracy enabled by new media (Trammell and Terrell 2016). However, the independence of the press is the ideal form of a Fourth Estate and one that is counter to state ownership or state control.

The Fifth Estate is a modern metaphor that builds on this metaphor of the Fourth Estate, with its foundations in the preindustrial, postmedieval age. And, similarly, the Fifth Estate is empirically anchored. While the potential influence of networked individuals is widely accepted or feared, the Fifth Estate remains a relatively new conception of the empirical reality and not yet understood as an ideal type. If the Fifth Estate could become a more salient normative model, it could enhance the role of networked individuals in holding the other estates more accountable as well as enable itself to be protected by law and policy. In such ways, the Fifth Estate could reframe discussion of the social and political role of the internet and social media in politics and everyday life in the digital age, providing both an empirical understanding of a new power shift and ideal type to guide the civic use of the new media and its regulation.

The Fifth Estate is a metaphor that connotes a new power shift—unique to the internet's digital age. It is composed of a moving, ever-changing collectivity of individuals who strategically use online networks to enhance their informational and communicative power vis-à-vis other actors. As a metaphor, the concept seeks to convey a new theoretical conception of how the use of the internet has changed the dynamics of communication and power in politics and society. To appreciate this metaphor, it is helpful to look back to the postmedieval or preindustrial age origins of conceptions of the Fourth Estate and draw their lose but clear functional equivalents in the digital age. I then move to contemporary research and discussion of the Fifth Estate to explicitly link my use of the term to alternative perspectives.

If you are content with my definition of the Fifth Estate in the introductory chapters, you may wish to move on to later chapters. However, I seldom talk about my work on the Fifth Estate without someone asking, What are the other four estates? If you are curious, this chapter offers my answer to this as well as natural follow-up questions, such as, Who are its critics?

THE FOURTH ESTATE

The concept of "estates of the realm" can be traced to divisions in the landed estates of Irish society between the clergy, nobility, and the commons—the three traditional estates. The Fourth Estate connotes an independent press and mass media that can hold governmental and other institutions accountable for their actions, such as exposing corruption or management failures. Its influence is based on the ability of the press to source information independent of governmental or commercial control and reach a large public, such as through investigative reporting.

The Fifth Estate is not simply an extension of the press. Nor are bloggers the embodiment of the Fifth Estate. The press and mass media are institutions that are distinctly different from the Fifth Estate, but which sometimes compete and sometimes cooperate in supporting greater democratic accountability. The chapter argues that while networked individuals, such as bloggers, have often been seen as critics of the press, the press has increasingly become more reliant on networked individuals and the Fifth Estate, such as in sourcing material during ongoing events, which is then authenticated and widely distributed by the press (Benkler 2013). Moreover, many of the policies and regulatory frameworks that support the press as a Fourth Estate, such as freedom from governmental or commercial control, have been supportive of the rise of a Fifth Estate. Threats to the independence of the press will be discussed as these highlight how the Fifth Estate can also be under threat on a variety of fronts.

The concept of a Fourth Estate is most often attributed to Edmund Burke, who was quoted by Thomas Carlyle (1831), who wrote long after Burke's speech to Parliament in 1787:

> Burke said there were Three Estates in Parliament; but, in the Reporters' Gallery yonder, there sat a Fourth Estate more prominent far than they all. It is not a figure of speech, or witty saying; it is a literal fact—very momentous to us in these times.

Burke and Carlyle popularized this concept not only among their contemporaries but also with leading public intellectuals for decades, such as Potter Stewart (1975). However, Thomas Macknight (1858: 462) argued that Burke was repeating an earlier observation as the origin of the idea could be traced to a British historian and politician, Thomas Macaulay.[1] It was Thomas Macaulay (1828: 165), who wrote, a few years before Carlyle: "The gallery in which the reporters sit has become a fourth estate of the realm." Decades later, John Thadeus Delane (1852) wrote an editorial as editor of *The Times* in which he used the Fourth Estate terminology to justify a separation between the press and government in order for the press to have the freedom to disclose information about events and public actions without fear of retribution or governmental sanctions (Cook 1915).

Whether Burke, Macaulay, or another originated the concept of a Fourth Estate during this postmedieval, preindustrial age of landed estates in Ireland and England, it has come to be associated over centuries with the press. The other three estates were the church or clergy, generally considered the first as it was established before the monarchy; the aristocracy or nobility; and the commons, or the established governing body of the time. I will keep referencing these estates of the realm, along with the fourth, as they have relevant analogies to power in the postindustrial digital age. In many respects, they are a wonderfully simplified framework for conceptualizing what has become known as a pluralist society or polyarchy (Dahl 1961, 1971).

MONTESQUIEU'S CONCEPTION OF THE SEPARATION OF POWERS

The French philosopher Baron de Montesquieu (1748) defined a "distribution" of political power between a legislature, an executive, and a judiciary. It has been treated as his tripartite system of governance, which greatly influenced the framers of the US constitution in defining a separation of powers between the legislative branch (Congress), the executive branch (president and the executive), and the judicial branches of the federal government (the courts). Parallel perspectives on the separation of powers exist as well in other liberal democracies, for example, Australia.

The idea of the distribution of powers in government preceded Montesquieu, but his work was among the most influential in the founding of the US Constitution and the notion of a separation of powers. Given this strong tradition in the United States, the Fourth Estate has long been used there as a complement to its constitutional doctrine of a separation of powers—as a new basis of power, independent of government, protected by the First Amendment to the Constitution, as the Fourth Estate. But whether we follow the path from Ireland's landed estates or the French distribution of powers, we end up adding a new Fourth Estate, anchored on the press.

Digital Age Parallels to the Preindustrial Estates

Given this brief sketch of the historical foundations of the metaphor of a Fourth Estate, I will build on the heuristic value of this metaphorical notion to imagine the modern-day—digital age—counterparts to the older estates of the realm and tripartite systems of governance.[2] You can see in Tables 2.1 and 2.2 how these historical entities might be transported into more contemporary digital age analogies.

I find the estates to be broader and heuristically richer than the separation of powers; they extend beyond the formal institutions of government to include powers that are no longer in formal positions of public authority but remain critical to a pluralistic range of different resources that provide bases of power, influence, and governance in liberal democratic societies. Montesquieu's tripartite system reminds us that government is most often not a monolithic entity but composed of separate bases of power, as are all the other estates or powers. The value of these categories is not in capturing the complexity and detail of historical changes—it is quite the opposite: capturing some fundamental similarities and continuities over time. They provide a simple structure for discussing the pluralistic bases of power in modern societies, which can be broken into far more fine-grained categories if relevant to a particular case.

Table 2.1 **Preindustrial Estate Metaphors for the Postindustrial Digital Age**

Preindustrial Estates & the Mob	*Postindustrial Digital Age Analogues*
Clergy	Public intellectuals, experts, technologists
Aristocracy, nobility	Business, industrial, economic elites, and internet industrialists, platform owners, internet celebrities
Commons	Government, politicians, and regulators
Press (4th Estate)	Journalists and mass media
Mob	Civil society, voters, networked individuals, mobs

Table 2.2 **Montesquieu's Tripartite Distribution and the Separation of Powers**

Tripartite	*US Parallel*	*Australian Parallel*
Courts, judiciary	Judiciary	Judiciary
Monarch, executive	Executive	Executive Government
Parliament, legislative	Legislative	Parliament
	Fourth Estate of journalists and mass media	Fourth Estate of journalists and mass media
	Civil society, voters, networked individuals, mobs	Civil society, voters, networked individuals, mobs

Given this breadth, it is fascinating that the historical estates continue to map well onto contemporary categories of powerful actors in the digital age (Table 2.1). The role of the church and the clergy has been diminished greatly over time, although this varies cross-nationally. However, the clergy remain significant among a larger group of public intellectuals who wield tremendous influence over public affairs in most postindustrial, liberal democratic societies.

Likewise, the aristocracy has been diminished over the decades in most postindustrial societies. In the United Kingdom, the continued existence of the House of Lords, a remnant of a more aristocratic society, has been challenged by many for being a body that is not popularly elected, despite it often being credited with serving a useful oversight role. However, the modern equivalent of an aristocracy is arguably better represented in contemporary societies by business and economic elites, including business leaders, industrialists, and the owners of the big tech companies. They possess enormous personal and institutional wealth, clearly one basis of their power, but their corporate and commercial interests need to be balanced with other values and interests.

In the digital age, the owners of the major internet and social media platforms, like Facebook, are viewed as increasingly powerful in shaping access to information and people online. These platforms can be seen as operating like a "master switch" to "a series of tiny choices whose consequences in sum we scarcely consider" (Wu 2011: 321). For far longer, there have been concerns over corporate ownership of media in the United States for example. Former US presidential contender and US Senator Bernie Sanders argued as recently as 2022 that the ownership of corporate media in America is far too concentrated and is restricting topics media companies can raise. For example, he tweeted a video on July 24, 2022, which said: "I want you all to know that we are looking at a situation in this country where a relatively small number of corporations control what we see, hear, and read."[3] He claimed that the press never asked about a number of topics because they were outside the bounds permitted by corporate media; he went on to enumerate these topics on a video posted online, which represents one small example of a politician seeking to use social media to circumvent the press.

Far more minor economic entities can yield powerful influences as well, particularly in the digital age. Internet and social media celebrities who can make financial gains based on many fans—their fandom—might also be included among the business and economic elites that could be motivated primarily by their entrepreneurial ambitions.

Similarly, the commons needs to be broadened as a power to incorporate all the various institutions of government—not only executive, legislative, and judicial but also the sometimes more independent regulatory agencies or authorities. That said, these public governing institutions remain distinct from the role of public intellectuals and the business and industrial elites as a locus of power in contemporary politics and society.

The press may have emerged as a Fourth Estate in preindustrial times, but its development over the centuries would have been unimaginable to Burke. In the United States, the First Amendment created a constitutional guarantee for a free press as an institution from control by government, which was interpreted in the 1920s to apply across all levels of government, from the federal to local levels. Potter Stewart (1975: 634) argued that the primary purpose of the founders of the US Constitution was to "create a fourth institution outside the government as an additional check on the three official branches." Likewise, Justice Brandeis had earlier argued that the distribution of powers established by the Constitution was designed to "save the people from autocracy" through the friction caused by a separation of powers.[4]

Over time, journalists have a far greater reach across new print, mass, and electronic media outlets locally and worldwide that increasingly builds on the advantages of the internet and social media. While some view the new media as an extension of the mass media, this transformation of the press and mass media is real but distinct from enabling a new power shift around the Fifth Estate, which can hold the press more accountable. Arguably, the networked individuals of the Fifth Estate are under the protection of the First Amendment's guarantee of freedom of speech of individuals in the United States, not the institution of the press.

ESTATES TRANSFORMED IN LIBERAL DEMOCRATIC SOCIETIES: EXPERTISE AND CIVIL SOCIETY

Thomas Carlyle was not a theorist of democracy or a proponent of democracy. He is known for his great man theory of world history.[5] During his time, most political movements outside the estates of the realm were tied to the "mob." Here you can see some of the greatest shifts over time. Not only did the press emerge as a new basis of power, given its ability to speak to the larger public, but there was also the rise of civil society, public interest groups, citizens, and the expanding scope of the public in voting and other forms of political and civic participation. Also the postindustrial, network society has witnessed a rise of experts with knowledge of a growing array of increasingly specialized fields and issues. Like information, the power to access expertise and experts is critical to informational power shifts, and every estate of the realm embodies many experts who can also play a role in the Fifth Estate. In fact, the internet and social media facilitate access to experts and expertise across institutions, sectors, and regions of the world.

Arguably, mobs—as large disorderly groups bent on causing trouble—still exist in real life and online, but the general public has become far more influential in multiple roles outside of the three estates, such as in civil society. Walls to defend the cities against the mob have indeed crumbled in modern liberal democracies.

Democratization has been one of the greatest aspects of political and social progress over the centuries. Just as the rise of the press and citizens has changed the political landscape of many nations, the rise of the internet and digital media has led to the emergence of networked individuals who are empowered by distinctly different resources and strategies than the other four estates—and can be envisioned as the Fifth Estate. When acting in a public-spirited role—independent of government, elites, public intellectuals, or the press—in holding others more accountable, they act from a new basis of power, the Fifth Estate.

THE PLURALIST NOTIONS OF THE SEPARATION OF POWERS

The Fourth and Fifth Estates are vital aspects of democratic accountability on their own terms—political accountability is their role as an ideal type. However, the existence of more independent bases of influence in liberal democratic systems are a virtue in themselves by creating a more pluralistic array of actors in shaping policy and practice. Pluralism has been viewed as a realistic perspective on democratic control as it envisions elites having greater influence than ordinary people, who are often uninvolved in politics, but without a monopoly of influence (Dahl 1956, 1961). In contrast to an autocratic system, a pluralist system achieves more or less popular control not by the equal participation of all—which is a myth—but through the interaction of separate and often specialized elites—a polyarchy—wielding power through their exercise of a variety of different resources, from the authority of the state to the expertise of public intellectuals to the financial resources of business and industry to the time, attention, votes, and protests of the general public (Dahl 1971).

NETWORKED INDIVIDUALS AND INSTITUTIONS ACROSS FIFTH ESTATE ARENAS

In the previous chapter, it was clear that there are complementary patterns in the use of the internet and related digital media across various institutional arenas, such as those identified in Table 1.2. For example, the press uses the internet and social media to maintain and enhance its role, but a journalist might well return home and write a blog, not as a journalist, but as a networked individual of the Fifth Estate. As the owner of Tesla, Elon Musk, is clearly among the business elite, but he famously used social media as an individual of the Fifth Estate in 2022 to great effect in his criticism and negotiations with the executives of Twitter and later in 2023 when he became its chief executive.

The internet is enabling networked individuals in each estate to associate in new ways—creating a Fifth Estate that helps them reconfigure and enhance their communicative power. Citizens, or civil society, in general, and experts and specialists in a particular area (e.g., medical professionals and patients), achieve this by going beyond their institutional sphere to reach alternative sources and contacts over the internet.

One of the most dramatic examples of a networked individual straddling different roles is the part played by the president of Ukraine, Volodymyr Zelensky, particularly in the aftermath of the February 24, 2022, Russian invasion of Ukraine. While president and representative of the commons—the government of Ukraine—he also spoke as a networked individual. During the Russian invasion of his nation, he spoke from his presidential offices and undisclosed bunkers in Kyiv, the capital of Ukraine, to the joint houses of the US Congress; the EU; the parliaments of Germany, Italy, Ireland, Israel, Japan, the United Kingdom; and more. In the United Kingdom, he channeled Shakespeare and Churchill. In the United States, he reminded elected officials of Pearl Harbor, Martin Luther King Jr., and Mount Rushmore. He spoke as a stateman for his nation and as a charismatic individual in ways unprecedented—via the internet. The UK journalist, Johnathan Freedland (2022), characterized Zelensky as "Churchill with an iPhone." He conveys information, does not hesitate to discuss what is at stake, evokes symbols effectively, and reaches across the world to appeal to a huge base of support for his nation's response to terror. He created an opportunity to win over the minds of a growing worldwide coalition of politicians and leaders of liberal democratic nations. Zelensky demonstrated an ability to powerfully reach leaders more directly during an ongoing Russian invasion of Ukraine over conflicting narratives of what was happening to his country and what help his nation required. He was president but also a networked individual of the Fifth Estate.

Of course, institutions rooted in the other estates, as illustrated by the press, can use online resources to maintain and enhance the communicative power of their organizations and institutions, such as print and broadcast media opening new online communication channels. In addition, institutional networking is supporting strategic shifts in organizational activities, including electronic government, internet commerce, working online, and online learning, but these are supporting existing institutions and are distinctly different from the activities of networked individuals, such as when the self-employed work from home.

As a result of these parallel developments—the digital transformation of existing institutions and the rise of new organizational forms, such as the Fifth Estate—there are challenges to traditional institution-based forms of authority. The Fifth Estate's network of networks, if independent of other estates and institutions, can complement or challenge existing institutions.

NETWORKED INDIVIDUALS VERSUS NETWORK INDIVIDUALISM

My use of the term "networked individuals" is similar to a related but quite different concept of "network individualism," a term coined by Barrie Wellman and his colleagues (2001) to refer to how the internet has created a hybrid form of networking that is distinct from traditional place-based communities or from individuals operating alone. For example, many critics of the online world argue that the internet is destroying place-based communities by substituting online communication for real community (Putnam 2000). Wellman and his colleagues argue that the internet complements and extends communities by allowing individuals to network with people outside of their neighborhood or school, for example, but it does not destroy the importance of community (Rainie and Wellman 2012; Hampton and Wellman 2021). In short, networked individualism is a sociological concept, which I find very useful, but it is distinctly different from networked individuals, which refers to the use of the internet in shaping one's informational or communicative power more than one's social network—a more technical and political, but also a sociological, conception.

A COLLECTIVITY OF NETWORKED INDIVIDUALS VERSUS A MASS SOCIETY

The Fifth Estate is also quite distinct from conceptions of a mass society. Institutional elites have long been skeptical of ordinary members of the public being sufficiently competent to participate in governance or public affairs. The three estates of the aristocratic feudal era viewed the public as little more than a mob. The press became viewed as a Fourth Estate because it could reach a large public and shape public opinion, giving it a unique source of influence. Yet institutional elites remained critical of the wisdom of public opinion, despite recognizing its significance. José Ortega y Gasset's *Revolt of the Masses* ([1932] 1952: 96) characterized the increasing role of the ordinary public quite bluntly as the "sovereignty of the unqualified." Such aristocratic views of popular participation in governance saw it as "rule by the incompetent" (Kornhauser 1959: 27).

That said, it is possible to see this viewpoint reflected in contemporary critiques of social media and the internet empowering ordinary people. However, such characterizations of the online world miss an essential aspect of the Fifth Estate. The internet and social media can empower ordinary people. They are not among the institutional elites directly involved in a particular decision or action. Nor do they necessarily represent mass public opinion. Instead, they are empowered by demonstrating an expertise or special relevance to the issue at stake through their voice online. The cliché that not every expert works in your organization can be extended in the digital age: not every expert participates in the process of governance as a member of one of the four estates.

The internet enables networked individuals to gain some informational or communicative power in issues where they have special relevance, such as having relevant expertise, being an eyewitness to an event, or being directly involved in an issue. A journalist might blog about an issue they are covering. A scientist might offer advice on a matter they have deep knowledge of. A witness might post a photograph from an event they were present at. A young person might express themselves in a uniquely powerful way. Throughout this book you will see many examples of ordinary networked individuals making a difference without either being among the institutional elites directly involved in a matter or one voice of the masses.

THE ROLE OF A COLLECTIVITY OF CIVIC-MINDED INDIVIDUALS VERSUS MALICIOUS ACTORS

Alvin Weinberg (1981) warned his readers of the risks tied to any technological fix. It is an illusion that technologies simply solve problems, as in doing so, they often generate new problems that require more technical fixes. If the internet empowers civic-minded networked individuals, it might enable malicious actors as well. In that sense the internet is rather democratic. Throughout this book, it is critical to keep in mind that the rise of the Fifth Estate is likely to be accompanied by the empowerment of malicious actors as well as those who are civil and public spirited. What to do about malicious internet users and the cybersecurity issues they raise is one of the major issues facing the future of the Fifth Estate.

MOBS AND THE FIFTH ESTATE

After the 2020 presidential elections, controversy over the outcome led those gathered for a rally by the US president, Donald Trump, with his family dancing on stage to a recording of 'Glory' from the 1983 movie *Flashdance,* to then march in protest to the US Congress to contest the election results. In the face of inadequate security at Capitol Hill, and malicious actors among the crowd, the protest transformed into a mob that resulted in property being destroyed, many injuries, and five deaths, including one police officer.[6] Disorderly groups of people intent on causing trouble happen in real life and online. Some commentators placed the blame on social media for the attack on the Capitol, creating a need for social research on the role of the internet and social media in this and other mob-like or violent actions.

Ironically, in the immediate aftermath, networked individuals went online to pore over selfies, other photos, and videos posted on social media by those participating in the events on Capitol Hill. This created some "270,000 digital tips to the FBI," contributing to the arrests of hundreds of participants (Zegart 2021: 168). However, the site they created, the Face of the Riot, "did not distinguish between people who broke into the Capitol complex and those who only attended protests outside it. Nor did the site's 'image dump' identify or remove mere bystanders, members of the press, or police officers" (Zegart 2021: 172). Did this crowdsourcing initiative turn into a group of vigilantes, a Fifth Estate, or another mob? Probably it was a mix of actors, with some individuals acting as a Fifth Estate in ways that could hold others more accountable, albeit not in a well-managed approach to collective intelligence (Chapter 6).

Similar blame was assigned to the internet and social media over the Arab uprisings, the 2011 England (London) riots, and some terrorist activities, such as the self-radicalization of individuals via social media. These claims have sparked calls for greater control of networked individuals, such as through content filtering, kill switches, and surveillance (see Chapter 9). As governments and commercial enterprises use the internet, social media, and big data as new means of gaining social intelligence and control over the public, an increasing number of scholars have dismissed its more democratic potentials, seeing the internet and related information and communication technologies as technologies of social and political control rather than technologies of freedom. The future of the Fifth Estate depends on how governments and other actors can respond to online or virtual mobs without creating greater problems (e.g., building a surveillance society). In part this means avoiding panic over social media and related technical innovations, which will be discussed throughout this book, and not confusing the Fifth Estate with the mob.

Enemies of the Fifth Estate

The vitality of the Fifth Estate within the space accorded by the internet is not inevitable and can be undermined or sustained by the strategies of the other estates in the internet realm. While the Fifth Estate can support and complement the other estates, it is most often viewed as a threat by existing institutions. In turn, it might be useful to quickly look at how these dual or alternative roles can be seen (Table 2.3).

PUBLIC INTELLECTUALS

For example, the modern equivalent of the First Estate of the clergy could be seen as the public intellectuals—individuals from the clergy, academia, the media, and other

Table 2.3 **The Fifth Estate and Other Institutions: Partnerships and Threats**

Preindustrial Estate	Post-industrial, Parallel	Opportunity for Fifth Estate to Complement	Perceived Threat of Fifth Estate
First: Clergy	Public intellectual	Worldwide research networks, science commons, experts' websites and blogs	Internet as amateurs' space without expert knowledge and analytical rigor
Second: Nobility	Economic elites	Collaborative network organizations, access to expertise, online interactions with customers	Centralization of information utilities, commercialization of Fifth Estate spaces
Third: Commons	Government	Innovations in engagements with citizens (e-democracy; e-government)	Censorship, regulation, and other controls that constrain and block internet access
Fourth: Press	Mass media	Use of Fifth Estate spaces to complement traditional media	Competition for audiences, funding, creating pay walls to online access and subscriptions
Mob	Civil society, including citizens, audiences, consumers, internet users, and the unorganized	Organized groups and interests; informed, helpful specialist forums (e.g., healthcare); greater democratic engagement	Putting the legitimacy of other estates at risk, undermining trust in the internet through malicious (e.g., spam, hacking) and accidental uses

sectors who are thought leaders with a national or international audience. These individuals yield influence through opinion pieces, essays, and interviews in the major media outlets and civil society circles, such as those created by business associations and nongovernmental organizations. Networked individuals can be viewed as a threat in several ways (Table 2.3). One is their use of media that many public intellectuals eschew, such as social media or blogs. Public intellectuals have most often come to prominence on other platforms, such as talk shows or newspaper opinion pages. Many could be threatened by a sense that they need to move to new media that are largely foreign to them.

Of course, the public intellectual is most likely to see their prominence earned by their intellect and training in developing and communicating their ideas. Not surprisingly, a prevailing criticism of new user-generated content is the argument that bloggers and networked individuals on social media are neither as brilliant nor as professional, lacking the training of those who should be interpreting events for a broad public. Instead, bloggers and social media commentators are claimed to be amateurs, over-occupying our attention with ill-informed and undisciplined views. User-generated content represents the "death of expertise" (Nichols 2017). For example, the subtitle of Andrew Keen's (2008) *The Cult of the Amateur* says it all: "How blogs, MySpace, YouTube, and the rest of today's user-generated media are destroying our economy, our culture, and our values." More generally, experts, such as medical and health professionals, might be equally threatened by social media users discussing issues that they are not adequately trained to address.

However, blogs or other user-generated contributions from networked individuals do not replace contributions from public intellectuals. They are a complement as there is no news hole on the internet that would limit the range of contributions. Moreover, networked individuals can be the public intellectuals' audience, and experts occupy every estate of the internet realm. Public intellectuals most often reach notoriety by their ability to synthesize and communicate the views of many experts, not based on their specialized expertise. Some of the cases in later chapters show how networked individuals can be the more qualified experts in particular cases, such as when they are at the scene of an event or accident or crime or are suffering from an illness. It is also possible that the internet and social media can enable experts to enter a public discourse when they have something new or profound to add to the conversation. Attention is a scarce resource, but that has always been the case, and the potential for a Greta Thunberg to draw the attention of millions and open a discussion of the climate crisis can be invaluable to experts on environmental issues in whatever estate and to public intellectuals. Again, they can complement one another.

However, to public intellectuals, amateur bloggers comment on issues that public intellectuals feel far better informed about and experienced in addressing (Keen 2008, Nichols 2017). To them, the internet and social media are somewhat of a Trojan Horse, which has snuck amateurs through the gates of intellectual respectability.[7] Not only that, but public intellectuals are also confronted with the criticisms of amateur bloggers and would-be experts, who hold them accountable. Stephen Fry, once threatened to stop appearing on Twitter because others on Twitter accused him of being boring, but he later decided to drop his threat and keep tweeting.[8] He himself—as a public intellectual in Britain—has been able to use Twitter to extend the reach of his work. Former UK

Prime Minister Tony Blair used the internet to get his ideas across and he was often critical of the government.

In such examples, it is clear that "user-generated content" on the internet and social media can be from experts from within any of the five estates, such as a former prime minister, an academic, or journalist addressing an issue, and their comments do not necessarily replace the contributions of the public intellectual—as they can be from a public intellectual as well. More often, they are likely to be complementary, such as when a blogger takes a public intellectual as the object of their editorializing.

Another criticism is that some bloggers or social media commentators might be popular, but the validity of information should not be judged on the basis of consumer choice online, rather it should be by one's peers in relevant communities of practice. To other public intellectuals, social media are simply a display of a worrying anti-intellectual trend toward consumer individualism, what others have called an "individualism fetish." As one physicist lamented, on social media, in discussing the United States and its culture of individualism:

> The fetish of exaggerated individualism is driving us to extinction. We in the United States seem to be in the vanguard of advocates for this type of atomization of humanity. We see this embodied in our overly compartmentalized suburban living spaces, social life and automobile centric transportation systems. This is also expressed in our growing rejection of all privileged viewpoints. So, for example, conclusions drawn from a large scientific consensus are rejected as "elitist" conspiracies upon which outright lies and quackery are permitted to cast doubt.[9]

However, a Fifth Estate perspective is not aligned with all viewpoints being equal, but more with notions of the value of collective intelligence, as discussed in Chapter 6, in which you would not expect every expert to be working in your community, institution, or nation. It is also based on the provision of more choice of content across millions of sources, as not everyone is interested in the same topics, issues, or problems. Search, as discussed in Chapter 3, helps individuals find the best sources for information about their particular interests in ways that cannot be replicated by traditional media. The best public intellectual in your nation might not be able to fix your washing machine, but that might be your problem of the moment. So, the expert or information you want is more likely to be online and findable. The experts are not the center of the world, but the individual is at the center online and able to source information from the experts they need.

Also, the Fifth Estate requires people to think about the nature of the actors and not the technology. Those outside the four established estates of the realm should not all be lumped with the mob but differentiated by the roles they play online, such as civil society versus the mob. All internet users are not the Fifth Estate, nor are all social media users. Too often, public intellectuals like Keen are wrong in attacking social media or user-generated content as the threat and fail to differentiate among the diverse abilities and interests of those online and using new media. This viewpoint dismisses valuable content on the internet and social media, possibly because established intellectuals are less informed and experienced online. Experts exist in every estate.

BUSINESS, INDUSTRIAL, AND ECONOMIC ELITES, INCLUDING THE BIG TECH GIANTS

The power base of twenty-first-century "nobility" is reflected in economic elites, for example, global corporations competing to dominate and commercialize internet spaces. Business and economic elites, such as the heads of the big tech industries, are often the objects of criticism by independent networked individuals. Growing numbers within institutions rooted in the other estates are networking beyond the boundaries of their organizations. This includes geographically distributed individuals networking together to form collaborative network organizations to co-create or co-produce information products and services (Dutton 2008). The online encyclopedia Wikipedia and open-source software products such as the Firefox web browser are examples of this phenomenon, becoming widely used and trusted despite initial doubts about the merits of their methods of creative co-production (see Chapter 6). This is just one way the Fifth Estate has a crucial transformative potential at all levels in businesses and other private-sector organizations.

There are concerns that collaboration online may blur the boundaries and operations of the firm or undermine the firm's productivity. Yes, working from home (WFH) has arguably enhanced productivity, particularly during the COVID-19 pandemic, and was enabled by the internet. Individuals in business and industry generally choose to use the internet and related digital media primarily to enhance their own productivity, performance, or esteem. Organizations need to understand how to capture the value of such innovations for the benefit of the enterprise as a whole, not simply for individual users. Moreover, as consumers become increasingly empowered to hold businesses accountable, such as through internet-orchestrated boycotts or better-informed consumer groups, the role of the Fifth Estate in business and industry will be even more visible.

Clearly, networked individuals of the Fifth Estate should not be confused with the owners of the big technology platforms that are central to the internet and social media across the world. The platformization of the internet has created new issues, such as around competition and content moderation by platforms, often demanded by governments. The platforms can undermine or support the Fifth Estate through the policies and practices they adopt, as discussed in Chapter 10.

GOVERNMENT AND REGULATORY AGENCIES

Government and regulatory agencies have viewed the users of social media and the internet as a problem because they do not fit neatly into traditional categories of actors subject to controls and regulations and are often protected by law and principles of free expression. The greatest threat to the Fifth Estate's enormous potential as an aid to democratic participation and accountability will be from the commons, such as if regulations, online gatekeepers, and other controls constrain or block the internet's original design as an open, end-to-end network allowing a free flow of content.

Many governmental administrations have made major strides in putting public information and services online, even though they have not generally kept pace with the commercial sector. This means that citizens and businesses can go online to complete tax returns or apply and pay for various public services. Many initiatives around the world have sought to build such e-government services. These e-government initiatives have been paralleled by innovations in e-democracy, including efforts to use the internet to support democratic institutions and processes (Coleman and Blumler 2009). However, in political campaigns, elections, and other democratic engagements, many still view the internet as largely irrelevant, marginal, or likely to undermine democratic institutions. Some critics suggest e-democracy could erode traditional institutions of representative deliberative democracy by offering oversimplistic "point and click" participation in public policymaking. However, these criticisms are normally aimed at institution-centric views of the internet.

Think of how politicians and public officials have used the internet and social media to have a more direct line to the public. Donald Trump did this from the White House and Oval Office while president of the United States. So did US Congresswoman Alexandria Ocasio-Cortez (OAC), such as when she posted a response to a tweet from Shell that went viral in which she criticized the oil company for gaslighting[10] and "lying about climate change for 30 years" (Carrington 2020:13). Even officeholders can move outside their traditional roles to speak and to hold others accountable online in ways that might well enhance their communicative power.

The Fifth Estate presents new opportunities and threats. It can enable political movements to be orchestrated among opinion leaders and political activists in "internet time." This can provide a novel means for holding politicians and mainstream institutions to account through ever-changing networks of individuals, who form and re-form continuously depending on the issue generating the particular network (e.g., to form an ad hoc "flash mob" at short notice through social networks and mobile communication). An example is the use of texting after the March 2004 Madrid train bombings to organize antigovernment rallies that challenged the government's claims and contributed to unseating that administration. Similar examples include the pro-democracy protests across the Middle East and North Africa in early 2011.

Politicians increasingly seek to use the internet to engage with citizens, including finding new sources of funding, as was successfully achieved during the campaign leading to the election of President Obama in 2008. A key element in open-government initiatives in the United States, United Kingdom, and other nations is to publish more information online in "user friendly" forms, such as linked data, including detailed departmental reports, plans and budgets, as a means for promoting greater transparency, enabling the public to hold politicians to account. In such ways, other estates are supporting the role of the Fifth.

THE PRESS AND MASS MEDIA

Traditional media are also competing with, co-opting, and imitating the internet's space of flows. The press is most obviously threatened by the rising influence of networked individuals as sources of news and information—even for the press (Cooper 2006). The internet has been criticized for eroding the quality of the public's information environment and undermining the integrative role of traditional Fourth Estate media in society. As noted, this includes claims that the internet is marginalizing high-quality journalistic coverage by proliferating misinformation, trivial non-information, and propaganda created by amateurs (Keen 2008) while creating "echo chambers" where personal prejudices are reinforced as internet users choose to access only a narrow spectrum from the vast array of content at their fingertips (Sunstein 2007). In the blurb to Greg Jericho's (2012) book on the Fifth Estate in Australian politics, it was vividly captured: "hell hath no fury like a criticised newspaper," reflecting how the press treated Jericho when he was blogging @GrogsGamut.

Such critical views of the Fifth Estate fail to recognize the two-edged nature of all communication technologies, including the traditional mass media's equivalent weaknesses (e.g., a focus on sensational negative news stories, its share of poor-quality reporting, and celebrity trivia). More importantly, there is often an unjustified assumption that the internet will substitute for, rather than complement, traditional media. Many internet users read online newspapers or news services, although not always the same newspaper as they read offline (Dutton 2009). And the internet and social media are often sources of news, such as in reports directly from participants in events, protests, and other activities. In these ways, the internet can be realistically seen as a source of news that in part complements, or even helps sustain, the Fourth Estate, given declines in journalists reporting from the field. At the same time, citizen journalists, bloggers, politicians, government agencies, researchers, and other online sources provide a related alternative that is independent and often competing. Moreover, the Fifth Estate can help hold the Fourth Estate more accountable, such as by identifying news outlets guilty of churnalism, that is, frequently disseminating press releases or prepared materials of politicians, governments, or business and industry, rather than doing actual and more costly reporting or even checking the facts of such material. Some websites even began counting the prevalence of news that was not original, such as a site designed to distinguish journalism from churnalism.[11]

MOBS, SPAMMERS, FRAUDSTERS, CYBERSTALKERS

Finally, there is the emerging force of the lay public and civil society, empowered by networked individuals—a modern and dramatic contrast to what Burke might have called "the mob." There may be mobs in contemporary society, and they can be enabled by the internet, such as a group of hackers in December 2010 calling themselves Anonymous, who sought to attack institutions that did not support WikiLeaks, via a YouTube video.[12] Anonymous argued it was the conscience of the internet and sought to play a positive role orchestrated online. That said, panic over the role of malevolent users online could drive disproportionate and inappropriate regulatory responses that could unintentionally undermine the Fifth Estate as well as every other estate increasingly dependent on the internet.

ATTACKS ON THE INTERNET AND SOCIAL MEDIA HIT THE FIFTH ESTATE

The perception of the Fifth Estate—or misleadingly, the internet and social media—as an enemy or adversary has fostered a number of critical attacks by the other estates.

Table 2.4 highlights criticisms of the internet and social media emanating from the others estates, particularly focused on user-generated content, that can undermine the vitality of the Fifth Estate. Public intellectuals, business and industrial elites, government and regulatory agencies, and the press, as well as the mob, have all attacked the internet and social media in ways that can undermine the Fifth Estate albeit often unwittingly.

Each estate, from a different perspective, can threaten the vitality of the Fifth Estate. Public intellectuals challenge the quality and motivations behind user-generated content. Economic elites can undermine competition online and vertically integrate in ways that undermine the ability of networked individuals to find the best information they are searching for. Government and regulatory agencies can develop policies that disproportionately regulate content, such as through filtering, undermining anonymity, or enhancing the ability of internet platforms to conduct mass surveillance of users. The press has at times sought to co-opt successful bloggers, imitate the free and open internet, and accuse social media of undermining quality information. And the Fifth Estate faces challenges from virtual online mobs, virtual vigilantes, bad hackers, trolls, spammers, fraudsters, cyberstalkers, and other malicious users who undermine the trust of networked individuals in the safety and integrity of the digital media (Table 2.4).

The enhanced communicative power of networked individuals has led to many attempts to censor and control social media and user-generated content, even by disconnecting the internet, equivalent to tactics used against traditional media. The internet's

Table 2.4 **Attacks on the Fifth Estate by Other Estates of the Realm**

Actor(s)	*Examples of Critical Attacks on the Fifth Estate*
Public intellectuals, experts	Viewing internet users as amateurs, without expertise in public affairs or topics of public discussion
Business, industrial, and economic elites	Vertical integration could undermine unbiased search; a monopoly over search could undermine quality, and increase advertised search and inappropriate or disproportionate content moderation
Government and regulatory agencies	Governments could disconnect users, usher in disproportionate or inappropriate content filtering (censorship), reduce anonymity, or enable mass surveillance
Press	News institutions critical of internet users and citizen journalists as amateurs; but they also hire and co-opt successful bloggers and online influencers; press imitating successful 5th estate roles and applications, such as online comments
Spammers, fraudsters, cyberstalkers	Undermining trust and confidence in the internet and social media; fostering content regulation; and incentivizing attacks on anonymity online

opening of doors to an array of user-generated content allows techniques deployed by governments and others to block, monitor, filter, and otherwise constrain internet traffic (e.g., Deibert et al. 2008). These are typified by the Chinese government's shift from open access to the global internet to adopting major legislative and technical approaches to filtering (censoring) and otherwise controlling access to internet content in China in what was called "The Golden Shield Project" or what has become more popularly referred to as the "Great Firewall of China".[13] Other examples are the Burmese government closing the country's internet service during political protests in 2007, and efforts by a number of governments to block internet access and create a "kill switch" to block the internet, such as the Kremlin shutting down most international social media in Russia and independent, nonstate broadcasters, after the February 24, 2022, invasion of Ukraine.

At the same time, networked individuals use the internet to challenge attempts to control access, such as by circumventing censorship. For example, from 2007–2019, a project at the Berkman Klein Center at Harvard University, called "herdict," accepted and published reports from internet users of inaccessible websites around the world, and the OpenNet Initiative and Reporters Sans Frontiers supports worldwide efforts to sustain and reinforce the internet's openness.[14]

Contemporary versions of mobs are putting pressure on governments and other estates to better control expression and activities online. And pressures emanate from the other estates, which perceive risks tied to the use of the internet and social media and want to defend their traditional role and activities. However, as suggested in this chapter, these actors should not panic as they could adapt to the rise of the Fifth Estate and change how they do what they do in ways that are not only complementary to and respectful of the legitimate role of the Fifth Estate but also further their own respective interests. To do so, they must know that such a thing as the Fifth Estate exists, a key objective of this book, and not focus their attacks on stereotypical visions of social media or user-generated content as harmful. The over 4 billion internet users across the world are composed of a diverse array of networked individuals—and their uses of the internet and social media should not be lumped together as some virtual mob, reminiscent of elitist views of the public as the mob of preindustrial societies.

The Power of Networked Individuals: Change from the Bottom Up

In preindustrial times, individuals outside the four estates were viewed as the mob. Industrial and postindustrial societies have enlarged economies to facilitate the expansion of education, incomes, and infrastructures, such as information and communication technologies, to ever-increasing portions of the population. In the digital age, as will be illustrated in Chapter 3, access to digital information and communication technologies has led most of the public in developed societies to feel informed, networked, and increasingly capable of forming opinions on public issues of the day.

Some fear this is associated with a rise of an extreme minority of populists. However, as discussed in the next chapter, our Quello Search Project (Box 3.3) found that in the

United States, United Kingdom, and five other EU nations, attitudes traditionally identified as populist are found in half or more of the general public of internet users (Dutton
and Robertson 2021: 425). Populism has become a new normal because—in part due
to the internet and social media—most of the general public believes they know more
and can find information about issues, and therefore deserve to be listened to by their
representatives. For example, three-fourths of networked individuals surveyed in the
seven nations of the Quello Search Project agreed that "elected politicians should follow the will of the people" (Dutton and Robertson 2021: 425). This view is no longer a
radical or populist perspective. The rise of these attitudes, civic organizations, and civil
society generally has meant that governments, business and industries, and public intellectuals are increasingly expected to be accountable to the goodwill of a critical mass of
ordinary people in an educated public.

If I could paraphrase Burke for our times, the idea that a critical mass of individuals
can play a powerful role in society is not a fanciful fetish of individualism but a literal
fact of life in liberal democracies. In studies of the role of the Fifth Estate, I have been
reminded of E. E. Schattschneider's (1960) brilliant perspective on the dynamics of
political conflicts. His ideas were based on traditional political strategies in liberal democratic politics—well before the digital politics of the internet. He offered his notion
of what he called the "semi-sovereign people" that has many contemporary ties to
mass media research around the role of agenda setting and issue framing (McLeod and
Detenber 1999). And work on agenda setting (Box 2.1) and issue framing (Box 2.2) has
proven valuable in relation to the role that active blogging communities can play (Shirk
2011, Hassid 2012). In addition, the ways in which issues are framed or presented by
contestants in debates can also shape initial opinions on the issue as well as the importance individuals place on resolving the issue. Consider President Vladimir Putin's effort
to frame what the West referred to as an unprovoked invasion of Ukraine—a war—as
a "special military operation" as one means of limiting public responses by the Russian
public to his actions in Ukraine.

However, Schattschneider's original conception linked agenda setting and framing,
as conceptualized in contemporary research, more directly to the outcome of political

---

Box 2.1 Agenda Setting

The concept of agenda setting has been one of the seminal ideas in the study of
the mass media and public opinion. Put simply, the argument is that the media are
less likely to influence the opinions of individuals or the general public than shape
the issues they care about. That is, the media tell us what to think about rather
than how to think about these issues. In an extreme example, the media coverage
of the September 11 attacks in the United States on the World Trade Center and
the Pentagon dramatically shaped what people were thinking about but were less
influential in shaping the opinions formed around this event. The issues people
think about are likely shaped by what issues the mass media cover. They serve an
agenda-setting function.

Box 2.2 **Issue Framing**

Politicians and media pundits often seek to present an issue in ways that will gain the most traction with their key audience—the most relevant stakeholders. For example, the advocates of abortion rights frame the issue as one of a woman's right to choose versus the opponents who frame the issue as the right to life. Many issues regarding the internet and social media could be framed in technical jargon to reduce the likelihood of the public engaging in the debate. Likewise, complex technical issues can be framed in simple and accessible terminology in order to draw more of the public into the debate, such as issues of network neutrality. How an issue is framed can shape the importance individuals place on the issue and their stance—for or against an issue (Nelson and Oxley 1999).

---

conflict. It therefore provides a useful language for discussing the role of the Fifth Estate in many of the examples discussed in later chapters (Dutton et al. 2015).

Essentially, Schattschneider (1960: 1) argued that the central aspect of politics in a liberal democratic society is that conflict can spread or become "contagiousness." The importance of this is captured by his analogy between politics and spectator sports, except—as he points out—in the game of politics, the spectators can join in the game at any time and on any side. And the outcome of the game or political conflict is shaped by the extent to which the spectators become involved and on what side they join. This dynamic makes the scope of a conflict one of the most important strategies of politics for contestants to control.

This is one reason why traditional political institutions place great importance on controlling communication. They do not want to accidentally create issues that bring more people into a conflict, as it could have unpredictable consequences on the outcome. For example, if someone is winning a contest, they would want to retain the present scope of conflict and keep all the spectators in the stands. In contrast, it is in the interest of those losing a conflict to broaden or otherwise change the scope, since they have nothing more to lose and can open up the possibility of more spectators joining their side or switching sides and thereby create the potential for a more positive outcome.

The scope of the conflict can be changed by socializing or drawing the attention of more people to the conflict (agenda setting) or changing the issue and how it is discussed or presented (reframing), which can lead some spectators to join a particular side or for some contestants to switch sides. This simple analogy provides a powerful perspective on why the internet can play a pivotal role in political and social processes. But for networked individuals to use the internet to shape the scope of conflict, they need alternative channels of communication, such as a blog, that are not controlled by those winning the game. It also requires the ability to source credible information that is independent of the media and other institutions that are controlling the agenda. It also helps explain why the existing estates of the realm are likely to perceive the Fifth Estate as a threat.

Conclusion

This chapter has provided a historical perspective on Edmund Burke's discussions of the mob and landed estates of preindustrial Ireland, which led him to identify the Fourth Estate of the press. It also introduced Montesquieu's conception of a tripartite system of power in France, which provided the basis for the separation of powers designed into the US Constitution, which became the basis for discussion of the press as a Fourth Estate in the United States.

These historically anchored ideal types provide useful analogies for understanding politics and other social processes in the digital age. Parallels can be drawn between preindustrial estates and the mob with twenty-first-century actors and institutions, with the addition of a new collectivity of actors that is captured by the Fifth Estate. By linking this new basis of communicative power to traditional conceptions of power, the Fifth Estate concept suggests that the changes wrought by the internet can be seen as more incremental than completely transformative. Even if the internet has not radically transformed the fundamental bases of power in society, characterized by the four estates, it has brought a new network power shift into play in ways that could enable a more democratically pluralist political and social system for the twenty-first century.

PART II

FIFTH ESTATE STRATEGIES

Access to the internet and related media, communication, and information technologies does not determine outcomes, such as the rise of a Fifth Estate. Inappropriate policies of censorship can undermine its viability. The choices of individuals, such as becoming bad actors to exploit the affordances of the internet are another way that the Fifth Estate can be undermined.

However, a Fifth Estate can emerge and thrive if ordinary individuals in particular contexts use the internet and social media in civic-minded ways that strategically empower them online. These strategies include the effective use of the internet in searching, originating, networking, collaborating, or leaking information. The importance of understanding the dynamics of these strategies has led me to focus on examining each one with examples that concretely illustrate their role at a particular time and place.

Part II begins with search since it is the easiest to grasp, as nearly all internet users employ search engines in a variety of ways to find information about nearly anything and everything. The technology that supports search is sophisticated and constantly evolving in a "cat and mouse" game as some internet users try to game the search algorithms of internet platforms. Nevertheless, most often search enables individuals to source their own information with tools equivalent to what many experts and journalists use. From the perspective of the Fifth Estate, this affordance translates into you—the networked individual—being able to source information that is not dependent on any one authority, but from a diversity of sources, giving you greater independence from other estates of the internet realm.

The remaining chapters in Part II look at the origination, networking, collaboration, and leaking of information in similar depth to convey how these strategies are interrelated and complementary to empowering networked individuals.

3

Searching

The societal implications of the diffusion and use of the internet and related information and communication technologies (ICTs) have been seen primarily through institution-centric perspectives on government, business, education, and other areas of the economy and society. For instance, government use of the internet started with initiatives focused on enhancing existing structures of government through "e-government" services and "e-democracy" initiatives around the world that were primarily focused on moving public information and services online (Fisher 2011). However, the internet has been more than a substitute for analog services. It has enabled a transformation in the ways that government, media, and other sectors do things, as well as giving rise to a genuinely new internet-enabled phenomenon—the Fifth Estate—that was not, and could not have been, foreseen from more traditional institution-centric viewpoints.

One of the most straightforward and concrete standpoints from which to see the role of the internet in enabling a Fifth Estate is by looking at internet use and search in everyday life. By understanding how internet users can easily and independently source information and network in areas such as business and industry, education, research, and health and medical care, it is possible to gain a sense of how a user's informational and communicative power can be enhanced online (Berners-Lee et al. 2006).

Mainly through surveys of how people use the internet for a wide range of activities, I discovered emerging elements of what I later called the Fifth Estate by observing changing patterns of behavior among internet users. Survey research and qualitative studies of the internet's use show how technical advances have enabled people to better source information and create their own networks of collective intelligence that can indeed empower them in everyday life in areas ranging from their health and medical care to politics. These include the internet's increasing significance across nearly all sectors of society, its use as a first port of call for information, the rise of search over the former reliance on specific authoritative sites, the rise of social media and the social cues and networks they offer, and the trust networked individuals have in what they can find online. The survey findings described in this chapter led to the conduct of a variety of case studies that highlighted the strategies of networked individuals in supporting their informational and communicative power, which will be described in this and later chapters.

The Fifth Estate. William H. Dutton, Oxford University Press. © Oxford University Press 2023.
DOI: 10.1093/oso/9780190688363.003.0004

Survey Research on Internet Use and Impacts

From the 1960s through the 1980s, the idea of individuals and households using computing and telecommunications in their everyday lives was largely a fanciful "blue skies" vision, only partly approximated by experiments with computer-mediated communication systems, such as around microcomputers and electronic bulletin boards. However, by the beginning of the twenty-first century, forecasts of the internet diffusing to a large portion of the public were viewed as increasingly credible, although from 2000 to 2003 when the internet began to spread more broadly, many continued to see it as a novelty, which would soon fail, analogous to an earlier fascination with citizen band (CB) radio (Wyatt et al. 2002).

That said, many academics and practitioners expected the internet to be a major development over the long term (Dutton 1999). At the Oxford Internet Institute, after I became its founding director in 2002, we conducted the first Oxford Internet Survey (OxIS) in 2003 (Box 3.1). With this survey, we also became a partner with the World Internet Project (WIP) (Box 3.2). These surveys allowed us to gain authoritative data on how people use or don't use the internet and related digital media and what differences they made in their lives.

OxIS surveys provided information on trends in internet use from 2003 through 2013 (Dutton and Blank 2013). And in 2019, we conducted another OxIS survey when

---

Box 3.1 The Oxford Internet Surveys (OxIS)

We conducted biannual Oxford Internet Surveys (OxIS) from 2003 to 2013 with a pause until 2019, when the survey was updated and repeated. OxIS was based on a multistage national probability sample of 2,000 individuals in Britain, enabling us to project findings to the nation as a whole. OxIS surveyed users, nonusers, and ex-users, covering internet and ICT access and use, attitudes to technology, and supporting demographic and geographic information. Each survey was a cross-section of the UK public fourteen years and older based on a multistage probability sample of households in which we randomly sampled an individual within each selected household. OxIS focused on three of the four nations of the UK (England, Wales, and Scotland), not including Northern Ireland due to the cost of reaching this nation across the North Channel of the British Isles. Given sponsorship from a variety of sources, we were able to conduct face-to-face interviews through 2013, leading to high-response rates, but we shifted to an online survey of a stratified random sample in 2019 as by that year over 80% of the UK population was online. Each survey was a new cross-section of respondents rather than a panel of the same individuals tracked over time, allowing us to randomly sample for each survey and thereby gain a more accurate estimate of internet use and nonuse. A more detailed overview of reports and methods of OxIS is available online at https://oxis.oii.ox.ac.uk/.

Box 3.2 The World Internet Project

In 2000, the World Internet Project (WIP) was launched as a global collaboration to track the use and impact of the internet. WIP was coordinated globally by Professor Jeff Cole at the University of California, Los Angeles. He and the project later moved to the University of Southern California, where he directed the Center for the Digital Future, part of the Annenberg School for Communication and Journalism. It was founded with the NTU School of Communication Studies in Singapore and the Osservatorio Internet Italia at Bocconi University in Milan, Italy. WIP enrolled partners from across the world to ask some common questions and meet yearly to share findings and plans. Together, the national surveys provided a rich data source for international comparisons, such as for gauging the commonalities between our findings in Britain and trends in the United States and other member nations (Cardoso et al. 2009, 2013: 216–36). Information about the WIP project is available online at https://www.worldinternetproject.com/about.html/.

---

over 80% of the UK population was online (Blank et al. 2019). Linking our findings to WIP studies, we compared results in Britain with findings in other nations.

Over the years, we were able to compare OxIS results with related research over time and in other nations, not only through the WIP but also through grants received to explore particular topics, such as the Quello Search Project survey of the United States and United Kingdom plus five other EU nations in 2016, focused on how people get information about politics (Box 3.3). Most of the findings discussed in this and other chapters are based on OxIS, WIP, or the Quello Search Project; the source of data will be identified in the context of the specific discussion of findings.

Patterns of Use Enabling a Fifth Estate

I did not look for the Fifth Estate on the basis of any preconceived theory or concept. Instead, I discovered an intriguing set of concrete patterns emerging and growing far more salient over the years. I found the concept of the Fifth Estate to be the best way to capture these patterns that were tied primarily to five separate but related trends in the use of the internet and social media. I will explain each in turn, but they include the internet becoming

- increasingly central and significant
- the first place people look for information
- increasingly navigated through search engines
- complemented by the use of social media and distributed collaboration
- trusted through experience gained over time

Box 3.3 The Quello Search Project

This study was based at the Quello Center at Michigan State University and funded by a grant from Google Inc. It addressed the question of how people obtained information about politics and whether search and related online media have a major impact on shaping their political opinions and viewpoints, such as whether they were biased by filter bubbles or echo chambers. Online surveys of respondents asked internet users how they used search, social media, and other important media for political information, and what difference this made for them. The project involved online surveys of stratified random samples of internet users in seven nations: Britain, France, Germany, Italy, Poland, Spain, and the United States. In addition, Google supplemented its support so this work could be presented in Montreal, Washington, DC, Mexico City, and Prague. Summaries of our project include presentations to academic, industry, and policy communities in Britain (London, Oxford); Germany (Hamburg, Berlin, Munich); Italy (Rome); Belgium (Brussels); Spain (Madrid); China (Beijing); and the United States (Arlington, Boston); and in a variety of publications, including Dutton et al. (2019). The report of this project (Dutton et al. 2017) is available online at https://papers.ssrn.com/sol3/papers.cfm?abstract_id=2960697/.

Over the years, these trends have become even more apparent and well understood. What was not understood initially was how these related trends, as explained below, were coming together to change how people do things that made individuals less dependent on traditional and local institutions and services, such as the local newspaper, shopping mall, doctor's office, library, school, or city hall. The communicative power of the networked individual was becoming less dependent on the information they gathered from these more traditional brick-and-mortar institutions and services and more dependent and connected with online sources. This gave networked individuals the potential to source information more independently and thereby enhanced their informational and communicative power.

GROWING CENTRALITY AND SIGNIFICANCE

As noted, even in the early twenty-first century, many thought the internet would be short-lived and marginal compared to traditional media, news, and entertainment outlets. In hindsight, it is clear that one of the most significant and obvious trends during the twenty-first century has been dramatically different—the growing importance of the internet to nearly everything. The longevity of the internet, its global diffusion, and its increasing significance across nearly every sector of society is almost unarguable. Far from fading away as a novel fad, the internet diffused to nearly two-thirds (63%) of the world's population, with nearly 5 (4.9) billion internet users and three-and-a-half (3.8) billion social media users by 2020.[1]

In Britain, for example, internet use exceeded 82% of the adult population in 2019, an increase from just under two-thirds (59%) in 2003 (Blank et al. 2019). But focusing on the mere diffusion of access can miss other fundamental transformations of the internet from 2003, when it was mainly based on a personal computer linked to the internet through a modem in the household, with a small portion of people on broadband, which has become nearly ubiquitous across the more economically developed world over recent years.

By 2020, most networked individuals had three or more devices, such as a laptop, smartphone, and tablet, some of which were mobile, that enabled them to use the internet from anywhere at any time. We called these individuals who had multiple devices, the "next generation users." The next generation users' ability to access the internet and related digital devices from anywhere at any time enabled their use to be even more central to a wider range of activities (Dutton and Blank 2011, 2013).

But looking back at the early years of the internet, its use was of significance primarily to academic networking, for which it was developed. Over time, its use became central to an ever-growing range of activities by all networked individuals. While these activities are too numerous to comprehensively list, the internet has become a key means for finding information about nearly any topic, product, or service, including using voice search over a personal digital assistant; entertainment and leisure activities, from surfing the internet to streaming movies; obtaining and providing services, from online shopping and banking to accessing governmental services; learning and education, such as in online courses; creating and producing information and communication for distribution online, such as in blogging, lecturing, or video conferencing with friends; and teleworking—working from home, while traveling, or in decentralized office spaces—a phenomenon that grew dramatically during the COVID-19 pandemic.

Perhaps nothing signaled the increased centrality of the internet and related digital media more than when, in the midst of the COVID-19 pandemic, the internet became a lifeline for many families and households, businesses, governments, and educational institutions around the world. Digital media became the way many households and businesses and schools were able to maintain themselves during the pandemic.

In other exceptional circumstances, such as in the midst of another crisis, the Russian invasion of Ukraine in 2022, threats of conscription in Russia led many potential conscripts to plan their escape from the war by searching online to find answers to their questions. What documents do I need? One community they could find through Telegram was called Relocation.Guide (Verma 2022).

Yet even during this time of tremendous reliance on services online, growing numbers of academics and media pundits were increasingly demonizing the internet and social media around issues of disinformation and political polarization. Rather than seeing these technologies as either an "unalloyed blessing" or an "unmitigated curse," to borrow from Mesthene (1981: 99), they were viewed as both, with seemingly little awareness of this conflicting duality, but certainly as a technology "worthy of special notice." For better or worse, there are few media of more significance to everyday life and once-in-a-lifetime decisions than the internet.

THE FIRST PLACE PEOPLE LOOK FOR INFORMATION

The significance of the internet is tied closely to it becoming a major source of information, but many fail to recognize just how important it has become as the first place people often look for information. In our second OxIS survey, in 2005, we began asking respondents, "Where would you go first, if you were looking for information on . . . ?" followed by a variety of topics. At that time, we wondered whether the internet was a significant source for people to go to for specific information. We almost did not ask this question because we assumed that so few would first go to the internet. We were wrong. While possibly obvious in hindsight, in 2005, we found, to our surprise, that a large portion of the public in Britain would go first to the internet for information across many areas, rather than first go to a specific book or place, as one example. This proportion continued to grow over time.

By 2013, as shown in Figure 3.1, more than half of all respondents (including even nonusers of the internet) would first go to the internet for information about topics such as researching an issue for a professional, school, or personal project; planning a trip; finding a book they had heard about; and getting information about local schools. There were many other examples. Very few topics did not have a majority going to the internet first, although there were some examples, such as finding information about a company or when encountering a problem with a product or service, as many would want to communicate in real time, for example, on the telephone. Even nonusers would often ask a friend or relative (whom we called "proxy users") to go online for them to get information or order something, among other things.

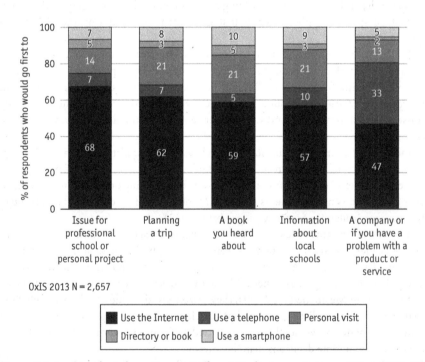

OxIS 2013 N = 2,657

Use the Internet   Use a telephone   Personal visit
Directory or book   Use a smartphone

Figure 3.1 Looking for Information on Different Media Source: Dutton and Blank (2013: 26)

In 2019, the OxIS survey again asked respondents where they would go first for information across a variety of topics (Table 3.1). The responses were similar to previous years, except that in 2019, mobile internet devices had diffused far more widely and were used far more to access the internet than in 2013. An increasing portion of networked individuals had become accustomed to using their mobile devices to search and find information about topics, not just on the move but also while at home or in the office. You can see from Table 3.1 that the internet via a computer or other device, such as a mobile phone or other internet-enabled device, remained the first port of call for information for just about any topic.

People may still use books and directories, but they are not the first place individuals go to for information about many topics (Table 3.1). Only 4% said they would go to a book or directory for information about a book they heard about. Likewise, few said they would make a personal visit for information in the first instance, such as going to a person's home or to a library or museum; however, nearly a fifth of the public did make a personal visit for information about a journey they were planning (18%), a book they heard about (16%), local schools (12%), or if they had a problem with a product or service (11%). About a quarter of the public said they would get on the phone first for information about local (council) taxes (25%), or if they had a problem with a product or service (29%). That said, the dominant source of information about every topic was the internet.

Table 3.1 **Percentage of Respondents Who Would Go First to Different Sources for Information About Selected Topics, Britain**

Information about	Telephone	Personal visit	Book or directory	Internet on computer	Mobile internet
Local minister of Parliament	12	8	2	41	37
Council taxes	25	8	1	39	26
Planning a journey	7	18	1	48	26
Book you've heard about	7	16	4	38	34
Local schools	13	12	3	41	31
Professional, school, or personal project	12	7	2	52	26
Problem with a product or service	29	11	1	32	26

The question: "Where would you go first if you were looking for information on ...?"
N=1,818

2019 OxIS

Mobile went from traditional mobile phone services to becoming a device for digital media and internet access. This made the mobile phone an increasingly important means for online information and services, furthering the centrality of the internet for individuals during any time and from any place. It almost makes little sense to ask about using a phone as opposed to the internet. For a time, people seldom used their mobile phones to make a phone call, although this increased with the availability of video calls and conferencing via smartphones and other devices.

INCREASINGLY NAVIGATED THROUGH SEARCH ENGINES

In early years, internet users most often went online to a few of their favorite websites. Over time, when people used the internet, they increasingly relied on search engines to find information. This growing reliance on search versus going to specific sources for information online, or offline, has real consequences for the rise of a Fifth Estate.

As late as 1998, Google was just starting as a research project at Stanford University. Since then, Google has become a dominant search engine in North America and Europe, along with other search engines such as Microsoft's Bing, and Baidu, the dominant search tool in China. The rise of search engines has become a major aspect of internet use.

OxIS asked people from 2005 to 2013 the following: "In general, when you look for information on the internet, do you go to specific pages, use a search engine, such as Google or Yahoo!, or do you do both about the same?" You can see from Figure 3.2 that networked individuals in Britain dramatically increased their reliance on search engines from 2005 to 2007, moving from 20% mainly going to a search engine to over half (56%) in 2007, and moving to 64% by 2009 (Figure 3.2).

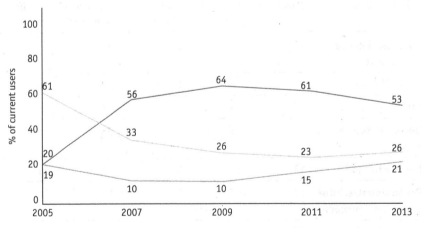

OxIS current users: 2005 N = 1,309; 2007 N = 1,578; 2009 N = 1,401; 2011 N = 1,498; 2013 N = 2,083
Note: Question changed in 2007.

— Mainly search engine   ---- Mainly specific pages   ---- Both about the same

Figure 3.2 Ways to Look for Information Online by Year Source: Dutton and Blank (2013: 26).

Just as going online rather than using the phone or visiting someone or some place to get information enhanced the information power of networked individuals, so did search. Instead of going to a particular institution's website, for example, or a specific page, such as Wikipedia, a networked individual could use search to go anywhere in the world that had information of value to the topic or question they wished to pursue. Search made the networked individual even more independent of prevailing institutions, such as a local expert, newspaper, broadcaster, or university.

In 2019, we asked our sample ($N = 1{,}818$) of the British public the following: "How often do you use any search engine to find information online?" About 10% said they used a search engine monthly or less than monthly, 25% used one weekly, but 35% said daily, and nearly a third (30%) used a search engine more than once a day. In Britain, use of a search engine translates into using Google search for nearly everyone, but search has become increasingly embedded in so many services and applications, making it more difficult to know which search engine is being used. In fact, while these responses suggest a strong reliance on search engines, they are likely to be underestimates, given the embeddedness of search in so many forms and applications. For example, voice search, particularly with the advent of personal digital assistants, shifted some search from text. Simultaneously, search via voice or text became built into nearly every service and application, enabling people to ask anything from anywhere at any time, thus often less consciously going to a "search engine." That said, this continuing and strong reliance on search enables individuals to be less dependent on particular institutions in particular places as they can go to sources identified through search—anywhere at any time.

RISE OF SOCIAL MEDIA, SOCIAL CUES, AND COLLABORATION

Of course, along with the rise of video and mobile and voice, there have been other dramatic changes in the use of the internet since 2013, such as the rise of social media—all of which shape the use of search engines. Social media became a major innovation in internet use, such as with the launch of Facebook in 2004 and YouTube in 2005. These innovations made the internet and related digital social media even more likely to be the first place to look for information and increasingly central to everyday life and work. In some nations, particularly in the developing world, social media, such as Facebook, virtually became the internet for most networked individuals. But worldwide, social media became increasingly central. For instance, during the pandemic, many individuals would ask their neighbors through local neighborhood networks about travel restrictions or for help in picking up supplies.

You can see in Figure 3.2 that reliance on a search engine—in the eyes of networked individuals—began to drop somewhat after 2009. One of the major countervailing trends that might explain this decline was the rise of social media. Many go straight to YouTube and increasingly use YouTube as their "search engine." The popularity of YouTube also links with the growing popularity of online video that enables individuals using YouTube to see/hear answers to their questions. I recall asking on YouTube how to right click a mouse on the Mac, which does not have a right click button as on a Windows mouse. I then listened to an adolescent speak for three minutes about how to accomplish this feat! He was enjoyable and informative.

Social media have been a focus of concern over disinformation (discussed later in this chapter and throughout this book), but that should not diminish the degree to which it remains a major source of information. Social networking enables individuals to ask their friends or the public questions and get immediate responses. During the pandemic, the residents of neighborhoods often had local social media sites where they could ask if anyone could go to the store for them or had a particular item or tool.

Again, the rise of social networking, such as on Facebook—still one of the most common social networking sites (about two-thirds of internet users in the UK use Facebook)—and others like Instagram, Snapchat, LinkedIn, and Twitter have enabled individuals to find information and ask questions online that empower them to source their own information, and thereby be more independent of traditional institutions and providers.

This does not mean that people rely and respond robotically to whatever they read or hear on social media. Quite the contrary. We asked respondents to OxIS in 2019 to tell us how reliable and accurate in general they found different sources of information to be. Social media were rated the most unreliable, with 25% of the respondents judging social media as "totally unreliable." At the same time, it is important to note that no media were judged to be totally reliable by more than 10% of the respondents (Table 3.2). While search engines might be judged more reliable by more of the public, the general point is that the public see no single medium as totally reliable or truthful (Dutton et al. 2017), which explains why most people rely on multiple sources of information—which is a good strategy.

By creating original information and providing content online (a focus of the next chapter), search and social media have further enhanced the communicative power of networked individuals relative to other institutions and certainly to those who are not online or using online resources. Networked individuals can obtain social cues, answers to questions, and develop collaborations with other networked individuals over social media in ways that complement other sources, as well as make themselves less dependent on traditional information providers.

Table 3.2 **Percentage Rating How Reliable and Accurate Information Is from Different Sources**

	Television	Radio	Online news	Social media	Search engine results
1 Totally unreliable	3	5	7	25	5
2	12	13	18	31	18
3	38	38	47	27	53
4	36	36	22	13	38
5 Totally reliable	7	7	5	4	10

N=1,818

2019 OxIS

A LEARNED LEVEL OF TRUST BASED ON EXPERIENCE

A frequent response to the internet challenge from traditional institutions, such as the Fourth Estate of journalists and the mass media, is to suggest that the mass media will retain their central position because of the trust they have built over the years. However, internet users say they trust what they can find on the internet at least as much as they trust broadcast news or newspapers (e.g., Dutton et al. 2009). Generally, the more experience people have with the internet, the more they develop a "learned level" of trust in the information they find and the people they meet online.

Internet users do not have blind faith in what they see online, any more than any other source of information (Table 3.2). Many remain skeptical, with more educated individuals relatively more so. However, the most distrustful are those who have never used the internet. This might be the case because the internet is what I have called an "experience technology" (Dutton and Shepherd 2006). As experience online continues to build, more users are likely to develop a learned level of trust and rely more on the internet as a source of information and expertise.

To understand the notion of "experience technology," think of your experiences online. Maybe you grew up using the internet and never questioned its value, but those who did not grow up online can probably recall the first time they ordered a book, tried to check a fact, or sought information about how to fix an appliance. A person can explain to another that you can use the internet to find information and do these things, but when a person actually does it online, they are generally surprised, "Wow, that was fast. I can do that!" When the book arrives on time and in good shape and the payments are handled quickly and easily, a person gains enough trust to order another book, maybe shops for other things online, and so on. Over time, that is how networked individuals develop a learned level of trust in using the internet and social media for a wide variety of purposes.

Of course, bad experiences online can and do undermine that trust. If and when there are problems online, such as a phishing attack, that trust is lessened. We found that individuals who had bad experiences online tended to have lower levels of trust. Experiencing problems online, such as with security, lessened a person's trust, but overall, most networked individuals retained a sufficiently high level of trust to continue to routinely use the internet and social media (Dutton et al. 2009). This means that the future of the internet and social media depends on maintaining and enhancing the reliability and validity and relevance of information that networked individuals can access and diminishing problems confronted when using these technologies. This is one reason why the providers of search engines and social media are constantly focused on improving the quality of search and reducing the potential for users to be victimized inadvertently or by malicious users.

Moreover, very few people rely solely on the internet or social media for information. We asked respondents to the OxIS survey of the public in Britain in 2019 to rate the importance to themselves of different media as a source of information (Table 3.3). For information, the largest portion of the public viewed television and the internet as "essential" sources. Fully a third (32%) viewed the internet as essential versus television (15%). Nearly two-thirds (64%) saw the internet as "very important" or "essential" as a source of information. However, most people in Britain attributed some importance

Table 3.3 **Importance of Different Media as Sources of Information, Percent**

How important as a source of information	Television	Radio	Internet	Print newspapers and magazines
Not important at all	5	14	14	18
Not important	27	35	5	36
Important	31	30	16	29
Very important	21	15	32	15
Essential	15	4	32	2

N=1,818

OxIS 2019

to television, radio, print newspapers, and the internet as sources. In an imperfect information environment, the public rightly sees a value in multiple complementary media.

Moreover, people find problems with a particular media or source of information. Your family and friends are sometimes wrong. Your newspaper might not report on an event of interest to you, stand behind a problematic report, or take a partisan position with which you disagree. Some might only read a certain newspaper or only listen to their favorite podcast for their news, but, generally, online sources are not usually used simply as a substitute for other media. They more likely are used to complement or supplement other media and information sources. The next section grapples with this and related issues in more detail.

Limits on the Reach and Centrality of the Internet and Social Media

Throughout this book, a major issue concerns a variety of actors and problems that threaten the vitality of the Fifth Estate. In closing this chapter, it will be useful to note several key issues and the questions around search that might shape and even undermine the future of the Fifth Estate.

DIGITAL DIVIDES IN ACCESS AND SKILLS: THE NEED FOR A CRITICAL MASS

The remarkable diffusion of the internet has brought access to search and social media to over half the world, but it has not erased local, national, or global digital divides between those who have internet access and those left without. As discussed throughout this book, these digital divides have become ever-more critical with the rising significance of the internet. Digital divides are deeper in that a lack of access is even more serious for those on the wrong side of this divide. But the Fifth Estate does not require universal access to online media. The Fifth Estate's vitality depends on gaining a critical mass of networked individuals. As you will see, across the various strategies of value to networked individuals, having a critical mass using search to source information more independently can create new forms of accountability.

MISINFORMATION: CHECKING FACTS

Disinformation has become a major topic of concern over the social implications of the internet and social media. News and information can be wrong or misleading, and individuals might use the internet to misinform the public out of ignorance or for their own purposes, such as in promoting a political candidate or narrative. As the famous American author Mark Twain is reported to have said, "A lie can travel around the world and back again while the truth is lacing up its boots." This captures the thrust of much discussion around misinformation, but, ironically, the source of this quote most often attributed to Mark Twain might actually be the words of Jonathan Swift, the author of *Gulliver's Travels*, who died in 1745—nearly a hundred years before Twain was born.[2] You can learn this through the use of search on the internet.

It is surprising that many journalists and academics focused on "misinformation" seem to have forgotten that finding good information that is valid and relevant has been an issue online since its inception. While the communication protocols on which the internet and many other networks are based were invented in 1973 by Robert Kahn and Vint Cerf, relatively few people outside of academia used the internet before the World Wide Web (the web) became available as a service in 1991. This was invented by Tim Berners-Lee and his colleagues at CERN to support sharing documents among a glob-ally distributed team of researchers. Moreover, while the web enabled more people to find the internet of value, it was not until early browsers were invented, such as Mosaic in 1993, which became commercialized as Netscape Navigator, that it became dramati-cally easier for the general public to use the internet through a graphical user interface.

However, in those early days, most of the information online was irrelevant to most of the public or of questionable origins and validity. It was common to see cartoons about the internet and web being portrayed as a big trash heap with people looking for a piece of useful information as if looking for a needle in a haystack. This was figuratively, if not literally, the case. This problem led internet enthusiasts to develop lists of useful sites on the web, such as a web page that curated useful information about politics or lit-erature, for example. I did that myself in my early years of using the internet. Networked individuals would share these lists and compile more comprehensive ones. Eventually, some of these lists became the basis of the earliest search engines.

However, prior to the major search engines, given the difficulties of finding good information online, the early commercial internet service providers (ISPs), such as Compuserve, The Source, and America Online in the United States, curated their own lists of websites. If you subscribed to an ISP, you could go to a page for—say—information about politics, and the ISP would have a set of web pages its team thought to be most helpful. Early internet content creators focused a great deal of attention on convincing an ISP to list their site in a prominent location. These early providers offered what might be classed as "recommender sites" that did not censor information but steered users to specific sites recommended by the provider. While this practice might have helped users avoid misinformation or being purposely mis-led, it limited them to those sites chosen by the providers. Not surprisingly, many users did not want to be caged and moved beyond these recommended sites to explore the open internet and web. This created more incentives for many projects to develop search engines, many of which remain in use.

It was not until 1998 that Google was launched, as noted above, initially as a research project. Given the promise of this project, one of its founders, Larry Page, is reputed to have offered to sell Google to Excite, the number two search engine at the time, and other ISPs, such as Yahoo! for a figure under a million US dollars. While a lot of money at that time, in retrospect, it was undervalued. In 2021, its net worth was estimated at about US$420 billion. But at that time, the fledgling internet industry did not see a way to make money with search, putting decisions not to buy Google's search engine among some of the world's most famous business mistakes.[3]

Yet Google and a number of other good search engines began to move search freely into the hands of internet users rather than the ISPs. In ways analogous to going online for information, by going to a search engine when one went online, networked indi-viduals enhanced their information or communicative power relative to the ISP, which tended to control what websites were likely to be visible to users. It did not take long for search engines in general, and Google in particular, to change the way people looked for information online and create a way for internet users not only to find information but also to check information—to do their own fact-checking. Search freed the internet and web from greater control by the early ISPs. Panic over disinformation online pressured the new ISPs, internet and social media platforms, and governments to again try to play a role of determining what is information—the truth—despite this failing to address the priorities of users in the earliest years of the internet.

FILTER BUBBLES AND ECHO CHAMBERS: THE VALUE OF MULTIPLE SOURCES

However, what if search engines are systematically biased in ways that prevent users from gaining access to the most relevant and accurate information they seek? This is the risk posed by some perspectives on filter bubbles and echo chambers.

Eli Pariser's (2011) notion of a filter bubble is that the algorithms designed to per-sonalize search—by ensuring that internet users get what they are looking for—tend to feed results that reflect the interests or location of the internet user or what they have searched for before. The fear is that personalization—which internet users value—might result in reinforcing a user's existing views on an issue, candidate, or political movement by not exposing them to a diverse array of countervailing information. In short, search engines could learn so well about what we look for that the software or algorithms that support search could be filtering what users see in ways that screen them from more diverse sources of information. The distortions of filter bubbles could happen without a user being aware of the limits of their search results. Rather than informing users, filter bubbles might cause search to systematically mislead them, such as by distorting their search results in areas like politics that benefit from a diversity of viewpoints.

The idea of an echo chamber is similar but brings the role of social networking into this logic. An echo chamber is primarily associated with the influence social media might have in restricting your access to a more diverse array of viewpoints. If your social network is a homogeneous group of like-minded individuals either online or offline, then you may not hear diverse views (Sunstein 2007, 2017). That is, social filtering by your network of associates could create a homogeneous bias much like algorithmic filtering bubbles (Nikolov et al. 2015). People generally like to have their views confirmed by others. They have a "confirmation bias" that attracts people to information that does not challenge their preexisting views (Nickerson 1998, Sunstein 2017).

These notions of a filter bubble and echo chamber are simple and intuitively attractive as we can see how they are plausible in a technical sense. However, they do not square well with how people actually get information. My colleagues and I looked at how people got information about politics (Dutton et al. 2017, 2019). We found that those interested in politics tended to get information from more than four different sources, including online sources, but also from TV, family and friends, print news, radio, charities, and religious groups. Only one of these sources was going online. And when they went online, they tended to look at more than four different sources of information, including the use of a search engine, as well as online sites of news and magazines, social media, online video platforms, email, and political websites (Dutton et al. 2017, 2019). The idea that a networked individual is trapped in a filter bubble—only seeing what they find on one search engine—or in an echo chamber—only knowing what their friends on their social networking site like—does not square with the multiplicity of sources people use when interested in a topic.

Also, most people create a social network on the basis of their family, friends from growing up through various schools and universities, and those whom they work with or know through work. They do not commonly cull their networks based on ideology or political viewpoints. Both notions are technologically deterministic and fail to look systematically at how people actually do things on and offline.

That said, there is greater merit in the concept of a "confirmation bias," but this is a social psychological proclivity versus a consequence determined by technical features (Nickerson 1998). A person might well choose or prefer to speak only with individuals they agree with, or they search only for information from sources they find more agreeable, such as subscribing to a newspaper or watching a TV news channel that has an editorial slant that aligns with their views. But this is of their choosing: it is not determined by the technology, but by their own decisions. Individuals could well be their own worst filter bubble or echo chamber, but this not the fault of search engines or social media. Your algorithm, not the search engine's algorithm nor your social media network members, could be the problem. In most parts of the world today, you have access to more diverse information resources than ever before through a global network of millions of sources available to you. Nevertheless, a large portion of the Russian public remained wedded to a narrative of a "special military operation" despite global sources discrediting assumptions underpinning this narrative.

Acceptance of this narrative will be a topic of discussion for the foreseeable future but it is the outcome of governmental censorship of state broadcasters, independent media, and the internet, rather than any internet filter bubble or echo chamber.

Many in the Russian public may have been subject to a confirmation bias, wanting to believe President Putin's narrative, but one of the only ways to access alternative news sites was through the internet, such as using an international platform not fully censored, such as Telegram, or circumventing censorship through a virtual private network (VPN).

Cybersecurity Divides: Developing a Mindset and Skills to Avoid Problems

At the extreme, malevolent individuals and organizations can undermine a person's trust in the internet and social media, such as through malicious hacking, trolling, hate mail, or phishing attacks, to name a few cybersecurity challenges. Networked individuals need to develop a mindset that is attuned to security, that is, using strong passwords, updating software and operating systems, developing skills to back up their computers, being cautious about clicking links from unwanted or unknown individuals, and more (Dutton 2017). The more central and significant the internet becomes, such as it did in working from home during the pandemic, the more likely that malicious users will try to exploit the vulnerabilities of networked individuals. Therefore, over time, cybersecurity will be of growing importance. As discussed in the final chapter, the challenges to enhancing cybersecurity present new opportunities for addressing online harms, a theme addressed in the concluding chapters. This involves moving away from media-centric perspectives to focus on the activities of civic-minded as well as malicious networked individuals, complemented by the efforts of internet platforms, software developers, governments, and information providers, such as banks and online shopping sites. The technologies, policies, and practices are in place that allow reasonably safe internet and social media use, but networked individuals need to be aware of and make use of them (Bispham et al. 2012).

Conclusion

In the short lifetime of the internet and social media, the development of facilities like high-quality search engines and social networking sites have enabled networked individuals to gain more independence over what they know and whom they know. They can use these technologies and skills to enhance their informational and communicative power such as by using search to find good information and fact-check problematic information. The new media can complement and supplement traditional media, which is generally the case, such as when you order a book online. But the key is whether networked individuals strategically use the internet and social media in ways that can enhance their power relative to other individuals, groups, and institutions. One strategy is to use search engines and social media to source information that is most relevant and appropriate to you as a networked individual. This is one step toward the development of a Fifth Estate as your own sourcing of information enables you to confirm or challenge the information and misinformation circulating on and offline in ways that enable you to hold other individuals and organizations more accountable.

Searching and networking to help source information is one strategy of the Fifth Estate. The next step involves the creation of information. Developing original content can be complex but also as easy as composing a microblog, such as a tweet, or using a mobile phone to post a picture. That is the focus of the next chapter.

4

Originating

The previous chapter described ways in which networked individuals have been empowered simply by their ability to use the internet and search engines to source their own information more independently. This chapter moves on to how the internet and related digital media, such as (micro-)blogs and mobile phones, have enabled networked individuals—bloggers, YouTubers, so-called Twitterati, TikTok influencers, and other producers—to create their own original content in ways that enhance transparency and accountability across politics and society. You may take it as given in the digital age that networked individuals can produce a live video of an event at which they were present, whether it is a pet, garden, police action, or public protest. However, this ability for ordinary people with little or no technical expertise to capture and distribute their own content as bloggers, YouTubers, Twitterati, and other content producers has risen rapidly in the recent history of media and with enormous consequences for democracy and the Fifth Estate. By empowering bloggers, citizen journalists, and other networked individuals, the internet is democratizing the creation of content in ways that enhance the role of the Fifth Estate.

Earlier chapters introduced how online posts of individuals like Greta Thunberg had dramatic consequences—in Greta's case, leading to worldwide implications for action on climate policy. This chapter revisits this case and brings in additional examples. However, we begin with a brief overview to provide a more historical and empirical sense of how dramatic this shift in the affordances of new media has been. The fact that nearly all networked individuals are increasingly able to produce and distribute information, including videos online, to a local or global audience is truly remarkable and should not be taken for granted. The chapter then provides an empirically anchored perspective on those networked individuals who take advantage of these affordances to create content to distribute online—not everyone online does so. These networked individuals provide a basis for understanding who is likely to join the collectivity of the Fifth Estate.

The chapter then moves to a few concrete but diverse examples of cases in which networked individuals have made a difference by tweeting, blogging, video (v)logging, and other methods to create content for online access. Of the major strategies of the Fifth Estate, including use of the internet for searching, sourcing, distributing, leaking, networking, and collecting intelligence, the creation of original content is perhaps the most protean, straightforward, and influential way networked individuals have enhanced their informational or communicative power.

The Fifth Estate. William H. Dutton, Oxford University Press. © Oxford University Press 2023.
DOI: 10.1093/oso/9780190688363.003.0005

Potentials, Realities, and Limitations

This form of witnessing is not entirely new. There are many historical examples of individuals bearing witness to events and capturing information that made a difference in policy or practice. Maria Seidenberger took photographs of Jewish, Roma, and others being marched to Dachau in one of what became known as the Nazi death marches. Her photographs and other people's helped validate the Holocaust and are available in the US Holocaust Memorial Museum, the Wiener Holocaust Library in the United Kingdom, and on online.[1] Another example is provided by photographic evidence of the massacre of over 300 Chinese workers near the city of Torreón, Mexico, by revolutionary forces and a local mob in 1911 during the Mexican Revolution.[2] Massacres and other atrocities carried out on Native Americans have been captured by written and photographic accounts, such as forty-seven massacres during the mid-1800s available online via Pinterest.[3] A number of online collections of photographs provide graphic evidence of the victims of lynchings and other forms of vigilantism against America's African American community. However, the scale and immediacy of accountability has changed dramatically with the rise of the internet and social media.

This is not to argue that every bit of information created or every blog is equally influential. This would be unimaginable given estimates of over 2.5 billion blog posts published worldwide in one year. Many blogs go unread or are read by few. Only a small portion of tweets are retweeted. Many videos are unseen by anyone but the producer and never shared. Many are purely for entertaining the creator and any reader. Moreover, many of those ideas, wishes, orders, and intelligence that are read or viewed, shared, and influential can be of little social or political significance. That said, a significant number of posts turn out to matter a great deal.

This chapter presents more examples that demonstrate the potential for different kinds of networked individuals to hold other individuals and institutions across society accountable. They also illuminate some of the limitations of networked individuals, such as in cases of failure. That said, this potential alone can have an influence on politics and society for the better, but also for the worse, such as if people post videos that can harm others or lead the public to feel they live in an Orwellian surveillance society—through what might be better called "sousveillance," in which everyone—not just Big Brother—is watching everyone else (Brin 1998).

The Pace and Magnitude of Technical Advances in Communication

By the 2020s, so many people were alarmed over the risks attributed to social media that email—rather than social media—received a resurgence in use, perhaps because senders and receivers felt more control of, or more informed about, those with whom they communicate. With that in mind, it is useful to begin with email to provide a sense of the short but rapid evolution of media enabling the creation of content by networked individuals (Box 4.1).

Box 4.1 **Innovations for Individuals to Create and Distribute Content**

1972 Demo of the ARPANET, forerunner of the internet, including email system
1978 First computerized bulletin board system (BBS) went online in Chicago
1980 Usenet (a "users network") established as a distributed system allowing users to read and post messages in newsgroups over dial-up networks
1983 Internet protocol suite, TCP/IP, adopted as standard for APRANET, enabling heterogeneous computers to communicate on a common, homogeneous network
1985 The Whole Earth "Lectronic Link" (the WELL) launched as a dial-up BBS
1991 World Wide Web becomes publicly available on the internet
1993 Mosaic web browser developed, commercialized as Netscape Navigator
2001 CompuServe launched, facilitating wider public use of email and the internet
2001 Wikipedia was founded, enabling networked individuals to edit content
2003 WordPress began, a popular blogging platform
2003 Friendster launch was a pioneer in social networking and gaming
2003 MySpace social network launched
2004 Facebook launched
2005 YouTube launched
2006 Twitter founded
2007 Tumblr, a microblogging platform and social media website, founded
2007 The iPhone was publicly released, popularizing mobile applications
2010 Instagram, a photo, photo-filtering, and video-sharing app, launched
2011 WeChat released as a mobile app by Tencent, creating one of the first Chinese microblogging, social media, and payment systems
2013 Telegram launched by brothers who founded Russian social network VK
2017 TikTok launched internationally around posting of short videos
2023 Artefact a text-based news app launched by founders of Instagram

---

One of the key origins of electronic mail (email) was the ARPANET's creation of a system in 1972. From the beginning, email was set up to be analogous to regular mail or post as used in business and industry, what some called "snail-mail," with such commands as send, receive, copy, carbon copy (CC), and blind carbon copy (BCC). I started using email in 1974 at the University of California, Irvine. At that time, I had to call individuals in academia to let them know I had emailed them so that they would look online. While many benefits and problems emerged in these early years of electronic communication, such as "hate-mail," its use was very limited.

Academics, primarily in the computer sciences and engineering, found email valuable for scientific collaboration, and those in the social sciences and humanities, along with many just enthralled with electronic networking, experimented with its use. But even into the 1980s, most businesses were still using teletype and telegrams rather than electronic mail. Executives of a major aerospace company in Los Angeles feared that email would be disruptive since too many seemed to use it for social and personal reasons rather than for strict business communications. In fact, this has been a continuing worry, although the uses of new media, like email, for social purposes can be quite valuable for effective networking and communication.

Email gave rise to systems that could capture and assemble sets of messages, such as electronic bulletin board systems (BBS). Analogous to a physical bulletin board, still used in many offices and neighborhoods, individuals could use a computer to post messages in groups by topic on a BBS. By capturing and enabling access to electronic messages, more distributed systems, such as Usenet, gained in popularity but still only among groups with relatively sophisticated levels of computer literacy, as early systems were essentially text, not as user friendly or graphical as later systems would become, and were largely dependent on dial-in networks and telephone modems to connect, which also made them more local and expensive than later networks. A truly innovative group of users formed the WELL in 1985, spawning many "blue sky" (optimistic) visions of a global public sphere emerging online (Rheingold 1994).

However, for over two decades, from 1972 until the launch of the internet browser in 1993, the creation and distribution of content online was limited generally to academics and a relatively small number of the pioneers (similar to Rhinegold's "homesteaders") of "cyberspace," a term popularized in the 1980s by William Gibson (1984), in his bestselling science fiction novel *Neuromancer*. The term "cyberspace" was used loosely to refer to the space inhabited in online computer networks, in contrast to physical spaces and the use of more traditional computer-based systems.

Even the invention of the World Wide Web (WWW or the web) did not really popularize the use of online networking as access was still not sufficiently user friendly and easy for nontechnically trained users. However, it fostered the invention of the internet browser in 1993 that became a key turning point in enabling nontechnical users in households, business, industry, and government to more easily access web pages and email online.

Innovations around the web in the 1990s led many individuals and institutions to develop their own web pages and learn basic "hypertext mark-up language" (html) and use "uniform resource locators" (URLs) so they could write and markup their stories, poetry, memos, and any text to be displayed and accessible on an internet browser—anywhere in the world. The concept of hypertext, a term coined by Ted Nelson in 1963, found concrete application in links within and across web pages that facilitated people moving in nonlinear ways through content, in contrast to how books are designed to be read linearly. By the early 1980s, students went to new media schools, like the Annenberg School at the University of Southern California, to learn about html and how to design and create web content more generally, as well as other new media, some of which would not be as successful, such as videotex (Box 4.2).

Creating a web page or blog was initially a manual process of coding or marking up text in html or other markup languages. But the creation of web pages and blogs was greatly facilitated by blog and web-hosting services that enabled nontechnical users to employ software platforms, like WordPress or Blogger, that helped users create their own web logs or blogs. Some early web pages were simply online diaries or logs of a person's life and activities, generally in reverse chronological order. This led to the use

---

Box 4.2 **Videotex(t)**

Videotex(t) was an alternative to the internet and web. Videotex(t) systems in North America used telephone lines to connect a keyboard for interactive communication while using the television set for displaying any text and video. In the United States, newspapers were very optimistic about this technology reaching households, as it appeared to complement television, one of the most important items in American homes. Using the internet to augment the phone and TV seemed unbeatable. However, news organizations in the United State that invested in videotex(t) became less optimistic when finding it was used for interpersonal messaging far more than for reading or viewing the news. In France, videotex(t) used a small terminal connected to the phone line—not the TV—and it was better designed for interactive communication. Called Minitel, their system survived longer than videotex(t) in the UK or US but nevertheless failed to compete with the internet in the longer term, once it gained the ease and color of a graphical, user interface through advances in browsers. This short but fascinating videotext phase of new media development is the subject of many books, including Mosco (1982) and Greenberger (1985).

Note: Some nations spelled it as "videotext" while others used "videotex".

---

of the term "web log," with Peter Merholz coining the phrase "we blog" in 1999, which spawned others to move to the simple term "blog," which remains in common use.

Early blogs were largely text based but soon added photos and later video. They were very diverse—shaped by whatever individual bloggers wished to write—but some genres began to emerge, such as politics, cooking, business, and news blogs, most of which commented on events, candidates, or news of the day available from mainstream newspapers and mass media. Major events, like the Iraq War from 2003, spawned blogs that featured the opinions of bloggers. During the early years of the twenty-first century, many journalists, politicians, scientists and citizen scientists, other experts, and computer enthusiasts created a wide array of blogs, ranging from playful observations to in-depth analysis of a topic or event.

WordPress became one of the most popular blogging platforms in 2003, which might have been near the height of excitement about blogging. It was one of the few ways networked individuals could communicate with the world. However, with the rapid launching of social media, such as Facebook, video sites like YouTube, and micro-blogging platforms like Twitter and Tumblr, the range of technologies for an individual to create content was mushrooming. While some were announcing the death of blogging, with a declining fascination with text-based blogs, the rise of micro-blogging and video blogging (vlog) was expanding the range of options available to networked individuals for creating and distributing their own content.

On top of these software platforms came the explosion of mobile internet access with the iPhone and other smartphones that enabled individuals to create short blogs and videos from anywhere at any time. Suddenly, bloggers were not simply at their desktop computers composing a critique of news stories; networked individuals were increasingly at the sites of activities, as they posted photos, videos, and textual commentary of developing events. For instance, in April 2010, BP's Deepwater Horizon Oil spill in the Gulf of Mexico created major environmental disasters for wildlife; these impacts were documented by individuals with video phones and blogging sites (Box 4.3).[4]

The diffusion of mobile internet-enabled content creation was global, such as with WeChat, enabling micro-blogging in China from 2011—bloggers in China documented a gas explosion in 2010 that authorities tried to block, even though it had been covered by a local broadcaster (Box 4.4).

Despite strict censorship in China, social media can get some information out. For example, in the days running up to a sensitive Congress of the Communist Party in Beijing, which would symbolize President Xi Jinping's third term in office, two protest

---

Box 4.3 Impact of the Deepwater Horizon Explosion and Oil Spill

On April 20, 2010, the Deepwater Horizon oil platform exploded, spilling 4 million barrels of oil into the Gulf of Mexico over eighty-seven days, causing incredible damage to wildlife. Images of what happened were captured by people on the beaches of the gulf and communicated around the world via blogs. A mobile offshore oil-drilling platform, Deepwater Horizon, owned and operated by Transocean, was drilling oil for British Petroleum (BP) in the Gulf of Mexico, southeast of the Louisiana coast. Its explosion killed eleven workers and led to one of the largest oil spills ever tied to oil-drilling operations. Individuals on the beaches across the Gulf of Mexico documented the damage to beaches and wildlife in photos posted online and in blogs in ways that concretely illustrated the damage and the cleanup efforts of the public. Many of these images and reports were picked up by mainstream press and media.

Box 4.4 News of the Gas Explosion in Nanjing, China

A major gas explosion in Nanjing, China, on July 28, 2010, was not covered by the press—as if it did not happen. However, it was covered by bloggers, and one video of resulting flames was shown on a local television news program. A government official at the TV station was then videoed storming up to the desk of the presenter, interrupting a live report, demanding, "Who gave you permission?" The local station did not have permission from the local government to report on the explosion. The case has been described in published articles (e.g., Huan et al. 2013), but to the public online, it officially did not happen. Links to this site result in the message: "Not Available." Nevertheless, the news reached the community that heard or saw the explosion and could not have missed the fact that its existence had been censored.

banners were hung on Sitong Bridge, which spanned a major road in the northeast of the capital of China (Davidson and Yu 2022). Plumes of black smoke were created to draw the motorists' attention to the banners, which were critical of the COVID restrictions and the Communist Party. Messages on the banners included "We want freedom, not lockdowns" and "We want a vote, not a leader" (Davidson 2022). Photos and videos of the banners soon appeared on social media, although they were quickly removed, they were still widely seen. Platforms accountable to the Chinese-government focused on controlling all posts containing the words "bridge" or "Haidian," the district in which the bridge was located. Posts then began to note "I saw it" to obliquely reference the social media posts; after nearly 200,000 views, these were removed, and some social media accounts that shared photos of the protest were disabled (Davidson 2022). McMorrow (2022) reported that WeChat and Weibo services deleted all mentions and images of the protest and "disabled thousands of users' accounts." Despite such powerful controls, there are limits on internet and social media censors, and China's "Bridge Man" became an international news story (Mao 2022).

Bloggers became an increasingly important global source of information and news content for the mass media, in contrast to pejorative images of them cannibalizing and criticizing mainstream media as some sort of "commentariat." Thus, blogging became arguably the most important way ordinary networked individuals gained a prominent voice online. Even though being able to search and source content is critical in itself, it is far more so once networked individuals are able to post and distribute their own information to a global network from anywhere in the world and at any time.

Estimates of blogging activity are problematic, given such issues as the very definition of what constitutes a blog; whether a blog is (in)active, free, or income generating; and because of the wide and growing number of different blog and video platforms. One prominent source estimates that there are over 500 million blogs among 1.7 billion websites across the world, with 2 million blog posts daily.[5] The United States has more newspapers than any other nation, but they amount to fewer than 1,500.[6] It is not surprising, therefore, that the generation of content by networked individuals has become a consequential source of new content across the world.

Networked Individuals of the Fifth Estate

Who has the potential to join this collectivity of networked individuals of the Fifth Estate? In 2013, I used the OxIS survey to estimate the likely scale of internet users who might be members of the Fifth Estate.

Based on the aspects linked to the Fifth Estate, individuals in the sample of all internet users were sorted by their answers to the following questions (Table 4.1):

- Where did they have access to a network, and if they did, was it only at home or from outside the home and at home (home plus)?
- Did they blog? That is, did they have a web or blog site and write blogs or post content rather than just reading content on the web?
- Did they post content in other ways, such as posting on chat or discussion groups online or posting their own photos or videos online, such as on social media?

Table 4.1 **Items Used to Estimate Likelihood of Fifth Estate Participation, 2013**

Items	*Categories*	*Weighted %**	*N*
Access to net	0 - No access	0	6
	1 - Only at home	32	579
	2 - Home plus	68	1,254
Creating and Producing Content			
Blogging	0 - Don't blog or read or have site	59	1,083
	1 - Don't blog but read and/or have website	21	387
	2 - Blog, read, have a blog/website	20	368
Posting: chat, discussion, post photos, their videos	0 – No posting	29	534
	1 - 1 or 2 activities	47	857
	2 - 3–4 activities	24	446
Sourcing Through Search			
Search	0 - Specific pages	22	405
	1 - Both the same	26	477
	2 - Search engine	52	957
Take cues from social media	0 - Don't know	5	86
	1 - Page respondent found	57	1,051
	2 - Page suggested by email, blog, or social media	38	701
Trust			
Trust information online	0 - Unreliable, refused, don't know (1)	3	62
	1 - Medium (2–3)	41	758
	2 - High (4 or more)	55	1,018
Trust providers	0 - None, refused, don't know	5	91
	1 - Medium (2–3)	50	917
	2 - High (4 or more)	45	830

Table 4.1 **Continued**

Items	Categories	Weighted %*	N
Centrality			
Importance of internet as source	0 - Not so important, not at all important	6	109
	1 - Important, very important	59	1086
	2 - Essential	35	643
Total		100	1,838

*N is weighted to better estimate population of Britain.

Source: 2013 OxIS Survey

- Did they actively use and follow search to source their own information or mostly visit specific pages?
- Did they collaborate with other networked individuals, such as following cues or links suggested by other users?
- Did they have a learned level of trust in the content providers they could find online?
- Did they trust internet service providers?
- Did they view the internet as essential for meeting their information needs, as opposed to being not important at all for information, such as merely a form of entertainment?

Those that were ranked high on most of these activities were classified as potential contributors to the Fifth Estate.[7] Those who were low (0–8) on all the activities (26%) were classified as spectators, and those with a mixed (9–11) profile (45%), were classified as attentives (Table 4.2). Less than one-third (30%) could be classified as having Fifth Estate potential (12–16, the maximum), but that was in 2013 (Figure 4.1).

While this is a rough approximation, these eight variables were used to determine characteristics of the sample relative to other internet users in Britain. Their socioeconomic status was similar to those most likely to use the internet—that is, they were more likely to be educated, middle or upper middle class, and with higher incomes.[8] They were also more likely to be employed in managerial/professional roles or be a student or unemployed. Put another way, they were less likely to have blue-collar or white-collar clerical jobs, for example. With respect to their attitudes, they were more likely to be high on political efficacy and have a strong sense of political empowerment. In these respects, except for the prominence of unemployed, this Fifth Estate group was also more likely to be young, urban, and a member of a minority group.

The prominence of the unemployed, young, urban, and minorities suggests that those with profiles closer to expectations of the Fifth Estate conformed not only to people most likely to be early adopters of the internet, such as those with more schooling, but also to people likely to feel less well served by the mainstream media. This is one possible explanation for the affinity of the internet and social media to minority communities across the world.

Table 4.2 **Devices and Activities in UK That Underpin Fifth Estate**

Devices	Percent No	Percent Yes	Total Percent	N
One or more computers	20	80	100	1,811
Mobile phone	8	92	100	1,818
Smartphone	21	79	100	1,679
Tablet or reader w/ touch screen	40	60	100	1,816
Smart speaker responds to voice	80	20	100	1,811
Activities				
Take videos/photos	8	92	100	1,325
Post photos/videos	28	72	100	1,327
Post photos/video you took*	23	77	100	1,818
Send photos/videos	14	86	100	1,328

*Not only on a mobile or smartphone

Source: OxIS 2019

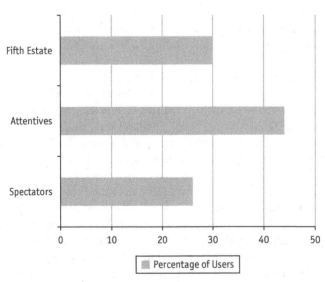

Figure 4.1 Percentage of Likely Spectators, Attentives, and Fifth Estate

THE FIFTH ESTATE AMONG MANY OTHER SPEAKERS

Networked individuals of the Fifth Estate are quite distinct from a number of other categories of online speakers (Box 4.5). They are not everyone online, even though nearly every person online might have the ability to create content as easily as liking a post on social media. They are not celebrities with millions of followers. They are

> ### Box 4.5 **Types of Networked Individuals**
>
> Networked individuals, that is, everyone with online access who uses the internet and social media for any purpose, include the following:
>
> Celebrities, in entertainment and other sectors such as business, who leverage their fame to reach followers online, such as Taylor Swift, to reinforce or gain recognition and promote causes
>
> Influencers who have built a large following of fans through their online presence and seek to leverage their base to promote brands, advertise, or influence public opinion, which increasingly includes computer-generated avatars, called "virtual influencers"
>
> Politicians who seek to reach their supporters and the public directly, unfiltered by the press
>
> Malicious users, who include online bullies, trolls, vigilantes, cybercriminals, and malicious hackers
>
> Fifth Estate, a moving, ever-changing collectivity of ordinary, civic-minded networked individuals who use online networks in ways that enhance their communicative power vis-à-vis other actors

not influencers who help market products or services—and certainly not computer-generated avatars that become "virtual influencers" (Li 2022). They are not high-profile political or sports stars seeking to have a more direct and unfiltered link with their fans. Nor are they malicious users who intend to attack others online without any concern for civility.

A Rising Potential for Networked Individuals

Since the diffusion of mobile internet with better quality as well as the ease of taking photographs and producing short videos, the potential base of networked individuals has become nearly ubiquitous around the world. Few nations do not have a critical mass of networked individuals present to witness and record major events.

In the United Kingdom, for example, we surveyed individuals in households in 2019, prior to the COVID pandemic, and gained a clear sense of the degree that devices in the hands of users were creating more capability for more individuals to contribute to Fifth Estate activities, such as posting original content. Over 80% of the adult population was online, and well over three-quarters of the public were using some form of mobile smartphone. Over half had a tablet or touch screen reader, and a fifth (20%) had a smart speaker in their household for voice search (Table 4.2).

The realization of this capability is evident in the proportions of the public taking videos or photos (92%), posting videos or photos online (72%), including their own photos/videos (77%), and sending photos or videos to others (86%). Most individuals in Britain are equipped and are able to capture aspects of events they witness or information they gain and then distribute it to others via online media (Table 4.2).

Moreover, the use of social media has also remained high, suggesting that internet users in Britain are well networked, not only in the sense of being online but also with other networked individuals. Over three-fourths (77%) say they browse or update social media (Table 4.3). While the most dominant platform in Britain in 2019 was Facebook, other social media like YouTube have over a majority of internet users, and many other social media platforms have over 10% of networked individuals using their services.

Table 4.3 shows the diversity of platforms supporting social media use in the UK—all of which and more are available in many other nations. Facebook became the dominant social media platform by 2019, but YouTube was also used by more than half of internet users with a sizeable number of platforms used by more than 10% of networked individuals. In short, networked individuals in Britain were enabled to create and distribute their own content in a variety of local and global networks.

Moreover, these trends continued in Britain and worldwide. More recent survey research in the UK found internet use to be as strong as in 2019, with only 6% of households not having access to the internet in 2021. While most users employed multiple devices to go online, 85% of internet users had a smartphone (Ofcom 2021: 1). Worldwide internet and social media use document the critical mass of internet users in most nations. Various cases speak to particular nations, but worldwide there are over 5 billion internet users amounting to over 65% of the adult population (WIS 2021). Regionally, Africa has the lowest proportion of internet users, but that proportion is 43%, which is sizeable. Asia has just under the average proportion of internet users, with 64% online, but has by far the largest number of

Table 4.3 **Social Media Use in the UK**

Use Social Media	Percent No	Percent Yes	Total Percent	N
Browse, update social media	23	77	100	1,325
Facebook	30	70	100	1,476
YouTube	39	61	100	1,484
Instagram	62	38	100	1,483
Twitter	75	25	100	1,476
Snapchat	75	25	100	1,484
Google+	81	19	100	1,476
LinkedIn	82	18	100	1,476
Pinterest	87	13	100	1,476

Source: OxIS 2019

internet users, over 2.5 billion. The potential base of a Fifth Estate is therefore huge and growing.

Concrete Illustrations of Informational and Communicative Power

This section moves behind the statistics to look at specific networked individuals empowered by the internet in ways reflecting the role of the Fifth Estate. It is impossible to fully describe any of these Fifth Estate actors and their activities, but the vignettes provided here seek to convey the basic role and impact of each, including failures as well as successes, in achieving some greater level of transparency or accountability. The seven examples described in this section are all exceptional cases—not typical but exemplary. They are among the better known but also emblematic of the potential and limitations of the Fifth Estate; I will refer to other examples in less detail as the stories of all or most can be further pursued online by interested readers (such as that in Box 4.6). They are not representative of all nations or regions or issue areas, but other examples populate other chapters of this book. Here the focus is on creating original content distributed in ways that shaped events.

WAEL GHONIM AND THE ARAB SPRING

A young Google executive in Egypt, Wael Ghonim, was able to use Facebook along with other internet sites to rally protestors against Egyptian President Hosni Mubarak. His efforts along with others fostered antigovernment protests in Egypt and may have prompted related protests across the Middle East, creating a vision of an Arab Spring and the role the internet might play in bringing democracy to the region. However, the government retaliated by blocking the internet and detaining Ghonim for twelve days. In the longer term, it became clear that the protests might have toppled the government but did not bring democracy, as autocratic regimes emerged across the region. Wael Ghonim was honored by many, including the CEO of Google, Eric Schmidt, and his efforts did galvanize a movement against an unpopular leader. After Ghonim was released from detention, Google welcomed him back. Eric Schmidt spoke to Wael Ghonim and said that the internet and collaboration tools like Facebook "change the power dynamic between governments and citizens in some very interesting and unpredictable ways" (Wortham 2011). He was very proud of what Wael had done.

Ghonim helped orchestrate protests that contributed to the resignation of President Mubarak. That said, the protests did not defeat autocratic rule and led to responses aimed at curtailing and controlling the internet and social media—a prominent response across regions of the world and in the more democratic regimes of the developed nations. But at the time, major expectations surrounded social media platforms as "global champions for facilitating the pro-democracy protests" across the Middle East and North Africa (Krishnappa 2011). While the internet did not bring democracy to the Arab world, the Arab Spring demonstrated the dramatic potential of networked individuals to convey messages and capture events that would not otherwise be portrayed from their perspective (Snowdon 2020).

Box 4.6 **Examples of Fifth Estate Actors Creating Impactful Content**

Fifth Estate Actors	Purpose	Implications
Wael Ghonim, a rising Google executive, in the Arab Spring	Used Facebook and other internet sites in 2010 to rally protesters in Egypt against President Hosni Mubarak	Internet blocked; Ghonim detained in Egypt for 12 days, but pro-democracy protests impactful; Mubarak steps down
Greta Thunberg, a young student protestor, in climate activism	Instagram post of her protest outside the Swedish Parliament	Reshaped global awareness of the climate crisis (Box 1.1)
Martha Payne, 9-year-old, in Scotland, in school nutrition	Developed NeverSeconds blog to complete a school project	Influenced reform of school lunch programs in Scotland and across UK
Ramsey Orta, son of a Puerto Rican father and African American mother, in Black Lives Matter	Recorded arrest and choking of Eric Gardner by a police officer on July 17, 2014, and posted video "Can't Breathe"	Orta and his family experienced harassment; Orta was imprisoned for carrying a stolen gun; Gardner's death fueled protests around BLM
Darnella Frazier, a 17-year-old teenager, in BLM	Walked on to the scene of George Floyd's arrest, used her phone to video a police officer with his knee on Floyd's neck for 9 minutes, posted video on Facebook	The viral video provided key evidence in the trial of the police and made George Floyd a symbol of structural racism and BLM
Hundreds if not thousands of individuals captured atrocities in photos and videos in the Russia-Ukraine war	Over 13,000 eyewitness accounts of atrocities from the Ukraine conflict were captured by an app, "eyeWitness to Atrocities"	Collected to be valuable in prosecuting war crimes at the International Criminal Court; supported Ukrainian claims and undermined Russian disclaimers

GRETA THUNBERG AND THE EXTINCTION REBELLION

As noted in Chapter 1, a young 15-year-old climate activist, Ms. Greta Thunberg, skipped school on Fridays to protest outside the Swedish Parliament. Her handwritten poster, which read in Swedish, "School strike for climate," encouraged other schoolchildren to strike until public officials took more aggressive action on climate change. The

Instagram post of her protest went viral as she inspired other children at her school and in many other communities across the globe to protest for action on climate change. Arguably, Greta became one of the world's most positive symbols for and catalysts of climate activism around the world. She brings to mind an earlier example of an even younger person making a difference in a more local and national context, the UK.

MARTHA PAYNE'S NEVERSECONDS AND ACTION ON NUTRITION IN SCHOOLS

That other young woman was a Scottish girl called Martha Payne. While attending school in Scotland when she was 9 years old, Martha challenged the way lunches were served across the United Kingdom through a blog she created. In 2012, she was assigned a school writing project by her teacher. Instead of a more traditional project, such as a paper, with encouragement and help from her father, Martha developed a blog. Entitled "NeverSeconds," the blog (neverseconds.blogspot.com/) included photos of her school lunches, which she took on her mobile phone, and the reviews she wrote about her lunches. Her original concern was about not being permitted to go back for a second helping of healthy food. However, the site quickly transformed into issues over the general quality of the food being served.

Her blog was so popular so quickly that it raised concerns among the primary school's governing council. Within months, in June 2012, the Argyll and Bute Council governing the school on a small Scottish Isle was concerned about the bad publicity, so it asked the headteacher to stop Martha from bringing her camera to school. This censorship by the school sparked even more interest in her blog, in line with what has been called the Streisand effect (Box 4.7). News of the ban led to a major increase in the views of her blog NeverSeconds and even a comedic song about the council.[9] Within days, journalists were showing up at their home, and UK celebrity chef Jamie Oliver tweeted about her blog. Views continued to grow internationally. Martha's original point was that children were not allowed seconds for their school lunch, but her photos and commentary on the lunches included details such as the hair content! The blog quickly transformed a child's critique of school lunches into a widely discussed, national issue. In less than

---

Box 4.7 The Streisand Effect

When people try to censor or hide information or avoid publicity, they can, and often do, make it even more likely to gain recognition. In 2003, the American celebrity entertainer Barbara Streisand tried to suppress aerial photographs of her home in Malibu, California. An aerial photo posted online showed an entrance to her Malibu estate, which she considered a security threat to her home. They were taken by Kenneth Adelman, a photographer for the California Records Project, whom her estate sued for tens of millions of dollars. Seldom viewed online, the photos became popular because of this attempt to block access. Trying to censor information online can have the exact opposite (Streisand) effect.

three months, the blog had 3 million views. It eventually attracted over 10 million views and played a major role in raising awareness and fostering debate across Britain over the quality of school lunches.

Martha followed the incredible success of her blog with a book co-authored with her father about their experience (Payne and Payne 2012). Produced by an independent publisher, the profits of its sale went to a charity in Malawi called Mary's Meals. Eventually, Martha Payne stopped blogging on NeverSeconds, as it was absorbing so much of her time, and she had many other interests to pursue in life.

This incredible story of a young girl's blog is a clear example of the internet enhancing her communicative power—and a fascinating example of the Fifth Estate.

NeverSeconds fostered debate over the quality of school lunches nationwide and worldwide and led to a variety of initiatives aimed at improving school lunches, such as through visits and tutorials by celebrity chefs.

RAMSEY ORTA VIDEOING ERIC GARNER'S ARREST AND SHAPING #BLM

On July 17, 2014, in the racially mixed Tompkinsville neighborhood of Staten Island, a borough of New York City, police approached Ramsey Orta, a Latino, and Eric Garner, a black Staten Island resident, who was illegally selling loose cigarettes. Orta immediately started videoing the interactions with police in what he described as "self-defense" (Jones 2019). The video shows Garner exclaiming to the police that he had done nothing wrong before an officer puts him in a chokehold (Lebron 2017: 5–6). The video documented Garner telling the police—eleven times—that he could not breathe, before he lost consciousness. He died in custody soon after his arrest. On the video, Orta's voice is audible, saying, "He can't breathe!" Garner's words—"I can't breathe"—became a rallying cry for protests, particularly for Black Lives Matter (#BLM).

Later in the evening of Garner's arrest, Orta reported police cars were parked in front of his home, shining spotlights through his windows. Orta felt that there was no proof of Garner's treatment other than his video, which had been posted online (although it is unclear who posted it), where it was viewed, shared, and discussed widely. He was the first of fifty witnesses for a hearing on Garner's arrest by a grand jury, where his video and a medical examiner's report were used at the trial to establish that a police officer had used an illegal chokehold that put pressure on Garner's throat and windpipe. After nine weeks, on December 3, 2014, the grand jury decided not to indict the police officer. However, the officer was eventually fired without a pension in 2019.

Ramsey Orta had a checkered past, such as being a member of a gang and a series of arrests prior to and following his video. Nevertheless, journalistic reports on Orta present a story of repeated harassment of his family and him, in and out of prison, since the time of his video (e.g., Jones 2019). He was released early from prison in May 2020 due to the COVID-19 pandemic, while serving a four-year sentence on drug charges (Ehrlich 2020). In hindsight, Ramsey was understandably of two minds, if not regretful, about filming this arrest—considering there was no conviction of the officer and the years of difficulties for him and his family with the police, which he attributed to payback for his video (Richardson 2020).

DARNELLA FRAZIER AND THE MURDER OF GEORGE FLOYD

On April 20, 2021, a police officer was convicted of murder in relation to the police-custody death of George Floyd on May 25, 2020. The evidence behind the conviction was based largely on video of the incident, mentioned by US President Biden in the aftermath of the guilty verdicts as a major contribution to the conviction.

George Floyd was born in 1973, one of five siblings, and grew up in a housing project in a historically black neighborhood of Houston, Texas. He was well over six feet tall and played basketball and American football in high school. He attended a college on a sports scholarship and moved to a major university in Texas but left before graduating. After returning to Houston, he was arrested several times on drug charges and theft before facing a more serious charge for an armed robbery in 2007, for which he served time in prison. In 2014, he left Houston for Minneapolis, Minnesota, to find work and make a new start. He worked for a time as a security guard, then as a truck driver, and then a bouncer at a restaurant before being let go when the COVID-19 pandemic closed the business.[10]

On April 20, 2020, in Minneapolis, a convenience store clerk saw that Floyd passed a counterfeit twenty-dollar bill to pay for his purchase. The store called the police, leading to the police confronting Floyd just outside the convenience store.

Darnella Frazier, a 17-year-old, who lived near the location of the store, was exiting the store as the confrontation with police began to unfold. As soon as she saw the arrest taking place, she shot a video on her mobile phone of a policeman kneeling on George Floyd's neck for over nine minutes. When she returned home, she posted the video on Facebook.

It was viewed and shared rapidly and globally, becoming a rallying cry for the Black Lives Matter #BLM movement in the United States and across the world. For this video evidence, Darnella Frazier received the 2021 Benenson Courage Award from PEN America, a leading literary and human rights organization (Fitz-Gibbon 2020). In the words of the CEO of PEN, "Darnella carried out the expressive act of bearing witness and allowing hundreds of millions around the world to see what she saw" (Fitz-Gibbon 2021: 1).

George Floyd quickly became a "global symbol" of racial injustice and the need for change in policing (Bushey and Aladesuyi 2021), and the jury verdicts in the Floyd case were seen as a "milestone in police accountability" (Chaffin and Rogers 2021), with the former Minneapolis police officer—the primary defendant—sentenced to over twenty-two years for murder. Capturing a widely shared view, the journalist Nesrine Malik (2021) argued that BLM had moved public discourse about racism to more "structural and institutional" versus personal and intentional racism. Years after his death, protesters continue to visit the site of his arrest in Minneapolis, where a mural has been painted of Floyd, depicted as an angel (Rogers 2022).

EYEWITNESS TO WAR AND ATROCITIES IN UKRAINE

In the early days of the Russian invasion of Ukraine on February 24, 2022, before Russians destroyed many mobile masts, many residents of Ukraine used social media to provide intelligence on the war. For example, citizens were able to provide information on the exact location (pinning it on Google maps) of Russian troops on a Telegram chatbot created by the security services along with screen shots of the troops (Judah 2022). While internet facilities were targeted by the invasion, internet access proved so valuable to the military that Elon Musk, at the request of the Ukrainian government, provided Starlink terminals to the country to provide satellite provision of broadband satellite services, mainly funded by donations through SpaceX's Starlink division and the United States support of SpaceX.[11]

Also, thousands of individuals in Ukraine have captured eyewitness accounts of atrocities committed during the Russian invasion. By July 2022, five months after the invasion was launched, more than 13,000 items were captured in an app entitled "eyeWitness to Atrocities."[12] Arguably, the Russian invasion of Ukraine was the most documented war in history given the number of individuals who could capture ongoing events and their aftermath on their smartphones, such as in the village of Bucha, Ukraine, where images taken by residents and journalists prompted accusations of war crimes against the Russian forces.[13] It will also be among the most transparent and subject to a greater level of accountability than any war in history. I'll return to this app in discussing collaboration in collecting intelligence, which makes the documentation by individuals even more powerful (Chapter 6, Box 6.3).

Risks of Empowering Networked Individuals

Before moving forward with additional strategies of a Fifth Estate, it is critical to acknowledge that there are indeed serious risks to the empowerment of networked individuals. There is a potentially damaging shift from seeing social media and the internet generally as "technologies of freedom" to disruptive and dangerous sources of disinformation controlled by malicious or naïve users. This is linked to a general move toward demonizing social media that could be detrimental to the future of the Fifth Estate. The central theme of this book is that such a demonization of the internet and social media would be misleading and masks the values it supports, such as the Fifth Estate. Nevertheless, it is useful to spell out some of the specific concerns so they can be addressed throughout the book.

THE DANGEROUS IMMEDIACY OF LIVE STREAMING: CHRISTCHURCH

Live streaming broadcast news coverage arrived in the late 1990s. In 1998, in midafternoon in Los Angeles, California, Daniel V. Jones, a 40-year-old man distraught over the circumstances of his health stopped his car on an elevated section of freeway transitioning from one to another freeway. Sitting next to his dog, he waved a shotgun at passing cars, drawing attention, and leading to calls to the police, including a 911 emergency call from himself. After unfurling a banner with a message criticizing his health provider, he ended up committing suicide on live television while households across the city were watching this news unfold. The *Los Angeles Times* headline read: "Man Kills Self as City Watches."[14] This was one of the first instances that led news organizations to institute delays in the broadcasting of live coverage to enable editors to avoid showing such disturbing scenes on live television.

Just over twenty years later, on March 15, 2019, using a camera on his helmet, Brenton Harrison Tarrant attacked Muslim worshipers in two mosques in Christchurch, New Zealand, killing fifty-five people. This 28-year-old white supremacist from Australia published an online manifesto he had written and live streamed his terrorist attack on Facebook. Here there was no news organization that could edit this footage, and police authorities could only warn the public on Twitter of "extremely distressing footage" if this incident was online.[15] A prominent journalist spoke of live streaming as a scary human invention that could not be controlled, analogous to Mary Shelley's Frankenstein (Bell 2016). With all the good that can be gained by networked individuals capturing unfolding events, in the hands of sick or disturbed individuals, online media organizations and governments face a real dilemma in how to prevent the inappropriate while enabling the civil and informative.

SHAMING AND THE POTENTIAL FOR REPUTATIONAL DAMAGE

Most social media users are increasingly aware of the potential for photographs or videos to damage or undermine their reputation. Some are frivolous, such as a video catching a professor teaching his students from "the wheel of his car,"[16] but some photos and videos have been nearly life changing for individuals, such as for the infamous "cat lady."[17] Such photos and videos range from shaming hunters who kill endangered animals to exposing evidence of sexist, racist, or threatening remarks. It can extend to the use of video to expose and attack a person or organization in a form of online or digital vigilantism, such as animal rights activists targeting those using animals in medical experiments and testing.

BULLYING, TROLLING, AND HATE SPEECH

Content can be created that is harmful in many other ways, for example, bullying an individual or trolling, that is, rude or inflammatory remarks/comments to provoke an emotional response or disrupt a conversation. These are aspects of a broader category of hate speech, directed at individuals, groups, or institutions, which has been propagated online from the earliest days of the internet (Strossen 2018). Social media and the internet promote spontaneity and personal perspectives on unfolding events, but if unintended slights or missteps lead to personal attacks by an online mob, then free expression will be undermined and self-promoting virtue signaling will be incentivized to everyone's detriment. Humor, sarcasm, and playful wording can be easily misunderstood online from short, abbreviated text often without any context. Reading online needs to be charitable and generous to speakers rather than hateful. Democratic discourse cannot thrive in constant threat of retaliation, censorship, or other sanctions.

DISINFORMATION

Another rising source of concern is over the potential for untrained, amateur, or malevolent individuals and organizations to use the internet and social media to spread misinformation, such as fake news (Keen 2008, McDougall 2019). As technical advances make it easier for anyone to post from anywhere at any time, it is possible to sow false or biased information. This is a growing focus of research, but research on users suggests that this fear is exaggerated by relying on technologically deterministic ideas about this potential without looking critically at how users actually read and view the internet, such as to check facts, select sources they trust, and read multiple accounts of information they care about. My own research tends to discredit these claims as fake news about fake news.

These concerns are illustrative of a wider array of problems tied to the power of online content creation that contribute to calls for interventions, such as greater online censorship and content regulation, that could undermine the internet, social media, and the Fifth Estate. In the next chapter, key strategies for users to protect themselves online, such as from disinformation, are discussed.

Words, art, books, and the internet can be maliciously used or unintentionally be harmful in different degrees over time and across different cultural contexts. No technology is uniformly positive, and while the internet can augment and network human intelligence, it can also be used to exacerbate such problems. Finding methods to enable the civil uses of the internet and social media while protecting individuals and society from misinformation, incivility, and cyber harms is one of the central challenges of our digital age—one that will be revisited throughout this book.

Themes Emerging from Cases of Network Power

These few examples are designed to illustrate some of the many concrete ways the Fifth Estate may or may not work for particular people in specific circumstances. Most Fifth Estate contributions are not seen by millions, thousands, or even hundreds, but they can nevertheless be impactful individually and collectively in creating a sense that people can be held accountable for their actions on and offline. You can see images of events in which hundreds are holding up their cameras to capture an important image to blog or post. There is a growing understanding of the empowerment of networked individuals to capture actions that might be subject to public scrutiny. How to balance the value gained by transparency and accountability with the threats of surveillance and the death of privacy are key issues for the Fifth Estate (Brin 1998).

While these examples help concretize the idea of a Fifth Estate, they also suggest several themes that run through the pages of this book.

THE INTERNET AND SOCIAL MEDIA CAN EMPOWER INDIVIDUALS

Individually and collectively, these examples show how the internet and social media can empower an individual, from a 9-year-old girl in a small Scottish Isle of about 3,000 residents reaching a global audience with her concerns about school lunches to surviving residents of a village in Ukraine documenting potential war crimes.

LIMITS ON FIFTH ESTATE POWER

That said, the examples also illustrate the limits of networked individuals to make a difference. Ramsey Orta did not save Eric Garner, nor did he realize a conviction of a police officer, but he enabled others to witness Garner's "I can't breathe" and help build the movement for BLM and police reform as did Darnella Frazier. Similarly, as you will read in Chapter 5, the water warriors in Flint did not get a response from the government, but they did contribute indirectly to getting others—citizen journalists, medical professionals, and scientists—involved in establishing the evidence behind their concerns over tainted water.

NO PUSH BUTTON OR SIMPLE POINT AND CLICK FOR DEMOCRACY

Much of the fear over social media and the internet is anchored in a sense that there is some claim that one tweet or photo can bring democracy to the Arab world or save the world from extinction. In each case, you can see individuals taking risks, often working very hard over an extended period, to leverage the internet in bringing facts to light. Greta Thunberg's Instagram post was one small piece of a range of actions and efforts to bring action on climate change to the attention of policymakers. Wael Ghonim helped make a difference to the fate of Egyptian President Hosni Mubarak, but rather than democracy, the Arab Spring evolved to the entrenchment of autocracies across the region (Howard 2011).

THE FIFTH ESTATE CROSSES SECTORS OF SOCIETIES WORLDWIDE

The examples also illustrate that the Fifth Estate is not limited to politics or government. They describe how the Fifth Estate can be seen in politics, such as the Arab Spring, but also environmental protection, nutrition in schools, holding police accountable, and solving crimes. As you will see with the many other examples described in this book, the Fifth Estate can be a factor in nearly any sector of society.

THE PROMINENCE OF VIDEO IMAGES AMONG REMARKABLE POSTS

These examples of remarkably empowered networked individuals are primarily linked to video images rather than detailed texts. One of the first books on the Fifth Estate focused almost exclusively on text-based bloggers (Cooper 2006), predating the rise of vlogs and the mobile internet's diffusion. It is suggestive of the power of an image to be trusted as a source of information but also to the ease of creating and seeing an image versus writing and reading a text. The growing popularity of applications like Instagram, WeChat, and TikTok, for example, which prioritize photographs and short videos, such as Instagram's photo filtering, and Facebook, to an increasing extent, capture this trend in the ease and popularity of video communication (Frier 2020, Richardson 2020). By 2022, young adults in Britain, 16–24 years old, spent more time on the social media app TikTok than they spent watching television (Barker 2022).

SOCIAL MEDIA AND THE INTERNET AS A SOURCE OF TRUTH

One of the major criticisms of user-generated information is the risk of misinformation, such as fake news and the undermining of truth. There are many ways patterns of internet use guard social media and internet users from disinformation, such as their ability to search and fact-check, which is discussed in other sections of this book. However, you can see in these examples that social media and the internet can also be the source of facts—witnessing and sharing events as they occur. Darnella Frazier's video was a primary source of evidence at the trial of the officer accused of kneeling on George Floyd's neck in broad daylight. In Flint, Michigan, as discussed in Chapter 5, residents on social media were a source of hard evidence about the tainted water in the city but were dismissed by emergency managers until more scientific evidence could be marshaled that backed the citizens not the managers. Ordinary residents across impoverished areas of Flint, Michigan, were reporting real problems with water and their health on social media that were erroneously ignored by public officials.

Points of Summary, Conclusion, and Related Problems

This chapter focused on describing how the internet and related social media enable networked individuals to source original content that can make a positive difference across many sectors of society. Technical advances are making the media more affordable and easier to use by more people around the world, creating greater potential for the Fifth Estate to emerge as a critical actor in key events and processes. All the chapters of this book will contribute to explaining and describing this potential in concrete trends and cases.

5

Networking

Social media like Facebook and other popular applications are a blessing to many. And, for some, particularly in developing nations, it is their only access to the internet. That said, to many others, social media is seen as nothing short of a "window into Hades"— something to be feared (Ganesh 2021: 21). This chapter focuses on showing how social media, and digital media more generally, provide a resource of value to networking socially in ways that also create a powerful infrastructure for sharing and supporting the rise of a Fifth Estate. The chapter briefly addresses some of the major worries raised about the potential harms of the internet and social media, such as around isolation and disinformation. Later chapters focus more directly and comprehensively on this issue, addressing the harms associated with the internet and social media, and how they might shape the future of the Fifth Estate.

The chapter begins with a simple overview of the rise and significance of networking and its centrality to social media. It then provides a brief introduction to the many social media that have been launched over the past decades, illustrating the emergence of a wide variety of concrete applications that support different kinds of social networking. This lays a foundation for illustrating the value of social media for the Fifth Estate through a few exemplary cases and related examples. The chapter then addresses key harms associated with social media, including social isolation, loss of privacy, surveillance, disinformation, and the threat of mobs. The chapter concludes by discussing proposals for blocking, censoring, and moderating social media that could kill it and undermine the Fifth Estate.

Innovation in Computer-Mediated Communication and Networking

The postindustrial information society has increasingly been understood as a "networked society" as communication has become as critical a resource as information to all sectors of society (Castells 1996). In this very broad sense, all the various strategies of the Fifth Estate are aspects of our postindustrial information or network society. But in this chapter, I use networking in its narrower sense, not as a macro-perspective on the digital age, but as the use of digital media to network with others as in the use of social media. That is, a wide range of concrete developments over many years in the use of digital technologies to network—connect—individuals and groups constitutes

The Fifth Estate. William H. Dutton, Oxford University Press. © Oxford University Press 2023.
DOI: 10.1093/oso/9780190688363.003.0006

one key force behind such macro-level perspectives as societies increasingly go online (Dutton 1999).

Of course, societies have long been organized around groups, but networks are not synonymous with groups as traditionally defined. As one of the pioneers of network studies put it: "In networked societies: boundaries are permeable, interactions are with diverse others, connections switch between multiple networks, and hierarchies can be flatter and recursive" (Wellman 2001: 227). Think of any group, such as your household or your coworkers, and then consider the myriad networks in which they are collectively involved. Networks do not erase groups but add other social connections, augmenting an individual's network in ways that are not likely to occur with groups anchored in a physical place, like a household or activity like a club.

In the early days of data processing, people communicated with a computer by using punch cards to enter data, for example. Computers were calculators for budgeting and accounting and scientific calculations. But individual users soon were able to communicate with a computer over a wire—transmitting electronic signals from a terminal to instruct and receive messages from the computer at a distance. Was this human-to-machine communication something that should be regulated, like the phone and other telecommunications? In order to foster innovation in computing, the United States and other governments argued that this was not a telecommunications service that should be regulated, as this could undermine further innovative developments.

The next and parallel development was how to enable computers to communicate with one another and share information and files so that scientists and others distributed across universities and labs could work collaboratively and share computing resources. Pioneering engineers like Vint Cerf and Robert E. Kahn and those we would later call computer scientists found ways to network computers through mechanisms such as packet switched networks and standardized rules—what became known as Transmission Control Protocol/Internet Protocol (TCP/IP) that enabled computers to communicate with each other over a network, like the internet. One of the early outcomes of connecting computers was the development of email systems, which allowed people on one computer to send messages to people on other computers anywhere in the world, if interconnected with each other. You could even send to lists of people who had email addresses.

In 1974, when working at UC Irvine, I had an email address and messaged some colleagues, but I had to call them to let them know to look for my message. I also sat with a computer science graduate student at that time, Walt Scacchi, who showed me how we could sit at a terminal at UC Irvine and use software on a computer at Stanford University, but software could be on any computer, anywhere in the world, that was linked on this network—which was then called the ARPANet. Yes, this was designed to support communication and collaborative sharing among scientists, but this was clearly a dramatic innovation in networking that would change the way people get information and communicate.

The Breadth and Fragmentation of Social Media

To many people in 2021, social media are almost synonymous with a particular application, such as Facebook in the case of Britain and the United States or WeChat in the case of China. But there are different kinds of social media, broadly defined, and different providers and applications within each approach to social media. Table 5.1 provides a selective and abbreviated overview of four different kinds of social media and representative applications, defined by whether they are primarily supporting:

- 1:1 or 1:many: one person to one person or one to many forms of communication, like email.
- Meeting or conferencing: group communication in real time such as in teaching or business or dispersed families during the pandemic.
- Social media: enabling an individual to find and connect with friends, family, or colleagues or a broader public.
- Private messaging: systems designed to more privately support smaller and more specialized groups, such as through encryption.

Table 5.1 provides some examples of applications of each type. Email might be the best example of person-to-person communication, but email has been greatly enabled for organizations and business by such applications as Constant Contact and MailChimp that make possible very efficient management of email lists and mailings that can be linked to other social media and marketing. Founded in 2001, in 2021, MailChimp sold for US$12 billion. Zoom might be the best example of a meeting technology, particularly during the worst periods of the COVID pandemic that led many divided households, classrooms, and business associates to meet online, often simply to reinforce their social network. Facebook might be the best example of social media in the United States and Britain, while Parler might be the most recent and most controversial. It is committed to free speech and opposed to Facebook's moderation policies, but its use by conservative supporters of Donald Trump, including some who stormed the Capitol, and proponents of conspiracy theories, such as QAnon, led Amazon Web Services to stop hosting the site. But it came back online with a new hosting platform promising to build a "reputable but contrarian platform" (Murphy 2021). In 2021, Facebook was among the most popular social media applications, but WhatsApp and other more private social messaging sites are rising in popularity as individuals become more guarded about whom they communicate with and more concerned over the privacy of their communication.

In many or most cases, a particular application, such as Facebook or TikTok, can be used in multiple ways and therefore span more than one type in Table 5.1, but I have tried to characterize each by its primary design features and how it is chiefly used. Users are notorious for employing technologies in unanticipated ways, so designs do not always match patterns of use. That said, all these technologies can support social networks that enable a Fifth Estate.

THE "SOCIAL" IN SOCIAL NETWORKS

From the perspective of the Fifth Estate, social media are particularly interesting and important because they are not designed or used to support a Fifth Estate. They are designed and used primarily to support or gratify any use of value to individuals and groups. For example, a person most often connects to Facebook to keep in touch with

Table 5.1 **Examples of Digital Networking Media**

Type—Focus	Examples (year launched)	*Description*
Interpersonal 1:1, 1:many	Email (1971)	Electronic mail was one of the earliest and key social media, not to be forgotten.
	Mailchimp (2001)	
	Constant Contact (2004)	
	Gmail (2004)	
	Facebook Messenger (2010)	
Group Meetings	Webex (1995)	Enabling groups of more than 2 to meet in real time began early with WebEx but soared during the COVID pandemic. Pre-internet examples include telephone conferencing systems.
	Skype (2003)	
	FaceTime (2010)	
	Zoom (2012)	
	Teams (2019), replacing Skype for Business	
Social Media	Friendster (2002)	These are core to how people view social media, enabling individuals to link with family, friends, and colleagues. Each places varied focus on public reach, private messaging, video, and other elements of their application. Technically, not all on this list are social media, in that some, like TikTok, with more than 1 billion users in 2022, essentially enable users to post short-form videos. But all enable user-generated content.
	LinkedIn (2003)	
	Facebook (2004)	
Myspace (2005–8)	Mastodon (2016)	
	Reddit (2005)	
	Twitter (2006)	
	Tumblr (2007)	
	Pinterest (2010)	
	Instagram (2010)	
	Snapchat (2011)	
	Pinterest (2010)	

Table 5.1 **Continued**

Type—Focus	Examples (year launched)	*Description*
	Google+ (2011–19)	
	TikTok (2017)	
	Parler (2018)	
	Truth Social (2022)	
(More) Private Social Networks	Nextdoor (2008)	Social media moved toward more private messaging in smaller and more focused groups and hyperlocal social networking, such as neighborhoods.
	WhatsApp (2009)	
	WeChat (2010)	
	Telegram (2013)	
	Slack (2013)	
	Signal (2018)	

A comprehensive "Timeline of Social Media" is available on Wikipedia: https://en.wikipedia.org/wiki/Timeline_of_social_media.

family and friends, such as childhood friends or classmates in college or at work. They may join social media, like Snapchat, because some of their friends are on the network or for myriad other reasons, but not to be a member of the Fifth Estate. However, despite whatever uses or gratifications that led a person to create a social network on a particular platform, it would not necessarily prevent that individual from using it strategically to support some civic purpose that is consistent with actions of the Fifth Estate, as some of the examples in this chapter will clarify.

Most social media allow users to post a short (in the case of a microblogging site, like Twitter) or long message (in the case of a blog such as on WordPress). On Twitter, for example, people can follow whomever they wish, while on Facebook, in contrast, a user can only follow other users who permit them to do so. If you are followed on Twitter, you do not need to follow the person back—it is not reciprocal. But on Facebook, if you permit someone to be your friend, then you are their friend—it is reciprocal. Twitter is also an open platform, such that users can see tweets even though they are not following you or vice versa. Facebook can be closed to friends or open to the public, and private networking systems are only open to members of the network. Most social media have means for sharing a post they like, such as with Twitter users retweeting a tweet "RT." Through such mechanisms as following, liking, sharing, forwarding, and retweeting, messages on social media can be propagated through multiple networks. Hashtags—a string of text preceded by "#"—are another mechanism, frequently used on Twitter. If someone wanted to see posts on developments around MeToo, for example, they might search for #MeToo. Everyone can see what anyone else is saying about the topic of the hashtag. In short, social media are designed for sharing information across an evolving network of networks.

This is powerful because an individual's network often includes individuals from other networks and therefore offers the potential to magnify the dissemination of information far beyond one's own network. And that network is at your fingertips at any moment that an occasion arises that would lead you to spread the word about an event, a problem, or an issue to you or your network. If you saw someone fly-tipping, for example, you are unlikely to organize a group against fly-tipping. But you might take a photo of the mess and post it on your social media site with a note on where and when it was seen. There is a website for collecting and analyzing such data, called Planet Patrol, discussed in Chapter 6. As the Chinese activist Ai Weiwei put it: "A small act is worth a million thoughts." It could make a difference to one or more other people in your network and not simply dissipate in your memory.

During the 2021 Tokyo Olympics, an Olympic sprinter from Belarus criticized her coaches on her social media for entering her in a track and field event she had never run competitively before the Olympics. Given the reactions of Belarusian authorities in Tokyo and the state media in Belarus, she feared being forced to fly home from Tokyo and sought sanctuary from city authorities, leading to an international incident that put her treatment in the public eye across the world (Ahmed et al. 2021: 1, 4). This young sprinter did not build her social network to expose the response of authorities, but she was able to immediately enlist the support of her network to let people know she was at risk and to help her find refuge.

NETWORKING GOES INTO BUT ALSO BEYOND SOCIAL AND POLITICAL MOVEMENTS

Networking and social media can often be conflated with political and social movements, and indeed they are becoming ever more critical tools for social and political movements, but such movements are organized and led. Therefore, like other organizations and institutions, they are subject to accountability by their members acting as a Fifth Estate. For example, individuals in a social movement, such as the Extinction Rebellion (XR) or Occupy Wallstreet, can use the internet, or social media in particular, to voice their support or dissent with the leadership of a movement. In this way, movements are like other institutions in many respects. There are examples of leaderless protests organized more on social media than by an organizing committee, and these come closer to the role of a Fifth Estate. Much has been written about the dynamics of social movements, and they are rising in significance due to the value of the internet and digital media to their outreach and impact. For example, Manuel Castells (2012) has provided incisive analyses of major movements such as Occupy Wall Street. They are important, but they are different from the less orchestrated collectivity of individuals that are the basis of the Fifth Estate. Examples in this chapter aim to clarify some of these differences.

Social Media and the Fifth Estate

During and in the latter stages of the COVID-19 pandemic, social media were roundly demonized as sources of disinformation and condemned for a litany of purported harms, largely captured by criticism targeted on Facebook, in the case of the UK. At the same time, during the pandemic, it was clear that networks of politicians in Britain were running the country in part by virtue of private messaging services, like WhatsApp, and the same applications were being used to support neighborhoods, sharing information on vaccine and lockdown guidelines and access to fresh food and vegetables from neighborhood gardens. As one political journalist argued, in Britain, WhatsApp has become "the political communication system of choice. Power flows through the thousands of one-to-one exchanges and informal groups that have replaced emails and formal meetings for decision-making" (Payne 2021: 22). Far beyond Britain, in the latter part of the war in Afghanistan, the Taliban used WhatsApp for a complaint hotline in cities they overtook. This was shut down by the owner of WhatsApp and Facebook after the Taliban took control of Kabul in August 2021.[1] At the same time that pundits and politicians are attacking social media, it is becoming a more central lifeline to communities and political elites across the world.

From the perspective of the Fifth Estate, social media are a gift. Social networks are not designed to empower individuals. Most are built to enable friends, family, neighbors, associates, and others to keep in touch and share photos and news. However, they provide an infrastructure that can be turned to other purposes, such as civic-minded efforts to hold individuals or institutions more accountable. This section provides a number of diverse illustrations of how social media can be turned from social and entertainment purposes to empower a collectivity of internet users.

THE #METOO SOCIAL RECKONING

Since its inception, the internet has long been credited with enabling individuals to find like-minded people anywhere in the world. On social media, the ability to assemble individuals with a common interest has been greatly facilitated by hashtags—a simple way for users to tag content so that it can be easily found and shared with others, one form of which has been called "#hashtag activism" (Jackson et al. 2020).

The MeToo hashtag is often viewed as synonymous with a social movement, but it is more than that, as it—and related hashtags it has spawned across the world—assembles a global collectivity of individuals and organizations in support of those who have experienced rape, sexual abuse, or harassment. The "Me Too" phrase was coined by Tanya Burke in 2006 in a post on MySpace (Table 5.2). A survivor of sexual abuse, she felt unable to adequately support a young child who told her of the abuse she experienced by the partner of the child's mother. Tanya introduced the child to a colleague who might have the training to help her, but on reflection, she thought she could have at least said "me too" so the child would not feel alone.[2] Tanya Burke then used this phrase on social media and to support her own MeToo movement.

In 2017, over a decade after the phrase was introduced, it went viral online. It was in the wake of accusations in the *New York Times* against Harvey Weinstein,[3] a famous American film producer who was later convicted of sex offenses tied to these accusations. In light of the accusations, an American actress, Alyssa Milano, used this hashtag on Twitter to encourage others to come forward with their own experiences. In this way, the allegations against Weinstein became a major catalyst for an outpouring of accusations from other survivors of sexual offenses, including many other celebrities. Suddenly, decades of silence about sex crimes were broken by a surge of allegations on

Table 5.2 **Illustrations of Social Media and the Fifth Estate**

Fifth Estate	*Purpose*	*Implications*
#MeToo	Empower women to share their accounts of sexual offenses and harassment	Contributing to a shift in the culture of relationships in the US and other nations
#BlackLivesMatter #BLM	Raise awareness of the deaths of black Americans while in police custody	Changes in training, recruitment, supervision, and accountability of police
#SaveSweetBriar	Lead students, alumnae, parents, and donors of Sweet Briar College to sustain the college	The college was saved from closure with innovations in its curriculum and tuition
LeeAnne Walters, "water warriors," and Amariyanna Copeny in Michigan's Flint water crisis	Posting photos on social media to expose pollution of drinking water in Flint and illnesses tied to it, demonstrating, and sending an email to US President Obama	Led to a network of citizen journalists, doctors, and scientists gathering credible evidence on lead-contaminated drinking water and actions to address the problem
Networked neighborhoods	Sharing information and support during the COVID-19 pandemic	Despite isolation, neighbors could support one another via personal messaging systems like WhatsApp
Video and audio meetings, such as via Zoom	Support and sustain interpersonal, family, and friendship networks	Major rise in the use of Zoom and other video-meeting applications to connect distributed groups

Twitter and other social media as well as in major press coverage that publicized a growing list of offenders (Farrow 2017).

The purpose and message of #MeToo was so simple and clear that individuals could readily act by coming forward with their own story and with the support of many other victims. Social media was not used to orchestrate a social movement so much as it was being used as a vehicle for individuals to act collectively. Rather than silently grieving alone without support, individuals could open up in the company of others with similar experiences.

The evolving impact of this reckoning was larger than anyone might have expected. It was credited with empowering individuals by communicating empathy and solidarity with victims of sex offenses. The conversations and controversies it fostered helped also to foster personal reflections on appropriate behavior and contribute to larger efforts to challenge and change cultural rules and norms defining appropriate sexual relations in the home and the workplace worldwide, such as in protest movements over the repression of women in Iran (Box 5.1). It has been credited not only with exposing many offenders but also with changes in law and policy that could be of long-term significance to reducing rape, sexual offenses, and harassment, as well as become a focus for social research on the political and cultural dimensions of sexual violence and behavior (Fileborn and Loney-Howes 2019).

#BLACKLIVESMATTER

The Black Lives Matter hashtag—#BLM—connected people and events that had dramatic consequences for public debate and discussions of racial justice. As in the case of #MeToo, #BLM is more than a social movement or an organization, although it embodies and supports various movements and organizations. It creates a collectivity of individuals who are anything from sympathetic to actively working to support racial justice in policing.

A Pew study found that in the days from May 26, 2020, the day after George Floyd died in police custody, to June 7, the #BlackLivesMatter hashtag was used 47.8 million times, almost 3.7 million times per day (Anderson et al. 2020). George Floyd was certainly not the first black American to die in police custody in circumstances that led to

---

Box 5.1 **The Cut: Social Media Protests Sparked by Repression in Iran**

Across the world, women posted videos or broadcast themselves cutting a lock of their hair to communicate their empathy with women in Iran following the death while in police custody of a 22-year-old woman, from the Kurdish region of Iran, Mahsa Amini (Kohli 2022). Mahsa was arrested on September 13, 2022, for violating Islamic dress codes—by not properly covering her hair. Hijabs are mandatory for all women to wear in public in Iran. The police took her to a detention center to receive training in appropriate dress; witnesses saw her being struck in the patrol car en route to the detention center. She died three days later, on September 16. Authorities claimed she had suffered heart failure while in custody. In response, prominent women, actors, and girls in Iran and across the world cut their hair in protest over Amini's treatment. A Swedish member of the European Parliament, Abir Al-Sahlani, cut her hair while delivering a speech in Strasbourg, France, on October 4 (Fine 2022). As effective as any hashtag, social media videos of women cutting their hair conveyed support for Amini and other teenage "martyrs" like 16-year-old Nika Shakarami, who died as well after being arrested for protesting the Islamic Republic (Bozorgmehr 2022). She was thrown off the top of a building. Protests following the death of Amini and other protesters contributed to one of Iran's major periods of unrest in recent years and have been replicated across the world, as illustrated in Strasbourg.

---

https://www.reuters.com/world/swedish-mep-cuts-hair-during-speech-solidarity-with-iranian-women-2022-10-05/

major challenges and protests. However, the documentation of his treatment in broad daylight (see Chapter 4) and the way this hashtag resonated with this and earlier incidents, while capturing a positive message that black lives should matter, generated levels of response on social media and on the streets that were unprecedented for such an incident. Prior to Floyd's death, the use of this hashtag never approached this level of use.

That said, the phrase "black lives matter" was first used much earlier, in 2013. It appeared in a Facebook post by Alicia Garza, following the acquittal of George Zimmerman. Zimmerman was a Florida resident accused, but later acquitted, of the fatal shooting of Trayvon Martin in 2012 (Anderson et al. 2020). Martin was walking through Sanford, Florida, wearing a hoodie and holding a soft drink, when seen by Zimmerman who was on neighborhood watch (Lebron 2017: xi–xii). Zimmerman called 911, was told not to approach the man who raised his suspicions, but he did, leading to a struggle that ended with the unarmed 17-year-old Trayvon being shot and killed. However, the verdict, based on a claim of self-defense, led to protests, and has remained a focus of controversy for years.

A friend of Garza, who was a Los Angeles community organizer, Patrice Khan-Cullors, replied to Garza's post with the first use of the hashtag of #BlackLivesMatter.[4] Other accounts argue that the hashtag was used to "cofound" an online international activist movement.[5] Allissa Richardson (2020: 43) saw the Zimmerman case as creating a "tipping point" that led to greater public and journalistic stories witnessing "violence against black bodies." However, at its inception, this hashtag was not international or a single movement (Lebron 2017). It may have come to signify a cause and connect individuals as well as one or more movements, but the initial use was independent of any organized social movement. And over time it spanned nearly all social media, many initiatives, many nations, and many languages.

Even before the surge in use of this hashtag in 2020, #BlackLivesMatter became the third most used "social-issue hashtag" in the first ten years of Twitter's history (Anderson 2016). It has been shortened often to #BLM and has become a meme, spawning related hashtags such as #AllLivesMatter and #BlackLivesVote, all of which attest to its significance as a boundary-spanning object that connects otherwise more loosely connected incidents, locations, and protests.[6] Its development has been the focus of a book: *The Making of Black Lives Matter* (Lebron 2017).

It is used by individuals, organizations, social movements, issues, and protests, but it is not synonymous with any one in particular, although it has been used to brand an official online website.[7] It spans them, and in doing so it serves to network individuals and events that might otherwise not be as connected and enables sharing similar and connected experiences. Some discussions of the hashtag are focused on illuminating that it is used in many ways for many purposes by many actors (Anderson 2016). Its longevity and prominence as a device for connecting individuals, events, and movements might stem from its meaning being so benign yet representing divisive and controversial issues, from opposing racism to defunding the police. Its most general impact seems to have been facilitating efforts to move the discussion of racial inequalities in policing and other sectors from traditional foci on racist individuals and mistreatment by prejudiced individuals to addressing more systematic and structural conditions that maintain and enhance unequal treatment of black and other minority groups over time.

SAVING SWEET BRIAR COLLEGE

Many universities and colleges use social media for outreach to complement newsletters and mail to their students, alumni and alumnae, and donors.[8] These institutions are not the Fifth Estate. However, individuals occasionally use the internet and social media to go outside the boundaries of the institution to protest or challenge institutional decisions, which was the case with students, alumnae, donors, and faculty of Sweet Briar College.

Founded in 1901, Sweet Briar is a small (500-plus students) private liberal arts college for women. Located in Sweet Briar, Virginia, the college occupies 2,800 acres of land in the beautiful green foothills of the Blue Ridge Mountains, which includes a 130-acre riding center, twenty acres of vineyard and farmland, in addition to the college campus and accommodations. It was founded by Indiana Fletcher Williams, who stipulated in her will that her home, Sweet Briar Plantation, was to be used to found a college in memory of her daughter, Maria Georgiana "Daisy" Williams, who had died in her teenage years. Given the small, female, and rural setting of Sweet Briar, its students spoke of studying in a "pink bubble."

Despite a sizeable endowment of US$84 million, the college was facing issues over declining enrollment in a context of demographic shifts and related problems besetting many private women's colleges across the United States. The board hired James F. Jones as an interim president in August of 2014. President Jones had stepped down in June 2014 from his previous role as president of Trinity College in Connecticut over controversies created by his plan to make its fraternities and sororities co-educational. His daughter was a student at Sweet Briar College, and he took on somewhat of a father figure role, such as by informally lunching with students.

However, on March 3 of his first year, without warning, the new president alerted faculty and staff at a hastily called noon meeting that the college would be closing in August. Faculty and staff would be laid off and students helped in transferring to other institutions (Leonard 2018: 2). Later that afternoon he let the top donors to the college know that the *New York Times* would be publishing an article announcing Sweet Briar's imminent closure—by August 2015. It was a surprise. He emailed alumnae and posted this news on the college's Facebook page on March 3, news that was shared widely across the community.

President Jones argued that the board had concluded that the college was not financially sustainable at a time when private liberal arts women's colleges were folding or struggling to recruit students, particularly given Sweet Briar's rural location when students were flocking to urban campuses. One professor wondered if the board had brought Jones in as "an axman" (Doner 2015).

The students, faculty, donors, and other stakeholders were shocked and angered, but they were activated by this news and did not accept the administration's decision to close the institution. On March 3—the very day of the announcement—a Facebook page was set up by a small group of alumnae and, within twenty-four hours, they set up an alumnae nonprofit group, Saving Sweet Briar, Inc. They also organized themselves into a set of working groups on legal, communication, and financial issues (Leonard 2018: 1). The nonprofit was formally incorporated by March 9.[9] Students "plastered their cars with a rallying cry—#SaveSweetBriar—in the school colors, pink and green"

(Dove 2015). Many alumnae who received a formal emailed letter from the president about the closure returned his letter in the post, overwriting his words with messages such as, "NOT IF I CAN HELP IT #SAVESWEETBRIAR" (Leonard 2018: 112).

The Facebook page, titled "Save Sweet Briar," provided a timeline of events, background on the effort to save the college, photos, and space for readers to post their views. Viewers could also invite others to "like" this page, further enabling it to reach a network of networks. It gained about 10,000 likes early in the campaign, supported fundraising, and helped those concerned with the college's future to bypass the administration of the college president and directly appeal to current and former students, faculty, and other friends of Sweet Briar College. Also, alumnae used their email lists to contact fellow alumnae about the closure and the Facebook page.

Nevertheless, the college president considered the campaign to be irrational, arguing that it would not go anywhere (Doner 2015). However, within seventy-two hours, the group had raised pledges exceeding $2 million, by April 12, $5 million, and within three-and-a-half months, $21 million.

The internet and social media not only enabled rapid fundraising but also provided a means for sharing news articles from around the country and creating decentralized networks of the college network. An alumna interviewed by Leonard (2018: 128) "recalled turning on the television and seeing 'Save Sweet Briar' posters and signs held up by audience members attending Good Morning America and the Today Show" in New York City.

Given the strong sense of community that existed within the college, a small alumnae team was able go around the administration to rapidly and strategically use their networks, social media, and email lists to directly reach multiple stakeholders to counter the administration's assumptions about the institution's sustainability and raise additional funding, rapidly organizing the Saving Sweet Briar Fundraising Campaign.

Providing evidence to counter the administration's assumptions, including raising additional funding, was key to a series of two lawsuits challenging the right of the college officials to unilaterally close the institution.[10] Legal resolution of these lawsuits resulted in an interim agreement in the form of a Memorandum of Understanding to keep the college open and support this by committing millions of dollars in donations and freeing some of the existing endowment to sustain its operations.[11] It also entailed electing a new president and board, with President Jones resigning on June 30, within seven days of the agreement gaining court approval of the settlement.

On July 2, a new interim president, Phillip C. Stone, stepped in on very short notice to keep the college open and stabilize its operations over the next two years while a new president was recruited (Poleski 2020). During this interim period, alumnae went beyond donating funds to help with a number of volunteer projects, such as "Sweet Work Days," a project to refurbish and clean the historic buildings. While the interim administration was able to keep the college in operation, the *New York Times* article announcing its imminent closure lingered online, adding to the prevailing negative mindset and evidence of other struggling liberal arts institutions closing, making the recruitment of new students more difficult (Shaker 2020).

Nevertheless, in 2017, the board was able to appoint a new president, Meredith Woo, a former director of International Higher Education Support Program at the London-based Open Society Foundation, supported by George Soros. In addition to this change in leadership, President Woo worked with faculty and alumnae on the controversial issues tied to transforming the curriculum, such as cutting the number of majors, and reducing finances, while dramatically lowering tuition fees to compete with the state's public universities—discovered to be their real competitors rather than other women's colleges—their previously imagined competitors (Joutz 2018). The new president sought to make the college more distinctive by focusing general education on teaching leadership and building on a sustainability theme by connecting the curriculum to experiential learning in their rural location, for instance, setting up a smart farm and using it and the college vineyard as sites for learning.[12] And in 2020, Sweet Briar sold 410 of its former 3,200 acres, its Mt. San Agnelo property, to the Virginia Center for the Creative Arts, which the center had leased for over forty years.[13]

By 2021, the college was back on track, recounting the "miracle" of saving the college, recovering from the pandemic closures, recruiting more students, and welcoming students to Sweet Briar College; the heading on their website stated: "Women Making History." Many individuals and events helped achieve this recovery, but social media were critical in enabling the proponents to move rapidly around and outside and subvert the president and his board's administrative control of outreach to directly tap into the support of donors, alumnae, students, and present and former faculty and staff. As one senior student told the *New York Times* in 2015: "We're at a liberal arts college that empowers women. Now we're finding ways to use that education to empower ourselves" (Dove 2015).

WATER WARRIORS TO LITTLE MISS FLINT: EXPOSING THE POISONING OF A CITY'S WATER

In 2011, economically distressed Flint, Michigan, was in a major financial crisis, driven not only by the 2008 global financial crisis but also by major losses of jobs in the auto industry, which had been central to the city with its links to Detroit, including the use of water from the Detroit Water and Sewage Department (DWSD). The flight of many well-to-do residents to the suburbs meant that the central city of Flint was increasingly poor and black, with many abandoned homes. Michigan's governor appointed a series of emergency managers to address the city's finances. One cost-saving measure was to obtain the city's water from a different source than DWSD, with an interim measure being the use of water from the Flint River that could be treated at a former water plant. This was seen as a win-win by saving hundreds of millions of dollars while allowing Flint to be more self-sufficient in the treatment and provision of water to its residents.

The switch was made on April 25, 2014. Soon after, problems with the water and its treatment became apparent to many Flint residents—primarily in the poorest neighborhoods—who shared stories on Facebook of polluted water in their households. The problems "more or less followed the patterns of inequality that dated back to Flint's development as a segregated city" (Clark 2018: 71). Local groups, such as the "water warriors," networked to inform neighbors and "pressured those in power to acknowledge the problems and continued to hold them accountable."[14]

However, for too long, as one participant noted, "the people of Flint were loud and organized and pressing all the buttons, but they were silenced, dismissed, and denied."[15] Given the lack of democratic structures under its emergency management, the actions of residents seemed ineffective. Residents posted photos of the orange-brown tinge in the water they bottled. They reported problems their children were experiencing, with evidence of problems such as hair loss and rashes. But their claims were not taken seriously until a whistleblower—a regulation manager in the Environmental Protection Agency (EPA), Miguel Del Toral—began investigating and raising alarms within the EPA over the Flint water supply. News of his work in the EPA leaked out to a few Michigan residents, including LeeAnn Walters, a mother of four, who contacted him.[16] This contact led Walters to discover that corrosion controls were not being employed during water treatment to counter old lead water pipes, and she helped lead other citizens to pressure authorities.

Also, Del Toral was able to connect LeeAnn Walters with a Virginia Tech professor of civil and environmental engineering, Mark Edwards, who had won an award for research on urban water safety. LeeAnne Walters helped Mark Edwards sample and distribute testing kits to households and conduct a defensible citizen science test of the water arriving in Flint households. The results were posted on the FlintWaterStudy.org website.[17] However, these findings were also dismissed by public officials. In this case, some officials did not trust Edwards, who they assumed was simply finding the same results as he had in other studies.

However, an American Civil Liberties Union (ACLU) investigative reporter—and citizen journalist, Curt Guyutte—teamed up with Mark Edwards to take on this issue.[18] His work, along with mounting concerns, prompted local journalists to cover this story, such as Ron Fonger with the *Flint Journal* and the Detroit journalist Anna Clark, who later authored a detailed and authoritative book about the crisis (Clark 2018).

Nevertheless, the coverage of developing findings continued to be viewed skeptically by public officials, with state authorities insisting the water was safe, and this view was reinforced by residents in more well-to-do areas of Flint who were not experiencing the same problems as households in less affluent areas—in hindsight, because less affluent areas had more abandoned homes and older infrastructures.

However, in 2015, a doctor at Michigan State University's Children's Hospital, Dr. Mona Hanna-Attisha (2016), affectionately called "Dr. Mona," saw the potential for analyzing existing medical records over time to determine whether children in Flint were registering higher levels of lead in their blood after the shift from Detroit water supplies to the Flint River. Dr. Mona's study painstakingly pulled together disaggregated records to perform an analysis, which found that children's blood lead levels had doubled over the time period of the switch in water supply (Hanna-Attisha et al. 2016). This evidence could not be dismissed by the authorities.

With the exposure of these problems, an 8-year-old-girl, Amariyanna Copeny, with help from her mother, emailed then President Barack Obama in 2016. On the day after reading the letter, President Obama decided to visit Flint on May 4, 2016, to speak with residents and federal officials.[19] By January, he called a federal state of emergency in Flint.[20] Amariyanna came to be known as Little Miss Flint.

There are book-length and far more detailed accounts of the Flint water crisis, the associated medical research, and the complex ecology of actors who needed to be informed and mobilized to make a difference (Clark 2018, Hanna-Attisha 2016, 2018). It was clear that no single blog or Facebook post would have mattered had there not been a persistent and talented array of networked individuals, local citizens, parents, citizen journalists, and scientists collaborating to uncover this tragedy and bring compelling evidence to the attention of politicians and other public officials who thought they knew otherwise. Ultimately, the failure of the city to properly treat the water was judged to have been the major problem.[21] Walters was later recognized with a Goldman Environmental Prize in 2018 for grassroots activists, and the citizen journalist Curt Guyutte was also recognized for his role.[22]

In these unfolding events, networked individuals like the water warriors did play a role, such as by organizing demonstrations, raising awareness of the issue, and creating the context in which journalists and scientists could be enrolled to investigate the claims of residents. However, a larger ecology of actors was critical to lead local, state, and federal authorities to take action to reduce the lead contamination across Flint's water supply. Arguably, there has been progress, although the legal and financial implications of this crisis has been ongoing into 2023.

NEIGHBORHOOD NETWORKS: ENABLING HOUSEHOLDS IN A PANDEMIC

In the early years of the internet, much of the fascination focused on the potential for reaching a global audience. That was what an open, free, and global network was all about, such as in the vision of a World Wide Web. However, this almost boundless potential is one reason why many individuals have been reluctant to use the internet for many purposes, such as local or family matters. In Britain, for example, there has been a long tradition of neighborhood and community associations. However, neighborhood groups have communicated most often in person and by leaflets and physical bulletin or noticeboards—not electronic but real bulletin boards erected along the sidewalks or pathways and roads of the neighborhood. In that tradition, neighbors could talk about a local garden party or event with, and only with, their neighbors.

The internet posed real problems for such locally bounded activities. The last thing households wanted was to be visible to the whole world. Many did not even want to be seen by people in other neighborhoods in the city or region. There has been a strong sense of privacy and security of communication that helps define the significance of local neighborhood communities. So, while much of the world was moving online, neighborhood groups were less enthusiastic about this potential and often stayed offline, lest their business be broadcast to the next neighborhood, much less the entire city or the world.

For such local networks, the rise of private social networks (Table 5.1) has been a major bridge to the digital age. Most discussions of networks like Facebook are focused on how powerful they can be for reaching a broad audience, but some groups set up on Facebook and more circumscribed private group networking have been central to such applications as WhatsApp and a neighborhood-focused application called NextDoor. Many local neighborhood applications have been developed for this purpose. Families can have multiple groups—locally or globally but restricted to a specific set of people—to facilitate sharing baby photos among close family members, or even smaller groups to keep in touch with a book group or a distant relative. Sending messages, phoning, video conferencing, and all the tools of networking are part of the toolbox of these more circumscribed private messaging and networking systems.

The user-defined boundaries of a private messaging or networking group are one of the key advantages of such online systems. During the COVID-19 pandemic, a neighborhood in Oxford, England, put together a WhatsApp group to support one another on a road of about one hundred households. Two members of a neighborhood association came up with the idea and, with another member, they set up a group on WhatsApp. The purpose of the group was "to enable residents [on and neighboring the road] to offer and request support when people are unable to get out." They used a traditional paper leaflet distributed to all the households to invite individuals to join.

Forty-five people signed up for the group after it was set up in the first lockdown of the pandemic in March 2020, when many were no longer able to safely meet face to face. Participating in the WhatsApp group enabled them to ask questions about government health advisories, find someone to pick up something for them when they went out, locate a home fix-it person to do minor repairs, look for a missing person, or provide some other service. As one commentator noted, in local areas, a neighbor can be better than an algorithm, such as on Google (Benedictus 2019). Occasionally the WhatsApp group was used to alert others to potential problems, such as teenagers loitering by the bus stop, or share pleasant news or sights, such as a fox sunning in a back garden.

One engineer with experience and skills online looked after the group, such as helping when someone wanted to be added to the list. The organizers did not control the agenda, as it was set up and used to enable internet users in the group to ask and answer questions—it was completely user defined within the provisions set for the purpose of the group. For example, it was not used for selling or advertising; it focused on supporting one another. It also supported a neighborhood watch function at times. While a modest innovation for the neighborhood, it gave added informational and communicative power to those who could support others and who needed support during the pandemic.

VIDEO AND AUDIO GROUP MEETINGS—THE ZOOM PHENOMENON

Video conferencing was demonstrated at the World Fair in New York in 1968. It was then launched in the early 1970s in the United States as what was initially called Picturephone Meeting Service (PMS), as it was anchored in the use of the Picturephone (Dickson 1973). This service did not succeed. It was expensive, and people had to congregate at a meeting site to communicate with others at another PMS site. Since then, video communication was repeatedly launched until finally it became a viable niche business service, such as with a few private services, like Skype and WebEx, which were available online. Further advances in software and speed issues limited video conferencing until broadband access and advances in compression and video transmission enabled video networking and video-calling apps on the internet and web and associated mobile and social media.

However, it was not until the COVID-19 pandemic and its related lockdowns that video communication skyrocketed with the use of Zoom, Teams, and advances of older services that could be used on a mobile smartphone or laptop. These systems were used in businesses, institutions, and education to enable group communication, such as holding business meetings and teaching courses online in real time.

But the pandemic led them to be adopted by households and networked individuals as well, given that they were essentially free to use in limited ways. There were teething problems, such as with Zoombombing, such as when a malicious user shared a vulgar image on screen. These problems were easily fixed through software updates and training. Rapidly, systems like Zoom became tools for networked individuals to have distributed group meetings, whether holding community group meetings or keeping in better touch with family and friends. They have been augmented by devices like video-conferencing platforms that facilitate hybrid—online and in-person meetings or events—more seamlessly.[23] The uses of these capabilities are too wide ranging to fully describe, but they clearly became another tool to empower networked individuals relative to other individuals and institutions.

Themes Across the Cases

Each of the above illustrations shows the ways networked individuals were at times able to gain relatively more informational or communicative power through the strategic use of social media. They also show the time and effort required to make a difference. There is no push-button Fifth Estate. The water warriors were unable to gain the attention of public officials but did prepare the way for citizen journalists and scientists to gather information that eventually made their case. Examples across the world parallel the Flint difficulties, such as the inability of residents in high-rise housing in sections of London to effectively convince authorities to address concerns over fire hazards (Yeginsu and Magra 2017).

In researching the social and political dynamics of each of these initiatives, the complex ecologies of actors and the confluence of multiple events become critical to explaining their success. Social media can support efforts to share information and network actors, but it is not some powerful silver bullet to fix a problem. The examples also demonstrate the many different geographies of activity that can be shaped by the Fifth Estate. From a neighborhood to a global audience, the internet and social media can play a role in networking and empowering civic-minded individuals.

Harms Associated with Social Media: Risks to the Fifth Estate

These examples illustrate positive roles that social media can play in creating infrastructures built to support communication among friends and families that can be used also for empowering networked individuals of the Fifth Estate. However, social media have been a growing target of criticism and policy initiatives aimed at preventing the risks tied to enabling access to user-generated content—the stuff of social media. It is important to note some of these challenges here, even if briefly, lest this chapter appear to present only the promise of social media for the Fifth Estate. Key issues tied to social media, in particular, include the potential to isolate individuals, undermine privacy and surveillance, foster disinformation, defame individuals online and hurt their reputation, and empower the mob. Any one of these risks could undermine the value of social media, but by understanding the claims and evidence in relation to each risk, it is possible to not become overwhelmed by the threats and better appreciate the promises of the Fifth Estate.

Isolation? Perhaps the most conventional worry is that social media—despite the label—will isolate individuals. They will spend time talking to screens rather than real people. There are individuals who clearly cut themselves off from others—walking through life with their headphones on and staring at their mobile phones. However, research on internet users has generally found that those who use the internet are more social than nonusers (Rice et al 2007). It is true that many develop social networks that are not identical to their friends at school or work, or their neighborhood, as internet users do meet people online with whom they share similar interests, for example. In the digital age, networks are a more hybrid set of online and offline relationships— what has been called "network individualism" (Wellman 2001, Hampton and Wellman 2021). But most often, online networks follow and reinforce real-world, face-to-face networks. For example, when children come home from school and go online, they are most likely connecting with those with whom they were just speaking at school. Social media generally reinforce and strengthen social networks rather than isolate individuals (Rice et al. 2007).

Privacy and surveillance? Neighborhood apps have been decried as a threat to privacy and peace of mind, such as when neighbors raise trivial issues or express concerns over pets or noise or BBQs (Benedictus 2019). But more generally, the use of social media to hold individuals or groups more accountable inevitably bumps up against restrictions on the privacy of individuals as it represents a form of social surveillance. In most cases, networked individuals are holding institutions more accountable, not individuals. For example videotaping a police officer taking a person into custody—the individuals are in focus but acting in a public place and performing a public service. How the public judges the balance between enhancing transparency and accountability versus privacy and surveillance can be an issue on a case-by-case basis in evaluating the role of the Fifth Estate in a specific locality with its own social norms. That said, there are social media uses focused that push these boundaries.

Defamation? Two examples of individuals being a problematic focus of the Fifth Estate have become so famous that they can be described without further exposing an individual. One involved surveillance video of a woman in Coventry, England, walking by a kitten in the evening before returning, petting the kitten, and then dropping the cat, Lola, in a garbage can (called a wheelie bin in the UK). The kitten survived, the RSPCA investigated the incident, and the lady apologized for her action, but the video went viral on social media and damaged her reputation in her community.[24] Another involved an American dentist from Minnesota, who shot Cecil, a famous, 13-year-old lion in Zimbabwe, after paying over US$50,000 to a professional hunter to help him get a trophy kill. But to do so, Cecil was lured out of the protected area of the Hwange National Park by fresh bait before being wounded when shot with a bow and arrow and suffering hours before his death. The dentist's photograph, posing with the lion, went viral, sparking global "outrage," and damaging the dentist's reputation in the eyes of many.[25] Others saw this differently. Some viewed the reaction on the internet as unacceptable—shaming, vigilantism, or mob justice (Capecchi and Rogers

2015). Others as meaningless clicktivism over one lion when so much wildlife is being destroyed without any action or outrage. Zimbabwe and the UN saw it as evidence of illegal hunting and poaching (Bilefsky 2015, Rogers 2015). Of course, posts relating to #MeToo and #BLM have been damaging to many of the accused. In many of these cases, the same events—even if first exposed online—have been covered by print and mass media and books. That said, the correct balance among transparency, accountability, and potential risks to an individual's or institution's reputation is a conundrum for networked individuals and the media, which often requires resolution on a case-by-case basis.

Disinformation? One of the most enduring concerns about the role of social media is around disinformation—fake news, misinformation, and an unprofessional approach to getting the facts (as noted in Chapter 2). The main weakness of this claim is that it is largely anchored in a technologically deterministic view of social media and its algorithms. The design of the technology is expected to create filter bubbles and trap social media users in echo chambers. My colleagues and I did a seven-nation cross-national survey of internet users that looked systematically at how people got information about politics (Dutton et al. 2019, Dutton and Fernandez 2018/19). We found that for those interested in politics, internet users would go to four or more sources, one of which would be online. And those who went online went to four or more sources, one of which might be social media (Dutton et al. 2019). So, the likelihood of being caught in filter bubbles or echo chambers is low for the large majority of users who consult multiple sources. Moreover, even if social media users produce content that is less professionally sourced at times than professional journalistic coverage, it is a complement and not a substitute for the mass media. Moreover, social media are a source on which the press itself increasingly relies. Users of the internet and social media are able to use search to check and find information they need, as discussed in Chapter 3, and they are best placed to determine what is valuable. Relying on social media platforms or governmental agencies to censor news and information and determine what is true and false is a huge risk to the diversity and overall quality of information online and to public trust in it.

Mobs? Finally, the Fifth Estate is not a mob—a point developed in Chapter 2. There are internet users who deserve to be labeled a mob for how they use the internet, but civic-minded internet users can act as a Fifth Estate to expose and critique those intent on causing trouble or promoting violence. As a Fifth Estate, internet and social media users can hold other users accountable if and when they act like a mob.

But do social media foster mob behavior? There were reports of mobs being driven in part by social media during disturbances in Tottenham, London, on August 6, 2011. Disturbances spread across London and other cities of England over the next four days leading some politicians to call for a social media blackout.[26] An innovative big data study of Twitter use during and in the immediate aftermath of these disturbances found that social media was used by some users to encourage participation, but it was also actively being used to challenge false rumors circulating among the crowds and in real time (Procter et al. 2013). In any street demonstration or riot, rumors are likely to spread, but social media have provided a means to challenge and correct false rumors more rapidly and in more detail than would be possible in the press and mass media without reporters on the ground. Moreover, this same study found Twitter was instrumental in organizing cleanups after the disturbances (Procter et al. 2013). A blackout would have prevented many false rumors from being challenged and undermined cleanup activities.

Win-Win Strategies for Social Media and the Fifth Estate

This chapter has highlighted the role that social media can play in creating a network for sharing information in ways that support the role of the Fifth Estate. Sharing through networking is one of an array of strategies at the fingertips of internet users. However, there are risks, such as those tied to disinformation and privacy and defamation, that internet users need to be aware of and address. The best approach is by developing digital skills, multimedia literacy, and social media competencies that enable users to understand and respect a set of social and ethical norms to guide and constrain their behavior in pro-social and pro-Fifth Estate ways. A far worse approach is governmental- or platform-driven blocking, censoring, or moderating social media, which denies the value of self-regulation and does not appreciate the degree to which users have multiple media and information sources and the means to check their own facts and assumptions, which will be discussed in later chapters.

6

Collaborating

Identified variously as distributed collaboration, collective intelligence, mass collaboration, crowdsourcing, open-source intelligence, or most famously as the "wisdom
of crowds" (Surowiecki 2004), distributed collaboration has been attractive to many
managers and professionals across all sectors of the economy and society.[1] A growing
number of visionaries have seen initiatives in this spirit as heralding a revolution in
how organizations can tap into the wisdom of crowds—the basic idea that the many
are smarter than the few (Surowiecki 2004, Tapscott and Williams 2006, Malone
et al. 2009). This vision captures the potential of using the internet, social media,
and mobile to exploit expertise distributed beyond those within any single organization. However, many are skeptical of its value, as distributed intelligence does not follow the incentive structures, confidentiality, and boundaries common to most formal
organizations.

Despite such controversy, collaborative networks developed around this vision have
been used to empower networked individuals vis-à-vis other individuals and institutions, such as holding them more accountable. This chapter explains aspects of such
applications of distributed expertise and describes a number of illustrations tied to the
Fifth Estate.

Capturing the Potential of Distributed Expertise

As discussed in previous chapters, the internet and web have expanded the potential
for distributed collaboration, such as by enabling networked individuals to share documents, contribute comments, and co-create information. If well managed, these functions can bring distributed expertise, eyes, and ears—often interchangeably referred to
as "distributed intelligence"—to the support of the Fifth Estate. To accomplish this, networks of individuals must be cultivated and managed—not as crowds or vigilantes but
as "collaborative network organizations" (Box 6.1).[2] Champions of such initiatives can
use a variety of networking platforms and management strategies to develop collaborative network organizations (CNOs) that can capture the value of expertise distributed
among networked individuals for sourcing expertise as well as tapping the "civic intelligence" of the general public (Schuler 2001), which might move beyond expertise to
such concrete contributions as being present as an eyewitness.

The Fifth Estate. William H. Dutton, Oxford University Press. © Oxford University Press 2023.
DOI: 10.1093/oso/9780190688363.003.0007

Box 6.1 **Collaborative Network Organizations**

The term "collaborative network organization" (CNO) was developed to convey findings from a variety of case studies of new, internet-enabled forms of distributed collaboration, what the study team originally called "distributed problem-solving networks" (David 2007, Dutton 2008, 2010). One central theme was that these networks were not like crowds. In contrast, they were well-managed collaborations. The wisdom of these collaborative networks was in their management. A variety of network levers were used by the managers of these networks, including the architecture of the network's design; its degree of openness; the controls employed, such as contributing and editing rights; and the approaches to the management and modularization of tasks. It is not magic that enables open distributed global collaboration to produce an encyclopedia or a film online, but serious interest in solving a particular problem and developing effective management of the collaboration are.

The centrality that collaboration can play has emerged from over fifty years of initiatives to harness distributed expertise. For example, the development in the 1960s by the RAND Corporation of Delphi techniques of forecasting sought to reduce the bias created by influential individuals in the social dynamics of co-located face-to-face groups of experts.[3] The potential for computer-based communication networks to enable the sharing of expertise accelerated the drive toward distributed collaboration in the 1970s, such as with computer conferencing, group decision-support systems, and later initiatives around computer-supported cooperative work.

One of the early innovations in computer conferencing, as discussed in Chapter 5, was driven by the ambition to create a platform to quickly network experts in the event of national emergencies and policy issues. In 1971, Murray Turoff and colleagues at the US Office of Emergency Preparedness, developed the EMISARI (Emergency Management Information Systems and Reference Index) system (Hiltz and Turoff 1978). At that early time, using teletype terminals, which linked to a central computer over telephone lines, the system used many features of contemporary collaboration technologies, including applications for real-time chat, polling, and threaded discussion.[4] For example, EMISARI was used to inform US President Richard Nixon's wage and price control program to tackle inflation.[5] In this same spirit, computer-based networks like the internet and social media could bring in expertise from anywhere in the world to solve any problems that go beyond what local experts are best able to resolve. Moreover, not only are the technical platforms to support distributed intelligence further advanced, but they are tied also to a critical mass of users—over half of the world or more than 4 billion connected to the web, a scale which could not have been foreseen in the 1970s.

However, for a time, the diffusion of personal computers across organizations shifted the focus away from computer conferencing and networking to the development of "groupware," executive boardrooms, and other applications to reconnect individuals fragmented within and across organizations by personal computer systems (Johansen 1988). Various groupware and computer-supported cooperative work projects in organizations pursued many of the same objectives tied to the networking of distributed expertise to share, jointly contribute to, and create information products and services. However, in academic research, private industry, and civil society, new forms of collaboration have begun to emerge, which offer real promise, not only for organizations but also for networked individuals of the Fifth Estate.

My colleagues and I have studied the advantages of distributed intelligence, what I have called "collaborative network organizations," compared to more traditional information systems in formal organizations (Dutton 2008). These include the potential to

- improve an individual's judgment by pooling the views of multiple people (provided they have no prejudice and a greater than even likelihood of being correct (Condorcet [1785] 1994);
- aggregate geographically distributed information and intelligence, such as experts remotely located;
- enhance diversity by bringing together more heterogeneous viewpoints, perspectives, and approaches (Page 2007);
- speed up questions and answers by permitting simultaneous rather than sequential review;
- counter the negative aspects of small-group processes, such as "groupthink" (Sunstein 2004), although, if poorly managed, networks could also expand the scale and scope of groupthink; and
- support greater independence of, and less control by, established institutions with entrenched interests and ways of thinking—key to a Fifth Estate.

Despite these possibilities, the "wisdom of crowds" has also been the target of much skepticism. Crowds include multiple people who are often prejudiced, particularly in the political settings of government and public policy, and often have a less than even probability of being correct—violating some basic assumptions behind the value of pooling judgments. However, in case studies of well-managed collaborative networks, this problem is addressed if not always resolved given the many cases in which a consensus on the facts and the complexity of the issues are politically fraught (Ford 2022). Crowds do not write Wikipedia entries. Instead, managed sets of networked individuals contribute to co-productions, like Wikipedia (Dutton 2015). In most case studies of crowdsourcing, a small minority of "core participants" are responsible for the majority of the activities within the network.

Case studies of crowdsourcing show that distributed collaboration can be used to solve a wide variety of problems, from rating products to writing an encyclopedia or producing a film.[6] However, it is more useful to focus on activities they support rather than the problems they solve. These activities include (1) sharing information, as networking in general; (2) enabling members not only to share information but also to contribute information, such as applications enabling the aggregation of judgments; and (3) co-creating information, such as jointly writing and editing a document.

Illustrations of Collaborative Fifth Estate Intelligence

This section moves to illustrations of distributed collaboration that involve different mixes of these key collaboration activities (Table 6.1). Each example is briefly described to show how each is potentially supportive of a Fifth Estate, with much material online that can complement these brief descriptions. The examples are very selective but not chosen to represent the most technically innovative. They were chosen primarily to illustrate a diversity of techniques developed to mine distributed intelligence for civic purposes that support collectivities of the Fifth Estate.

CREATING AN ENCYCLOPEDIA: WIKIPEDIA

The best example is one of the most remarkable stories in the development of distributed collaboration online—Wikipedia. It is the most successful online, free encyclopedia as a website written primarily by volunteers around the world. It was launched in 2001 by Jimmy Wales and Larry Sanger as one part of Nupedia, an earlier online encyclopedia, but within weeks set off on its own separate website. The aim was for anyone to be able to suggest additions or changes to entries, following standard guidelines and layouts for pages. For example, Jimmy Wales set some criteria for inclusion in Wikipedia, such as a person who had done more than one thing—no one-trick pony, and entries should be anchored in an unbiased, "neutral point-of-view."[7] However, content creation has been moderated and managed by Wikipedia editors who can review and referee suggested changes, do sub-editing, close entries to further changes in highly contested cases, and ensure that its development meets rigorous standards. It has over a thousand "administrators" to manage the editing and nearly 1 billion registered users. It has been called a "global, virtual, collaborative knowledge community" (Earl 2005: 19).

In its early years, university professors would commonly criticize students for citing Wikipedia in their papers, preferring them to have more authoritative sources. Initially, in 2001, many academics questioned the future of the internet and web and were even more skeptical of a free online encyclopedia designed apparently to be more democratic than meritocratic (Earl 2005). However, within a decade of its launch, university professors began to consult and cite this online encyclopedia themselves as an authoritative source, although issues remained over the accountability of authors and the quality of entries, particularly on controversial or politically charged topics. No entry was judged to be complete, so quality was expected to evolve over time, but different biases could also emerge over time as well; so many anonymous authors can mean that no author is held accountable.

Nevertheless, with the website being open to anyone challenging entries and suggesting amendments, it has demonstrated the potential for open sourcing of content, even being peer reviewed to be just about as authoritative as a more traditional encyclopedia, although errors were found in scientific articles in both sources (Giles 2005). It has been threatened with lawsuits, such as by a person linked to the assassination of John F. Kennedy in a hoax article posted on Wikipedia but subsequently corrected (Seelye 2005).[8] As noted earlier in this chapter, crowdsourcing is ideally suited for

Table 6.1 **Fifth Estate Collaboration of Networked Individuals**

Fifth Estate Actors	Purpose	Implications
Wikipedia	Open "wiki" encyclopedia creation, allowing users to collaborate—add, edit, and use online content—using Media Wiki	Supports global scope of free online content in hundreds of languages, demonstrating potential of distributed collaboration
Teacher Ratings	Early student initiatives for students to provide ratings of college professors and lecturers	Led many colleges and universities to open and systematize their student assessments of teachers
I Paid a Bribe website	Providing the public of India with a place for reporting bribes	Raised the priority placed on addressing corruption by governments of India
Beijing residents and workers monitoring pollution levels	Providing distributed monitoring to analyze air pollution levels in Beijing	Challenged more optimistic press and other public pronouncements
Planet Patrol	Enabling individuals to identify and report litter	More systematic data on the levels and types of litter spoiling the environment
Sermo links licensed physicians in the US to share information and assist each other and sponsoring organizations	Providing a resource for doctors and physicians to ask questions of peers and share insights and opinions among experts in a field	Created a sustainable international ecosystem that is supportive of physicians, particularly in small or remote practices without local experts to consult
Patients Like Me	Enabling patients to link with other patients with similar problems	Attracting 800,000 patients, adding to search and interaction with physicians to get information
Crowdsolving detective in finding the Golden State Killer	Paul Haynes conducted online research from home on crimes tied to a serial killer in California	Worked with crime writer to raise profile of an FBI case, leading to identification and conviction of Golden State Killer

topics free of bias, problems like guessing the number of balls in a jar, not a politically contested topic. Not surprisingly, therefore, there are controversies surrounding the editing of many articles that are politically and personally significant that have at times been judged biased by some readers (Ford 2022). The virtual anonymity of key editors can therefore pose an issue of accountability, but networked individuals are not reluctant to hold Wikipedia accountable online.

By 2011, Wikipedia had over 18 million pages available in nearly 320 languages. The English edition of Wikipedia is the largest, but all Wikipedias total to more than 3.5 billion words, according to the site.[9] It became the largest encyclopedia ever by 2007, when the English edition passed 2 million articles. In 2021, it included 6,365,978— over 6 million—articles, with nearly 600 added every day.[10] It is owned by the nonprofit Wikimedia Foundation, supported largely by grants and donations, with the leadership continually campaigning for contributions to support the free content.

Wikipedia has empowered networked individuals around the world to produce and use a free and authoritative encyclopedia in addition to other complementary content, such as news. It also gives networked individuals the ability to contribute to the content, such as in becoming one of the first ports of call for posting real-time accounts as eyewitnesses to unfolding events occurring around the world. This role of Wikipedia became so prominent and frequently used, such as in realtime eyewitness accounts of events like school shootings, that Wikipedia created a news section. The site's popularity and scale promise a continuing focus on methods and criteria for ensuring quality while also enabling volunteers to write and edit.

COLLEGE STUDENTS RATE THEIR TEACHERS

The evaluation of teachers has been an enduring issue. From the 1960s into the 1980s, there was strong support for student ratings of college and university teaching, mainly driven by students, along with other forms, such as ratings by other faculty and administrators, based on visits and review of teaching materials. All were physical paper and pencil questionnaires unless more informal. Faculty has been notoriously skeptical of the validity of student ratings, suspecting that they would be based on criteria irrelevant to the quality of the material being taught. Generally, faculty blocked the development of student rating systems unless they were systematically designed and controlled by the faculty and kept confidential.

However, when I was a professor at the University of Southern California, I can remember when a colleague approached me about how upset he was over finding that his teaching was rated online by some students and not all that favorably. He found himself criticized in ways he was unhappy about and wondered how this could happen and be publicly available.

The answer was that online networks created platforms on which students could organize their own surveys and report the results for their fellow students to see. Colleges and universities no longer had a monopoly over the capacity to design and use systems for soliciting and aggregating student evaluations. Students could create a collaborative network to evaluate their teachers. Systems like my colleague saw became popular, leading to a couple of major consequences.

First, many colleges and universities started more formally developing student evaluation systems that would be visible to students who wanted some guidance on whose courses to enroll in and which faculty's courses to avoid. When such evaluations were undertaken by academic institutions, the university faculty gained more control over the questions asked and the responses reported, for example, being able to censor or moderate insulting comments. Student initiatives drove universities to develop more open and accessible systems to evaluate the teaching faculty.

Second, the popularity of these systems led to the development of larger scale systems on the internet and web, such as Rate My Professor in 1999. One of the other early initiatives was Rate My Teacher (RMT) in 2008, originally developed for high schools in the United States, that was adapted to college ratings. RMT "disappeared" after being purchased in 2018, later replaced by Rate My Teachers (with the plural "Teachers"). It was given a new look and "sanitized" by removing comments since the original site's inception, some of which were considered damaging, if not slanderous, to the reputations of some teachers.[11]

As noted, from the earliest days of teacher evaluations, faculty worried about evaluations. Faculty and administrators remain skeptical of such systems. They worry about them being based on irrelevant criteria, such as the teacher's looks, the potential for students to "stuff the ballot box" with multiple entries, or for their evaluations to be biased by how hard the course was for them or how well or poorly they did in the course (Costin et al. 1971). Also, angry students might well be among the most motivated to post comments that could damage a teacher's reputation.

Such issues did not go away, but the internet and social media have provided platforms for students to evaluate their professors, despite the concerns of the faculty and administrators that had prevented them from openly conducting them and making them available to students, up to that time. These include Rate My Professors, the revived Rate My Teachers, Rate Your Lecturer, and Uloop. The very existence of such sites provides the potential for students to rate a particular professor or lecturer that they found particularly bad or good, empowering students if they felt that the institutions were not listening, or would not listen, to their views on teaching performance.

TRACKING BRIBERY: IPAIDABRIBE.COM (IPAB)

Ipaidabribe.com[12] (IPAB) has been an innovative application launched in India that helped initiate the development of bribery websites.[13] It is a crowdsourced platform for reporting incidents of bribery, enabling individuals to report bribery in ways that can create public information at the level of specific offenders but also aggregated to identify the kinds of services and regions of a nation that are most plagued by bribery, as one key indicator of other aspects of corruption.

This website has been hosted by a not-for-profit organization in India known as the "Janaagraha Centre for Citizenship and Democracy," based out of Bangalore (now Bengaluru), since 2011. The center has sought to improve lives in urban India such as through "JanaOnline" that is focused on bringing offline communities online and helping them to interact in more significant ways in addressing civic issues.[14] JanaOnline developed "Ipaidabribe" and "Ichangedmycity," the latter of which is focused on resolving citizen grievances online.

The "I Paid a Bribe" website is a crowdsourced corruption-reporting platform aimed at exposing the prevalence of bribery. India has experienced high levels of corruption, particularly in the judiciary, police, and public services and procurement, with bribery being one of the more prominent forms of "retail corruption," as it is based on small exchanges.[15] Many drivers in India stopped by a police officer for a minor traffic offense, for example, would assume that a bribe could help avoid a fine or other punishment. However, no data or other traces of these practices existed to foster remedies.

The I Paid a Bribe website provides a place people can go online to report when and where they paid—or refused to pay—a bribe. Through this website, a person can report the nature of the bribe they paid (or didn't pay) and even identify an honest officer they may have encountered. The editors of the site authenticate the claims, such as by speaking to those accused of accepting a bribe. The website then seeks to use this information to improve practices and reduce corruption. It seeks to raise awareness among citizens with regard to how to deal with bribery-related exchanges and provide information that puts more pressure on public officials to deal with bribery. In addition to following specific reports, the totality of reports is analyzed over time, such as by the type of bribery and its geographical location. This creates visualizations of the prominence of bribery reports that is newsworthy and helps keep government officials focused on bribery and corruption issues.

When members of the public go to the I Paid a Bribe website, they are asked to submit their experiences in detail, such as the time and place they were stopped and to whom they paid the bribe. If the complaint is specific enough, at the very least a query is raised to verify the incident. This process itself is time consuming for victims as well as those at fault. In strong cases, victims would be asked to come to a government office, speak with officials about the accusation, and find a resolution. There are some journalistic I Paid a Bribe stories that go into the investigation and authenticity of claims.

The website was originally limited to India, but the source code has been widely shared in more than a dozen countries to create partner sites, enabling the websites to be adapted to each country's unique legal and administrative procedures. It was such a success that it became a Harvard Business School case.

In 2011, shortly after I Paid a Bribe was launched in India, I spoke about it in China. A week later, before I left, I was told that a group of bribery-reporting websites had come online in China—at least eight reported by the press (Jie 2011). They were then taken down, and some reemerged, but clearly these sites were more problematic in the regulatory regime of China than in India. Also, in China, web platforms hosting these sites were not anchored in an NGO like the Janaagraha Centre, as China does not have a strong civil society online from which they were able to generate support for such functions as editing and authenticating, which could trigger, if not invite, accusations of libel and defamation (Ang 2014). As a result, they did not have the resources to verify claims and therefore did not report those accused by name to protect their privacy and reputation and prevent their sites from being subject to claims of defamation or libel. For such reasons, IPAB sites in China were subject to government shutdowns, revocation of website approvals, and closures, but for a variety of internal, regulatory, and cultural issues beyond freedom of expression, such as lacking a culture of civic participation online (Ang 2014). In this case, the success of IPAB was dependent on the national regulatory and vitality of the civil society context of each nation.

MONITORING POLLUTION IN CHINA

There has been a history of controversy over the accuracy of reporting pollution levels in China, particularly in Beijing and other large cities. One consequence was the launch of pollution-monitoring applications, often tied to mobile phones and smart watches. One example is the "China Air Pollution Index" developed by Wang Jun. Individuals could install the app on their phone or smart watch to track local air pollution levels. Data downloaded from the US embassy and China's Ministry of Environmental Protection could be aggregated by geographic areas to estimate pollution levels, frequently documenting an underreporting of pollution in official media outlets. The use of Wang Jun's app increased dramatically during a prolonged period of pollution in Beijing in 2013 (Kan 2013). Within a year, there were reports of pollution-monitoring data from the US embassy being blocked by authorities in China, which instructed websites to only use data released from the Chinese Environmental Protection Ministry (Watt 2014).

The COVID-19 pandemic has spurred the further development of mobile apps for networked individuals to enter location and other data and follow government guidelines in Britain and other nations. Such mobile applications are likely to enable networked individuals to monitor and capture data that could be uploaded to sites for reporting detailed accounts of medical, health, smog, and air pollution data. However, as in tracking pollution in China, access to these sites will be dependent on the practices, policies, and regulations of each nation.

MONITORING AND HOLDING SOURCES OF LITTER ACCOUNTABLE: PLANET PATROL

Many members of the public have been annoyed, if not upset, when finding litter in public places, such as on walkways and parks, but are left unable to do little more about the problem than complain or pick up the litter. Planet Patrol created a free litter-tracking app in 2016 that enables networked individuals to collect and record litter they see. The data is reviewed, cleaned, analyzed, and aggregated to create a database that can track litter over time and cross-nationally to help stimulate and inform solutions by industry and policymakers. Researchers can request data for use for not-for-profit purposes, creating the potential for selective free use of agreed data. Planet Patrol was founded in 2016 by Lizzie Carr, a paddleboarding enthusiast, who cataloged over 3,000 photos of litter she found on a 400-mile journey through England's waterways. From her own work in founding Planet Patrol, it has developed into an effort involving about 35,000 people recording litter in eighty-five countries (McCallum et al. 2021: 2).

As you see litter on a walk, for example, Planet Patrol encourages you to take a photo with your mobile phone, identify the litter, such as using a barcode function on the app to identify the type and brand of the litter automatically. As they instruct: photograph pollution; upload your photo with the number of pieces, type, and brand; then see your photo pop up on an interactive map of pollution in your area (McDermott et al. 2021). Photograph it, pick it up, record type and brand, and map it.

Simply by having a smartphone and capturing photos and details on litter, networked individuals become key to crowdsourcing data that supports citizen science and community action, such as by enabling Planet Patrol to provide evidence of the relative prominence of different kinds of litter. Researchers at two UK universities (University of Glasgow and University of Nottingham) are involved in this citizen science project. Its 2020 report, for example, shows that nearly a quarter (22%) of litter types consisted of plastic packaging. Greenpeace UK's head of oceans, Will McCallum, has argued that the UK government should establish targets to radically diminish the use of single-use plastic, and data provided by Planet Patrol can support such efforts (Hodgson 2021: 3).[16]

Many other projects have emerged around monitoring and tracking a wide range of problems to identify their scale and more about their social and geographical prominence. Related initiatives include the Peach Tech Lab developing approaches to tracking incidents of violence, domestic abuse, and terrorist attacks.[17] Generally, there is clear evidence from successful projects that students and others among the public enjoy and value participation in citizen science projects (Piesing 2020). They can feel empowered by supporting such civil society initiatives but also by doing something that enhances their informational power.

ANSWERING PHYSICIANS' QUESTIONS: SERMO

Sermo began as a US-based collaborative network that had over 200,000 physicians in the United States in 2014.[18] Nearly a decade later, by 2021, the network was international, engaging 550,000 members, healthcare physicians, in 150 countries.

"Sermo" is Latin for "conversation." It was originally designed as a discussion board by a physician, Daniel Palestrant, in 2005 to report "adverse effects" of treatments, such as drugs. It grew to enable a self-described conversations among an authenticated community of physicians who could both contribute to and filter professional knowledge. Members of the community, the physicians, could post questions to other physicians within the network and provide answers to questions posed by other members, as well as by paid members of the community, such as pharmaceutical companies, who pay Sermo to ask questions of the physicians that the companies cannot answer. As of October 2007, Sermo was open to physicians across the United States, who could authenticate that they were registered physicians. In 2012, it was sold by the physician founders to WorldOne, Inc. and expanded to other countries. It remains a private social media network for physicians, only open to licensed physicians, such as those having an MD (Doctor of Medicine) or DO (Doctor of Osteopathic Medicine) degree.

By vetting prospective community members, Sermo is an internet-enabled, closed community of experts within their specific field. It is closed to registered members to ensure that members are qualified to answer and ask questions, even though it is free to licensed physicians. It is also valuable when some elements of confidentiality are necessary.

Licensed physicians who are registered on the Sermo website may choose to be anonymous to others on the website. Anonymity is the default option as one means of protecting the confidentiality of the symptoms or details of patients they may discuss online. Moreover, anonymous participation can discourage vote buying, extortion, or other influence that might distort the answers of physicians. Also, individuals might feel reluctant to voice concerns or opinions if attribution was required. That said, anonymity can raise concerns about the qualifications or validity of the individual voicing an opinion or issue. However, members of Sermo can rate the quality of answers to questions, creating a system within the community for identifying more or less trustworthy sources.

Sermo is similar to many other social networking sites emphasizing user-generated content, mechanisms for peer review and comment, and the rating of content. However, the problem emphasis—answering questions of other physicians—of the Sermo model is relatively unique in seeking to cultivate a network that can collectively address emergent health and medical treatment concerns relevant to medical practitioners.

From its beginning, Sermo has sought to facilitate valuable conversations—the sharing of observations and knowledge—about healthcare and medical practices. At the same time, Sermo seeks to foster a sense that physicians on Sermo are in a community of peers. Networking physicians proved to be valuable, particularly among those in rural or small practices, where they had fewer proximate colleagues with whom to discuss novel, rare, or difficult cases.

The business model of this system was creative and sufficiently successful for it to become a private enterprise. Government, academic, finance, and healthcare industry experts could pay to access Sermo and observe activity online. (When my colleagues and I were studying Sermo, we were given free guest memberships.) Most creatively, these non-physicians can pay to ask questions of the physicians, such as whether any had seen or suspected a specific set of side effects associated with a particular drug. Physicians would then have up to two weeks to answer the question, with their answers not being visible for a specified period of time so early answers would not influence later responses. Physicians could even suggest amendments to a question or its answers, such as by adding a side effect of a treatment that they had administered. The answers would then be available to those asking the question. In this example, a company might get early evidence of a side effect from these answers in two weeks, while they might wait years for the more authoritative results of a controlled clinical trial.

ANSWERING QUESTIONS BY PATIENTS LIKE ME

In contrast to Sermo, Patients Like Me focused on building networks for communication and support among individuals with similar health and medical conditions.[19] It began in 1998, when 29-year-old Stephen Heywood was diagnosed with a progressive nervous system disease called amyotrophic lateral sclerosis (ALS). His two brothers started crowdsourcing information from others with ALS to learn more about how to manage and live with this disease. A family friend learned of what they were doing and launched Patients Like Me to connect ALS patients with one another online. Since 2011, it has been "welcoming any person living with any condition to connect with others, learn, and take control of their lives."[20] It has over 800,000 people with over 2,900 conditions.

In 2019, it was acquired and became an independent company backed by Optum Ventures, a UnitedHealth Group affiliate. Patients can use the site free of charge by virtue of agreeing that the site can sell research services and aggregated, de-identified data to pharmaceutical companies and other partners. A platform enabled networking among patients in ways that complemented other information and advice on their health and medical care.

This same logic of connecting individuals with similar problems was built into the site so that individuals could identify their health and medical conditions and be linked with information and people like themselves. This has been done by others, such as families with children with type 1 diabetes.[21] Some problems like this are severe but not so common that all physicians and clinics can keep up-to-date with the latest treatment regimes. However, the families, by networking together, can share information and experiences in ways that provide new insights to families and patients, such as helping them ask their physicians better questions. This case illustrates how some private companies can support networked individuals of the Fifth Estate just as some private internet and social media platforms do.

CROWDSOLVING A SERIAL MURDER CASE

This example is a dramatic illustration of someone in a remote location and well outside a formal organization being able to contribute to problem-solving. Here an ordinary member of the public in the United States used the internet, web and—at the time—innovative approaches to geographic mapping to help raise the priority of a criminal investigation, reignite FBI investigations, and secure the conviction of a serial killer.

A citizen detective, Paul Haynes, was an insomniac. Paul was an unemployed 30-year-old from South Florida, with an MA in media studies. He began doing research a few hours each day, rising to ten to fifteen hours per day from his bedroom at his standup desk. He became focused on a set of mysterious murders on the other end of the United States, in California. Over time he focused on finding the serial rapist and killer in California who was first called the Night Stalker, then the East Area Rapist, before the perpetrator was branded as the Golden State Killer by the crime writer Michelle MacNamara, with whom Paul began to collaborate.

His work with the Michelle MacNamara began as a result of following his research. Both were circling the same crimes. Paul Haynes contributed to the killer's identification through his ability to source his own information online. To search for the serial killer, and aspects of his identity, such as a connection with a "Bonnie"—a name that arose in previous investigations—and he used many online resources, such as Classmate. com and Ancestry.com, and geo-mapping of crime scenes—innovative at that time (geo-mapping has become a staple of contemporary crime and detective thrillers). The insights gained from his crowdsourcing resulted in new leads that created an incentive for the FBI to reopen the case, refocus their investigation, and employ online forensic genealogy based on DNA data sourced online to find the individual, who was eventually convicted.

Based on old DNA at an early crime scene, Paul was able to identify possible relatives of the killer by using publicly available applications, such as Ancestry.com. The suspect left DNA at early crime scenes so the FBI were able eventually to match his DNA. DNA samples provided to Ancestry.com led to the identification, not of the killer, but of four cousins, whose family trees eventually filtered down to Michael de Angelo, living in Sacramento, California. Then, DNA obtained from de Angelo's trash was found to match with this person of interest.

Box 6.2 **Malaysia Flight 17 Shot Down over Ukraine in 2014**

A domestic airliner, Malaysia Flight 17, came down in Ukrainian territory in 2014, killing all 298 people on board. The Russian government placed blame on Ukrainians and promoted problematic narratives to support this. A pioneering CNO focused on open-source intelligence, Bellingcat, investigated the downing of Flight 17. The name of the group, Bellingcat, is based on a cat and mouse story in which a bell is hung on a mouse to alert all the mice when the cat is approaching. Founded by a college dropout and video game enthusiast, Eliott Higgins, Bellingcat's staff and thousands of online volunteers established that the flight was shot down by pro-Russian separatists, possibly believing Flight 17 was a Ukrainian military aircraft, with a Russian Bak surface-to-air missile, supplied by a Russian special forces unit. The open-source intelligence is described by Zegart (2021: 170): Bellingcat "used pictures and videos . . . posted on social media; dashboard camera footage . . . posted on YouTube . . . an app called SunCalc, which measures shadows in pictures to pinpoint the time of day of an image, and Instagram selfies of a Russian undercover solder posing at the border." This is an example of how Bellingcat uses open-source intelligence to challenge disinformation and be an "intelligence agency for the people" (Higgins 2021).

This led eventually to the arrest and conviction of a former police officer, Joseph James DeAngelo, who was sentenced in 2020, at 74 years of age, to life in prison for at least thirteen murders and many more sexual assaults between 1973 and 1986. In the process, Paul also helped in the research for Michelle McNamara's (2018) bestselling account of the search for this serial killer, which provides far more detail on the investigation.

Crowdsolving has become more commonly referred to as open-source intelligence as more initiatives seek to exploit data such as photographs and text available online from multiple sources. Elliot Higgins (2021) has written an informative account of his work, from his home office in Leicester, UK, as Bellingcat, which has used open-source intelligence to examine a growing number of mysteries, including the downing of Malaysia Flight 17 (Box 6.2). In this and other cases, including the identification of agents sent to poison the Russian defector, Sergei Skripal, in Salisbury, England, and of Russian use of cluster munitions in civilian areas of Ukraine, his CNO was able to refute claims of the Russian government and gain the reputation as the "world's most celebrated Internet sleuth" (Campbell 2022: 23).

Themes from the Illustrations

In different ways, each of these examples illustrates how distributed collaboration can empower ordinary individuals or a particular group of users: how students, to amateur sleuths, to licensed physicians and patients can be empowered by strategic use of the internet. Crowdsourcing represents another strategy for supporting the Fifth Estate. That said, this approach has well-known problems that need to be addressed. For example, evidence collected online can be altered, raising questions about the authenticity of information sourced by networked individuals. This problem has been addressed by many of these sites, but another powerful example is "eyeWitness to Atrocities." As explained on its Twitter site, @eyeWitnessorg, eyeWitness "seeks to bring to justice those who commit international atrocity crimes by offering an app to take verifiable video and photos" (Box 6.3).[22]

Likewise, ratings have sampling and other validity problems, as discussed in the case of teacher ratings. But all these issues can extend to other rating applications, such as on Amazon Seller and Product Ratings or eBay Ratings of Suppliers. Those managing such systems need to continually monitor and address potential distortions of the crowd. That said, if well managed, these forms of collaborative networking can be of value to the Fifth Estate. Clearly, they build on the role of networked individuals in sharing information in ways that magnify their influence.

Box 6.3 eyeWitness to Atrocities

The mobile camera app eyeWitness to Atrocities enables eyewitnesses to war crimes and other self-evident cases of atrocious criminal conduct to post their pictures or videos with a time stamp so it can be preserved, authenticated, and used to prosecute the perpetrators. By downloading the mobile camera app, videos and photos are embedded with metadata that provides evidence of their authenticity. The International Bar Association with support from LexisNexis launched this app in response to the formidable challenges of authenticating and protecting evidence gathered by citizen journalists across the world that could be admissible evidence in future trails. For example, the app prevents the evidence from being altered until used as evidence. The developers initially worked with civil society organizations but later realized the potential for ordinary networked individuals to be eyewitnesses, which the site makes available to a global public. Websites provide instructions to those who might document atrocities and make the app available to download and use. The vision of the developers is to enable a "world where those who commit the worst international crimes are held responsible for their actions" (https://www.eyewitness.global/). This platform has been used to support twenty-eight dossiers to investigative bodies around the world that are pursuing those responsible for acts for which there is self-evident presumptions of an atrocity, such armed groups attacking civilians in the eastern region of the Democratic Republic of Congo in 2012 (UN 2012). More recently, it has been used effectively in Ukraine in one of the most documented wars in history. The director of the UK-based charity eyeWitness estimated that the evidence gathered during the first six months of the Russian invasion of Ukraine was comparable to "three years of the usual evidence captured around the world" (Siddique 2022).

A TRANSFORMATION IN THE COMMUNICATIVE POWER OF INDIVIDUALS

As described in previous chapters, through search and social networking tools, networked individuals of the Fifth Estate can source their own information and build virtual networks within and beyond any given organization. However, through distributed collaboration, networked individuals, like organizations, can also capture the value of distributed intelligence. Contributions to distributed intelligence can come from individuals who are close to the actual event, service, or problem to be solved. As a result, the people who are best informed about a particular topic or activity can become involved in and contribute to the resolution of problems. Whether it is making a Wikipedia entry or documenting litter, individuals involved with the topic or picking up the litter are becoming information sources of real value.

MOVING BEYOND CITIZEN CONSULTATION TO SOURCING ADVICE

It is also important to note how these examples demonstrate a departure from more traditional forms of citizen consultation. Generally, governmental initiatives have tended to focus more on engaging networked individuals as citizens rather than experts. For example, one of the first commercial experiments with interactive cable communication, the QUBE system in Columbus, Ohio, experimented with permitting viewers in Columbus to be polled during the broadcasting of debates, such as on town-planning issues. One example was the use of a network of QUBE systems to poll viewers on their relatively negative reactions to President Jimmy Carter's "malaise" speech in 1979 (Davidge 1987: 92–93).

Interactive cable systems were eclipsed by the use of electronic bulletin board systems (BBS) and computer conferencing systems, such as the Public Electronic Network (PEN) in Santa Monica, California (Guthrie and Dutton 1992). PEN was organized by the city and enjoyed a limited period of success, but it declined with the rise of the internet, which moved users away from this local system, and because of the inability to establish rules of order for discussion (Dutton 1996). PEN was used to foster discussion among residents of Santa Monica, in line with the concept of citizen sourcing of expertise. In fact, polling and voting was not a function provided on PEN to avoid situations in which public officials would feel at odds with public opinion. Instead, hundreds of more specific topics were raised, such as how to help the city's homeless, on which residents and employees in the city could express their views.

However, since this early period of experimentation with electronic city halls and forums, attention has shifted to citizen consultation, such as in enabling governmental units, like parliamentary committees in the UK, to obtain public feedback on issues (Coleman 2004). Citizen consultation is one clear role in which the internet can support the public sector, but it is primarily organized by and supportive of governmental institutions, such as departments and regulatory agencies, to complement and enhance the institution through electronic participation of the public. Unfortunately, it has become an expected part of policymaking in the United States and other liberal democracies that citizens will be consulted, but often too mechanistically to have a real impact on the substance of policy.

There has also been discussion of the potential for crowdsourcing in the public sector, such as through conceptions of "Wiki government" or "collaborative democracy." Again, while these imply a move beyond consultation, these concepts blur distinctions between citizen consultation and expert advice. For example, Beth Noveck (2009: 17) has defined collaborative democracy as "using technology to improve outcomes by soliciting expertise (in which expertise is defined broadly to include both scientific knowledge and popular experience) from self-selected peers working together in groups in open networks." This is a useful definition, incorporating both consultation and distributed expertise. From the perspective of the Fifth Estate, it might be useful to draw a sharper distinction between these two very different roles that networking can and should play in government.

One is gauging opinion, which comes closest to "collaborative democracy," that might ask citizens to respond to policy options, for example, on the basis of their experience. The other is engaging expertise, which might be based on scientific, technical, or experiential knowledge, such as being at the location of a problem (Benveniste 1977). Citizens are more than constituents whose opinions are equally legitimate. Citizens also have the potential to have expertise, and some citizens have more expertise than others, for example when they possess specialized knowledge or particular experience relevant to a specific subject.

Viewed as experts, the challenge for government is not to air public issues and gauge public opinion. The problem is to find relevant experts, based on merit and a spirit of voluntarism, wherever they live or work. The next problem is to find ways to bring their expertise to bear on a particular question in a timely and effective manner. Nevertheless, that is different from networked individuals determining that there is a problem and organizing a collective effort to crowdsource a solution, from litter to racial injustice—initiatives more central to the Fifth Estate.

SOCIAL LISTENING: INITIATIVES IN MACAU AND HONG KONG

My interviews with a former colleague on his initiatives in Macau and Hong Kong provided an example of an innovation in what his team calls "social listening" that is innovative and clearly magnifies the contributions of the people commenting on social media posts.[23]

Decades ago, in research on governmental and management use of computing in the 1970s, I found that some of the most consequential management information was gained by mining operational data (Dutton and Kraemer 1978, Kraemer et al. 1981). For example, there was a complaint process in a large city in the midwestern United States that aggregated complaints to the city in a single integrated list. Simply by looking at what residents were complaining about, the city managers could get early warnings about problems, such as what departments, functions, and areas of the city were experiencing what problems. It was valuable management information.

My colleague from Macau, Angus Cheong, who developed this new approach to social listening, had branched off from survey research on internet use to become a more independent entrepreneur, providing social research support to the government of Macau and business enterprises. In addition to using surveys, he often focused on content analyses of complaints and comments on social media. From this work, he developed a multinational business in Macau and Hong Kong with Chinese and English versions of the tools and processes for mining social media data.[24]

Across social media, like Twitter, Facebook, or LinkedIn, comments of individuals, such as about a political candidate or public issue, are scattered across multiple posts and platforms. The comments are so highly fragmented that they are seldom consequential beyond occasionally indicating a strong positive or negative sentiment toward a new development. Angus Cheong and his team developed the tools and processes to text mine multiple social media platforms for comments that can be tied to particular topics, like a candidate or issue, and then content analyzed to discern what people in the aggregate are saying in their comments. They call this "intelligent cross-platform data technology." As he is a social scientist, Angus and his colleagues understand research methods, such as data sampling, testing the reliability of indicators, coding qualitative content, doing automated content and text analysis, as well as statistical analysis, and visualization. It can be done quite systematically.

Suddenly, information otherwise virtually lost in cyberspace is accessible and interpretable in ways that can be informative for marketing, campaign evaluations and management, evaluation of public programs, customer experiences with products, monitoring brands, sensing responses to public policies, and so forth. It is supported by artificial intelligence (AI), but their process is using AI and text mining to augment human coders. For instance, as coders make decisions, such as coding one term as equivalent to another term, the analysis can quickly work through the coding decisions to reanalyze and visualize the results across the entire corpus of comments.

As comments are anonymized and aggregated, social listening is not a tool for surveillance but for discerning messages from the noise of too many public comments to humanly read or digest. As long as the results and the process are transparent and accountable, it has the potential to capture the messages buried in the aggregate of comments individuals make when reacting online to events, people, and issues in ways that can inform decision-making, much like the complaint system I saw in the 1970s but far more powerful.

They call this "social listening," while I have referred to it as "social intelligence." Aggregating comments across platforms and posts can enable the individual comments by ordinary users to be far more meaningful for policy and practice. Moreover, as the public increasingly knows that their comments are being listened to and acted on, then social intelligence might encourage more individuals to give more thought and care to their posts. They could make a difference to policymakers or practitioners across many sectors.

ACCESS TO TECHNOLOGIES FOR SHARING, CONTRIBUTING, AND CO-CREATING INFORMATION

Open-source software has contributed a variety of tools for collaborative network organizations, such as MediaWiki, software that can be used to create wiki-based collaborative environments. These infrastructures are being built. The public internet itself represents an open platform for distributed collaboration, using tools such as mobile apps, wikis, and collaborative software, which is widely available as a service, such as collaborative editing tools, like Google Docs. The current availability of such platforms and tools is one of the major enablers of collaboration among networked individuals. An individual does not need to start from scratch but can tailor existing tools to their particular purpose. The internet platform and the tools of collaboration, from email to wikis, are increasingly accessible to growing segments of the public.

In this sector of innovation, there are new technologies using the web, social networking sites, and even mobile phones and texting (SMS) to enable networked individuals to develop collaborative networks, which support a Fifth Estate. If individuals can obtain governmental and other information online and collaborate with others over the internet, they have the potential to hold government and other institutions more accountable. Even serious games have been developed online that are designed to better inform and engage citizens in public policy issues, such as the environment, or to solve practical problems, such as tagging photographs or other images on the internet, through what are called Games with a Purpose (GWAP).[25]

INNOVATIVE FAILURES

However, the illustrations of this chapter leave out many failures and dashed expectations. Individuals have sought to create a collaborative network without anyone joining them. Collaborative networks are not the inevitable outcome of technological, generational, social, and economic change (Tapscott and Williams 2006). The successful development of networks that can solve problems is difficult. The advice provided is not always the best and can be bad. However, the illustrations of collaborative networks in this chapter might stimulate others to consider the potential for embarking on this strategy and improving approaches to managing collaboration. In the right context and if well managed, collaboration can be successful as illustrated in some examples in this chapter.

THE IMPORTANCE OF MANAGING COLLABORATION

Collaborative networks reconfigure who communicates what, to whom, and when, within a network. The illustrations should demonstrate that these are seldom viewed simply as "crowds" involved in collaboration but managed interactions among networked individuals—regulated in part through the architecture and in part through management of the network, such as the assignment of editing rights and privileges. For example, a Wikipedia entry is likely to be written, edited, and updated by a small group of experts in a particular subject area, not a crowd (den Besten, and Loubser 2008). In addition, most of the successful collaborative networks have very strong leaders or champions, like a Jimmy Wales, sometimes taking on the role of a "benevolent despot," able to timely resolve issues and move ahead (Cassarino and Geuna 2008). Just as democracies have armies, which are not democratic organizations, many successful collaborations depend on learning from experts and managing contributions rather than gauging public opinion.

BUILDING A CRITICAL MASS

Successful networks build a critical mass of users. This often takes time and work in recruiting members who form a community, feeling a sense of ownership and value within the network. Alternatively, it is possible to bring a problem to an existing community of users. However, while many users are necessary, a small minority of "core participants" often make most contributions to the network, conforming to the so-called power law—where only a few are most active, with levels of activity quickly trailing off to form the long tail of the distribution, with most people making very few contributions. Fifth Estate initiatives around collaborative networks need to focus simultaneously on developing a core set of users to drive content development and a critical mass of users who follow and occasionally contribute to the network.

Engaging many often entails a key strategy of modularizing tasks, such as networked individuals simply photographing litter and uploading details about its type and brand. Successful systems often need to be extremely modular in their allocation of work or tasks. For instance, one of the earliest and still successful uses of email has been for broadcast search. A typical query is: Does anyone know someone knowledgeable about a particular topic? Questions like "Who knows?" can be ignored by those who do not know the answer and quickly dealt with by those who do know. Particularly when dependent on voluntary contributions, the key is to develop tasks that can be done quickly and easily. This happened often on neighborhood networks.

For example, when a reader of Wikipedia reads an entry and sees a mistake or the need for an update, it is possible to edit the entry and complete the task in a matter of minutes. It is the cumulative contributions of many editors making small contributions that have resulted in the unpredictably successful growth and quality of this online encyclopedia. By keeping tasks modular and easy to complete, it is possible for a multiplicity of individuals with a plethora of diverse motivations to drive collaboration.

The Distributed Intelligence of a Fifth Estate

Expertise is distributed geographically, institutionally, and socially. It has become a cliché, but no less correct, that not every expert in any given field works for your government or company or lives in your neighborhood. In a multitude of cases, expertise can often be located closer to a local problem or be distributed across the globe. Governments and other institutions, but also networked individuals of the Fifth Estate, can realize the potential for networking with others, not only as an audience, friends, or colleagues but also as experts or as people directly involved or affected by a problem. Achieving this potential will require more recognition of the role that CNOs can play in the empowerment of the Fifth Estate, as well as advances in the processes being learned on best practices and ethical norms on how to employ and manage distributed collaborative networks.

7

Leaking

Leaking is one of the most powerful but arguably also the most problematic strategy of the Fifth Estate. On the one hand, from the perspective of the Fifth Estate, leaking can be a key strategy for leveraging the internet and related media and technologies to hold powerful individuals, authorities, celebrities, or institutions more accountable. In this respect, it is a strategy that can further the public interest. On the other hand, leaks most often involve an insider within an organization or institution disclosing confidential or even highly classified information to the public—if not the world. It is an act that can be unethical, if not illegal, and can fail to balance the right to know and the value of transparency with other established rights to privacy and confidentiality.

It is impossible to unequivocally balance these conflicting values and interests as a general principle, but it is possible to get closer to a resolution by looking carefully at specific cases, which this chapter seeks to do. Even when specific cases are examined, the issues are not always neat and tidy; they are often complex and often further obscured by uncertainty over the facts of each case and the calculus of specific individuals: Why did they leak information? How individuals eventually balance these conflicting facts and values often comes down to a politically judgmental process—deciding who did the right thing in the specific circumstances of the case. That said, a major issue in discussing leaks is that in some cases, such as instances of leaking covered by the US Espionage Act, motivations might not matter. In that case, the issue is whether a person leaked classified information and the motivation can be viewed as irrelevant.

Leakers, Gossips, Malicious Hackers, and Other Actors

Governments, business and industry, the press, and civil society organizations have information that is often not public, such as confidential conversations or memoranda. Those inside these organizations who pass confidential, secret, classified, or other restricted information on to others are often vilified as gossips, snitches, or informants. In contrast, a whistleblower is a person, usually an insider or an employee, who calls attention to wrongdoing, such as information or activity within an organization that is perceived to be illegal, harmful, an abuse of power, or otherwise against the public interest. They call attention by making it public, going to the press without the permission of their organization for example. Individuals within organizations might well

The Fifth Estate. William H. Dutton, Oxford University Press. © Oxford University Press 2023.
DOI: 10.1093/oso/9780190688363.003.0008

pass confidential information to the press for strategic reasons, such as to demonstrate that the organization was being truthful, but that is a strategic communication strategy rather than an unauthorized leak.

Foreign state actors can pay or otherwise incentivize individuals to leak information, but those individuals would be better classified as foreign agents, or conspirators, not leakers, such as Julius and Ethel Rosenberg and Morton Sobell who were charged with leaking US military secrets to the Soviet Union, during the Cold War, in 1950.[1]

Likewise, malicious actors or cyber attackers might illegally breach the computer systems of any organization to access data or information for monetary gain, but they are malicious individuals, crackers, or cybercriminals, not leakers. Some call them hackers, but that can be misleading (Box 7.1). Such security breaches are serious and growing as data is so easily stored on simple devices and distributed on computer systems in ways that make it likely that accidents occur, such as leaving a laptop on a train or mistakenly including confidential information in an email.

Leaks of relevance to the Fifth Estate are focused on those perpetrated by an insider to support the public interest, for instance when the leaker believes the public has been lied to or deceived by the organization for whom they work. Some of the most notorious leaks that fit this description include Daniel Ellsberg's leaking of the Pentagon Papers, FBI agent W. Mark Felt's (Deep Throat) leaks to *Washington Post* reporters about the Watergate scandal, WikiLeaks' release of the leaks obtained from Chelsea Manning, including the Iraq and Afghan War Logs, the PRISM leak by Edward Snowden, and the leak of a National Security Agency (NSA) report on Russian meddling in US elections by Reality Winner.

Box 7.1 Hackers

The early use of the term "hacker" was in reference to the behavior of a set of very smart and dedicated programmers at MIT in the early 1970s. An MIT professor at that time, Joseph Weizenbaum, found them working night and day on developing computer programs, routinely to the point of missing sleep and proper meals, to progress their work. They were so obsessed with coding their programs that he called them "compulsive programmers" (Weizenbaum 1976). He was concerned that their final products might be less than optimal because of their approach to continually try to fix and refine the software until it worked. They hacked away at their coding rather than taking a more systematic, preplanned engineering approach, hence the term "hackers." However, since these early days, the term has frequently been used to refer to malicious individuals trying to inappropriately breach or crack into computer systems. Some refer to "ethical hacking" that is purposively employed to determine if a system is secure. Can the program withstand attempts to hack into the system? Notwithstanding, the term "hacker" is not the best label when referring to malicious networked individuals seeking to breach cybersecurity. Hacker clubs are often prestigious and lawful.

The Pentagon Papers and Watergate leaks did not involve the internet or social media. In these cases, a copy machine was used by Ellsberg and human interpersonal communication employed by Deep Throat. And these early leaks were primarily directed to the press as the means to make them public. What has changed in the digital era is the role that the internet and social media can play by enabling a whistleblower obtaining access or distributing information directly, instantly, and globally to the public as well as to the press. The press is no longer the only or proverbial "middleman" or gateway in such leaks, raising questions about the degree that rights of free expression might apply to leakers as well as the press, such as in the United States, where the press has largely been more protected by the First Amendment, and in many other nations.

Leaks Relevant to the Fifth Estate

Table 7.1 provides an overview of the leaking examples discussed in this chapter. I begin with a pre-internet case involving Daniel Ellsberg, since his leak of the Pentagon Papers has become one of the most famous and discussed examples of leaking, even if he was empowered over a half century ago by a copy machine rather than the internet. As is the case in other chapters, there are many other leaks than those discussed here that provide

Table 7.1 **Illustrations of Leaks Tied to a Fifth Estate Strategy**

Leaker · Whistleblower	The Leak	Implications
Daniel Ellsberg and Tony Russo	Photocopied classified documents on US involvement in Vietnam, i.e., the Pentagon Papers	Excerpts published by *the New York Times* in 1971; affected debate over Vietnam War and press freedom
Chelsea Manning · Julian Assange	WikiLeaks	Undermined the credibility of the US government and military
Daniel Domscheit-Berg	OpenLeaks	Demonstrated the challenges in creating an institution for a website accepting leaks
Edward Snowden	PRISM and related surveillance initiatives	Focused on potential for mass surveillance and pushing telecom and internet firms to be more transparent about data requested by government
Reality Winner	Arrested for leaking an NSA report on US election security, which she mailed to *The Intercept*	Report described Russian attempts to hack US voting systems before 2016 elections

---

Box 7.2 **The UK's Phone-Hacking Scandal**

A few rogue reporters and consultants of one or more newspapers in the UK hacked into the telephone messaging systems of many celebrities and others in the news to obtain personal information that might be of interest to the readers of the tabloid press, including the voicemail of a young murder victim, and without any rationale grounded in law or the public good. Many individuals with an answering machine or other voice messaging systems can routinely record messages left by callers. They are normally protected by passwords but are often weak default passwords provided with their purchase. If accessed illegally—maliciously hacked—it is possible to obtain personal information about relationships and other private and confidential matters. The discovery of unauthorized phone hacking by agents of the UK's *News of the World* led to a public inquiry into the conduct of the press. The inquiry resulted in a major four-volume, 2,000-page report presented to Parliament (Leveson 2012). Controversy followed on the wisdom of legislation on press regulation.

---

good examples of the role of a Fifth Estate and even more that are not entirely centered on leaks by individuals within institutions, such as newspapers involved in the UK's phone-hacking scandal (Box 7.2).

The press often performs a watchdog role vis-à-vis governments and corporations, much like the Fifth Estate, and invented many of the strategies used by Fifth Estate actors, including the publication of leaks. I will refer to a few cases to illustrate similarities but focus on those cases in which networked individuals versus institutions are the key agency behind efforts to hold institutions more accountable.

DANIEL ELLSBERG LEAKING THE PENTAGON PAPERS

On June 13, 1971, speaking to then US President Richard Nixon in the Oval Office of the White House, near the end of a discussion of casualties in the Vietnam War, the president asked General Alexander Haig, Nixon's White House chief of staff (Brinkley and Nichter 2014: 171): "Okay. Nothing else of interest in the world?" General Haig replied: "Yes, sir. Very significant. This goddamn *New York Times* exposé of the most highly classified documents of the war." Nixon said he saw the story but had not read the exposé. Haig explained its origins and added: "This is a devastating security breach of the greatest magnitude of anything I've ever seen." And this remains one of the more dramatic security breaches in US history, with the leaker, Daniel Ellsberg, being known fifty years later as the "patron saint of whistleblowers" (Smith 2021: 36).

Ellsberg was a Harvard graduate in economics, who enlisted in the US Marine Corps and became a company commander. After being discharged in 1957, he returned to Harvard as a junior fellow for two years, during which time he began working for the Rand Corporation, a major think tank based in Santa Monica, California. Rand invented the Delphi technique as one of a number of methods designed primarily for forecasting military and defense needs over a long-time horizon. Ellsberg then moved to a permanent position at Rand in 1959, while also completing his doctorate in economics at Harvard in 1962.

From 1964, he worked at the Pentagon, under Secretary of Defense Robert McNamara and then for General Edward Lasdale at the State Department, which took him to South Vietnam to visit sites and conduct a study of counterinsurgency. During that time he came to question the wisdom of US involvement in Vietnam. He returned to Rand and from 1967 collaborated with others on a top-secret study of US involvement in Vietnam (1945–1967) for Defense Secretary McNamara, which was completed in 1968. The lessons he learned from this study further eroded his support for US involvement, as the papers led him to conclude that successive presidential administrations had misled Congress and the public about the conduct and prospects of the Vietnam War.

Despite his experience in the military, he became increasingly sympathetic with anti-war activists and draft evaders, coming to see them as having what he called "civil courage" (Smith 2021: 37). Some 7,000 pages of a forty-seven-volume study called "The Pentagon Papers," once completed, were sitting in Ellsberg's safe at Rand.

Initially, Ellsberg tried to get legislators, William Fulbright and then George McGovern, to read and publicize them, such as through hearings or the *Congressional Record* (Greenberg 2012: 34). That failing, he decided to leak them to the press. As in the case of draft resisters he admired, he knew this could land him in prison, but he viewed it as his own act of civil courage (Smith 2021).

This was pre-internet and email access, but a friend of a friend of Ellsberg had an advertising agency with a Xerox photocopier. At that time, a Xerox was the brand name of a copy machine that became synonymous with any copy machine. Over eight months, Ellsberg, with the help of a colleague at Rand, Tony Russo, spent nights at the ad agency making copies, with some help from Ellsberg's 13-year-old son.

On March 2, 1971, he gave a copy to a *New York Times* reporter, and on June 13 the first excerpt was published in the newspaper, leading to General Haig's comment to President Nixon, quoted previously. The papers focused on the administrations of Presidents Kennedy and Johnson, reflected in Haig's comment that the leak was "going to end up in a massive gut fight in the Democratic Party" (Brinkley and Nichter 2014: 171). It was not about Nixon's administration. Nevertheless, in a conversation the next day with H. R. Haldeman, Nixon said that such a leak not only undermines the security of classified information generally but also "shows that people do things the president wants to do even though it's wrong, and the president can be wrong."[2] It quickly came to be seen by Nixon as a threat to the power of the president. Members of Nixon's team invented strategies to suppress Ellsberg and the papers (Greenberg 2012: 41), including a burglary of the office of Ellsberg's psychiatrist.

Nixon's attorney general, John Mitchell, ordered the *Times* to halt publication then brought a lawsuit against the paper when it refused. Moreover, Ellsberg had given the papers to eighteen other newspapers. Daniel Ellsberg and his colleague, Tony Russo, were charged under the Espionage Act of 1917 among other charges, but all were dismissed when evidence emerged that the FBI lost evidence of the wiretapping phone conversations between Ellsberg and others, which were recorded without a court order, making them illegal, as well as finding that burglars had broken into Ellsberg's psychiatrist's office. All this was discovered during the Watergate scandal. These and other misconduct charges against the administration led the case against Ellsberg and Russo to be dismissed on May 11, 1973. But in line with the Streisand effect (Box 4.7), the government's efforts to block publication brought far greater attention to the Pentagon Papers than they might otherwise have engendered.

Like many cases of leaking, there were issues over the legality of leaking the documents, as Ellsberg did, and the right of the press to publish documents obtained from these leaks, which was the primary issue raised with the courts. While associate justice of the US Supreme Court, Potter Stewart (1975: 636) observed years later, the US court could find no constitutional basis for "prohibiting publication" of "allegedly stolen government documents."

At his trial, Ellsberg and his attorneys argued that the First Amendment protects freedom of speech and the press and therefore supports the right to publish the papers.

Ellsberg also saw himself acting in the spirit of the First Amendment in leaking the report, claiming that the government was suppressing information that should be known by the public—that is, privileging openness over secrecy. However, the US district court judge ruled this argument "irrelevant," and therefore it was not presented to the jury (Ellsberg 2014). His lawyer complained to the judge, saying he had never heard of a defendant not being able to tell the jury why he did what he did. In response, Ellsberg (2014) recalled that the US district court judge said: "Well, you're hearing one now." Nevertheless, as mentioned in connection with the Watergate case, the chargers were dismissed.

WIKILEAKS' CABLEGATE

Julian Assange was born in Australia in 1971, one year after his mother, Christine, met his father, John Shipton, at an anti–Vietnam War demonstration. [3] John disappeared, and Julian was raised by his mother, who later married Bret Assange, who traveled with an organization staging and directing plays, with Julian's mother helping at times. Christine then became linked with Keith Hamilton, who was connected to an infamous Australian cult, led by Anne Hamilton-Byrne, accused of imprisoning and brainwashing children in the 1970s and 1980s. From 1982, when Hamilton became abusive, she and her son, Julian, spent years as fugitives, trying to evade Hamilton who pursued her.

In the 1980s, out of this remarkable childhood, Julian became active and highly regarded as an exceptionally smart and charismatic member of Melbourne's hacking underground, which was an "almost entirely male group of self-taught teenagers" (Leigh and Harding 2011: 40). This added up to a relatively nomadic life that typified Julian's upbringing. He continued to live a life that might be an early example of a digital nomad, when he founded Wikileaks.

Assange founded the whistleblower website called WikiLeaks in 2006, inspired by his rising crusade for the transparency of information. The WikiLeaks website explains that the mission of this group was to analyze and publish large data sets composed of materials that had been censored or for which access has otherwise been restricted.[4] It receives documents, authenticates them, and, if judged significant, leaks them, and holds them in an archive for public access, despite efforts to censor their contents. Assange said that WikiLeaks gives "asylum" to these censored documents.[5] In turn, WikiLeaks works actively to make these materials accessible to the public, such as through collaborating with media outlets.

Despite his talents, Assange developed a reputation for being a difficult person to work with, known for his eccentric behavior. Nevertheless, WikiLeaks gained many partners supporting the organization and some funding from sales of material but mainly from gifts and contributions from the public. The organization received over a dozen awards for its activities, such as the Amnesty New Media Award in 2009.

Probably, the most famous name associated with Wikileaks was Chelsea Manning. Born in 1987, Manning was named Bradley at birth but identified as female, changing her name to Chelsea in 2013. Chelsea Manning lived her first thirteen years in a small, rural, conservative Christian religious community in Crescent, Oklahoma. Manning's American father was in the US Navy, meeting his wife while he was stationed in Wales, UK. After service, the couple moved to Oklahoma, where Manning and her elder sister were born. Manning was smart and sociable, participating in the school band and quiz team and staying out of trouble (Leigh and Harding 2011). As Manning approached her thirteenth year, she became more introverted and began realizing that she did not identify as a heterosexual male. Even earlier she had questioned religion, despite growing up in a small religious community. Rebelling in ways from her community, she expressed herself through symbolic gestures such as refusing to reference God when reciting the Pledge of Allegiance at school (Leigh and Harding 2011: 23).

Around the same time, her father left his wife and the family home. Manning's mother then returned to Wales, where Manning found herself the only American in the local school. She was a target of some bullying, but participated in a computer club, and became engaged in discussions critical of American foreign policy, particularly the invasion of Iraq.

At age 17, Manning left school in Wales to return to the United States to live with her father. Manning found a job in a photo-sharing software company, but this lasted only four months. When Chelsea's father discovered that she did not identify as male, she was pushed out of her father's house, leaving Chelsea homeless and jobless, until she enlisted in the US Navy in 2007, following in her father's footsteps.

In the navy, she trained as an intelligence officer and gained the security clearance that would enable her to access classified files. While stationed at the Fort Drum military base in Upstate New York, she met Tyler Watkins, later her boyfriend. Tyler was going to Boston University and helped introduce Chelsea to the hacker community in Boston and Cambridge, Massachusetts.

As an intelligence analyst in her early 20s, Manning was stationed at a military camp in the Iraqi desert outside Baghdad, working with highly classified national security materials, including files from communication networks of US embassies and US intelligence. While there, Manning became disillusioned with her unit for not being professional and motivated and not adhering to basic security protocols.

Experiences in the service also disenchanted her with the US mission in Iraq, much in the way Daniel Ellsberg became disenchanted as he learned more about the Vietnam War. Since Manning realized that little attention was paid to what she brought in or out of the offices, Manning carried a Lady Gaga CD to work, erased the disc, and copied classified material onto the it, which she carried out of the workplace.

In 2009, Manning learned that WikiLeaks was streaming pager messages that had been captured on September 11, 2001, the day of the 9/11 attacks on New York City and Washington, DC. Manning assumed that this leaker group must have received these files from a NSA database. Manning concluded that she might be able to trust WikiLeaks and came to see WikiLeaks as a channel she could use to get the information she had copied exposed to the public—including video from a helicopter gunship, Afghan and Iraq War Logs, classified diplomatic cables, and more. She approached Assange, and then she told what she had done to an American computer hacker called "Lamo" (Leigh and Harding 2011: 93). Manning also told Lamo that she did "counter-counterintelligence" to reassure herself that her leaks had not been discovered, using her security clearance to delete records that provided evidence of her leak (Greenberg 2012: 43).

On June 21, 2010, Julian Assange met with several journalists at the Hotel Leopold in Brussels, Belgium. He opened his laptop, typed, and then handed a napkin from the table to the journalists with the password to the whole set of files, saying, "No spaces" (Leigh and Harding 2011: 99). Days later, American officials were looking for Assange to prevent the publication of the diplomatic cables among other files. By this time, Manning's leaking had been discovered and he was already being held in a military prison.

Julian Assange and WikiLeaks became internationally famous after releasing a classified video Manning had provided that showed night-vision images from a helicopter gunship over an Iraqi suburb as it located, targeted, and gunned down over a dozen people, two of whom were discovered to be Reuters news staff, not terrorists. This was but one piece of documentation of many contained in what were called the Iraq (391,832 documents from 2004 to 2009) and Afghan (over 91,000 reports from 2004 to 2010) War Logs consisting of classified verbatim reports from US military in the field, and more, amounting to over a million documents (Leigh and Harding 2011: 99).

These were followed by a release of diplomatic cables that provided the materials for WikiLeaks "Public Library of US Diplomacy," described by the organization as the largest searchable collection of US confidential, or formerly confidential, diplomatic communications. The leak of US diplomatic cables—what came to be known as Cablegate—was among the most controversial and consequential of the material leaked by WikiLeaks. Of the documents, 251,000 were classified and sensitive US State Department communications between 1966 and 2010 by its consulates, embassies, and diplomatic missions around the world. The potential implications of these leaks were serious, given that they contained personal and candid assessments of host nations and officials that could undermine decades of international diplomacy.

An early release of a few files began in February of 2010 and was followed by a larger and more organized release in November of 2010 consisting of cables redacted by WikiLeaks in collaboration with news agencies, including *The Guardian*, *New York Times*, and *der Spiegel*.

In November 2010, Sweden issued an international arrest warrant for Assange, accused of rape by one woman and sexual assault by another following a WikiLeaks conference held in Stockholm in 2010. Assange denied these allegations, arguing this was a guise for returning him to the United States.

Then, in 2011, additional cables were released that failed to be redacted in ways that could protect individuals involved. It was not clear that WikiLeaks sought to release these unredacted files. Ironically, it could have resulted from a hack of WikiLeaks, as the original documents were held in password-protected files. There were allegations that Assange had not been sufficiently professional, for example not updating and carefully managing passwords, and this is alleged to have led to their release. That said, the later distribution of unredacted files was associated with a breakup of WikiLeaks, such as with the departure of Daniel Domscheit-Berg, a technical architect of WikiLeaks.

In 2013, Manning was convicted of the theft of the cables, which entailed violations of the US Espionage Act. Since the act was committed while she was a member of the armed forces, Manning was court martialed and sentenced to thirty-five years' imprisonment. On the day after sentencing, Manning announced on the *Today* talk show in the United States that she was transgender, introducing herself as Chelsea Manning. Eventually, Chelsea Manning's sentence was commuted by President Barrack Obama, leading to her release in May 2017 after seven years of confinement.

In 2012, Julian Assange was granted political asylum in the Ecuadorian embassy in London, where he remained until 2019. On April 11, 2019, he was arrested by the London Metropolitan Police for failing to appear in court and was facing possible extradition to the United States. The US indictment was a lesser charge than Manning's: conspiracy to commit computer intrusion by helping Chelsea Manning gain access to information that he intended to publish via WikiLeaks. However, within a month, a US grand jury added eighteen federal charges to the original indictment. In 2022, the UK's home secretary gave a "green light" to Assange's extradition to the United States (Croft 2022). On October 8, 2022, supporters formed a human chain outside Britain's Parliament to protest his extradition and to free Assange.[6]

As of this writing, Assange remains in the UK. However, twelve years after major news outlets, including the Guardian, New York Times, Le Monde, Der Spiegel, and El País, published selected excerpts from "Cablegate"—distributed to them by WikiLeaks—the editors and publishers jointly opposed charging Julian Assange under the US espionage act. As they put it: "Publishing is not a crime." Prosecution would undermine freedom of the press.[7]

DANIEL DOMSCHEIT-BERG AND THE VISION OF OPENLEAKS

When Daniel Domscheit-Berg left WikiLeaks in September 2010, he set out to create a new website that would be better engineered to address problems he encountered with WikiLeaks. He found Julian Assange's vision compelling but not well engineered. Three months after parting company with Julian Assange and WikiLeaks, he began developing a website called OpenLeaks that was almost famous. It stalled early in its development and failed to be successfully implemented and go live (Greenberg 2012). However, this example dramatically illustrates the difficulties of creating a formal organization to support leaking as a Fifth Estate strategy.

Domscheit-Berg sought to engineer and write the code for his website that would be legal and enable more democratic, transparent, and secure processes. Also, he wanted it more focused on collaborating with media and civil society organizations rather than directly publishing or distributing leaked material—a role that might resolve some legal issues.[8] If a leak was sent to a media outlet, for example, the outlet could provide it anonymously to OpenLeaks, which could create a protected space for ensuring its anonymity, authentication, and distribution to other outlets. His website would not itself be directly receiving leaked documents or be a publisher but a middleman in a larger ecology of actors. The idea was that a news outlet could use all or aspects of a leaked document for its readers and benefit by providing it to OpenLeaks, which could help with authentication and preservation to enable use by other outlets from different angles or for other purposes.

Following in this spirit, for example, the Tow Center for Digital Journalism at Columbia University developed guidelines and tools for sending and receiving documents from anonymous sources online, which they call SecureDrop,[9] "an open-source whistleblower submission system." This system was originally developed by *The New Yorker* as Strongbox, furthered by the Freedom of the Press Foundation as Deaddrop, and then as SecureDrop. In such ways, ideas that motivated OpenLeaks were later developed and implemented by others, if not Domscheit-Berg.

WikiLeaks was run by a benevolent dictator, Assange, and so have many other distributed collaborations and open-source intelligence sites—collaborative network organizations, as described in Chapter 6. OpenLeaks aimed to be a more democratically governed organization by having a board overseeing and approving critical decisions, which had not been the case for WikiLeaks. Daniel sought to create a managed network organization that permitted transparent distributed collaboration in authenticating and redacting leaked material among its members. Supporting this collaboration while protecting the files would be possible via sophisticated encryption and decryption by authorized collaborating members.

OpenLeaks was to be part of a larger system, involving the press, media organizations, selected nongovernmental organizations (NGOs), and civil society groups. They would receive and distribute leaked information, possibly removing responsibility from OpenLeaks, while making the system distributed, which would therefore be more difficult to build, manage, and secure.

The major crisis at WikiLeaks stemmed from breaches of security that enabled malicious internet users to get access to unredacted files. Data protection of all aspects of this system proved difficult. Domscheit-Berg set up an opportunity to demonstrate how OpenLeaks could survive penetration testing at an international hackers' camp, the Chaos Communication Camp, in August 2011, but his team failed to reach the point that a penetration test could be conducted (Box 7.2).

In addition to security, OpenLeaks needed to have good newsworthy leaks, which are not easy to attract. Collaboration with media organizations could help. But consider the small number of individuals identified with seriously important leaks, people like Ellsberg. And the submissions must not be traceable, accepting uploads that are anonymous, while seeking to authenticate them, which is one aspect of evaluating the source. The press and other media organizations occasionally work with anonymous sources, such as Watergate's Deep Throat, who turned out to be an FBI agent, but journalists were able to authenticate the credibility of his leaks over time as they followed his clues.

Moreover, such a credible informant leaking is rare and suspect in a profession where trust is hard won.

The vision of a not-for-profit organization that would enable public access to a portal to support those who wished to distribute information that exposed unethical, immoral, or mendacious activities occurring behind closed government or corporate doors remains a valid goal of sites designed to accept leaks. However, OpenLeaks found the required engineering feats to be insurmountable in the time frame Domscheit-Berg set for himself, which was particularly difficult given its complex ecology of actors. Collaboration with the hacking communities, media organizations, foundations, civil society, and leakers, while fenced off from the intelligence communities in ways that could be trusted by hackers and leakers as well as be on the right side of law enforcement proved to be a Herculean task for the team.

The prospective launch of OpenLeaks was riding a wave of optimism about the future of whistleblowing in 2011 (Greenberg 2021). However, its failure to realize the vision undermined the momentum behind such initiatives, making websites accepting leaked materials difficult to create or even find online over the following years.[10] This stumble by OpenLeaks left leaking to the surviving websites accepting leaks, including WikiLeaks,[11] and the whistleblowers, such as Edward Snowden.

EDWARD SNOWDEN AND PRISM

In 2013, Edward Joseph Snowden leaked information about a secret surveillance pro-gram of NSA called PRISM and a related mass collection of telephone records. He has been a fugitive ever since, living and working in Russia, as I write, critiquing information policy in the US and worldwide.

Ed Snowden was born in North Carolina in 1983, but he was raised during his early years in Maryland.[12] He was a high school dropout who studied intermittently at a com-munity college but never received a college degree. He did complete requirements to obtain a General Education Development (GED) test score certifying that he had high school–level academic skills. In 2004, he enlisted in the army reserve and later joined the special forces, only to be discharged after four months. After this stint, he worked as a security guard at a University of Maryland facility affiliated with NSA. Regardless of lacking the credentials of an impressive formal education or career path, he was able to demonstrate skills and promise in computing that led to a position with the Central Intelligence Agency (CIA) in 2006, resulting in him obtaining a security clearance in 2007. He worked for the CIA as a network security technician in Geneva.

In 2009, Snowden left the CIA and began work in Oahu, Hawaii, as a data analyst for one of the NSA's private defense contractors. This work gave him access to classified intelligence of the NSA. While in this position, he blogged posts critical of government surveillance programs, but it is unclear whether he pursued his concerns through any formal mechanism open to whistleblowers within his organization or the US govern-ment, such as contacting an ombudsman or his congressional representative.

Later, in 2013, he chose to download classified information onto a memory stick before taking a medical leave, and he left Hawaii for Hong Kong. In Hong Kong, he began developing channels of communication with journalists who had reputations for concerns over privacy and surveillance, such as American journalist Glenn Greenwald. Under an alias—"Cincinnatus"—he sought to create a secure encrypted email channel, even coaching a journalist on how to set up common encryption software, called PGP (Pretty Good Privacy), to keep their communications confidential (Greenwald 2014: 7–12). He was soon speaking with journalists about NSA's information gathering. In June 2013, newspapers, including *The Guardian* and *Washington Post*, published information that was disclosed by Snowden, along with an interview with him, conducted in Hong Kong, which argued that this unwarranted mass surveillance program (PRISM) violated American citizens' right to privacy.

From interviews then and since, Snowden saw himself and has been widely regarded by others as a whistleblower in the tradition of Daniel Ellsberg.[13] Also, Snowden admired the actions of Julian Assange, the founder of Wikileaks, as well as Chelsea Manning (Snowden 2019). Wikileaks sought to advise and support Snowden. Throughout his ordeal following his leak of NSA information, Snowden has conveyed a commitment to transparency and the value he places on the public's right to personal privacy, which he saw at risk from programs supported by NSA.

Snowden's leaks exposed US government surveillance programs, including PRISM, which was launched in the aftermath of the 2007 Protect America Act and the Foreign Intelligence Surveillance Act (FISA), along with other NSA programs. PRISM leaks detailed the existence of mass surveillance of data, including emails, browsing histories, social media records, records of voice and video chats, phone calls, and multimedia files that raised legitimate concerns of privacy and surveillance. A system used by the British Government Communications Headquarters (GCHQ) for surveillance of communications data, called Tempore, was also exposed by Snowden's leaks.[14]

In some respects, these programs were a continuation of earlier surveillance of international communications, which had long entailed links between telecommunication carriers and the NSA (Laprise 2013). However, advances in network and computational capabilities allowed surveillance to move beyond tracking international phone calls to track email, the web, and other digital communication networks in ways that could identify who is communicating or linking with whom. Did this program reasonably balance the protection of the privacy of American citizens with national security needs, as President Barack Obama argued, or was it a disproportionate response of a surveillance state? Was this a courageous act of a patriotic whistleblower or the reckless illegal behavior of a romantic who betrayed his country? Was he a heroic whistleblower, patsy, or pawn?

To address such issues, it is critical to investigate the exact nature of PRISM and similar surveillance programs conducted by nations around the world. What information is collected from what sources and how is it analyzed in ways that might infringe on or protect the privacy of individuals, whether citizens of the United States or other nations? Is surveillance limited to metadata, information about the contents of a message, such as to whom it is addressed, or more inclusive of the contents of messages, for example? How does the information gathered by government differ from that collected by private ISPs and social media companies, and what difference might this make? However, debate seldom dived into this level of information and analysis. Instead, the press coverage tended to focus on issues that largely distracted the public from the core concern over privacy in a democracy—missing an opportunity for the media to educate the public.

It is doubtful that the press intentionally sought to distract the public. It is more plausible that the press simply followed what they saw as the public's appetite for the personal and international intrigues and conspiracy that enveloped this story. The early press accounts discussed and asked, Where is Snowden? Where will Snowden take refuge? Was Snowden under the influence of a foreign government? Does the NSA have adequate safeguards over intelligence operations? There were even discussions of how his "ex-girlfriend" felt about his absence.

There are many reasons why journalists would not spend much time discussing PRISM. It is possibly unpopular in the post-9/11 world to delve into such issues (Susca 2017), particularly in proximity to incidents prominent at the time of this leak, such as the bombings at the Boston Marathon or the brutal murder of Lee Rigby in Woolwich, England, which raised the priority of fighting terrorism. Moreover, it has long been the case that while the public cares about privacy, they are also likely to surrender their privacy to achieve other values, from health and safety to even personal convenience (Dutton and Meadow 1987). For instance, most people willingly support airport security systems because they place safety and security above their personal privacy.

Also, many may view the potential for intelligence agencies to care about, or observe, their behavior online as infeasible, if not impossible, particularly given the billions of people using digital media during everyday life and work. Of course, the advances in networking and computational analytics that support big data analytics are making mass surveillance increasingly feasible, but these analytical techniques are not easily conveyed to the public.

In the aftermath of the Snowden leaks, and his taking refuge in Russia from US authorities, discussion of the leaks and mass surveillance programs died down. However, among privacy advocates, he became a hero, winning numerous prestigious awards, including recognition as president of the board of directors of the Freedom of the Press Foundation, became a trusted go-to expert on issues of privacy and surveillance, and published his personal memoirs (Snowden 2019).

In September 2022, after the February 24 invasion of Ukraine, Snowden was one among a group of foreign-born individuals granted Russian citizenship.[15] While he has continued to criticize the human rights record of the United States, he does not, and probably cannot, risk addressing Russian actions in Ukraine. But he continues to occasionally blog on Twitter, apparently over a VPN, and participate remotely in online events relevant to human rights.

REALITY WINNER AND US ELECTION MEDDLING

Reality Winner was a 25-year-old intelligence contractor. After the 2016 presidential elections in the United States, she printed a classified NSA report on Russian attempts to meddle in the 2016 elections, such as hacking voting systems prior to the election, which she emailed to *The Verge*. She was arrested in 2017 under the Espionage Act and pleaded guilty to espionage in 2018.[16] In 2021, following the 2020 election of President Joe Biden, Reality was released from prison to serve her remaining sentence in a halfway house (Robertson 2021). A documentary, entitled *United States vs. Reality Winner,* provides an account of her leaking this document about attempted Russian interference.[17]

The Mueller Report (2019) of the US Department of Justice reinforced evidence that a Russian military intelligence unit, the GRU, had sought to interfere with state elections, such as in Florida, by placing code on election websites that would enable the extraction of information, and working to access information from companies producing US voting machines and their companies' executives. However, the report found no evidence of an impact on the outcome of US elections. The same GRU unit was responsible for attacking Hilary Clinton's personal email server and a server for the Democratic National Committee (Mueller 2019).

Leaking and the Fifth Estate

These brief sketches of some notable initiatives aimed at leaking in the public interest are suggestive of themes that cut across one or more of these examples. Some reinforce recurring themes across the chapters, such as the empowerment of individuals. Daniel Ellsberg made a singular contribution to exposing the Pentagon Papers, but he also needed help. He even enlisted one of his sons as well as his associate, Tony Russo. Manning worked alone but did need connections to get his material to WikiLeaks. But just as networked individuals are always working in a larger ecology of actors when searching, creating, networking, and collaborating, so are they when leaking information. They are one of a number of key actors but empowered by the internet and social media in ways that earlier leakers could not have replicated.

Unique to this focus on leaks has been the role of "insiders." Insiders leak, while discovery by outsiders is news. Almost by definition, all the major leaks were committed by insiders, underscoring the significance of the boundaries of institutions. Networked individuals of the Fifth Estate operate outside of the institutions, or in a different role, such as the journalist blogging in the evening. The leaker is one of the few roles inside an organization that reflects the role of networked individuals, albeit raising more serious ethical and legal issues.

These examples raise other key themes of relevance to the Fifth Estate.

THE CHALLENGES OF INSTITUTIONALIZING THE FIFTH ESTATE

The outcome of the OpenLeaks initiative illustrates the difficulty of institutionalizing the reception and distribution of leaks but also the Fifth Estate more generally. Domscheit-Berg thought he could solve issues of security and redaction by developing a better engineered process, which pushed him to create a real organization with some permanence. However, this also forced him to deal with the complexities and other challenges of the multitude of actors involved in a more democratic, distributed, and secure process that will pass tests of legality. Consider simply the issues of any formal organization being infiltrated by law enforcement, the intelligence community, foreign agents, and hackers. The organization would be difficult to build and difficult to maintain in such a no-trust environment.

Institutionalizing this process does not fit well with the Fifth Estate. As a function becomes institutionalized, it moves away from the ability of networked individuals to make a difference and creates the ability of other estates to exert more control—it is easier to close down an institution. A bribery website can and has been removed only to be replaced in hours or days later. The actions of networked individuals are more difficult to regulate, control, or destroy.

SPEED AND REACH AND SCALE OF DIGITAL AGE LEAKS

The contrast between the leak of the Pentagon Papers and Snowden's revelations or WikiLeaks underscores the degree that digital technology has sped up the process and greatly expanded the reach of leaks. It took weeks for Ellsberg to copy the report he leaked to the press, while it took seconds for Manning or Snowden to download the materials that they were able to immediately deliver to online sites like Wikipedia and many more press outlets. Physically copying hundreds of pages is far different from downloading files onto your blank Lady Gaga CD, as Manning did, or sending to your printer, as Reality Winner did. Leaks in the digital age can involve millions of files—a scale unimaginable in the copier era—which create major issues for redaction, synthesis, and redistribution.

CIVIL COURAGE TO TAKE LEGAL AND ETHICAL RISKS

Each example of leaks in this chapter illustrated the real risks and costs of leaking important information. Had it not been for the Watergate scandal's fallout, Daniel Ellsberg might have gone to prison. Chelsea Manning did go to prison, and Julian Assange was taken into custody by the Metropolitan Police in London after taking refuge in the Ecuadorian embassy in London for nearly seven years and leaving to face a probable sentence for breaking conditions of his bail agreement and array of other charges. Edward Snowden sought refuge in Russia, where he remains after being granted permanent residency in 2020 and citizenship in 2022. In most of these cases involving the leak of government information, the leakers were not oblivious to the legal and ethical choices they faced, and they knowingly put their freedom at risk to expose what they believed to be violations of the rights of citizens. Ellsberg said it when he noted the civil courage required to expose secret information. Similar courage was exhibited by the celebrities and gymnasts who exposed abuse in their organizations, like Olympic gymnastics medalist Simone Biles. Snowden's silence on Russia appears to be an exception to this pattern, although he is unlikely to have any privileged information about Russian actions that is not available to others in Russia public with limited access to uncensored foreign media.

ETHICAL UNCERTAINTIES AND GRAY AREAS

Daniel Ellsberg went to trial thinking he had a defensible case for leaking the Pentagon Papers, believing the government had deceived the public. However, the judge did not care about his ethical calculus in light of the US Espionage Act, which is blind to motives or the perception of the individual but focused on the act of leaking. However, in other areas, the ethics of leaking are less black and white and subject to debate. Nevertheless, when successful in establishing their case, leakers have become heroes and heroines, as in the case of others in the Fifth Estate.

The legal-administrative traditions of different nations create distinctive contexts for resolving the legality and lines drawn around the leaking of governmental and corporate information. The First Amendment in the United States, as seen in the Ellsberg case and since, has been used to support the publication of leaked documents. As WikiLeaks argued, if leaked documents are in our possession, WikiLeaks is not legally bound to prevent their publication any more than the press would be. For better or worse, in the UK, in contrast, the Official Secrets Act places a higher hurdle for the release or leaking of governmental information. And the United Kingdom and United States are among the more liberal democratic nations in the world. The risks and costs of leaking are far greater in many other nations, illustrating the degree to which this strategy of the Fifth Estate requires a level of respect for freedom of expression and privacy to enable even courageous individuals to risk releasing secret or classified information.

Arguably, in the United States and other nations, governments and corporations are working hard to make leaks more difficult and more costly to whistleblowers. Margot Susca (2017) has argued that governments and the public, at least in the United States, are becoming more focused on plugging leaks, in part due to the increasing threats posed by the use of new technologies such as WikiLeaks as well as revelations of classified documents being found in the residences and offices of former US President Trump and US President Biden. In addition, she argues that public opinion has been relatively uninterested or "increasingly wary" about leaks. While there might have been what she called an unspoken bargain between governments and the press about classified or secret information, that bargain is disappearing in light of the growing threat of an increasing number of leaks.

RESPONSIBILITIES OF LEAKERS AND THE PRESS

The adage "with great power comes great responsibility" applies to whistleblowers. While many if not most leaks entail the violation of organizational agreements, such as for confidentiality, or laws, such as the Espionage Act, there remain expectations that leakers need to protect the public if they purport to serve the public interest. For example, in the leak of the diplomatic cables by WikiLeaks, Julian Assange and his colleagues worked with and enlisted major media organizations to redact material to protect individuals for whom personal communications were reported. Reputations, jobs, even lives of innocent people could be at stake if unredacted files were widely distributed. WikiLeaks took on this responsibility but, in the process, failed to adequately protect the unredacted files, which—ironically—were hacked and distributed on the internet. This failure led some WikiLeaks staff to depart as they lost confidence in the organization.

These examples illustrate the variation in the attention of leakers to communication about the material they released. At one extreme, Ellsberg worked with the press to ensure that key content of the Pentagon Papers was communicated accurately to the public, along with his central message about the mendacity of the government. Manning discussed the rationale for his leaks with others but never in a way that could reach the public, particularly given his rapid detention. Edward Snowden also went to some length to schedule and hold interviews with journalists to convey his findings in understandable ways, eventually writing his own memoir to discuss these issues (Snowden 2019). Arguably, a responsibility of whistleblowers should extend to clarifying and explaining why materials were released and what they in fact show that could challenge or correct oversimplified headlines. Whistleblowers cannot control how the press treats their material, but they can put effort into communicating and summarizing what it shows and why it is important.

LEAKING AS ONE OF MULTIPLE STRATEGIES

The limitations on leaking, which are many, need to be balanced by recognition of them as one of many strategies of the Fifth Estate. In discussing the emerging trends in the use of technologies for greater transparency, Andy Greenberg (2012: 316) describes an interview with a 23-year-old software developer, Rich Jones, who had created smartphone apps to capture live incidents in protests and other events, two of which he called "OpenWatch" and "Cop Recorder," supporting what has been discussed here as "originating" content (Chapter 4) and collaborating on witnessing atrocities (Chapter 6, Box 6.3). As discussed in previous chapters, leaking is one of a set of strategies the Fifth Estate can use to hold other individuals and institutions more accountable, including originating, searching, networking, and collaborating—all strategies for empowerment, transparency, and the Fifth Estate.

PART III

SHAPING THE FUTURE OF THE FIFTH ESTATE

This final part of the book turns to the implications of the Fifth Estate and its future. Do the multiple strategies of Fifth Estate actors add up to real-world outcomes for democracy and society? Chapter 8 develops the case that the combination of Fifth Estate strategies of searching, originating, networking, collaborating, and leaking is enabling greater democratic and social accountability. Fifth Estate actors are playing significant roles in shaping major outcomes online and in the offline world of government and politics as well as everyday life. You can see how Fifth Estate actions are distinctly different from putting existing structures and functions online. The internet is empowering a new collectivity of actors to initiate actions from the bottom up to hold individuals and institutions more accountable and effect change.

If the Fifth Estate was a gift to democracy, then the platformization of the internet has been a gift to politicians, regulators, and others who seek to control content and expression online. Governments have powerful incentives to control platforms, whether to protect children's safety or the state's narrative, as illustrated by Russia's regulation of a virtual technosphere in support of its "special military operation" in Ukraine. As I write, the prominence of techno-deterministic media perspectives versus user-centric perspectives is leading to exaggerated claims and depictions of the implications of the internet within a harms framework, which marginalizes the value of being online in an increasingly networked society, where nearly all information, people, services, and technology are increasingly networked. Even when well-intentioned, such as in child protection, these techno-deterministic and harm-framed perspectives are leading to approaches to governance and surveillance that are likely to over-control online content and undermine personal privacy. In an effort to tame a purported "Wild West" of the internet realm, the proponents of control are empowered by the platformization of internet and social media, just as governments seek to create geopolitical technospheres to support the narratives of the state. These threats combine to raise questions over the future of the internet, social media, and the Fifth Estate.

That future is the subject of the concluding chapter. I remain optimistic about the future of the Fifth Estate by virtue of its growing prominence across the world, as described throughout this book. It is not a fanciful vision, but a reality that is documented in major trends and a multitude of examples. However, while this estate is far from being a utopian vision, it has yet to be widely recognized and understood. Greater awareness of the Fifth Estate will enable Fifth Estate actors and all the other estates of the internet realm to better experience, protect, and sustain its role in supporting greater democratic and social accountability.

8

A Power Shift for Democracy and Society

Countervailing Views

Since the financial crisis of 2008 and the EU membership referendum (Brexit) and US presidential election of 2016, optimism about the internet and democracy has declined across most of the Western world, if not worldwide. To a rising number of journalists and researchers, Ithiel de Sola Pool's (1983) vision of the internet as a "technology of freedom" has been turned upside down, with digital media being linked to the rise of autocracies and even the "end of democracy" (Runciman 2018). Similarly, the wider social implications of the internet and social media have become characterized in equally catastrophic ways.

Since 2016, discussion has begun to concentrate on the harms of the internet and social media to democracy and society as policy has shifted to a focus on how to prevent a growing litany of risks to children and the larger society. Social media are particularly demonized even by research, which has turned increasing attention on the bias of algorithms and the disinformation being sown online—two of many factors claimed to be undermining the role of the internet in the digital age.

A CASE OF HARM? FRANCES HAUGEN, FACEBOOK'S STAR WHISTLEBLOWER

The dramatic claims of the Facebook whistleblower Frances Haugen precisely follow this line of critique, arguing that Facebook had misled investors in her filings to the US Security and Exchange Commission (SEC), state attorney generals, and then in her appearances before the US Congress and the UK Parliament in 2021. She argued that Facebook's management were prioritizing profit over safety from harms that put children and democracy at risk (Box 8.1). Her argument was that the company knew there were problems with its online engagement strategy—the algorithms shaping what users see online—that endangered users, such as those linked to children's use of Instagram. She claimed Facebook knew that "content that gets an extreme reaction from you is more likely to get a click, a comment or reshare" (Stacey and Bradshaw 2021: 10). Her logic is that its algorithms were designed to maximize online engagement rather than minimize harm to users, such as damage to children's mental health and adverse effects on those with body image problems; failed to address safety issues, such as protection from bullying; and was undermining democracy by polarizing the public.

The Fifth Estate. William H. Dutton, Oxford University Press. © Oxford University Press 2023.
DOI: 10.1093/oso/9780190688363.003.0009

Box 8.1 **Facebook's Whistleblower Frances Haugen**

In 2021, whistleblower and former Facebook employee Frances Haugen leaked tens of thousands of pages of internal Facebook documents to the *Wall Street Journal,* which she claimed showed inconsistencies between the company's public statements and its private communication among staff (Bradshaw 2021: 10). She unmasked herself in filing a complaint with SEC and appearing for a televised *60 Minutes* interview, followed by her testimony to a US congressional subcommittee about the documents she obtained while an employee of Facebook's civil integrity unit, a unit that had been axed by the company after the 2020 US elections. She argued that Facebook's own research showed that popular services like Instagram "harm children, stoke division, and weaken our democracy," yet the company did not adequately address these issues (Milmo 2021a: 32).

Born in the American Midwest, in Iowa, Haugen was an outstanding student with a "glittering academic background," including a Harvard MBA (Perrigo 2021: 28). Her career ambitions took her to Silicon Valley with work for a time at Google, Yelp, and Pinterest before joining Facebook in 2018 with the aim of tackling misinformation, having lost a friend who succumbed to conspiracy theories, and landed a position with exactly this mission (Perrigo 2021: 30). However, she told a reporter that in her first months she complained about not getting the team or support she needed and felt her concerns were dismissed by her engineering manager and others at the company. Her team was eventually disbanded, and she started gathering documents that supported her concerns over the limited efforts of the company to address the harms of social media.

Facebook is large, with over 70,000 employees, and a culture of hierarchy among the founders and their social circles (Marwick 2013). Moving from settings since childhood in which she was a star to become a small fish in a big pond must have been difficult. During the pandemic, she first went to live with her parents and then to work remotely from Puerto Rico, which she could afford from her successful investments. When Facebook told her she could not continue working remotely from a US territory, she resigned, but not before trawling Facebook's internal employee forum for documents related to harms linked to social media (Perrigo 2021).

She then went on to raise whistleblowing to a "higher plane" (Waters and Murphy 2021). She worked with advisors to come out with a public website, https://www.franceshaugen.com, and talking points, collaborating with John Tye, the founder of the whistleblower aid organization that represents her—a new development in the area. She filed with the SEC to put her under the agency's whistleblower protections, which opened up the potential for receiving 10–30% of the proceeds from any penalties (Haugen 2021). Another "whistleblower strategy" advisor, Harvard Law School Professor Lawrence Lessig, whose expertise has been intellectual property law, compared Facebook's hiding harmful effects with that of tobacco companies,[1] with US Senator Ed Markey also comparing Facebook to big tobacco. In fact, her very polished—perhaps too polished—testimony had the hallmarks of a brilliant Larry Lessig script. Those who dislike Facebook were pleased, with Senator Markey calling her a "twenty-first-century American hero" (Milmo 2021a: 32).

Pundits claimed her case was based on hard evidence (Cadwalladr 2021), but the evidence appears to be internal research and communications, such as from the Facebook forum, Workplace. Attributing dramatic impacts to specific applications, like Instagram, seems very difficult if not impossible to substantiate—she was an MBA data scientist, not a social psychologist or social scientist. Likewise, it is difficult to imagine real evidence to support her link between engagement algorithms to genocide in Myanmar or to the Capitol riots in January 2021 following Trump's electoral defeat, which followed the demise of her civil integrity unit.[2] And there is no logical way engagement is in direct opposition to safety. Information could be—and should be—engaging as well as true or safe—imagine making information about COVID-19 dull or unengaging!

However, despite doubts over credible empirical support and the reasonableness of her claims, Haugen and her whistleblowing team gained support from Luminate, backed by the founder of eBay, Pierre Omidyar, and convinced journalists and politicians across both parties in the United States and internationally that they had the goods on Meta and its Facebook and Instagram platforms. Meta (then Facebook) argued that from Ms. Haugen's limited position in the company, she could not know the company's strategy and that the company was continuing to develop better approaches and increasing the staff responsible for reducing harmful content. That said, it is difficult to ever know if the claims made in her whistleblowing case could have stood up to credible independent social research on social media users.

THE INTERNET AS A LIFELINE

At the same time, the internet has proven to have been a lifeline during the COVID-19 pandemic, enabling work and education to continue online for example. And with nearly two-thirds of the world's population online, governments and NGOs around the world are even more focused on addressing digital divides in access to the internet than ever before—striving to get rural populations online as well as the next 2–3 billion people to create an internet for all.[3] Adding to the irony, for many people in low-income, developing countries, Facebook is in essence their internet.

How can we square these dueling perspectives with the Fifth Estate? Is the idea of a Fifth Estate an overly optimistic vision? While in line with continuing efforts to address digital divides, the idea of a Fifth Estate must appear to be a lone voice in a rising chorus of concerns over the catastrophic social and political implications of the internet and social media.

The next section of this chapter focuses on briefly reviewing the argument of this book before moving to focus on the role of the Fifth Estate in government and politics and then across every sector of our increasingly networked societies. Pulling together a synthesis of the various strategies enabling the Fifth Estate, it is clear that it is not a utopian vision but a real, observable development that spells a positive power shift for democracy, government, and society. The next chapter moves to a discussion of the major threats to the Fifth Estate in the context of these dualling perspectives.

The Fifth Estate: A Perspective on the Network Power Shift

Since the early days of computing and networking, people have debated the implications of computers and telecommunications, and in turn, the internet, on the relative power of different actors in organizations and society. As explained in the introduction to this book, the dominant findings of research up to the rise of the internet, including my own, were that technological innovations in computing were usually adopted and implemented in ways that followed and reinforced existing structures of power in organizations and society—what we called "reinforcement politics" (Laudon 1977, Danziger et al. 1982). Reinforcement politics was in line with a critique of technological determinism as it countered the idea that computerization would have a systematic and predictable bias across all organizations, such as empowering technocrats or top managers. In contrast, it underscored the importance of empirical studies of the actual use and implications of technologies like the internet.

This did not mean that technologies made no difference. When successfully adopted in organizations or societies, information and communication technologies (ICTs) like the internet reconfigure how people get information, communicate with others, obtain services, and do what they do. In the process, they also reconfigure what people know, who they know, from whom and where they get services, and what know-how they require in their work and everyday life. These are major social implications. Even if ICTs were to entirely reinforce existing patterns, such as making even closer connections with a person's family and friends, this would be an important social effect. However, in the case of the internet and social media, empirical studies demonstrated time and again that these relationships are not simply reinforced but are reconfigured—people get different information, meet new people, get services from different providers in different locations, and require new skills and levels of know-how. The internet is not simply reinforcing existing information and communication practices—it is changing them. How are they changing?

Most generally, the internet and related digital media are enabling networked individuals to source their own information and configure their own social networks in ways that enhance their informational and communicative power relative to other individuals and institutions. In fact, a critical mass of ordinary networked individuals has the devices and skills at hand to access information and network with others that are as powerful as, or essentially equivalent to, that available to politicians, leaders in business and industry, and public intellectuals. Networked individuals can strategically use the internet and related social media to search, originate, network, collaborate, or leak in ways that enhance their communicative power vis-à-vis governments, business and industry, and other actors and institutions. The evolving and ever-changing collectivity of networked individuals who have the civic courage to use these techniques in the public interest are what I've called the Fifth Estate.

In such ways, the collectivity of networked individuals of the Fifth Estate is becoming as significant in the twenty-first century as the Fourth Estate of the independent press was in the earlier industrial age of print technologies, when the press could hold other institutions more socially and politically accountable for their actions. The early preindustrial estates of the clergy, aristocracy, and commons are reflected in contemporary public intellectuals, business and economic elites, and elected and appointed public and governmental officials, along with the press. Each of these sets of powerful individuals and institutions can be held more accountable by civic-minded networked individuals of the Fifth Estate, who use the internet and related media strategically to search, create, network, collaborate, and leak in the public interest.

Most accounts of the political role of the internet are focused on government and politics, such as political campaigns and protests. However, the power shifts linked to the Fifth Estate extend beyond politics to encompass nearly every sector of society. Therefore, I will discuss government and politics in the next section and then move to how these implications are far more general across society.

Democracy: The Fifth Estate's Gift to Governance and Politics

The Fifth Estate provides a new perspective on the transformation of governance and politics, shifting attention to a new collectivity of networked individuals acting for the Fifth Estate—as a new player in an expanded pluralistic ecology. Mainstream research on the internet in governance and politics has focused on the role of new technologies in supporting existing democratic institutions, primarily governmental institutions, such as legislatures and parliaments.

For example, early internet research on politics and governance asked how the internet was augmenting or transforming traditional institutions and processes (Tsagarousianou et al. 1998). In line with this, the internet was generally adopted and implemented by public institutions to support the provision of information, such as guidelines on public health; e-government, such as in the provision of government services; policymaking, such as by enabling citizen comments, consultations, and petitions; and in campaigns and elections, such as polling and voting (Box 8.2).

These functions remain important. It was right that research on the internet in politics and government focused on whether these traditional functions have become more effective or efficient online, and, in some cases, how online applications have created new services or failed in ways that lessons could be learned. My early work focused on the impact of nascent computerization of governmental processes, finding evidence that it often fell short of expectations (Kraemer et al. 1981).

Critiques of the role of the internet in politics often dismiss as insignificant the actions of networked individuals through such concepts as "clicktivism" and "slacktivism." The ease and satisfaction of clicking "like" buttons or emojis or retweeting microblogs from the comfort of one's home is most often compared with the serious politics of people making the effort and sacrifices to protest in real collective actions. However, online activities on social media, email, and other digital media are analogous to aspects of traditional politics, such as flyers, and most often complement rather than substitute for other forms of collective action (Karpf 2012).

Electronic voting, for instance, has had a fascinating history. The Clinton administration called for studies of the feasibility of online voting in 1999, only to be followed in

> ### Box 8.2 Arenas of Digital Innovation in E-Government and E-Democracy
>
> Information: electronic voter guides, online forums and debates, dissemination of public information via websites, email, and social media, such as COVID-19 guidelines.
>
> E-government: provision of online or electronic services for licenses, taxation, registration; administration, such as online complaint systems and analysis; administrative rulemaking, such as e-rulemaking; and analysis, such as data and computational analytics for service provision, such as police manpower allocation.
>
> Policymaking: online forums and consultations, online e-petitions, online submissions of comments on policy, such as network neutrality.
>
> Campaigns and elections: using the web and online media in campaigns; polling and voting online, such as experiments in remote internet voting.

the Gore-Bush presidential election in 2000 with a full-blown crisis over the integrity of voting in Florida, with its discussion of hanging chads confusing counts based on the use of counter-sorters in Florida with now antiquated punch cards. But varieties of schemes have been used, such as poll-site kiosks and more distributed multimedia kiosks, with remote internet voting always being the most controversial. Yet all e-voting options tended to be critiqued regarding risks to proving the integrity of the vote, given technical vulnerabilities to fraud, manipulation, and cyberattacks; and the effect on turnout, such as advantaging the "haves" of the digital divide while disadvantaging the elderly and technophobes; and legal challenges, such as requirements for a paper ballot (Simons 2004, Simons and Jones 2012).

That said, over time, computer-mediated systems like the internet allowed some traditional functions—even voting—to be done in new ways. For example, the Democracy Network was a new form of voter guide that used the web to enable candidates to define the issues at stake and clarify their positions online and in their own words in ways that would help voters to better compare candidates (Docter et al. 1999). This was created by Tracy Westen at the Center for Governmental Studies in Los Angeles and later adopted by the League of Women Voters.

Another example is how the City of Santa Monica, California, developed an electronic city hall on a dial-in network, called the Public Electronic Network (PEN), which was useful for hosting electronic forums for discussing policies for the city, such as how to better serve the homeless (Dutton and Guthrie 1991). While successful, its use declined in part due to conflict over how to moderate the forums but also due to networked individuals shifting to the internet and World Wide Web—linking to the world rather than only their community. However, networked individuals have continued to develop initiatives in the spirit of PEN but increasingly outside or at arm's length from the control of government, such as Virtual Taiwan (vTaiwan) and Polis, described later in this chapter (Box 8.3).[4]

Box 8.3 **Polis and Taiwan's Gov Zero Civic Hackers**

Since 2014, student activists and protesters in Taiwan set off what became known as the Sunflower movement (Ho 2019), involving a standoff between the government and protestors over a trade bill with the mainland (C. Miller 2020). In light of these protests, some activists despaired how polarized debates often led to little or no meaningful interaction with government representatives. One "civic hacker" in Taiwan, Audrey Tang, a coder since she was 14 years old, had become involved in multistakeholder internet governance initiatives and gained experience as an entrepreneur in Silicon Valley. She brought this experience back to Taiwan to join with other civic hackers in g0v, called gov zero, a decentralized civic tech community, founded in 2012 (https://g0v.tw/intl/en/). They sought to apply lessons learned from internet governance to debate over mainstream politics. Specifically, they saw the value of finding areas of consensus to foster more meaningful citizen input to government. As public officials were impressed with the early hackathons and success stories of g0v, they asked g0v for help in creating a Public Digital Innovation Space (PDIS) with Tang as the digital minister of Taiwan (Miller 2019). Tang and her colleagues worked with the government to employ interpersonal and online approaches to generate citizen engagement in a virtual "vTaiwan" to address questions posed by the government as well as raise questions for the government, often applying Polis (https://pol.is/home) to map attitudes and beliefs to find areas of consensus. The online tools help them identify and include more of the public's views in debate, be more transparent in how they interpret input, and find areas of consensus—the commonalities—that they make more visible to all stakeholders through Polis and their internet-empowered approach to governance.

Likewise, traditional democratic institutions, like parliaments or legislatures and regulatory agencies, increasingly used the internet and related ICTs to reinforce and extend their processes, for example by creating electronic consultations such as for the US Federal Communication Commission's consideration of regulatory measures on network neutrality. These and many other innovations along with many failures in e-government, e-democracy, and e-participation have been important and have helped transform how governmental and political institutions, such as campaigns and consultations, are conducted.[5] An entirely new field of democratic innovation has developed to critically assess their implications for participatory democracy (Elstub and Escobar 2019), particularly around increasing citizen participation in decision-making processes in existing institutions (Smith 2019).

One key issue that has constrained the use of the internet and social media by traditional democratic institutions has been the digital divide. If a large proportion of the public is not online, then political activities that are online could be inherently biased in favor of the online community and viewed as undemocratic. Along with security concerns, this has long been a factor slowing moves toward online voting, for example.

That said, the Fifth Estate only requires a critical mass of networked individuals—not universal access. This makes it a more realistic advance in democracy than many more traditional functions that would require more universal access, and even this constraint is diminishing as more people move online.

Fifth Estate Innovations in Governance

However, the rise of networked individuals enabled other innovations outside or around traditional democratic institutions, such as developing e-petitions to initiate policy change from the grassroots (Briassoulis 2021). Another illustrative case, following in the spirit of the PEN system, is the development of open-source software, called Polis, that can help find areas of consensus potentially buried in public debate and discussion.

Polis (or pol.is) has been called a consensus-generating mechanism. It does not require funding from government or industry and can be used by individuals, civic groups, and governments, giving it an independence from other estates. It empowers networked individuals by giving their voices a greater likelihood of being considered in processes organized to elicit public input. Three founders and their small team of technically sophisticated activists in Seattle, Washington, created Polis as open-source software that has been used by many organizations across the world to collect and analyze the views of a large group of people concerned about a policy issue.[6]

Eliciting the views of networked individuals in their own words, Polis employs machine learning and statistical analyses to interpret and sort the fog and divisions that can arise from many views expressed. Its aim is to find areas of consensus by analyzing the text of online posts. Rather than identifying issues that divide, Polis seeks to identify, show, and incentivize areas of agreement to those involved in the discussion. In this way, Polis software and data can discover and visually map opinions—creating an attitude map—as a debate evolves. By being able to see that there are clusters of individuals emerging who agree on similar statements or saying essentially the same things but in different words, Polis can target discussion on areas where a consensus might be reached. Identifying these points of consensus and where there might be areas of agreement that connect different clusters of individuals, such as for or against an initiative, it seeks to enable compromise. Finding areas of consensus across diverse opinions is also supported by features of the software, such as not enabling replies that may foster debate. Polis has been used by a variety of groups, including an initiative in Taiwan that has had some demonstrated successes (Box 8.3).

Fifth Estate Enabled Campaigns

Barack Obama's campaign in the 2008 US presidential election demonstrated the potential of social networking. It was one of the first major initiatives that used social media to decentralize the national campaign, enabling supporters of Barack Obama to use email and social media networks to extend and democratize the campaign, such as by providing their own reasons for supporting their candidate. In the UK, a roughly comparable social media campaign organization formed, called 38 Degrees, which

---

Box 8.4 **The Internet and the Madrid Train Bombings**

Three days before Spain's general election, on the morning of March 11, 2004, multiple bombings occurred on a commuter train in Madrid: 193 people were killed and as many as 2,000 injured. Controversy arose immediately after the attack when the governing party attributed the bombings to the Basque separatist organization ETA (Euskadi Ta Askatasuna), while the opposition blamed militant Islamists, retaliating over the Spanish government's alignment with the United States with respect to the invasion of Iraq. Nationwide demonstrations and protests were orchestrated online, accusing the government of hiding the truth. This controversy has been linked to the loss of the general election by the incumbent. Since the election, despite investigations, responsibility for the bombings remains unattributed, with no direct link established to ETA or al-Qaeda, albeit with more connections made to leaders of al-Qaeda (Reinares 2017). A Fifth Estate might have had an influential impact on the election but was not necessarily correct.

Box 8.5 **Tweeting the 2016 Trump-Biden Televised Presidential Debate**

Focusing on the first televised US presidential debate between Donald Trump and Hillary Clinton in 2016, we studied how members of the public joked, derided, and fact-checked candidates on Twitter as the debate happened. We found several different types of participants, whom we called "the fandom," who enjoyed communing with like-minded others: partisans, wishing to support their candidate; virtual mob, relentlessly denigrating one or all; the public sphere, who invoked discussion of issues; the viewertariate, focused on providing live commentary; and finally, the Fifth Estate. The debate audience used the Twitter platform primarily to post humorous quips and attack candidates with negative comments. However, many users also shared substantive critiques and fact-checks and sought to hold not only Trump and Clinton accountable but also the debate moderator for their performances. By sharing fact-checks and substantive critiques, many Twitter users acted as a Fifth Estate (Robertson et al. 2019).

---

created systems for members of the public to launch online petitions and other social media campaigns. Other examples range from the role of the Fifth Estate in the aftermath of the 2004 Madrid train bombing (Box 8.4) to participating in live tweeting of the televised debates between Trump and Biden in the 2016 election (Box 8.5).

The Fifth Estate Is Not a Political Movement

The diffusion of antigovernment protests across the Arab world in the early 2010s led to unexpected uprisings and unseating of such heads of government as Colonel Muammar

Gaddafi in Libya in 2011, leading some to ask if it heralded "democracy's fourth wave" (Howard and Hussain 2013). Wael Ghonim, then a 30-year-old executive from Google, the administrator of an anti-torture page on Facebook, was discussed in Chapter 4 regarding his role in creating content that made a difference in helping organize the first day of protests in Egypt on January 25. He was clearly an actor who approached the ideal type of the Fifth Estate.

Nevertheless, the uprisings that followed failed to bring democracy to the region, and over the decades since the Arab Spring such failures have demonstrated the degree to which online protests could ignite protest or destabilize a government but not necessarily sustain the momentum for change. They could not overpower traditional institutions in nations, which have been repeatedly found to have staying power far more difficult if not impossible to sustain online (Lin and Dutton 2003).

Online actions like protests can be rapidly organized and influential but far more difficult to sustain. In contrast, traditional institutions can sustain activity while protest diminishes (Lin and Dutton 2003). However, the idea that the internet can be used in ways that enhance the informational or communicative power of networked individuals vis-à-vis other individuals and institutions, does not mean that they become more powerful than the legitimate institutions of government and politics of a nation. That would be preposterous.

In fact, the political response to the Arab uprisings and other disruptions, like the 2011 UK or London riots, mentioned in earlier chapters, and the US Capitol riots in 2021, sparked immediate calls for content filtering and social media kill switches, aimed at controlling networked individuals even in liberal democracies, when each set of events was far more complex and multifaceted than being driven by social media. Online social movements as well as the rise of the Fifth Estate can spur people to action but also be undermined by leading authorities to further restrict freedom of expression online and institute surveillance or regulation.

Nevertheless, the Fifth Estate is distinct from these online campaigns and protests, as described in cases in this book. Even democratic grassroots movements and protests are most often led by a few individuals—illustrative of Robert Michel's (1962) "iron law of oligarchy." In the digital age, every protest movement or march has individuals able to source and share their information and viewpoints in ways that can support or challenge the leaders. Just as Haugen can leak about Facebook, individuals in movements can challenge their movement and its leadership. For instance, videos and social media created by participants in the January 6, 2021, Capitol riots were used in bipartisan congressional hearings on the roles of individuals and groups in the event, focusing on former President Trump. The committee released its findings in December 2022, which formally asked the US Department of Justice to bring criminal charges against the former president on a number of referrals, including "inciting, assisting, or aiding and comforting an insurrection" (Select Committee 2022).

Democracy, Autocracy, and Pluralism

Cases in this book provide many concrete examples of Fifth Estate actors shaping politics and society through their effective use of searching online, such as sourcing their own information; creating content, such as blogging or posting a photo; networking with others, such as through hashtags or social networks; collaborating in sharing data and observations, such as in aggregating data about bribes, litter, or the climate; and in some cases leaking inside information, such as about racial or gender biases or even Facebook's engagement strategy (Box 8.1).

However, the Fifth Estate differs from the more traditional perspectives on the internet and democracy. It takes the internet as a significant political resource that is changing patterns of governance across multiple sectors, but it does not view this impact as inevitable or an inherent feature of the technology; rather it is the result of a pattern of use observed over time in particular contexts that can be undermined by other estates. It differs from reinforcement politics by not seeing any single actor or the other four estates controlling the internet and its political use and implications. The existence of a Fifth Estate does tend to ensure a more pluralistic interplay among a more diverse ecology of multiple actors in governance.

Is the internet a tool for a more pluralist democracy, autocracy, or anarchy? I have found that the Fifth Estate enables a more pluralist array of actors in nearly every type of political system. In that sense, it is a force for more pluralistic accountability and governance. However, there is no inevitable or inherent outcome of technical change. Nor is technology determining the rise of the Fifth Estate. The Fifth Estate is enabled and made possible by virtue of networked individuals having sufficient privacy and freedom of expression to strategically use the internet and related digital media, but it is also shaped and constrained by legal, regulatory, cultural, and economic contexts as well as by patterns of use by you and other networked individuals and institutions across the world. It can enhance democratic processes by adding a new set of actors to the pluralist ecology of politics in liberal-democratic societies.

THE FIFTH ESTATE IN AN ECOLOGY OF ACTORS IN PLURALIST DEMOCRACIES

How does the Fifth Estate fit into theoretical perspectives on pluralist democracy? One problem with pluralist theories of democratic politics is the degree of stability assumed in specialized areas of policy and governance, where a pluralist array of multiple actors is focused on an issue. No single actor or group is likely to control the outcome of a particular issue area over time, nor all areas of policymaking or governance, as those whose time, attention, and other resources are focused on one area or issue are not likely to be as focused on others.

However, in the case of many political issues, the dynamics of processes are shaped not only by different actors focused on one issue but also different, complex, and sometimes overlapping arrays of heterogeneous and evolving sets of actors distributed in unpredictable ways over multiple issues. The choices of actors are not fixed and deterministic. Instead, they are more often unpredictable as they emerge, change, and mutually influence each other. They interact in a set of "actor networks" (Crozier and Friedberg 1980) or what Norton Long (1958) called an "ecology of games," where games define different sets of objectives, rules, and players, all of which can change over time (Dutton 1992). In an ecology of games or actor networks, the outcome can open or constrain the strategies available to players of another game. In such ways, heterogeneous actors with diverse aims and objectives can jointly shape outcomes, even though some actors might attempt to move them in alternative directions. This kind of ecology of games is often more descriptive of the actual political processes of decision-making than one in which all participants seek to influence the outcome of a particular issue (Dutton and Zorina 2021).

Like the idea of a Fifth Estate, the ecology of games is a qualitative, sensitizing concept that provides a simple way to capture the complex dynamics that can evolve around multiple actors pursuing a variety of objectives. The Fifth Estate can bring a new set of actors into the political process; they may literally come out of nowhere to shape the outcome of events. Recall the discussion of Schattschneider (1960: 1) in Chapter 2, who argued long ago that a central aspect of politics in a liberal democratic society is that conflict can spread or become "contagious." Politics is like spectator sports, except that in politics the spectators can join in the game at any time and on any side. In that spirit, the outcome of political conflict is shaped by the extent to which the spectators become involved and on what side they choose to join. This dynamic makes the scope of a conflict one of the most important strategies of politics for contestants to control. It also makes the Fifth Estate a potentially influential actor and one difficult to predict or control even in the short term.

In politics, following the logic of an ecology of games or actor networks, if someone is winning, they would want to retain the present scope of conflict and keep all the spectators in the stands. In contrast, in the case of those losing a conflict or left out of the political process, it is in their interest to enlarge the scope of the conflict. They may have little to lose and potentially open the conflict up to more spectators joining their side or switching sides, thereby creating the potential for a more positive outcome.

In considering the dynamics of an evolving ecology of actors, all the strategies of the Fifth Estate come to mind. The internet enables networked individuals to search and source information new to them that could either keep them in the stands or encourage them to join one or another team. They can create new information, such as a video of a police action, that could lead others out of the stands. They can network with others to save a college or, as in the #MeToo #BLM hashtag cases, network in ways that lead individuals to feel supported and more confident to leave the stands to join a team. They can collaborate to share information on pollution or litter that creates new evidence that could cause individuals to switch teams or join the contest.

As an insider, they might leak information, perhaps breaking a rule of the game, which can be done in real life as opposed to board games, in ways that undermine Facebook, or the US government after Manning's or Snowden's leaks, or Russia, in the case of Reality Winner (Chapter 7) or the so-called Surkov leaks (Box 8.6). In such ways, the Fifth Estate can shape the outcomes in politics and government in addition to the most obvious role of the Fifth Estate in holding actors more accountable.

A DIGITAL CULTURAL SHIFT?

There might well be a cultural shift in the digital age that supports the role of a Fifth Estate. Many pundits in the West worry about the rise of populism. But if you ignore the beliefs sometimes associated with populism, such as a right-wing nationalism, and

---

Box 8.6 **The Surkov Leaks**

Russia has been the alleged victims of leaks with the so-called Surkov leaks (Mackinnon and Standish 2020). Vladislav Surkov was appointed in 2012 to oversee the Russian-backed separatist region in Georgia and came to oversee planning and micro-manage communication tied to Russia's hybrid war in eastern Ukraine's pro-Russian separatist regions of Donetsk and Luhansk. He advised and coordinated communication with pro-separatist officials on how to destabilize Ukraine, such as being sent the names of individuals proposed for appointments by the pro-separatist governments. Prior to this position, he had worked in public relations and advertising before becoming a political operative and advisor to Putin in the Kremlin. Over 2,000 emails from his office account from September 2013 to November 2014 were obtained by a Ukrainian hacker group, Cyber Hunter, which passed these on to an open-source journalism investigative group, Inform Napalm, before many were published online in October and November of 2016. Some recipients of these emails validated their authenticity, and a digital forensics lab at the Atlantic Council validated many of the leaked documents and emails, although the Kremlin claimed they were fake. Leaks of Vladislav Surkov's emails provided evidence of covert strategies, such as black PR, that is, malicious disinformation aimed at destroying reputations. The Kremlin was using such strategies to subvert and control developments during the hybrid war in eastern Ukraine and other former Soviet states (Shandra and Seely 2019). Surkov was "sacked" from his post overseeing Ukraine policy by the Kremlin in 2020.

---

look at the indicators of populism, they reflect an anti-elitism and a belief that ordinary people are knowledgeable about policy issues and should have a greater force in governance. In our surveys across seven liberal-democratic nations, we found that most networked individuals held some beliefs in line with the legitimacy of more public involvement in governance. It is not only a perception; the role of the internet has possibly fostered greater confidence in larger proportions of the public that they are more informed and have views on policy that merit consideration (Dutton and Robertson 2021).

I suggest this is a potential cultural change in that it may extend well beyond politics. One career service expert in the UK has noted that talented college graduates of the Generation Z era, having been educated in a digital age, are different (Black 2022). First, they are well-informed about employers having the ability to source their own information about them online. Second, they reject standard applications and questions addressed to all applicants for a position. They expect a dialogue in which they can ask questions about the purposes, work practices, and diversity of the firm or institution as well as whether they will find it intellectually engaging. They feel and are empowered in the digital age of the internet and social media. In this and other ways, the Fifth Estate power shift is not limited to politics and governance.

Society: A Network Power Shift Across All Sectors

Importantly, the concept of the Fifth Estate is not limited to politics and government in its application. Access to the internet enables individuals to enhance their informational and communicative power across every sector of society. As noted in Chapter 3, the internet is what I have called an "experience technology" (Dutton and Shepherd 2006, Dutton and Meyer 2009, Blank and Dutton 2011). As people gain experience with the internet, performing searches for example, they not only gain a learned level of trust but also a personal sense of how it empowers them. Even though I have used the internet since the 1970s, I continue to have frequent experiences with its use that still pleasantly surprise me—leading me to think, "Wow, this is incredible!" Mundane instances build this sense, such as when I could not find one of my old papers in my file cabinets— possibly misfiled, so I searched online and found it in milliseconds over the World Wide Web. Repeated experiences like this bring home the degree to which those with access to the internet and the skills to use it are advantaged—they gain informational and communicative power over those who are not online. And they have resources in some respects quite comparable to those in far more powerful positions of authority.

Consider some of the following ways networked individuals are empowered in every-day life. Individuals can answer questions online or reach out to a friend or colleague anytime from anywhere. In the trivial case of two people enjoying a meal together, a question or argument can be easily resolved, often simply by searching the internet from a mobile smartphone. An individual feeling lost can use their smartphone to find out exactly where they are on a map as well as get directions to where they wish to go. A colleague of mine in the United States has a mobile app his whole family uses to simultane-ously map where everyone is located, which helps coordinate travel to sports and school among other uses. Countless other examples exist of how online access empowers indi-viduals to get information or reach people anywhere at any time.

This book has provided examples of individuals creating new information, such as Martha Payne blogging about her school lunches, or a bystander posting a video of a man being choked while in police custody. Women in the #MeToo movement felt so empowered through networking that more have come forward—they knew others had similar experiences. Mothers in Flint, Michigan, posted photos of tainted brown water pouring from their kitchen taps. During the pandemic, neighbors networked with each other when someone needed information or help, such as with groceries, via a private network set up for their local community. Individuals walking or hiking can collaborate through Planet Patrol to share and aggregate information on litter and plastic pollution. Many more examples exist.

ENVIRONMENTAL MONITORING

Lizzie Carr, the founder of Planet Patrol (Chapter 6), enjoys paddleboarding. She pad-dleboarded as sport for the joy of exploring the canals and waterways of England. It was on these trips that she became aware and increasingly concerned over the plastic and other litter she would see as she traveled. Lizzie began photographing litter and tracking it on an interactive map during a 400-mile journey. She continued using the map to log litter through her mobile phone. She turned this map, which only she could add to and edit, into a prototype of the crowdsourcing app, which became the original version of the app used into 2022. Set up in months, she kept refining and expanding the tracking app over time until she was completely comfortable with its functionality and was able to track litter anywhere.

She found the experience of building this application and using it to track litter to be personally satisfying, but that was not her primary motivation. She sought to create a space for like-minded people to take action and turn frustration and concern into something positive and meaningful. She quickly found that other people wanted to be involved, not only from her local community but also from around the world. In the United States, over 100 billion plastic bags are used each year, equivalent to 300 bags per person, and worldwide, 500 billion to 1 trillion plastic bags are used in one year.[7]

She realized that this crowdsourcing was generating important information and that she could realize her vision of building a base of undeniable evidence to affect policy and practice, especially with the "polluting brands," documenting a significant increase in bags designed for long-term reuse not just single-use plastic. Otherwise, she thought, we "would be litter picking forever."[8] As Lizzie said, "Individuals can immediately see their contribution" appearing on their map. Her own contribution has been acknowledged by the UK's prime minister.

This experience led her to see how she could expand the data collected, such as to start monitoring water pollution in England's waterways. Again, this can spread and engage others who gain a sense of real empowerment. They can do something about the pollution by measuring and reporting and holding those responsible to account.

EXPERTS IN AND OUT OF ACADEMIA, EDUCATION, AND RESEARCH

The internet has long been relevant to education and research (Dutton and Loader 2002). Arguably, the internet pre- and post-pandemic is one of the most important technological innovations in education and academia. But with the COVID-19 pandemic enabling so many educational institutions and research enterprises to continue online, it is a useful time to focus on the role of the internet in this context as one example of another sector reshaped by the Fifth Estate.

Online learning normally follows and reinforces existing institutional structures, such as with the teacher as the primary authority and gatekeeper in a multimedia classroom, virtual learning environment, or a new hybrid classroom that enables a mix of in-person and online access—facilities available to well-funded institutions. However, online learning—especially informal learning—can move beyond the center and boundaries of the classroom or university. Students can and do challenge their teachers by bringing in other authorities and views through their networking with one another and with a variety of experts and knowledge they have sourced themselves. They are empowered. This can be a positive force, better engaging students in the learning process, or a disruption in teaching, depending on how well preparations have been made to harness online learning networks.

Universities with adequate resources are building hybrid classrooms (to simultane-ously reach online and on-campus students), as well as campus grids, digital library col-lections, and institutional repositories to maintain and enhance their productivity and competitiveness vis-à-vis other institutions. Teachers and researchers are also increas-ingly collaborating through internet-enabled networking, often across institutional and national boundaries (Dutton and Jeffreys 2010)—a phenomenon that skyrocketed during the pandemic with Zoom and other video-networking technologies, such as for online learning. But even in-person classrooms can benefit, such as when a teacher can bring experts from industry or academia into the classroom more easily via video links to add interest and authority to a subject. And past the height of the COVID-19 pan-demic, hybrid classrooms have empowered faculty and students who are ill, symptom-atic, or disabled to stay home when it is safer or wiser to do so.

Teachers and researchers—not just their students—are more likely to use an inter-net search engine before they go to their library; as likely to use their personal computer to support network-enabled collaboration as to meet their colleagues in the next office; and tend to post work in an accessible way on websites, such as disciplinary digital repositories and blogs, rather than only in institutional repositories or academic jour-nals, which often have restrictions on access to their content.

Most major universities have developed websites that allow access to the publications of their faculty and staff. These facilitate free online access to other academics when many publications are still behind pay walls of various academic journals. Citations of their faculty's work is a credit to the institution, so much work is focused on ensuring that the work is easily accessible online to read and cite. However, many subject-matter repositories are also valuable in enabling free online access, such as the Social Science Research Network (SSRN), but some of these repositories make it more difficult for academic institutions to track and garner the recognition that comes with the value of their academics' publications. All have merits, but academics and their institutions value online access to their publications, and their availability provides a resource to all estates of the internet realm. Moreover, an increasing number of individual academics and researchers understand the value of being accessible online—it can enhance their informational power in academia.

Freely available social networking sites offer tools for collaboration that could be as, or more, useful to researchers than systems for collaboration in which universities and governments have invested more money, such as institutional repositories. Academics are engaged as participants in their own Fifth Estate, for instance by online mobiliza-tion around both local issues, such as university governance, and more international topics, such as copyrights and open science. However, the major role of the internet in empowering academics and researchers as well as students is in gaining informational and communicative power in learning and research.

The Digital Divide

This book has underscored the degree to which the Fifth Estate does not require uni-versal access to the internet. Once there is a critical mass of users, good things can hap-pen for empowering individuals to search, originate, network, collaborate, and leak information in ways that enhance their informational or communicative power. They are not voting on candidates for office or public policy but generating opportunities for more diverse information and communication networks. But as you can see in this chapter, the empowerment of networked individuals is not a neutral outcome. True, a Fifth Estate can help hold institutions and the powerful to account and this can be for the good of the public at large. However, it is also true that the empowerment of networked individuals comes with access to the internet and related digital media, which is not distributed equally—it is distributed unequally because of differences shaped by wealth, education, and geography.

In education, as just discussed, access to the internet enabled many institutions to maintain and persevere through the pandemic, but those individuals and institutions without access were severely disadvantaged. This applies across all sectors of society. The fact that the internet enables networked individuals to gain informational and communicative power undermines the power of those on the wrong side of the digital divide—those without the devices, skills, and other resources necessary to use and exploit the technology. More than half of the world is online, and billions more are likely to be online soon. However, at least a third of the world is not online and has no opportunity to experience or gain directly from the informational or communicative power that could be enabled by searching, originating, networking, collaborating, or leaking information independently and through devices at their fingertips.

9

Threats to the Fifth Estate

Major problems threaten the vitality of the Fifth Estate. These threats include the predominance of a media-centric focus on new technologies, the increasing propensity to frame implications of the internet around harms, the rise of big tech and platformization of the internet, the surge of regulatory governance imperatives, and the internet's geopolitical fragmentation. Reasons why each is real and substantial are discussed in this chapter, and examples are provided to make them more concrete.

A Media-Centric Focus on New Technologies

One central aspect of this book has been to move away from "media-centric" perspectives, central to many perspectives on social media regulation (Napoli 2019), to focus on the identification of the different actors in the internet realm. There are the diverse members of the first three estates, the Fourth Estate of the press, and the Fifth Estate. Likewise, networked individuals are a mix of different actors, including journalists, experts, witnesses, elected officials, candidates, advocates, consultants, and more, but also what might be called malicious users. In turn, malicious users might include vigilantes, the mob, cybercriminals, producers of malware, computational propagandists, and malicious hackers, trolls, online bullies, and more. This assortment of actors and networks compose complex ecologies, what some emerging researchers have called an "assemblage" that builds on the social shaping of technologies and related work on actor networks (Müller 2015).

Technologies are clearly part of the ecology of actors online, but many new media regulatory initiatives take what is arguably too narrow a focus on technologies, such as social media, or user-generated content (UGC), and internet platforms, rather than the people who use, produce, or regulate them. Even the Facebook whistleblower Frances Haugen (Box 8.1) makes a point of her love of social media while focusing her concern on its engagement algorithm, a more specific technology. A focus on technology is understandable given the history of the regulation of radio and television, which focused on one too many broadcasters—broadcast regulation. The producers of content were a few licensed or otherwise regulated broadcast organizations. Regulators could oversee and regulate broadcast media, often by focusing on instances that generated consumer complaints or that were patently offensive or otherwise outside the remit of the broadcaster.

The Fifth Estate. William H. Dutton, Oxford University Press. © Oxford University Press 2023.
DOI: 10.1093/oso/9780190688363.003.0010

In the digital world, every user (there are 5 billion in 2022) is potentially a content producer. Contributions from a small portion could enable more freedom of expression and valuable contributions to social and political accountability, such as illustrated by the Fifth Estate. But effective regulation of this new and more complex ecology of actors requires a very different model, such as one based on identifying and regulating malicious users and producers, rather than regulation of the new media as if we were back in the age of print newspapers and broadcasting. To illustrate some aspects of this more complex ecology of actors, it is useful to look closely at the Cambridge Analytica case. It was a scandal generally attributed to Facebook, but that press coverage was an oversimplification of a complex case involving a larger assemblage of multiple actors that share responsibility. (Readers familiar with this case may nevertheless appreciate the following effort to dig into this complexity that illustrates the complex assemblage or ecology of the actors tied to the scandal.)

THE CASE OF CAMBRIDGE ANALYTICA

The Cambridge Analytica scandal erupted in the wake of an insider at Cambridge Analytica, Chris Wyle, leaking information about how this political consulting firm used Facebook data to support the 2016 Trump presidential campaign. The allegations generated calls for greater regulation of social media (Lapowski 2018, Rosenberg et al. 2018). It has been called Facebook's "massive data breach."[1]

However, the scandal oversimplified and exaggerated Facebook's role while failing to address the role of other actors, including the whistleblower, Chris Wylie, connected by a complicated ecology of decisions with an array of individuals across multiple institutions and companies. To paraphrase John Ehrlichman in 1971, speaking with President Nixon, going after a whistleblower is "a little like trying to catch a skunk," as everyone ends up smelling bad (Brinkley and Nichter 2014: 333).

This is certainly applicable in this case. Journalists' efforts to sort out exactly who did what and when have created conflicting accounts that have changed over time. Nevertheless, the scandal involved many actors beyond Facebook and issues beyond security, such as research ethics. Table 9.1 lists the actors as simply as possible, by entity, individuals, and their role(s). The case clarifies how the scandal had less to do with social media as a malicious technology than it being the product of a far wider set of actors engaged in a set of activities that lacked transparency.

A pivotal role was played by a data scientist with a neuroscience lab at the University of Cambridge, Alexandr Kogan. He was a Moldovan-born American lecturer in the university's department of psychology. After a postgraduate degree at UC Berkeley, he earned a PhD from Hong Kong University. Kogan was one of the investigators of a big data initiative spanning multiple departments of the university.

In his university, colleagues were working with Facebook likes and other data to predict personal attributes (Kosinski et al. 2013). Kogan established the Prosociality and Well-being Laboratory (the CPW Lab) in the university, during and after 2013, collaborating on the collection and analysis of Facebook user data for academic research.[2] He used a Facebook app he helped develop, the CPW Lab app, called "This Is Your Digital Life," to collect personal data from individual Facebook users, who logged onto his app, and answered questions tied to personality scales.

Table 9.1 **Actors Involved in the Cambridge Analytica Story**

Entity	Units/Individuals	Role
Cambridge University, Dept. of Psychology	Aleksandr Kogan (married name Spectre)	Lecturer since 2012
Aleksandr Kogan	Established Cambridge University's Prosociality and Well-Being Lab (CPW Lab)	Research creating CPW Lab app to collect Facebook data, e-personality data set
Aleksandr Kogan and colleagues	Established Global Science Research (GSR) in 2014, not affiliated with Cambridge University	Consultant to SCL, parent to Cambridge Analytica, creating GSR Lab App, repurposed CPW Lab app to collect anonymized Facebook data
Institutional Review Board, Cambridge University	Reviewing and approving all Cambridge University research, involving human participants	Rejected 2015 application for ethical approval to use data collected by GSR for Kogan's academic research
Eunoia Technologies	Chris Wylie's company, 2014–2017	Data science, consulting, guiding, and advising Kogan, obtained complete access to the GSR data set
SCL Group	Set up SCL Elections Limited	Parent company to Cambridge Analytica
SCL Elections Limited	Chris Wylie hired as part-time intern on student visa	Set up Cambridge Analytica
Cambridge Analytica (not affiliated with Cambridge University)	Alexander Nix (CEO), Steve Bannon (VP), Rebecca Mercer (board member), and Chris Wylie	Established project with Kogan's GSR to create data set for a targeted digital ad campaign
Mercers	Robert and Rebecca Mercer	Financial support for GSR Facebook data mining
Qualtrics	Staff and systems for providing email samples and fielding online research	Paid for emails for survey by GSR, which collected psychometric data and permission to access Facebook accounts

(continued)

Table 9.1 **Continued**

Entity	Units/Individuals	Role
Facebook	Thousands of users who agreed to allow GSR to access their accounts	GSR mined Facebook accounts for data to collate with psychometric data collected by surveys
2016 Trump Campaign	Steve Bannon	Aimed (probably failed) to set up targeted ad campaign based on psychometric profiles
Peripherally Involved		
St. Petersburg University	Aleksandr Kogan	Visiting lectures, promoted the use of psychometric modeling techniques
The Observer, The Guardian, New York Times	Chris Wylie leaks to *The Observer* (2017), *The Guardian* (2018), and the *New York Times*	Anonymous whistleblower (2017) then publicly (2018)

But to get to this app, individuals were recruited via email to complete a survey that generated data based on questions designed to provide indicators of a person's psychological and personality profile. Importantly, the survey enabled respondents to approve the use of their Facebook accounts by the research team to gather information, including information about their "friends." A link on the login page to the app outlined the terms and conditions of their use of this app, which indicated that the data would be used for "academic purposes" (Kogan 2018). The lab drew on the data harvested from Facebook to create a myPersonality data set. Kogan seemed to exaggerate the power of data such as this to provide insights on the behavior of individuals through a few lectures he gave at St. Petersburg University and tried to develop a project there that was like what he developed with Cambridge Analytica (Cohen and Ilyushina 2018).

In 2014, the research changed course after Aleksandr Kogan was introduced to Chris Wiley, who worked for SCL Elections Limited, a parent company to Cambridge Analytica, both of which have since been closed.[3] Chris Wiley described himself as a data scientist and was interested in acquiring the myPersonality data set developed by Cambridge researchers. One of these colleagues objected to sharing this data because it was collected for academic purposes. Therefore, Kogan (2018) created a private company, called Global Science Research (GSR), that was set up as organizationally separate from his university. This would allow him to receive private funding to collect more data in ways analogous to what he collected with his colleagues at the university.

SCL agreed to fund GSR to cover the costs of Qualtrics, a reputable survey research platform, in collecting new data, enabling them to offer respondents a few dollars as an incentive to answer their survey. Two rounds of surveys were posted online through

Qualtrics, for which Qualtrics was paid "about $800,000" (Kogan 2018), which would have allowed the firm to provide and incentivize up to 300,000 respondents, with as many as 270,000 downloading the app (Schotz 2018). The Qualtrics survey obtained personality and demographic data, and one item on the survey led respondents to the CPW Lab app, that was renamed the GSR app, from where they would log into their Facebook account and be presented with GSR's terms and conditions, which included granting GSR "an irrevocable, sublicenceable, assignable, non-exclusive, transferrable and worldwide license to use your data and contribution for any purpose" (Kogan 2018). After respondents clicked "OKAY," they were returned to the Qualtrics survey. This allowed survey (Qualtrics) data to be merged with social media (Facebook) data collected through the GSR app to permit personality profiles, for example, to be related to the use of Facebook, such as pages liked, which could be used to find correlations with different personality traits.

Given these terms and conditions, and his trust in Chris Wiley, who dictated the terms and conditions, Kogan (2008) was convinced it was legal to collect this information and share it with SCL. SCL was given demographic information, personality profiles, and a "limited" set of page likes. However, GSR provided the data to a related company, Eunoia (owned and set up by Chris Wiley) along with a similar data set that also included all page likes. Kogan also shared an "anonymized" copy of the GSR data with his CPW Lab and researchers at the University of Toronto.[4] These data sets may or may not have made their way to Cambridge Analytica to provide a basis for data collection and a social media campaign by the political consulting firm. Crucially, it was enabled by GPS, which was led by an academic researcher, working in a consulting capacity, and Chris Wiley, who established his own company, Eunoia Technologies.

Wylie was a bright 27-year-old entrepreneur. He orchestrated this research collaboration and sharing, but nevertheless he became disenchanted with the enterprise while listening to focus groups of voters at Cambridge Analytica. This led him to blow the whistle on the use of Facebook data by Cambridge Analytica, claiming that it helped shape the 2016 Trump campaign.

Kogan has said that it was never his intent for his research on the happiness and well-being of Facebook users to be deployed as a political tool.[5] Moreover, he argued in hearings, the data collected would not have been useful in targeting voters because it had little predictive power at the individual level.[6] As Kogan himself argued, it would have been far better for Cambridge Analytica to have simply purchased Facebook ads, for which it would have been unnecessary to collect any Facebook data. However, principals at Cambridge Analytica and in the Trump team, such as Steve Bannon, seemed to have been sold on the hype surrounding the use of psychometrics in targeting voters. Kogan claimed he was a "scapegoat," and he was not the only actor although a key person in a larger ecology of actors who contributed to this debacle (Weaver 2018).

Facebook has strict guidelines outlining what can and can't be done with user data,[7] which appears to have been violated by passing the personal data collected by GSR to Eunoia Technologies, Cambridge Analytica, and others. This is what would be called sensitive personal information on what is alleged to be thousands if not millions of Americans, only a fraction of whom might have granted Kogan permission to use it for a political campaign. In this respect, the process raised ethical and transparency issues.

Facebook may have permitted Kogan to collect data for research at the university, but this is clearly not the case for his private company, separate from the university, and for a political consulting firm. Here the researcher is disclosing personal data without the informed authorization of Facebook or the users, as even those survey respondents who authorized this collection were not informed about its use for a campaign. Moreover, Facebook argues that once it learned of this data set and its use, it insisted that the data be deleted—which appears not to have been done until a major lawsuit was settled. Andrew Bosworth, a vice president at Facebook, reported that the scandal was a "non-event" but noted that Cambridge Analytica had been "shopping an old Facebook dataset that they were supposed to have deleted" (Kobie 2020).

With respect to Facebook, in its early years, having been launched in 2004 when Facebook was a cool innovation, it was a gold mine for network and internet researchers who could, for example, get permission to retrieve users' social networks—their friends and friends of friends to see a social graph of how they are linked with one another—for research. Similarly, researchers teaming with Facebook could experiment with tweaking features of Facebook pages to study certain effects, such as shaping voter turnout (Corbyn 2012). However, as the company and its reach grew, Facebook and researchers quickly became aware of privacy and other ethical issues of harvesting such data and exploiting the power of the network for experimentation that could be deceptive, leading the company to progressively restrict its use for research.

The complex ecology of actors in the Cambridge Analytica case illustrates why the protection of personal data is a difficult issue in the digital age. If many of the claims described in the press occurred, then it would have violated rules set by Facebook on the use of these data and the university's guidelines on academic research, which would have clear limits on how personal data about individuals is gathered, used, and shared. Who had or used the data remains clouded in a virtual shell game involving multiple companies and their representatives. That said, in describing the scandal, the *New York Times* simply indicated that Trump's "consultants exploited the Facebook data of millions."[8] The UK's Information Commissioner's Office said their models were "exaggerated and ineffective" (Afifi-Sabet 2020), which is undoubtedly the case. Whatever your view of Facebook, this was a major oversimplification of the case by the press and pundits that had a dramatic impact on perceptions of the harms tied to social media.

Much can be done to demystify big data analytics and help internet and social media users to be more aware of how data is used, by whom, and for what research. Moreover, cases like this provide a greater impetus for ethical and institutional review boards in universities to bring their policies and practices into the digital age. Many university review boards have been anchored in medical research, where personal data is more obvious, and some do not fully understand how digital data on the internet, social media, and the coming Internet of Things can create privacy and ownership issues, such as in the context of computational analysis. Likewise, review boards need to fully understand the ways that academic institutions can connect the potentially complex relationships between university staff and their outside entrepreneurial roles that raise conflicts of interest and blur the boundaries of the institution.

Researchers need to understand the social and ethical issues of personal data as well as they understand the algorithms and visualization of data. Increasingly, computer and data scientists are social scientists. And as this case makes clear, Facebook as well as all the internet and social media platforms should focus more attention on ensuring that the researchers, who seek to use data, are not just smart data scientists, but ethically aware and responsible researchers.[9]

Framing Harms: The Mean World Online Syndrome

The internet can not only empower civic-minded individuals in ways that support the public interest but also empower malicious individuals who can undermine the public in numerous ways. There is a veritable litany of risks and harms that come with using the internet. However, they are not inevitable and can be addressed by strategies of all the estates of the internet realm to follow pro-social norms and govern the internet and social media in socially and politically responsible ways. The fear is that concerns over the risks and harms attributed to the internet will lead to inappropriate actions that undermine the benefits as well as the harms—throwing the proverbial baby out with the bathwater.

As in many other areas of technology and society, threats can be exaggerated or overly hyped (Fazal 2021, Mueller 2021). For example, there is a stream of media research on "cultivation theory" that argued that mass media coverage can cultivate a disproportionate level of fear among the public (Gerber et al. 1986), what the late George Gerbner, a major originator of this theory, sometimes called the "mean world syndrome" (Morgan 2012: viii). For example, longitudinal study of the public in Philadelphia found that viewing local television, which often focused on crime, was associated with increased fear of crime—leading the public to believe that their streets were more dangerous than they were as based on declining crime rates (Romer et al. 2006).

This mean world syndrome might well have parallels in moral panics over news media coverage of online harms to individuals and society that are attributed to the internet and particularly social media. Panic over these harms arises from genuine, serious concerns being misunderstood, overblown, and exaggerated in a narrative that has begun to define all debate over the internet and social media. Each harm can be real—it encapsulates serious issues—but each needs to be tempered and balanced by empirical understandings of the actual harms as well as the actual benefits of the internet and social media to children and adults across the world.

Most generally, social implications of the internet and social media—particularly UGC—have been increasingly framed as harms. To be fair, for decades, scholars and pundits have focused on the benefits of internet adoption, with the major concern focused on the risks tied to inequities resulting from digital divides in access to the internet and related digital media (van Dijk 2019). The very idea of an industrial to postindustrial information society (Bell 1973) or network society (Castells 1996, 2001) is focused on the need to transform education, employment, economies, and culture to adapt to change in technology and society around the growing centrality of information and communication to control, build on, and revive industrial and agricultural economies. Individuals, communities, and nations left behind in the information/network/ digital age will be disadvantaged, as in Pippa Norris's (2001) concept of the "information poor." Concerns over digital divides and inequalities have continued. Major efforts have been undertaken in the United States at federal and state levels as well as other nations across the world to get access to the internet and associated skills to the minority of individuals and communities of the information poor on the wrong side of the digital divide.

However, in parallel, the framing of the social implications of the internet is being reshaped by a powerful narrative around the harms associated with the internet and the related technologies that underpin them, such as UGC and the design of algorithms. You can see this most dramatically in the case of the UK's debate over the regulation of new media, but it is not limited to the UK, as New Zealand's Harmful Digital Communications Act illustrates.[10]

THE UK CASE

From the early years of the internet, the UK was among the leading nations to support an open, global internet, such as by explicitly not placing internet regulations among the responsibilities of a newly created independent regulator of telecommunications and broadcasting, the Office of Communications (Ofcom), when founded in 2002.[11] However, concerns over privacy led the UK to create a data protection commissioner as early as 1984, which later became a function of the Information Commissioner's Office (ICO). The UK also established a process in collaboration with the Internet Watch Foundation (IWF) for the telecommunications provider to filter or remove web pages deemed threatening to child safety.[12]

The protection of children from harm was widely accepted as a legitimate rationale for internet filtering in the UK and worldwide. While largely limited to its explicit purpose, child protection was an exception to a broader perspective in support of innovation and diffusion of the internet. That said, child protection always carried the risk of being used as a wedge issue for wider internet filtering and censorship (Nash 2014). However, in the early 2000s, when Ofcom was established, internet regulation was largely limited to privacy and child safety. Only later would it be framed within a model for regulating cyber harms.

The risks of harms were the principal motivation behind the UK's Online Safety Bill—safety from harms. In fact, it was originally developed as an Online Harms White Paper (DCMS 2019), which transformed into an Online Safety Bill.[13] Facing early criticism, the bill's authors nearly eliminated the word "harm" not only from the title but also from its 230 pages. Nevertheless, the Safety Bill stated that regulation of the internet and social media—particularly media based on UGC

> must take into account the likely impact of the number of users of a service, and its functionalities, on the level of risk of harm to individuals from illegal content, content that is harmful to children and content that is harmful to adults disseminated by means of the service. (DCMS 2021: 126)

In addition to illegal content, the Safety Bill required the regulator to focus on any content "harmful" to anyone—children or adults. Over many revisions, a controversial phrase concerning the policing of "legal but harmful" content was dropped from the bill.

Box 9.1 **Harms Covered by the Online Harms White Paper**

Harms with a clear definition: child sexual exploitation and abuse; terrorist content and activity; organized immigration crime; modern slavery; extreme pornography; revenge pornography; harassment and cyberstalking; hate crime; encouraging or assisting suicide; incitement of violence; sale of illegal goods/services, such as drugs and weapons (on the open internet); content illegally uploaded from prisons; and sexting of indecent images by those under 18 (creating, possessing, copying, or distributing indecent or sexual images of children and young people under the age of 18).

Harms with a less clear definition: cyberbullying and trolling, extremist content and activity, coercive behavior, intimidation, disinformation, violent content, advocacy of self-harm, promotion of female genital mutilation (FGM).

Underage exposure to legal content: children accessing pornography, children accessing inappropriate material (including under 13 using social media and under 18 using dating apps; excessive screentime).

Harms outside of the scope of the Department for Digital, Culture, Media & Sport: privacy and surveillance, which were under the responsibility of the UK's Information Commissioner.

Source: DCMS (2019, Table 1)

So, what could be harmful in this broad sense? The original White Paper enumerated the many harms of concern (Box 9.1). Some are almost unarguable, such as incitement to violence, but some or most are problematic, such as excessive screentime. Moreover, the original White Paper noted that this initial list is not "exhaustive or fixed" and that the regulator could add harms as "new technologies, content, and online activities" arise. This created such an exceptionally broad and open-ended agenda for regulators that the paper generated criticism.

You—particularly if you are an American—might read this list of harms to be controlled by a regulator as unfeasible because many imply levels of censorship that would be clearly unconstitutional in the United States, given the First Amendment protections of freedom of speech. Likewise, to know what users are saying and reading online would most likely involve levels of surveillance that would fall afoul of safeguards on privacy. Moreover, it is not clear exactly how some of the harms would be defined and successfully regulated, and whether the actual harms are seriously exaggerated. This chapter will return to the Online Safety Bill in discussing regulation while considering a few specific examples.

DISINFORMATION: A CASE OF EXAGGERATING HARM

Disinformation is one harm that became a major focus of debate since the 2016 US presidential election and the 2016 UK–EU membership referendum (Brexit). Inevitably, discussions about stopping disinformation falter when turning to who determines what is true or false. Should a government official, an intelligence agency, an independent regulator, a judge, a social media platform, or someone else determine what is disinformation? Also, are we sure that the levels and consequences of disinformation are not exaggerated?

There is disinformation—including fake news, misinformation, conspiracy theories, and more—online. In fact, in the early days of the internet, most of the content online was viewed as rubbish—a garbage heap. That is why search engines were invented—to find the needles in this proverbial haystack. Moreover, search engines work very well for most users most of the time (discussed in Chapter 3).

However, empirical research has shown that users themselves are more critical of information than is claimed by many pundits and academics, who ignore, for example, the degree to which individuals use the media, the internet, search, and other tools to sort out what is informative and what is misinformation (Dutton et al. 2017, 2019). In fact, as noted in previous chapters (see Chapters 3 and 8), people who are interested in politics tend to go to over four sources of information, where only one of which is going online. Moreover, when they go online, they visit over four sources of information online (Dutton et al. 2019).

Consider those search practices in relation to the most prominent claims. Some have claimed that search engines distort what internet users see and what they don't see by creating "filter bubbles" that feed users more of what they like (Pariser 2011). Others claim that due to a human bias to find information confirming rather than challenging our views, this confirmatory bias leads social media users to network with only like-minded individuals and disconnect from those individuals and content they do not agree with, putting themselves in a virtual "echo chamber" (Sunstein 2017).

The likelihood is low that an individual would be literally or technically trapped in a filter bubble, since they read, discuss, and view material that goes beyond online sources. It is also unlikely that they would be living in an online echo chamber when they visit multiple sources online and seldom curate their social media around their political views as opposed to their friends and family. If they are trapped in either way, it is less likely that it is due to internet, social media, or search algorithms than to the user creating their own filter bubble or echo chamber by ignoring information or people who disagree with their views. For example, in the highly polarized politics of Hong Kong, my colleagues and I found that individuals have tended to disconnect from those with whom they disagree on key issues, such as the status of Hong Kong (Zhang et al. 2022), but this is not at all a worldwide phenomenon and misses other key "uses and gratifications" that explain why people use social media, such as surveillance and to kill time (Blumler and Katz 1974). Researchers have focused on the uses and gratifications sought by those using "political media," but social media are not primarily used for politics (Holbert 2017).

Arguably, there has probably been no time in the world that people have been able to get access to as huge a diversity of information than today. It is not the fault of the internet, social media, or search that some individuals might choose to ignore information. In fact, the opposite is more likely to be the case. A major collaboration on the factors shaping a person's willingness to be vaccinated during the COVID-19 pandemic found that in the UK and US, controlling for demographic characteristics and other explanatory factors, the level of internet use was positively correlated with the number of health media used, which was in turn positively related to a willingness to be vaccinated.[14]

In addition, how would one address disinformation? Internet and social media companies are not public service broadcasters, like the BBC, even though many would like them to behave as if they were. But then they would lose their claim to being neutral intermediaries and be subject to litigation in ways that a newspaper or other edited publications would face if they published false or libelous information. Through online search, networked individuals can access millions of sources anywhere in the world at any time, even though they also can access their local newspaper and broadcasters more easily than in the print era.

Of course, there have been some dramatic disinformation campaigns, such as the post-February 24, 2022, Kremlin narrative of a "special military operation" in Ukraine as opposed to the West's view—Russia invaded a sovereign nation unprovoked. But if a nation seeks to block one or another narrative, as Russia did, then it is likely to undermine the public's trust in the censor. But this is Russian governmental censorship and disinformation, not an internet filter bubble or a social media induced echo chamber.

Harms Drive Key Research Areas

The exaggeration of issues such as disinformation often stems from a failure to conduct or draw from empirical research that incorporates systematic study of internet users. In this respect, the concerns raised over specific harms should provide a basis for programs of research on the social implications of the internet and social media along with specific applications. The harms delineated by the White Paper (Box 9.1) could be addressed through multidisciplinary research in order that policy draws less on anecdotal evidence and extrapolations of impacts based on the nature of the technology. While I've noted research on how people get information about politics, a few examples beyond disinformation might help illuminate broad areas for research on the actual implications of these technologies that can move the discussion of harms beyond conventional wisdom, anecdotal cases, and technically deterministic forecasts.

Media Use: The Allocation of Time

The Harms White Paper (DCMS 2019) identifies screentime as a potential harm.[15] Everyone who has been annoyed with a child or friend looking at their mobile phone rather than who they are with in person can tell their own stories. That said, in the case of children as well as adults, time online is most often used to reinforce relationships offline. The internet and social media do not isolate individuals. Instead, they tend to reinforce community (Hampton and Wellman 2021). Moreover, in this worry over time online, many seem to have forgotten about television. While time spent watching broadcast television has declined, in the UK almost a third of waking hours are spent watching TV and streaming television and films.[16] Serious scholars have focused on conceptualizing what some have called the "attention economy" and far more needs to be focused on how people allocate their attention (Williams 2020).

While the internet and social media might have overcome many earlier scarcities, such as space in newspapers, numbers of TV channels, and space on bookshelves, it has made our time a scarcer resource. How much time are people across social and cultural categories spending on different media and how is this changing over time, for better or worse? Some platforms might report your screentime, but many individuals use three or more devices, making aggregate use difficult to gauge. Likewise, a few minutes spent emailing friends might be more important time than the hours watching streamed movies. However, systematic empirical study of adolescents has found that being disconnected from the online world could be more harmful to their well-being of adolescents than even heavy social media use, such as evidenced in lower levels of self-esteem (Hampton and Shin 2022). This should give pause to any panic over screentime. That said, research on time allocation has been a major issue of sociology and other social sciences, and more work in this area is valuable to keep up with the complexities introduced by new technologies and changing media practices.

Human Rights: Privacy, Freedom of Expression, and Anonymity

Privacy has been one of the earliest and enduring foci of social research on computers and the internet. Yet threats to privacy and related human rights, such as freedom of expression and anonymity, are becoming more complex and multifaceted and therefore more difficult to track and research (Diebert et al. 2008, MacKinnon 2012). Anonymity is arguably essential to protect freedom of expression, but some level of anonymity might need to be sacrificed to protect networked individuals from harmful content, for example. There is almost universal acceptance of privacy and freedom of expression as an abstract value in the networked society, but there are also powerful critiques of policy and practice suggesting that these values are being lost in the rise of a surveillance society (Brin 1998) and surveillance capitalism (Zuboff 2019, also Rifkin 2000). Considering the central framing of online harms, these issues of freedom, privacy, and anonymity need to be examined in the context of concerns over hate speech, cybercrime, and online vigilantism—how can these public values be saved while addressing these various concerns over harms?

Powerful arguments have been made in opposition to legislating against and censoring hate speech, as censorship can result in more harm to freedom and equality than the harm it is intended to regulate (Strossen 2018). Indeed, initiatives to regulate the internet and social media to reduce harms are likely to undermine the key values of privacy, freedom, and anonymity that have supported the internet's vitality. An alternative would be for young people to be empowered along with their peers to tag, respond, and counteract online hate speech, completely in the spirit of the Fifth Estate.[17]

In the process of years of discussion over the Online Safety Bill, which continues as I write, it has been more focused on protecting the safety of children online and dropped some of its most controversial measures, such as dealing with legal but harmful content, but has remained tied to a "duty of care" mandate, discussed later in this chapter, that will threaten tech companies with huge fines if they fail to enforce child protection standards, which they have "yet to define" (Criddle and Murgia 2022), which is likely to lead to disproportionate levels of censorship. Some late amendments being considered go beyond parental controls and age verification, each of which raise complex issues of enforcement, to include the incorporation of the means to hold the senior executives of platforms criminally liable, following regulatory initiatives in Ireland, if they fail to protect children online.[18] Critics of the bill see this as further incentivizing senior executives of these firms, who do not want to serve jail sentences, to institute "general monitoring and over-removal of content."[19] Moreover, the bill is expected to permit the regulator to order tech companies to install yet-undeveloped software that will permit them to de-encrypt and find inappropriate material (Criddle and Murgia 2022), which suggests major risks for privacy and surveillance online.

Political Implications: Polarization, Populism, and Empowerment

As the internet and social media have become more widely used and increasingly linked to politics, as illustrated throughout this book, a variety of themes have risen around their political implications. Most often, academics, journalists, and political commentators have blamed the internet and social media for apparent trends toward greater polarization and the rise of populism (Howell and Moe 2020, Tumber and Waisbord 2021).

But as argued in this book, the rise of networked individuals with a greater sense of empowerment is not necessarily a sign of populism. Our own research found it to be an outcome enabled by the internet and social media—feeling more informed and knowledgeable about issues—rather than some resurgence of a radical ideology (Dutton and Robertson 2021). However, political pathologies, trends, and problems will need to be studied increasingly in the context of the use and impact of digital media, communication, and information technologies and its substitution and complementarities with traditional media and communication systems.

As you can see from the Cambridge Analytica case, many of the issues tied to social media result from assemblages of actors that range far beyond the executives of the social media firms. Moreover, the new media enable huge benefits as well as harms, but benefits are brushed aside by a focus on the harms of new media that have no agency in themselves. An algorithm might be blamed for a problem, but algorithms are computer programs that evolve over years shaped by multiple individuals and processes in ways that they are often "incomprehensible programs" (Weizenbaum 1976). But while becoming incomprehensible over time, they often work very well, for example in the case of constantly evolving search algorithms through machine learning.

A focus on new media technology is as likely to undermine the benefits as well as the harms associated with it unless it is systematically addressed and studied in terms of how particular actors have used it for malicious reasons or for good reasons with unintentionally harmful outcomes. It is most often not malicious software—malware—but valuable software used for malicious purposes by bad actors. The focus needs to be more on the actors than the technology, which I return to in the final chapter.

Big Tech and the Platformization of the Internet

A third threat has arisen from the changing architecture of the internet, which has transformed dramatically since its inception. For example, the web was designed for a globally decentralized internet with intelligence and content at the endpoints—the websites on millions of internet servers around the world. However, the rise of popular platforms has been one of the most dramatic trends online. Technically, a server that is used by an internet provider to support access by their users or customers is an internet platform. There are different kinds of platforms, distinguished by how applications are developed for the platform's users, but they tend to be highly scalable.

Think of a blog or website of your own, for example. It is so easy to use that you can post content to be read by only a few people, if anyone. That said, it will cost no more if it is read by hundreds or thousands. The costs to platforms, which are great in supporting staff and technology, declines per user or reader dramatically as the number of users increases. Economies of scale are important in media industries generally, but online they are an even more dramatic engine of development, given that they have a more global application that includes more producers, such as yourself.

The nine tech giants—Google, Amazon, Apple, IBM, Microsoft, and Facebook in the United States, and Baidu, Alibaba, and Tencent in China—are powerful (Webb 2019). There are many search engines, but Google has a 92% share of the search engine market, with the second most popular search engine far behind it.[20] With respect to social media, just over a third (35.6%) of the global population uses Facebook, but that is composed of nearly three-fourths (71.3%) of people in North America and about two-thirds of people in Latin America/Caribbean (69.5%) and across Europe (62.4%).[21]

On October 4, 2021, someone at Facebook made a single mistake in updating the company's Border Gateway Protocol (BGP) records, which instruct computers how to find its various sites online, like Facebook.com. The error left computers around the globe not knowing where to find sites, causing users worldwide to be unable to communicate with one another or use any Facebook applications, including Facebook's other media platforms, Instagram and WhatsApp.[22] Particularly for many internet users in low-income and emerging economies, where Facebook is essentially their internet, the scale of Facebook could be experienced, if only for a few hours of no access.

The flip side of this concern over concentration in the industry growing because of such economies of scale is the degree to which companies like Meta (the Facebook company) and Alphabet (the Google company) can control how much of the world experiences the internet, for better or worse (Wu 2011). On the bright side, such economies of scale enable these companies to provide Facebook to users for free, but most often balanced by an agreement that their data can be used to support services or passed on to other providers. While this entrepreneurial approach to data extends internet and social media access to many who might not otherwise be able to afford its use, it has a dark side. Many critics view this data surrendered by users for their free use of the internet as exploiting the personal information of the user, including where they go online, for the profit of the companies—what has been called "surveillance capitalism" (Zuboff 2019). In this instance and others, a more competitive industry is in the public's interest as it could help mitigate some issues tied to the big tech platforms, giving users more choice.

For the Fifth Estate, this dual effect is real. It means there are more networked individuals who can use the internet and social media to gain informational and communicative power. At the same time, it puts a few big tech firms in a position from which they can know who does what online—in a position from which surveillance is also a real potential. For years, the potential for the effective surveillance of individual internet users seemed infeasible given the levels of use worldwide. As one example, over 500 hours of video are uploaded to YouTube every minute! How could any company or government agency track individual users given such huge levels of activity online?

However, issues such as privacy need to anticipate future potentials and not only what is currently possible. In that respect, with advances in artificial intelligence (AI), which all the big nine tech giants are developing, the potential for more fine-grained mass surveillance is becoming increasingly feasible. In the course of time this could undermine the anonymity of networked individuals and therefore diminish freedom of expression and the vitality of the Fifth Estate, which depends on networked individuals feeling safe in searching, creating, and sharing content.

The increasing dominance of a few social media giants could also undermine the freedom of social media through the design of its software—software that limits the freedom of—that is, the control of—its users (Stallman 2015, Wu 2011). On the one hand, any software tends to exert some control by defining what users need to do to use it. However, control can be advanced by making the creation of content far more restricted than at present, such as by incentivizing and pushing networked individuals to point and click and like but not truly write or create original content. Instead of writing a blog about a problem, you might simply use a sad emoji to express your thoughts. In such ways, the free, open, and interactive online media might become more like other consumer technologies, like the television or radio, with far less UGC, one of the principal new potentials of the internet and social media. It was the limited interactivity allowed on one-to-many broadcast media that inspired the development of new media, so this freedom should not be lost without a clear understanding of its social and political implications.

In the early days of the internet, blogging was one of the most prominent avenues for UGC to be produced. Platforms like WordPress enabled users without programming skills to create their own blogs quite easily with choices of backgrounds, fonts, and features, such as the addition of photos and videos. The transition to micro-blogging, as an additional option, reduced the number of characters expected for a blog. This might have made blogging easier and attracted far more people to blog, but it also moved some from blogging more substantial content to tweeting—because it was easier and less time consuming. Of course, a tweet can be linked to a video or an encyclopedia of information, but on balance, the micro-blog has probably reduced longer forms of blogging. These issues are not just academic—they are critical to the vitality of a Fifth Estate.

Another problematic aspect of all the platforms is the major role that critical events and fads can play. Fads have moved many people from blogging to messaging on social media, and from one social media platform to another. Events can have major impacts. Take the impact of Elon Musk, the pioneer in electric vehicles and private sector space ventures, on Twitter. Musk's tweets about Twitter and his rocky effort to first buy, then not buy, then to acquire the company shaped perceptions and the economic evaluations of the platform, leading some avid Twitter devotees to move onto other social networks, like Mastodon However, his interventions played a role in loosening Twitter's policy on user bans, which some argued to have been disproportionate (Murphy 2022). Since his acquisition of Twitter in October 2022, when he tweeted "The BIRD is freed,"[23] Musk continued to communicate directly to Twitter users and the public about his plans as "Chief Twit", while searching for a new CEO, bypassing the press and other intermediaries in line with the approach of a Fifth Estate actor. While controversial, his purchase will be consequential to Twitter's success over the coming years.

Perhaps the major threat from the big nine tech firms is that they have become a gift to regulators. When the public raised concerns with politicians over the internet or social media, they would simply say: "Do something about it!" But for politicians and regulators, the sheer scale of the internet—millions of web pages, billions of users—made it unimaginable to control or regulate. Today, politicians can turn to regulatory agencies, who can turn to the big platforms and say: "Do something about it!" A government-big-tech complex? At once, the infeasible becomes possible, but also a possibility of increasing governmental and industry control of the internet in ways that would undermine ordinary people of the Fifth Estate. There is more discussion on this below in considering the regulatory imperative.

The Regulatory Governance Imperative

In the context of a greater focus on harms, as discussed above, there has been a clear imperative across the world to regulate the internet more rigorously, and social media, in particular (Tambini 2021). Anecdotal but serious cases of harm attributed to social media have led the public in Europe and the UK to demand that their representatives "do something" about social media abuse, such as with hate speech and online bullying. Such demands were largely what led to a consultation in the UK, initially around the concept of online harms—most often from a technologically deterministic perspective.

The consultation began with a focus on the UK's Harms White Paper, seeking to find a way to stop illegal or "unacceptable" content and activity online.[24] However, after meeting with serious criticism, the paper was reconceived as online safety, leading to the Online Safety Bill.[25] While the bill had been through multiple revisions and included in proposed legislation that had progressed to the report stage, it was put on hold when Boris Johnson was stepping down, until the autumn of 2022 when a new prime minister (PM) replaced him. Only one candidate for PM openly opposed the bill, even though the exact text of the bill remained obscure—sequestered as the bill was refined. The new PM, Liz Truss, indicated that she had reservations about aspects of the bill. This process has continued with the resignation of Liz Truss and selection of Rishi Sunak as PM. As the bill has moved into its final stages, the public argues that protections on harms to children should be expanded to include content harmful to adults online, as early critics feared (Milmo 2021b).

On its face, the objective of safety is difficult to challenge. Prior to this consultation, the problem was finding acceptable and legitimate methods to proportionately address various harms, such as without infringing freedom of expression and privacy, particularly considering the scale of content encompassed by the internet and social media. For example, Statista estimates that there are 4.75 billion items shared by Facebook users each day.[26] Over one and a half billion (1.62 billion) people use Facebook nearly every day.[27] It is essential to keep this in mind when the UK's regulator, Ofcom, and other media regulators can spend days reviewing one short segment of one broadcast they have had consumer complaints about. Is policing the internet and social media in such a qualitative, deliberative, and time-intensive way feasible for a regulator? Is there a new approach that would make content regulation feasible? The UK thought they had found an approach through a "duty of care."

The big idea behind the UK White Paper consultation was to apply a "duty of care" responsibility on the social media companies, the intermediaries between content producers and those who read their content online. The idea builds on the EC's call for regulating video-sharing platforms by adding a duty of care obligation. Companies that allow users to share or discover "user-generated content or interact with each other online" will have "a statutory duty of care" to be responsible for the safety of their users and prevent them from suffering harms. If they fail, the regulator can act against the companies, such as fining the social media executives or threatening them with criminal prosecution.

The UK's Safety Bill addresses these issues by changing the rules governing intermediaries—by creating the duty of care provision—occasionally euphemistically masked by referring to it as a "duty of impartiality" (Foster et al. 2020: 3). It also recommended several technical initiatives, such as flagging suspicious content, and educational initiatives, such as online media literacy.

However, the duty of care responsibility is the key innovation as well as the most problematic issue. In fact, such threats have been leveled at social media executives before passage of the Safety Bill. The UK culture secretary named top executives of Facebook's Meta in Parliament, saying that they and others would see corporate fines and criminal sanctions. They may want to "take off into the metaverse" but her advice would be to "stay in the real world because this . . . bill is going to be an act very, very soon, and it's the algorithms which do the harm, and . . . you will be accountable to this act" (Milmo 2021b: 15).

Generally, internet platforms as intermediaries, like telephone companies in the past, would not be held responsible for what their users say or do. As intermediaries, however, their liability would be limited, unless the platforms were creating harmful content. The internet community has looked to intermediaries to foster freedom online (MacKinnon et al. 2014). Imagine a phone company acting as a common carrier being sued because a pedophile, drug dealer, or terrorist used the phone. Instead of the police asking for information about a suspected offender, the phone company would have to surveil all telephone use to stop or catch offenders, and the telephone company would risk being subject to fines or criminal action if it failed to do so. Likewise, internet intermediaries will need to know what everyone is using the internet and social media for to stop illegal or "unacceptable" behavior—behavior that might result in one or more harms.[28]

Moreover, the algorithms of search and social media platforms cannot easily be shared and transparent without enabling malicious users to exploit them, such as for optimizing their visibility through search, and without being inaccurate as most are constantly changing through machine learning.

Nevertheless, a combination of multiple actors were attracted to come off the sidelines to lobby for internet regulation because they saw their own goals tied to addressing one or more of the specific harms identified by the consultation, whether it be child protection or disinformation. In such ways, the consultation aggregated many with a dedicated interest in ridding the internet of specific harms to generate support for instituting new rules for protecting internet users from a wide-open range of harms, including their own concerns. In the process, the rising focus on cyber harms fundamentally changed the range and centrality of different actors, objectives, and strategies entailed in controlling the internet in ways that challenge, if not undermine, traditional notions of internet freedom and online privacy.

The risk is that by approaching the regulation of social media and the internet to address these and future harms, policies will undermine privacy and freedom of expression and have a chilling effect on internet use by everyone in the UK. As expressed in a response to the cyber harm consultation as a "deeply flawed" proposal, one critic noted:

> By including both subjective individual harms and nebulous harms to society, the government has brought upon itself the very problems, notably damage to legitimate online freedom of expression, that are avoided by the deliberately crafted limits to offline duties of care. (Smith 2019: 5–6)

The problems with the proposed approach have been addressed by other critical reviews (Dutton 2019, Voipicelli 2019) but has continued on a track to becoming law in the UK as the Online Safety Bill in ways that have generated equally critical reviews (The Spectator 2022: 3).

Specifically, the Online Safety Bill entails a number of risks: it covers a very broad and potentially open-ended range of cyber harms; requires surveillance to police this duty that could undermine the privacy of all users; incentivizes companies to overregulate content and activity to avoid prosecution or huge fines, resulting in more restrictions on anonymity and chilling effects on freedom of expression; potentially generates more fear and panic among the general public, undermining adoption and use of the internet and widening digital divides; and necessitates an invasive monitoring of content, facing a volume of instances that is an order of magnitude beyond traditional media and telecoms, as mentioned, for example, over 500 hours of video are posted on YouTube every minute (Clement 2020).

However, adding to the potentially unanticipated outcomes of the ecology of choices by multiple actors that drove this approach, not all internet industries were tied to this duty of care. The White Paper went beyond its focus on cyber harms to support information and communication startups and companies in Britain. Remarkably, it targeted American tech giants almost exclusively (no British companies) and even suggested subsidies for UK companies. This illustrates a direct link between the framing of harms and big American tech companies.

Notwithstanding these risks to an open and global internet and the potential to exacerbate digital divides, this push found support from actors focused on each of the respective harms, such as child safety or disinformation or the impact of algorithms. One more general driver has been the rise of a dystopian climate of opinion about the internet and social media over the last decade and less confidence and support for freedom of expression. This has been exacerbated by increasing concerns over child protection as well as concerns over disinformation in elections in the United States, as well as across Europe, such as with the Cambridge Analytica debacle and Brexit in the UK, which, taken together, created the specter of interference in elections and a need for content moderation (Murphy 2020).

Europe generally and the UK have not developed internet and social media companies comparable to Facebook and Google and all the so-called big nine tech giants of the United States and China (Webb 2019). (While the UK has a strong online game industry, this industry was not mentioned in the White Paper, except as being a potential recipient of subsidies.) In the UK as well as most nations across the EU, the internet and social media companies are viewed as foreign, primarily American, companies that are politically feasible and often popular to target.

In this context, the platformization of the internet and social media has been a gift to regulators. It created a politically feasible way for regulators to force companies to police a large portion of traffic, providing a way forward for politicians and regulators to meet the demands of the traditional mainstream media, the press, and the public for them to "do something" about the new media.

The public has valid complaints and concerns over instances of online harms. Politicians have not known what to do, but this duty of care approach will not be the silver bullet for politicians and regulators. Politicians might believe they can simply turn to the companies and command them to stop harmful consequences from occurring or the companies will suffer the consequences, such as their executives facing steep fines or criminal penalties. But this remedy carries huge risks, primarily in leading to overregulation of platforms and the internet and inappropriately curtailing privacy and freedom of expression of all digital citizens across the UK and other nations that could well follow their lead.

Ironically, given the UK's early role in fostering an open internet, the new approach genuinely reflects aspects of internet control in China, which has been widely viewed as having a chilling effect on privacy and freedom of expression.[29] As a critique of the Online Safety Bill puts it: the "Chinese government has shown how the big state can suborn big tech" (The Spectator 2022: 3). This is a fair assessment in that threats of steep fines and criminal indictments could lead to a similar outcome in the UK, despite being a more liberal democracy, making it not the safest place to be online, but a place one would not want to be online with one's content, with even screentime potentially under surveillance. UGC would be dangerous. Broadcast news and entertainment would be "safe."

Despite such reservations, the ideas proposed by the consultation in 2019 remained under consideration and destined to be approved by Parliament in 2022. Ironically, this is just as the internet and social media have been proven to be a lifeline: key to working at home, online education, and networking public services amidst the COVID-19 pandemic.

Internet users across the world value their ability to ask any question, voice any concern, and use online digital media to access information, people, and services they like. It was been called a "technology of freedom," as Ithiel de Sola Pool (1983) argued, in countries that supported freedom of expression and personal privacy. If citizens of the UK decide to ask the government and regulators to restrict their use of the internet and social media—for their own good—through a duty of care, they might well undermine their freedom of expression and the value of the internet to its nations and regions and in other nations that might follow its lead.

BROADER EFFORTS TO TAMING THE WILD WEST OF THE INTERNET

The UK focus on harms helps provide a concrete understanding of the guiding logic of regulatory intervention in social media. Around the world, governments have been moving away from no or light-regulatory approaches to the internet and social media to far more regulation as a solution to problems attributed to the technologies and the industry. Europe has been leading developments in internet regulation, early on with its Privacy Act and later with a Digital Services Act. These efforts have fostered a new focus in academia on the translation of law and policy into the digital sphere around the concept of digital constitutionalism (Celeste 2021, 2022, De Greggorio 2021, 2022).

The Digital Services Act

The European Union's Digital Services Act (DSA) could be a step in a similar direction but a lighter touch than the UK's Online Safety Bill. It seeks to codify efforts to ensure that content moderators, such as social media platforms, take responsibility for ensuring that what is illegal offline is not permitted online. While it uses platforms to enforce public policy analogous to the Online Safety Bill, it also places limits on monitoring users, such as asking platforms to respond to specific notifications from trusted actors and limiting the liability of online platforms for the speech of others, such as social media users. While forcing the tech giants to police illegal and harmful content on their platforms, through the threat of fines or criminal sanctions, the DSA has defined some limitations on sanctions and codifies the critical value not undermining freedom of expression online.

As with the Online Safety Bill, this legislation seems to have responded to the alarms raised by politicians and by the Facebook whistleblower Frances Haugen. In line with her pleas, the DSA will require platforms to be more transparent around their content moderation algorithms, for example, and to give users more control over algorithmically curated search, so that they are not left with only the platform's results. Options for users are a good step, but the transparency of algorithms fails to sufficiently recognize that malicious users and even well-intentioned but overly ambitious content providers can use information about algorithms to optimize the likelihood of their content being found through honing search engine optimization (SEO). SEO can result in distorting search such that many users fail to find the information of most value to their organic search results (Box 9.2).

The bill was tentatively supported by the EU Parliament in 2022 but has yet to reach the stage of approval at which it will come into force. Incredibly, the actual text

---

Box 9.2 Search Engine Optimization

Since the early days of search, for example, there has always been a cat-and-mouse game between search engines and content providers to game the system to optimize their findability or exposure online. Early in the evolution of search engines, certain elements, such as a particular word, were used to gauge the community's interest in a post. So websites might embed the word in their background, invisible to human readers while catching the eye of search engines. When search engines realized they were leveraging an aspect of the search algorithm to their advantage, the search engine would revise the algorithm. In this cat-and-mouse game, transparency will be a gift to those gaming search engines and other algorithms to their advantage.

has not been open for scrutiny during the last stages of legislative negotiations. The legislation remains unclear to experts even as the DSA approaches the final stages of adoption (Allen 2022). So, from what the DSA purports to accomplish—what is on the tin, so-to-speak—it appears to be a step in the right direction. The question is whether the language of the actual legislation and its implementation does what is advertised by the EU. This must be a focus of research and public accountability in the coming years.

The internet and social media have always been subject to regulation as what is illegal offline is illegal online. It is not a so-called Wild West. In the United States, the First Amendment is regulation. But more regulation is being focused on enabling governments or industry to moderate and control the production and sharing of content on the internet and social media that runs counter to traditions of freedom of expression and privacy, as best exemplified by the Online Safety Bill. The movement for digital constitutionalism seeks to ensure that what is illegal offline is translated into policies and regulations to ensure they are prevented online.

DIGITAL CONSTITUTIONALISM OF THE INTERNET'S WILD WEST

No longer is the internet viewed as an innovation that will be enabled by not applying regulations that were applied to common carriers, like the phone companies or broadcasters. As it has become a major infrastructure of nations, governments view regulation as imperative create regulations to protect the public interest. But inappropriate or disproportionate regulations, such as based on a duty of care regime, present risks to undermining this national and global infrastructure and the vitality of the Fifth Estate.

Since the early years of the internet's diffusion, there has been a rise of efforts to develop rules to govern and regulate the use of the internet that are anchored in legal norms and precedents. In 1996, John Barry Barlow, a lyricist for the rock group Grateful Dead, reflected the zeitgeist of many pioneers of this new virtual network of cyberspace in the Declaration of the Independence of Cyberspace, asking governments to "leave us alone." For decades, many critics of cyberspace reflected the view that the internet was a "Wild West"— it was ungoverned, lawless, and dangerous. In fact, it was never ungoverned or lawless and was safe by any reasonable comparison with the physical world. For example, it gained freedom in the United States because of legal precedents such as the First Amendment, and individuals who used the internet to commit fraud or another crime could be held accountable by the law.

However, the early years were governed by a sense that the internet was a promising technological innovation that could have major social and economic benefits. It should be encouraged. So early networks were treated as if they were more like a computer than a telecommunication network, which would have placed them under regulatory restrictions that could have choked their development. This innovation mindset drove early regulation of the internet to encourage its diffusion. Even today, major efforts to close the digital divide between individuals and nations without adequate access to the internet are a high priority of governments worldwide. This is because it is an essential infrastructure of our networked information age.

In such ways, legal norms and policy principles of nations, such as the First Amendment, have long driven the regulation of the internet. Over the decades, efforts to explicitly translate these rules into the governance of the internet in local, national, and international contexts have fallen under a framework generally referred to as "digital constitutionalism," led in many respects by politicians, regulators, and legal scholars of Europe and the EU in particular (Celeste 2019, 2022, De Gregorio 2021, 2022). Edoardo Celeste (2019: 77) views it as a "theoretical framework" that is essentially an "ideology that adopts the values of contemporary constitutionalism to the digital society" that seeks to embed the "norms of constitutional law in a given legal order" to digital technology.

Its proponents see it developing in ways that move away from technologically deterministic choices being made by key actors, such as social media platforms, to reflect rules that are derived from law and policy in particular legal contexts, such as states and regions, like the EU, with the aim of protecting the rights of individuals and balancing rights with potential threats to individuals, such as privacy threats. It can balance powers by putting law and policy in place to protect individuals and institutions in the digital age. An example is the development of rules designed to protect personal data through the ninety-nine articles of the EU's General Data Protection Regulation (GDPR).

John Parry Barlow died in 2018, so I can only imagine that he would find digital constitutionalism exactly the kind of development he feared. The risk is that as regional and country-specific policies and regulations develop across the world, the internet will either be sanitized to the lowest common denominator, "cat photos," or become an increasingly fragmented "splinternet" (Alba 2017, Ball 2022). The promise would be for digital constitutionalism to develop in ways that appropriately balance benefits and harms in ways that protect a more global internet and the Fifth Estate. As one proponent of digital constitutionalism puts it, there is the potential for an "internet bill of rights" (Celeste 2022). If digital constitutionalism lives up to its potential as an internet bill of rights, then it might well support the vitality of the Fifth Estate rather than create national and regional technospheres of regulations, a likelihood furthered by the Ukraine conflict.

Geopolitical Fragmentation of the Internet

China's firewalls, which seek to reinforce a more national internet, and the aftermath of the Russian invasion of Ukraine raise new and steeper barriers to an open global internet. While the fragmentation and filtering of the internet began before the February 24, 2022, Russian invasion of Ukraine, the war brought nearly instant recognition of a Russian geopolitical silo around the its narrative of a "special military operation" in contrast to a narrative accepted by the US, UK, EU, and other Western liberal democracies of an unprovoked and unjustified Russian military invasion of a sovereign nation. It is too soon to understand the long-term implications of the level of censorship and surveillance of broadcasting, the internet, and social media applied by the Russian Federation. However, it has highlighted the limited role the internet could play in holding the state-controlled press and mass media in Russian accountable for disinformation within Russia and to the rest of the world.

The great firewall of China was created in large part by language barriers but also from censorship and government control of the media and internet providers and platforms in China. This was an issue long before the invasion of Ukraine. However, the stark battle of competing narratives surrounding the war in Ukraine made it impossible to ignore parallels in China that had been ignored by most of the world up to that point. It is likely that the war will be a game changer not only for international relations but also for the internet and global communication and information order. Certainly, visions of an open global internet were dashed immediately with new scenarios of a world fragmented into more geopolitically isolated technospheres by an increasingly plausible "splinternet" dividing autocracies and democracies (Alba 2017; Ball 2022, Stokel-Walker 2022).

Interrelated and Cumulative Threats to the Fifth Estate

These threats are interrelated. For example, the censorship conducted and propaganda generated by the Russian Federation in the aftermath of its invasion resulted in initiatives, such as in Europe, to target and respond to "fake news" and propaganda (Espinosa 2022). Thus, the invasion and geopolitical splintering of the internet has reinforced regulatory initiatives and a push against big tech that could further surveillance and censorship of the internet and social media across Europe and other regions.

Cumulatively, all these threats are woven into a developing narrative across all the estates about the risks and harms of social media—a narrative that could undermine the Fifth Estate. As discussed previously, governments in liberal democratic states are increasingly focused on the regulation of UGC anchored in the use of social media to prevent a growing litany of harms. Added to this challenge, the dystopian narrative about social media has been taken on by all the other estates.

Public intellectuals including world-class and media-savvy academics are largely onboard with this narrative. For example, the founder of Citizens Lab at the University of Toronto, Ronald Deibert (2021), claimed he agreed with "an emerging consensus about the problems related to social media" Deibert (2021: 7–8) and lists other scholars with whom he agrees about the "painful truths about social media," as if it were a scholarly opinion poll. Unfortunately, there is indeed a strong consensus, which is problematic on several fronts.

A media classic, *The Boys on the Bus* (Crouse 1972), exposed the development of pack journalism on the bus full of journalists following President Richard Nixon's re-election campaign against Senator George McGovern. Communication networks were so closely connected on the campaign bus that major stories across many papers tended to follow the same news agenda about the campaign. Instead of independent thinkers, the journalists became more of a pack with a common narrative. Today, the journalists are not all boys and there is no bus, but not only journalists but also public intellectuals, journalists, and economic and business elites are all networked via the internet and—yes—social media that they increasingly read and follow the same narratives. The moral panic about social media has generated such a strong narrative that it garners widespread public support.

It is a problem for public intellectuals, particularly academic scholars, because it often lacks a clear analytic skepticism. Scholars in academia are not only expected to be independent thinkers but also skeptical of taken-for-granted assumptions, whether they are positive or negative. This does not seem to be happening in the present context, when those holding positive views of social media tend to be swimming upstream.

This would be more acceptable if empirical research supported this social media narrative. However, many who have empirically studied how people use social media and the internet have found evidence that contradicts key assumptions underpinning the social media panics as discussed in relation to work on disinformation. But even anecdotally, there should be far more skepticism about many claims. Diebert (2021: 3) suggests the election of Donald Trump in 2016 was an impact of social media, yet Trump has risen in polls since his accounts were suspended by social media companies like Twitter and Facebook. By 2021, it seemed clear that the polarized partisan divides in the United States cannot be so simply attributed to social media—they are real rather than manufactured by social media.

Professor Diebert (2021: 28) believes social media "degrades the quality of public discourse on the platforms," but the internet and social media have never really supported public dialogue—that was a naïve vision of the internet creating some variant of Habermas's public sphere even in the heady days of experiments with e-democracy before the turn of the century (Dahlberg 2001).

A final example is the lament that social media are "antisocial," isolating adults and children, which ignores research studies that show that people who are socially isolated are not online and that the use of the internet and social media tends to reinforce and maintain existing social networks while enabling people to make new friends as well (Rice et al. 2007, Hampton and Wellman 2021). And yes, children are engaged by mobile smartphones and other computing devices, but only a romantic would think that children were pulled away from books and writing with pen and paper by the internet. The computer scientist Seymour Papert (1980) discovered what he called the "holding power" that computers had for children, which he thought could be turned to make computing a powerful tool for education and training by holding the attention of children learning how to read, write, and create.

Whether computers are addictive or have holding power is an example of the inherent "dual effects" of nearly any information and communication technology, from the telephone to the internet (de Sola Pool 1977). A recent study of children in the state of Michigan found that adolescent self-esteem is more problematic for those disconnected from social media than for those who are heavy users (Hampton and Shin 2022). If we uncritically focus on one side of this duality, we will dismiss the social, economic, political, and cultural benefits of living in a networked society. For such reasons, the development of a networked narrative—a modern equivalent of pack journalism—about the harms of social media is a challenge not only to the Fifth Estate, which can strategically harness social media, but also to society at large in the digital age.

These categories of threats—a media-centric focus on new technologies like UGC, framing social implications around harm, ever-bigger and more concentration on a few tech platforms, following a regulatory imperative, and countering an increasing geopolitical fragmentation of a splintered internet—are creating challenging issues for the continued development of a Fifth Estate. That said, each threat raises problems, but with the pundits and established critics focusing on techno-media-centric blaming, framing discussion around harms, targeting big tech, regulating the Wild West rather than ensuring an internet bill of rights, and creating geopolitical digital curtains or technospheres that fragment the internet and the world's information order, then social media, the internet, pluralist democratic processes, and the Fifth Estate are facing serious threats to their future vitality.

However, given the degree that key assumptions underpinning these threats lack real evidence or conflict with prevailing research, such as around disinformation, it is possible to remain optimistic. The longevity of these threats could be short-lived once they are forced to confront systematic evidence of internet use and impact in the digital age ahead. That future is the focus of the next and last chapter.

10

The Future of the Fifth Estate

Will threats diminish significance of the Fifth Estate or will networked individuals muddle through to sustain its role? Alternatively, will a broader understanding of this power shift enhance the role of the Fifth Estate in this digital age?

This final chapter addresses these questions. It begins by briefly summarizing the idea of a Fifth Estate and its role across sectors of society followed by a brief discussion of the many issues and challenges that raise questions about its future. Three scenarios are outlined on the future, including a diminished, sustained, or expanded role. These scenarios reflect the open future of this phenomenon while presenting a normative view of the need to not simply sustain but to enhance the vitality of the Fifth Estate and move from an overly media-centric regulatory imperative to securing the Fifth Estate at multiple levels. The chapter closes with discussion about how research and policy can monitor the vitality of the Fifth Estate and support its growing prominence.

Revisiting the Concept of Fifth Estate and Its Elements

The internet is used to complement governmental, business, press, and social institutions, such as in supporting a protest or social movement. As important, if not more so, are the ways the internet enables ordinary people to enhance their informational and communicative power through searching, originating, networking, collaborating, and leaking. This makes them relatively more powerful vis-à-vis other individuals and institutions worldwide that can make a difference for politics and society. But doesn't the internet and social media just transmit data, words, or images? "Blah, blah, blah"—as Greta might say.

Over 130 years ago, when the telegraph was the new medium, the US Supreme Court (1887) heard a case that hinged in part on the degree that laws governing interstate commerce between persons, such as through transportation networks, were "visible and tangible." Could they be applicable to the telegraph, which only transmitted invisible and intangible signals? The Court's answer was insightful, saying:

> The telegraph transports nothing visible or tangible; it carries only ideas, wishes, orders, and intelligence ... which passes at once beyond the control of the sender, and reaches the office to which it is sent instantaneously.

The Fifth Estate. William H. Dutton, Oxford University Press. © Oxford University Press 2023.
DOI: 10.1093/oso/9780190688363.003.0011

The telegraph was a remarkable media, communication, and information technology (ICT) of the nineteenth century that in many respects has evolved into the twenty-first-century digital media central to this book. And in some respects, it still "carries only ideas, wishes, orders, and intelligence" that were equally immediate but increasingly from any networked individual or institution to anyone, at any time, from any place, with potentially enormous consequences, as described in many examples in this book. The internet and social media are literally reconfiguring one of the most significant informational and communicative power shifts of the digital age.

Caught in an Internet Trust Cycle

The growing trust in the internet relative to other media has been one of the most remarkable developments of the first decade of this century. As early as 2009, internet users in Britain viewed the internet as being more essential as a source of information than television or newspapers. Moreover, users trusted the information they could obtain online as much as they trusted broadcast news and more than they trusted what they read in newspapers (Dutton et al. 2009: 31, 34). Over the internet, networked individuals could access information from many traditional sources as well as much more content produced anywhere in the world.

Over time, the value of the internet became such a fact of life in liberal democratic states, particularly among high-income countries, that it was increasingly taken for granted. Evgeny Morozov (2013), a renowned journalist-scholar of the digital age, even concluded that the internet was of no special importance. The new-new thing became data. It had transitioned from a problem, captured by the threat of a data deluge, to a new form of capital created by computational analytics in research, business, and industry (Dutton and Jeffreys 2010). This shift from problem to opportunity was captured by the concept of "big data" (Mayer-Schoenberger and Cukier 2018).

However, during the second decade of the century, governments and the press grew more concerned over the misuse of the internet and personal data online, a new threat to privacy and surveillance (Zuboff 2019), as illustrated by data protection initiatives of the European Commission, even though data may be of little value or even dysfunctional, outside of the application it is designed to support. Also, with the advent of social media and the growing reach of Facebook since its launch in 2004, concerns rose as well over the influence of social media as one of a growing litany of harms, such as around misinformation, being attributed to the new media. In parallel, national security threats arose also over WikiLeaks, Edward Snowden, and Reality Winner's leaks of highly classified information from the United States (Chapter 7). Increasingly serious questions were being raised about the unintended consequences of the internet for individuals, the media, and national security. I wrote about the creation of an internet "trust bubble" that threatened to burst if problems continued to be perceived as induced by the internet (Dutton et al. 2013).

In this context, the Cambridge Analytica scandal (Chapter 9) became a lightning rod for critics of the internet and social media. Disinformation sowed in large part by social media became a convenient yet superficial explanation for the surprising results of the British European Union (Brexit) referendum and the election of Donald J. Trump as president in 2016. Revelations of the disinformation campaign launched against the nation of Ukraine by the Surkhov leaks (Box 8.6) made these threats even more salient given the Russian invasion that followed. Since 2016, a continuing stream of dystopian concern was expressed over the harms that could be attributed to the internet, potentially undermining trust in these technologies and their use in everyday life.

. As discussed in Chapter 9, the framing of the social implications of the internet in terms of harms as opposed to benefits of the postindustrial information or network age has come to dominate discourse and policy.[1] The optimistic era of the internet seemed to have come to an end in Britain, in the United States, and around the world. By 2022, even the rise of Facebook user numbers among younger age groups appeared to stall but was often accompanied by rising numbers moving to newer platforms like TikTok.

In this dystopian context, in which the internet and social media are frequently demonized as the cause of multiple harms, it is reasonable to question the sustainability of one of the most positive perspectives on the internet since its inception—the idea of it fostering a Fifth Estate. At the same time, a survey of the public in Britain, commissioned by the UK's media regulator (Ofcom), which sought to gauge the levels of concern over harms, found that "a majority of internet users believe that the benefits of going online outweigh the risks" (Jigsaw 2019).

Major threats to the Fifth Estate were described in the previous chapter. They include a techno-media-centric perspective that overlooks the diversity of choices available to individuals online, the framing of internet social implications by harms, the rise of the big tech platforms too concentrated to be trusted, a trajectory of regulatory initiatives that could result in inappropriate and disproportionate regulatory responses if not balanced by the protection of rights, and the impact of the war in Ukraine on geopolitical fragmentation of the internet.

As a consequence, "you" are not likely to again be the person of the year on the cover of *Time*. Fewer thought leaders celebrate the empowerment of ordinary people in democratic societies. To the contrary, concerns are rising over the enhanced communicative power of networked individuals, generating efforts to censor and control user-generated content (UGC) on social media.

And while the internet has opened doors to many user-generated innovations and content, it also provides the platforms and tools for critics of the Fifth Estate to block online access, surveil users, and filter internet content (Deibert et al. 2008, 2010), including efforts to virtually shut down the internet—the so-called internet kill switch. Notwithstanding this resistance, the internet is used in repressive regimes by networked individuals to challenge such controls, such as by circumventing and exposing the Kremlin's efforts to filter internet traffic that challenged its narrative about Russia's "special military operation" in Ukraine. Up to three-fourths of the Russian population watched state broadcasters that parroted this false narrative about the war in Ukraine. Despite blocking social media, such as Facebook, Russia criminalized coverage that challenged the government's narrative, threatening to prosecute anyone charged with spreading false information about its invasion of Ukraine, such as by calling it a "war" (Troianovski 2022), forcing internet users to work harder to get information online, such as through virtual private networks (VPNs) and a few less censored social media, such as Telegram.

Perhaps the Fifth Estate has and will continue to face efforts to limit its influence, just as the Fourth Estate of an independent press and courageous eyewitness journalists have continued to experience. However, the democratic implications of the Fifth Estate are broader than such parallels between the new and traditional media. Internet users increasingly go online as their first port of call when looking for information on all types of subjects (Dutton et al. 2009). Networked individuals can also mobilize political campaigns effectively, as social media were used to boost the election of President Obama in 2008 and have since been used increasingly in local and global campaigns across the globe, such as the Extinction Rebellion (https://rebellion.earth).

Comparable developments have risen in nearly every sector of society, such as in access to medical and health information, such as enabling medical professionals to reach trusted online sources of information and services in their field of interest and not be limited to their local practice or organization, such as by sharing information on Sermo (Chapter 6; https://www.sermo.com). Patients can go online for medical information to complement what they receive and discuss with their traditional providers. The internet is often the first place the head of household goes for health and medical information, a fact that is putting increased pressure on health and medical institutions to have stronger, more responsive, and trusted online services as well as improvements in doctor-patient communication processes, when their patients are sufficiently informed to ask better questions.

This is true across many sectors, not just healthcare, where trust in institutions is declining (Zuckerman 2017, 2022). Growing numbers of networked individuals are coming together online across geographical and organizational boundaries of their fields to create products and services, such as the online encyclopedia Wikipedia and open-source software products across nearly every sector of society. Civic media and the Fifth Estate can provide a greater level of accountability that could help restore trust in institutions (Zukerman 2022).

Protecting the Fifth Estate

Tensions with other estates resulting from the internet's role in challenging traditional institutions could undermine the Fifth Estate (Chapter 2). Threats emanate from each of the four estates. Public intellectuals, a contemporary equivalent of the clergy, have attacked the Fifth Estate as amateurs, not worthy of serious attention, and responsible for misinformation (Nichols 2017). However, experts as well as amateurs are given greater voice as a Fifth Estate, and they can complement and enlarge the public agenda since they are not part of the network of journalists analogous to earlier forms of "pack journalism" (Crouse 1972). Economic elites, today's nobility, including owners of the big tech companies, are generating wealth through the internet but are placing the Fifth Estate at risk by building monopolies and reducing transparency in ways that jeopardize trust in search and information sources (Zuboff 2019).

Governments, representing the commons, are placing increasing controls on freedom of speech and information, often applied by internet platforms. While often well-intentioned, designed to protect children and consumers, as illustrated by the UK's Online Safety Bill (Chapter 9), the implementation of their approach could undermine freedom of expression and privacy while necessitating online surveillance. Beyond the

UK, as Samuel Greengard (2021) notes: "Governments around the world are taking steps to limit access to information, or even shut it [the internet] down using tactics like site blocking, URL throttling, restricting mobile data, and regulatory and legal threats." The democratizing potential of the Fifth Estate could be lost if inappropriate forms of internet regulation are introduced that restrict its content, openness, and creativity.

The Fourth Estate is emulating aspects of the Fifth Estate, such as in efforts to engage readers and viewers online, but also seeking to co-opt successful networked individuals and producers, such as by hiring them as journalists, while at the same time portraying networked individuals as sources of disinformation. Unfortunately, the war in Ukraine reminded many of the potential dangers of state control of broadcasting and the internet, which the Kremlin was able to use to reinforce the Russian Federation's narrative of a "special military operation." However, in less extreme cases, contemporary problems with the quality and polarization of mainstream media in pluralist democratic states could be undermining trust and fostering more reliance on the Fifth Estate.

Finally, among its wide base of users are malicious individuals, who might have been called "the mob" in an earlier era—far from the ideal type of a Fifth Estate. The activities of malicious users are among the key threats that have spurred efforts to impose greater control over internet content and use. But even the malicious users, such as those using inauthentic accounts, can be the target of Fifth Estate accountability as illustrated by Bellingcat (Chapter 6) and intelligent and targeted censorship of orchestrated disinformation campaigns as discussed later in this chapter (Box 10.2).

In this context, dystopian views persist about the internet and social media and more positive viewpoints are increasingly silenced. Even the inventor of the Web, Sir Tim Berners-Lee, complains about his creation being abused by large companies.[2] As public intellectuals like Berners-Lee and members of the lay public demand that politicians do something about social media, politicians are finding ways to put pressure on regulators and big tech platforms to do something, such as in response to Frances Haugen's whistleblowing. Where will this lead?

Notwithstanding these concerns, faith in democracy (Helm 2022) and trust in traditional institutions is also strained in the United States and worldwide (Zukerman 2021). In this context, the potential for the Fifth Estate to provide another source of greater transparency and accountability could make a positive contribution to all estates and their institutions.

Future Scenarios

Three plausible future scenarios include the demise, continuation, or expansion of the Fifth Estate, which I will call, respectively, the Lost Horizon, Routing Around, and On the Horizon.

DEMISE OF THE FIFTH ESTATE: A LOST HORIZON?

The Fifth Estate might have been a temporary phenomenon driven by the early users of the internet and social media. As increasing proportions of the public moved online, the internet also attracted less responsible and more malicious users along with civic-minded users, leading to a growing number of problems associated with the many harms that have been attributed to the internet. The empowerment of ordinary internet users, in this scenario, was viewed as too dangerous as it empowered the mob, cybercriminals, terrorists, and all sorts of malicious users spreading disinformation, hate, and abuse online, often over inauthentic accounts. A promised vision of a more democratic technology receded and was replaced by a realization of the need for control and regulation of the internet and social media that better supports government, business and industry, and public intellectuals as the source of information and accountability in liberal democratic societies—reinforcing an elitist theory of democracy, where—ironically—the public relies on elites rather than ordinary citizens to protect the values and processes of democratic institutions (Bachrach 1967). Policy and regulatory initiatives like the UK's Online Safety Bill and the EU's Digital Services Act might enable regulators to incentivize internet platforms to potentially reduce disinformation and other harmful content online, albeit in ways that hold the prospect of undermining the many benefits of the internet in the digital age (Chapter 9).

SUSTAINING THE FIFTH ESTATE: ROUTING AROUND?

Emerging policy and regulatory initiatives in response to the contemporary moral panic over online harms and threats to democratic institutions could undermine the Fifth Estate. They are also driven by specific incidents that shock the public and politicians, such as a suicide or an attack on a public figure, that are claimed to be linked to use of the internet or social media rather than being anchored in systematic empirical research of internet users. For example, there are testimonials of people being saved from committing suicide by support they've found online, but a parent's insistence that a child committed suicide because they were encouraged to do so online is a far more powerful story that can shape policy and practice. But bad policy can arise from being inspired by specific cases, however heartbreaking, serious, and well intentioned, which could be the problematic driving force behind inappropriate regulatory responses.

That said, even if inappropriate policy and regulation of the internet and social media arise, users are likely to find ways to route around and through barriers to freedom of expression and privacy. For instance, most scrutiny will be applied to the big tech platforms, where most users are concentrated. This may move more users away from the big tech platforms to alternative platforms that are moderated but less subject to censorship of content and surveillance of users. As the proverbial saying goes, the internet is built to route around problems, and this might well be the case if regulation is disproportionate or otherwise inappropriate.

Also, while politicians and pundits are often ill-informed about the technologies of the internet and social media, regulatory bodies like the US Federal Communications Commission (FCC) and the UK's Office of Communications (Ofcom) have experts who are well informed about relevant technology, law, and policy. Moreover, in the implementation of policy and regulation, more reason and discretion might be exercised in ways that enable the continued vitality of UGC and the Fifth Estate. As discussed in the previous chapter, efforts to develop digital constitutionalism seek to protect and even develop an internet bill of rights that would help support the Fifth Estate.

EXPANDING THE FIFTH ESTATE: ON THE HORIZON?

An optimistic scenario is that we are only at the beginning of the Fifth Estate—only beginning to recognize the role of this collectivity of independent networked individuals and its potential to support accountability and empowerment. As more individuals—the next billion—move online, there will be a continuing critical mass of civic-minded users empowered by the internet and social media. Technological advances, such as in artificial intelligence, continue to create a wow factor around the potential of the internet and related media, such as over an AI system called ChatGPT that can answer natural language questions, accompanied by panics over what it could mean for teaching and education. Competition across rival social media, like Facebook, Twitter, TikTok, Mastodon, and many other networks will keep the social media world in play. And with recognition of this Fifth Estate empowerment, more efforts will be placed on instilling greater social responsibility on the part of all users and actors in the ecology of internet provision and use (Cohen-Almagor 2015). Furthermore, the digital divide will be narrowed in ways that diminish inequalities in the empowerment of the networked public.

In many respects, this scenario does not require major legislative or regulatory initiatives but a refinement of current law and regulatory policies that aim to support regulation and appropriate content moderation of the internet, web, and social media. Tech platforms and firms will continue to win over time in the cat-and-mouse games with malicious users to refine search and other relevant algorithms. In addition, the public will stop framing the use of the internet from the perspective of harms. As discussed with respect to a UK survey, most internet users saw the benefits of using the internet outweighing the risks, even before the COVID-19 pandemic (Jigsaw 2019). During the pandemic, the whole world realized that the internet was indeed a lifeline; it became a basic infrastructure of contemporary networked societies. Balancing harms and benefits, the narrative will shift to a more positive framing around security—securing networked individuals, organizations, and nations from malicious users—to reap the benefits of the digital age.

Governance of the Internet for a Fifth Estate

A shift away from governmental policy and regulation that carries risks of many unintended negative consequences is possible through a broader focus on governance that could be an outcome of moves toward digital constitutionalism. Governance is broader than government as it recognizes the role of all actors, including internet users, to reinforce the benefits of networked societies and recognize and protect the ideal of a Fifth Estate, along with other estates of the internet realm, from malicious actors.

It is impossible to return to a position of no or minimal regulation of the internet. Too many legitimate concerns have been raised, for example regarding child protection. Moreover, the internet has always been subject to regulation, albeit positive regulation such as the First Amendment in the United States and content moderation to maintain the civility of communication. Regulation and governance of the media and internet need to protect freedom of expression, privacy, and related rights. But there are alternatives to a narrow focus on the regulation of media, which could undermine freedom of expression and privacy through censorship and surveillance, such as has been the case in countries without a democratic pluralist tradition, China for example.

BUILDING AWARENESS OF A NETWORKED SOCIETY AND THE FIFTH ESTATE

First, it is important not to take the fact that we live in a networked information society for granted. We are no longer living in primarily agricultural or manufacturing societies, but societies and economies in which agriculture, manufacturing, and new information and communication jobs and industries are anchored in and enhanced by the internet and related media, communication, and information technologies (Bell 1973, Castells 1996). Social scientists have been documenting this shift for decades, but a public understanding of this shift is critical for both ordinary people and elites to ensure the innovations required to maintain and enhance its vitality. Living in a network society has been taken for granted by so many that leadership and the public have become too complacent about digital innovation and inclusion.

Second, the idea of a Fifth Estate is the focus of this book, but it is not a concept that many in the public are aware of, understand, or act on. It is difficult to protect a phenomenon that is unknown or misunderstood. The Fifth Estate is an ideal type based on patterns of internet use across the larger population of users. As an ideal type, it does not refer to all internet or social media users, many of whom do not create or share content. It refers to the collectivity of networked individuals who approach this ideal and are therefore informationally and communicatively empowered through strategically searching, originating, networking, collaborating, and, yes, even leaking online that creates a new form of social and political accountability.

The Fifth Estate may well be as important if not more so than an independent press in an earlier era. But protection and enhancement of the Fifth Estate might require greater awareness among a broader public of its existence and role in society and politics. You cannot see the Fifth Estate in the same way you can see institutions of the press. Greater awareness can stimulate and network individuals who understand and see a future for the Fifth Estate.

EMBEDDING THE FIFTH ESTATE IN EDUCATION

One promising example of awareness raising has been introducing students to the Fifth Estate. Educational researchers have discussed the potential of social media and the Fifth Estate as an underutilized approach to a variety of content areas in elementary and high school education, such as in civics and language arts.[3] Civics training in the United States is focused on the rights and responsibilities of citizens, along with efforts to address social media, given its centrality to students. However, training is through sites closed off from the outside world and from a safety perspective, such as teaching students how to protect their reputations online, stand up to cyberbullies, and understand how information can spread online (Greenhow et al. 2020). English language arts (ELA) classes cover subjects such as argumentative writing, which opens another door to social media training (Askari 2022).

Emilia Askari (2022) took social media training to another level by experimenting with the use of the Fifth Estate perspective to introduce a more proactive, action-oriented approach to digital citizenship and ELA. She developed her doctoral thesis in the top-ranked College of Education at Michigan State University by bringing the concept and strategies of the Fifth Estate into Kindergarten–12th grade (K–12) education. Dr. Askari worked with several teachers and then focused primarily on working with an ELA teacher, who had the freedom to experiment with a high school class in Flint, Michigan, the location of the Flint water crisis (discussed in Chapter 5). The ELA class was affiliated with the University of Michigan's Flint campus "early college" courses, designed to give high school students some experience in college courses (Askari 2022: 53). Dr Askari (2020: 53) wanted to show students how they could use social media to "create positive change" for the good of their community.

K-12 institutions in the United States have been cautious about any use of social media, particularly involving students communicating with individuals or audiences outside the school. However, the researcher's interviews with teachers and their administrators found many open to applying social media in ways that could show students how social media could be used for the public good, such as voicing concerns whether about their neighborhood or the world.

Working with an ELA teacher and administrators, the researcher found safe ways to adapt to restrictions on student use of social media for one class session per week over about twelve weeks. For example, they created a class account to keep students from using their own personal accounts. They also set up a system for students to compose their own posts, but which ensured that the teacher posted for their students on one or more of the platforms students were familiar with—using Twitter, Instagram, and TikTok. Students could then see how their posts were commented on, viewed, or shared online, and adjust their social media strategies accordingly.

The mascot of the school, "Owls," was used to create an "Owls4Justice" project to experiment with the concept and strategies of the Fifth Estate in ways that overcame conventional restrictions on social media use in the schools and the unconventional restrictions on students and schools during the COVID-19 pandemic. This enabled the doctoral researcher to develop a case study of one class with embedded case studies of four selected students from the ninth and tenth grades from mid-December 2020 through late January 2021, spanning the US Capitol riot of January 6 and the pandemic.

In interviews, questionnaires, and analysis of student posts, it was clear that students experienced how the internet and social media could be empowering and not simply a playful social medium. They could see and experience how they could search, share, originate, and network with others in ways that could positively affect their community.[4] They also experienced the challenges of reaching a significant audience in a meaningful way on social media. The potential of this approach was reflected in the findings, including post-project interviews in which students spoke specifically of feeling empowered (Askari 2022).

TAKING SELF-REGULATION AND CIVILITY SERIOUSLY

A depressingly common refrain of the times is that self-regulation of the internet has not worked (Napoli 2019). However, while much is focused on content moderation by internet platforms, the processes for self-regulation by internet platforms and networked individuals have not yet been taken seriously by governments, intellectuals, business and industry, the press, or the public at large. Amid the pandemic, hospitals and other frontline service providers had signs posted everywhere to not abuse the staff. Even in real-life person-to-person contexts, people can be frustrated, frightened, angry, or so distraught that they are not polite in communicating with others. People, particularly when stressed or upset or otherwise difficult, need to be constantly reminded of the need for civility, courtesy, rules of order, and understanding.

More can be done at all levels to underscore the need for platforms, individuals, teams, organizations, and nations to moderate and otherwise act civilly in what is a globally connected society (Cohen-Almagor 2015). Consider the rising levels of public awareness on the need for acting to protect the environment to avoid a climate catastrophe. This model suggests that far more can be done to teach children, families, friends, colleagues, and others on the need for civility in politics and society, online as well as in person. Digital ethics, etiquettes, rules of order, and norms could complement initiative around digital constitutionalism (Dutton 1996; Turk 2019).

More research could be done on mechanisms to enhance civility online. In the early days of the internet, much discussion focused on the phenomenon of flaming, usually on email (Box 10.1). Today, flaming is largely a problem of an earlier era.

With advances in artificial intelligence (AI), for example, it is increasingly feasible to flag email or social media messages like hate mail that violate norms of civility. These warnings are already employed by many platforms. Networked individuals can then choose to avoid, report, or look at them. Offensive language is not illegal, and in the United States, it is protected by the First Amendment. But offensive language, obscene words, or gestures could be telegraphed to recipients so that they can decide how to treat them depending on their source and their tolerance for different forms of offensive speech.

Box 10.1   Flaming

Early email users often encountered abrupt and rude or other aggressive reactions to messages online. Most often, this resulted from misunderstandings of short, cryptic messages. The receiver interprets a quick response as rude or offensive and fires back with an equally or more aggressive message, resulting in a pattern of flaming. One remedy was to raise awareness of this phenomenon and encourage users to be clear and polite online and avoid overly abrupt emails or other electronic messages. Another was to make email more visibly human, such as by embedding a person's photograph with the message so that an angry insult was less likely the result. However, privacy concerns have tended to reduce the use of personal photographs, moving to alternatives like generating a personal avatar, which can be even less personal. Another strategy is to use symbols, such as emojis, to indicate that an abrupt answer might be in jest ☺ so as not to be misunderstood.

RETHINKING THE REGULATORY PARADIGM

Finally, the most significant change might be to move away from overreliance on traditional, media-centric regulatory paradigms (Napoli 2019). The frameworks and agencies that regulated the telecommunication and broadcasting systems might not be the most appropriate for the internet and social media, despite the social "media" label. Initially, the internet was so innovative and different from traditional media that it was viewed as a service that was not at the core of common carrier or broadcast services and would not be regulated in traditional ways, such as under common carrier or broadcast regulations in the United States. Increasingly, communication regulators are moving rapidly toward greater regulation of the new media, as if it were a common carrier or broadcast media, which it is not.

There are two reasons for falling back on a broadcast regulatory framework. One is that the communication regulatory agencies work primarily with common carrier (telecommunications) and broadcasting (radio and television). A new communication technology is then subsumed within its remit. Another reason is that this is their background: many regulators come from the common carrier or broadcast industries. This makes them more conversant with traditional regulatory models.

However, it is possible that a more appropriate model to consider is outside the broadcasting arena—in computing.

In the early days of computing and data processing, computing was designed for batch processing. Users would enter instructions with stacks of punch cards, and computer operators would use a keyboard on the computing machinery. When terminals emerged to enable people in another room or office building to interactively provide instructions and enter data via a remote terminal, connected by an electronic channel, the question arose: Is this wire an artifact of telecommunications or computing? This was resolved by not calling it telecommunications or computing but a "value-added service." Otherwise, the wire would have been seen and regulated as if it were a phone line, and innovation would have been stopped. Or if seen as part of a computer, the lack of any regulatory framework might have undermined its future as well, such as by not protecting intermediaries—not holding them legally responsible for what others say or do on their networks.[5]

Today, you can watch television on a TV, receiving broadcast radio signals, or on a computer streaming service, like Netflix. Is this broadcasting or computing? You might believe that since you are watching television shows or channels on your computer, it is another device to watch TV—it's broadcasting. But the content is sent from computer servers to your computer, so you are using an interactive computer system, or value-added network. Therefore, it might be useful to move outside the media regulation box to find a framework tied more closely to computing, as suggested in the following section, that could augment if not substitute for more traditional broadcast regulatory approaches.

ONLINE SAFETY, ONLINE SECURITY

Many initiatives to reduce online harms, disinformation or hate speech are two examples, are based on using censorship of content on the internet and social media, particularly UGC. And this censorship increasingly relies on surveillance of internet users. Governments seek to achieve this through pressuring internet platforms to eliminate harmful content and discussions, such as through the duty-of-care provision of the UK's Online Safety Bill.

However, there is an alternative path to safety online, which is through building the capacity of individuals, households, organizations, and nations to generate a greater capacity for protecting their cybersecurity. Cybersecurity may seem too narrow or technical, but it is all about preventing bad things from happening, such as online harms, or creating the capacity to not be harmed by such events. One widely accepted definition of cybersecurity is "about technologies, processes, and policies that help to prevent and/or reduce the negative impact of events in cyberspace that can happen as the result of deliberate actions against information technology by a hostile or malevolent actor" (Clark et al. 2014: 9).

Contemporary and commonly accepted definitions of technology include more than the hardware. To paraphrase Emmanuel Mesthene (1981: 102), technology is the organization of equipment, people, and techniques for practical purposes. Any accepted definition of information and communication technologies today includes individuals enabled to use the equipment through various techniques as part and parcel of the technology.

Online harms are negative impacts of events in cyberspace caused by deliberate actions of hostile or, more often, malevolent actors, such as someone distributing hate speech or purposively spreading disinformation. In such ways, online harm reduction and cybersecurity are genuinely overlapping in their coverage, yet there is surprisingly little communication and sharing experiences across what might be viewed as two cultures of the internet—a broadcasting and computing culture.

This is not only the fault of broadcasters and regulators. The computer science community seldom views itself as overlapping with the broadcasting community or communication sciences. But the convergence of media information and communication technologies has been a dramatic consequence of the digital age that seems too often to be missed as a consequence of "disciplinary silos." Do approaches to cybersecurity, which evolved from earlier approaches to computer security, have anything to offer those considering online harms? I believe they do. Consider the following.

For over a decade, initiatives in cybersecurity capacity building have been developed by multiple centers, such as the Global Cybersecurity Capacity Centre (GCSCC) at Oxford University with which I have been involved. The rationale for these initiatives assumes that it is impossible to protect any entity completely from cyberattacks and security breaches or related harmful acts by malevolent actors. However, it is possible to build the capacity of actors to be resilient in the event these problems occur, such as through developing techniques to reduce their likelihood and increasing preparations for recovery to minimize any lasting damage. And they work: nations with higher levels of cybersecurity capacity have fewer problems and more positive implications stemming from the benefits of internet use and (Creese et al. 2021).

There are various models for how to build cybersecurity capacity, such as the GCSCC's cybersecurity maturity model, which defines policies and practices across five dimensions of capacity building (Box 10.2).[6] Some dimensions may seem applicable primarily at the national level, such as legal and regulatory frameworks, but even in many households there are rules about being online. Together all these dimensions have relevance across multiple levels and can be applied to "you" (Box 10.2).

Box 10.2 **Aspects of Cybersecurity Capacity**

1. Cybersecurity policy and strategy, such as respecting freedom of expression, privacy, and intellectual property policies and practices.
2. Aspects of culture and society, such as developing a cybersecurity mindset that supports more secure practices, such as strong passwords.
3. Knowledge and capabilities online, including knowledge and training in protecting yourself online.
4. Legal and regulatory frameworks: developing rules of engagement for not only legal but also civil and appropriate use of the internet and social media.
5. Standards and technologies: using spam filters, antivirus software, and avoiding pirated software and untrusted actors, texts, email, and websites.

Adapted from the GCSCC's Cybersecurity Capacity Model at https://gcscc.ox.ac.uk/cmm-dimensions-and-factors#/.

For instance, an individual, household, or business should have rules in mind about how to comply with relevant laws and regulations, such as on freedom of expression and privacy and data protection. Some dimensions are most applicable to internet users, households, and business and industry, but they extend to a nation, such as a culture and society aligned with cybersecurity and the knowledge and capabilities to protect cybersecurity, such as that built through education, awareness raising, and training.

The dimension of maturity defined as "culture and society" involves building a cybersecurity mindset to ensure that networked individuals routinely prioritize security in their day-to-day use of the internet and social media, build a learned level of trust and confidence in using online services, and understand personal information protection online (Dutton 2017). I have used the analogy of a bicycle to convey the idea of a security mindset, which might be particularly appropriate considering a quote of Steve Jobs, suggesting that the computer is like "a bicycle of the mind" in the ways it can enhance the efficiency of humans.[7] In Oxford, where bikes are a major mode of transportation, everyone has a bicycle-security mindset. They park their bike in a prominent place, buy a lock and use it, and even purchase used bikes because they are less attractive to bicycle thieves. They don't need to think about these activities: it is part of their mindset.

Other aspects of a cyber culture and society include developing a learned level of trust in online technologies and services. Networked individuals need to be trusting enough to use online tools but not have blind faith, trusting everything they see online, as discussed previously. Users need to learn how to check the authenticity of actors and the validity of information. Another aspect is understanding that personal information protection online is critical for making informed decisions about what information to provide whom, such as whether Facebook users should have given access to their Facebook accounts through an online survey connected to Cambridge Analytica (Chapter 9). These and related aspects of a cyber culture and society can be fostered through education, awareness raising, and training, which should be supported by governments, business and industry, civil society, and educational institutions across networked societies.

During the COVID-19 pandemic, my colleagues and I interviewed cybersecurity experts and support staff in business and industry to understand whether the move of many executives and staff to working from home caused new or greater problems with cybersecurity. We did find problems, such as more phishing emails, but overall, the development of cybersecurity capacity by governments and business and industry over the years enabled more people to work at home without major issues for cyberse-curity (Bispham 2022). Just as broadband to the home, sometimes called fiber to the home (FTTH), enables more people to have access to the internet, so has cybersecurity enabled more people to work from home or on the move or from remote work centers, supported by years of education, awareness raising, and training. For example, many organizations routinely train executives by simulating phishing attacks and other cyber-security threats and provide them with equipment for use in their work.

A major advantage of understanding cybersecurity in addressing online harms is that it focuses on actors and is not as media centric, albeit media regulation is one aspect of effective legal and regulatory frameworks (Box 10.2). For example, rather than focusing on governmental or platform censorship of content, a cybersecurity framework oper-ates at multiple levels, from institutions to individuals, and is more attuned to identify-ing malicious actors or fake/inauthentic accounts and to mitigating the damage they can do. Internet users have been well served, for example, by advances in spam filters and ant-virus software that identifies and eliminates malicious content or software before it is accessed by the user.

Past broadcasting innovations, such as incorporating a violence-chip (V-chip) in a TV set, sought to provide technical filters to violent content as an approach to child protection, as one example. Analogous appliances for computing devices, like those for TV sets, could be far more successful and enable users and households to establish their own standards for broadcasting across different members of the household. This is already a standard for many streaming services, allowing households to tailor access to content for specific individuals, such as children.

The use of computational tools to read the web and social media are increasingly capable of detecting sources of disinformation, such as illustrated through the research of Oxford's Computational Propaganda project at the OII (Box 10.3). Rather than try-ing to block information sent to millions of internet users, strong detection techniques can be used to locate and block sites at the sources of the disinformation. Focusing on a few malicious users must be superior to mass censorship of content and surveillance of users across the internet and web.

Cybersecurity capacity building at multiple levels—networked individuals, house-holds, organizations, and nations—could augment or replace approaches based on a media-centric regulatory framework. Efforts to adapt cybersecurity approaches to the concerns over online harms could benefit communities of researchers, practitioners, and policymakers as they learn from each other. If successful, the future of the internet and Fifth Estate will be brighter. Moreover, the very idea that individuals can develop the skills and awareness valuable to be part of the solution to protect their security online is perfectly in line with the rise of a Fifth Estate. It is another way networked individuals can be empowered.

Box 10.3 **Targeted Censorship of Disinformation Chinese Consul General Campaigns**

Marcel Schliebs, a doctoral researcher on the Oxford Internet Institute's Computational Propaganda Project, in collaboration with NBC News, discovered a set of about 500 "inauthentic" accounts blogging a patently false narrative: COVID-19 had been imported to Wuhan, China, from the United States in Maine lobsters. It began with a tweet from the Chinese Consul General that was followed by hundreds of verbatim tweets in nearly two dozen languages. The timing and rhythm of the tweets indicated they were produced during workdays in China. They often hijacked abandoned but formerly popular accounts that still had many followers. Nevertheless, the impact was small because they were detected very early, and Twitter quickly suspended the suspect accounts. Suspended accounts can be replaced, and the Chinese embassy indicated that China was opposed to "fabrication of information," but this kind of process can detect and block other disinformation campaigns.

Source: Olivia Solon, Keir Simmons, and Amy Perrette, "China-linked disinformation campaign blames Covid on Maine lobsters," NBC News, October 21, 2021: https://www.nbcnews.com/news/china-linked-disinformation-campaign-blames-covid-maine-lobsters-rcna3236/.

Canaries in the Institutions of Liberal Democracies

The popular story of coal miners bringing a canary deep into the coal mines to warn of dangerous levels of poisonous gases might have a modern-day parallel.[8] Liberal democracies across the world saw the diffusion of the internet in the twenty-first century giving rise to a Fifth Estate—a collectivity of networked individuals who could use the internet to hold institutions across all sectors of society more accountable. Might the rise of the Fifth Estate have been a sign of the online vitality and openness of liberal democratic institutions? Likewise, might the demise of the Fifth Estate signal dangerous risks to open access to information and to freedom of expression and assembly so central to liberal democracies? If so, can the vitality of liberal democracies be empirically monitored by tracking the prominence of the Fifth Estate?

The Fifth Estate is alive and well. Take the incredible "Greta Thunberg Effect" since 2019, significantly launched by her Instagram posts, as but one clear example along with others in this book. But how might we systematically and empirically track the vitality of the Fifth Estate amidst multiple efforts to curtail its influence?

One approach would be to build on the strategies and tactics of the Fifth Estate to collect information on national and global trends. For instance, it is possible to monitor trends in all the strategies important to empowering the Fifth Estate.

First, being connected to the internet is critical to enabling ordinary people to enhance their communicative and informational power. There is no controversy over the advantages gained in being online in our digital age, and this has spurred campaigns to reduce digital divides in nations and worldwide. However, Fifth Estate actors are not simply passive consumers of the internet. As you have read, they variously search, originate, network, collaborate, and leak information in strategic ways.

Searching is a key tool, and surveys and data analytics could track any declines in the use of organic search. For instance, search could be diminished by greater reliance on mainstream news media, advertised search, or by increased confidence in stronger algorithms that decrease the propensity to search, such as by the growing prominence of mobile apps or voice search.

Originating information for the online world is another key Fifth Estate resource, so it could it be possible to follow trends in the origination of online content. Research could track mentions of internet and social media sources cited in news coverage to detect any rise or decline. Sample surveys of networked individuals could detect changes over time in the creation of online content as well as the use of search.

Networking can be tracked by the growth and decline of a variety of social media. For example, Facebook grew from its start in 2004 to approaching 3 billion users by 2020.[9] WhatsApp had 200 million active users in 2014, when it was acquired by Facebook, but grew to over 2 billion users by 2021. By 2022, TikTok registered over 1 billion monthly active users.[10] The clear growth in number of users and number of online networks suggests the continued vitality of the Fifth Estate, but will these trends continue?

Collaborating in the development of collective civic intelligence is another key strategy. It would be possible to monitor the vitality of distributed intelligence, such as by tracking the vitality, growth or decline of prominent sites, such as Wikipedia. Are new tools for networking distributed expertise, like WikiMedia, being developed and other collaboration tools, such as mobile apps, being used more frequently to support collective intelligence?

Leaking is an important strategy even if the public does not support leaks that they view as unjustified or vengeful. It would be possible to trace the incidences of leaks, such as by mentions in major news sources. News and reports of arrests of whistleblowers could be another indirect indicator, comparable to statistics on the arrests of journalists as some evidence of problems with the Fourth Estate.

These are only a few suggestions of how empirical research could track the rise or fall of the Fifth Estate. It could be as important as efforts to track the fate of press freedom around the world—potentially even more significant in this digital age. Arguably, the fate of the Fifth Estate will be one indicator of the fate of liberal democratic institutions—the proverbial canaries in the coal mine. In an era when pundits talk about the death of democracy, with the "broken" internet cited as a key driving force (Bartlett 2018), it is hard to propose a more important trend to empirically study in the digital age.

Conclusion

The internet's broad social roles in government, politics, and other sectors of society have similarities with those of more traditional media, information, and communication technologies from the telegraph to telephone and contemporary mass media. However, the internet has also enabled the rise of the Fifth Estate—networked individuals who can enhance social accountability in the governance of important institutions, including the press—what Stephen Cooper (2006) called "watching the watchers." This contributes to significantly distinctive features of the Fifth Estate that make it worthy of being considered a new estate of at least equal importance to the Fourth—and the first to be anchored in networked individuals rather than being institution centric.

The underlying dynamics of the Fifth Estate result from the role networks can play in altering the biases of communication systems, such as by changing cost structures, eliminating and introducing gatekeepers, and expanding or contracting the geography of information and communication. These new and positive biases of communication reconfigure access to information, people, services, and technologies in fundamental ways with many positive outcomes (Dutton 1999, Amichai-Hamburger and Furnham 2007).

Access to information and communication has been reconfigured in ways that networked individuals and institutions are able to build and exercise their own informational and communicative power (Garnham 1999, Dutton 1999). They can use ICTs to reconfigure networks in ways that can lead to real-world power shifts. For instance, the relationships among media producers, gatekeepers, and consumers are changed profoundly when previously passive audiences generate and distribute their own content and when search engines point to numerous sources reflecting different views on a topic.

Moreover, networked individuals can use searching, creating, networking, collaborating, and leaking to create new, more independent, and additive sources of information and collaboration that are not directly dependent on any one institutional source or any single institution within in single estate—whether public intellectuals, business and industry, government, or the press. Even internet-enabled individuals whose primary aims in their networking activities are social can often break from existing geographical, organizational, and institutional networks, which themselves are frequently being transformed in internet space, to hold other institutions more accountable, as did the young woman who happened to be an eyewitness to George Floyd's arrest, which she captured on her phone and posted on social media (Chapter 5).

The digital choices institutions and individuals make will afford greater or lesser control to citizens, viewers, consumers, and other networked individuals. Appreciating how the use and diffusion of technologies is socially shaped reveals how the development of any particular outcome was not inevitable, including those supportive of a Fifth Estate. They have evolved through the unpredictable interaction of strategic as well as unintentional decisions by many actors, with many different competing and complementary objectives. For instance, the ability to forge local and global networks is illustrated by the mobilization of political and financial support around the world for causes as varied as climate change, antiterrorism, and struggles about state control, disaster relief, and disinformation.

Since the early days of private bulletin board systems (BBS), some moderation of platforms has been critical to their survival, just as filtering spam and antivirus software are critical to individual internet users. There are serious issues related to online harms, but the centrality of the internet to network societies demands that harms are addressed in ways that maintain a commitment to freedom of expression and privacy, as well as the protection of personal information.

This cannot be accomplished by generating fear as this might well lead the most marginal in society to disconnect from the digital world (Dutton et al. 2022). It can be done through digital governance that will protect the rights of internet users, as argued by proponents of digital constitutionalism (Celeste 2022, De Gregorio 2022), but also by supporting online safety through building multiple levels of capacities to support cybersecurity as opposed to an overreliance on top-down censorship and surveillance of the internet. This more security-based approach to safety could enable individuals and organizations to build their capacity to be resilient to hostile actors, disinformation, and malicious actions, without disconnecting or surrendering their freedom of expression and personal privacy. Security is not only in the spirit of an empowered network individual, but it can also further empower the Fifth Estate.

THE OPEN FUTURE OF DIGITAL CHOICES, THE CRITICAL MASS, AND DIGITAL DIVIDES

Use of the internet will continue to diffuse to the next billion users across the world, and in the variety of applications it supports, and in the devices that can be used for access (e.g., see www.worldinternetproject.net). As a result, the internet has become such a crucial infrastructure of everyday life in our network society that disparities in its availability and take-up are of substantive social, economic and—increasingly—political significance, placing great emphasis on reducing digital divides that often follow and reinforce socioeconomic inequalities in society (Hargittai and Hsieh 2013).

However, social and economic factors do not explain all patterns of adoption and use of the internet (Rice et al. 2007, Rainie and Wellman 2012, Ellison and Boyd 2013). Geography also matters with even high-income developed nations focusing more attention on remote rural areas and distressed urban areas, where internet access has reached fewer individuals and households (Reisdorf et al. 2020). In addition, "digital choices" about whether to use the internet also come into play. For example, many people still choose not to use the internet even when they have opportunities to do so. It may be generally understandable that elderly citizens are significantly less likely to use the internet than younger generations who have appropriate skills and greater familiarity with the technology. Yet, many people in homes with access to the technology and other support are still not motivated to go online or engage in pro-social forms of online activity, such as networking (Dutton et al. 2022).

Despite these continuing digital divides, the internet has achieved a critical mass in most nations that enables networked individuals to become a significant social and political force. A major strength of the Fifth Estate is that its existence does not depend on universal access but on reaching a critical mass of users. This enables the Fifth Estate to play an important political role in nations such as Indonesia, with less than three-quarters (70%) of its population online but amounting to nearly 200 million users— clearly a critical mass.

That said, as the Fifth Estate becomes recognized as an important source of political and social accountability and empowerment, the digital divide will also be a more prominent political divide—a growing source of inequality in politics and society. And conceptions of the digital divide will expand to include knowledge of how to effectively search, originate, network, collaborate, and even leak information, when necessary, in ways that enable you to play a Fifth Estate role. The informational and communicative empowerment of networked individuals should not be divided between the haves and have-nots of the networked society. By addressing and expanding our understanding of global digital divides, this network power shift of our digital age can enhance the vitality of all sectors of societies across the world.

Notes

Introduction

1. ARPA stood for the Advanced Research Projects Agency of the U.S. Department of Defense.
2. Communication networking over the early APRA network was at 50-kilobit-per-second speeds.
3. Solid is a technology designed by Sir Tim Berners-Lee through a project he directed at MIT that has moved to an official website at: https://inrupt.com/solid/.
4. Elaine Tassy (1993), "Shwashlock Helps Homeless Prepare for the Working World," Los Angeles Times, November 18: https://www.latimes.com/archives/la-xpm-1993-11-18-we-58017-story.html/.
5. E.g., Eric Schmidt was reported to argue that the internet could undermine if not bring down corrupt governments, making a case for internet power. See https://www.telegraph.co.uk/technology/eric-schmidt/9285827/Eric-Schmidt-internet-will-bring-down-corrupt-governments.html/.
6. See this CNN coverage of his 2019 talk at https://edition.cnn.com/videos/tech/2019/10/18/mark-zuckerberg-facebook-social-media-fifth-estate-sot-vpx.cnn
7. This is a concept underpinning a 2022 conference on the challenges to public service broadcasting by the new digital media platforms in Vienna, Austria, in September, entitled "Between the Fourth Estate and the Fifth Power."

Chapter 1

1. Greta Thunberg, on Twitter, @GretaThunberg, December 1, 2022. Also see: https://www.instagram.com/gretathunberg/.
2. Daniel Ellsberg quoted by Smith (2021: 37).
3. Helen Roxburgh and Laurent Thomet, "Chinese Doctor Who Raised Alert on Coronavirus Has Died, While the Outbreak Continues," Science Alert, February 2020, https://www.sciencealert.com/doctor-who-alerted-world-to-wuhan-coronavirus-tragically-succumbed-to-the-virus/.
4. Editorial Board, "The Unanswered Questions of the Peng Shuai Case," Financial Times, November 25, 2021, https://www.ft.com/content/f84280ae-5f65-49ff-be75-58f08ca9b164
5. Joe Hernandez, "Read this Powerful State from Danella Frazier, Who Filmed George Floyd's Murder," NPR, May 26, 2021, https://www.npr.org/2021/05/26/1000475344/read-this-powerful-statement-from-darnella-frazier-who-filmed-george-floyds-murd
6. The use of phones in disturbances in the Arab-Israeli conflict, such as documenting settlers attacking Palestinians, provides one example, see Kerr (2021).
7. On Demand News, "Woman Throws Cat into Wheelie Bin," YouTube, 2010, https://www.youtube.com/watch?v=eYdUZdan5i8&ab_channel=OnDemandNews.

8. Patrick Barkham, "Cat Bin Woman Mary Bale Fined £250," *The Guardian*, October 19, 2010, https://www.theguardian.com/world/2010/oct/19/cat-bin-woman-mary-bale.

9. A major contribution to the "Killing of Cecil the Lion" is provided by Wikipedia: https://en.wikipedia.org/wiki/Killing_of_Cecil_the_lion/.

10. Office of Public Affairs, "Six Russian GRU Officers Charged in Connection with Worldwide Deployment of Destructive Malware and Other Disruptive Actions in Cyberspace," US Department of Justice, October 19, 2020, https://www.justice.gov/opa/pr/six-russian-gru-officers-charged-connection-worldwide-deployment-destructive-malware-and. (Last accessed 6 January 2023).

11. Code For America, "Civic Hacking 101," December 1, 2022, https://codefordc.github.io/resources/what-is-civic-hacking.html.

Chapter 2

1. A number of colleagues who are historians, and one a Burke scholar, provided valuable insights to the uncertainties surrounding the identity of the various landed estates and the origin of the concept of the Fourth Estate, including Mark Bruce, Martin Millerick, and Kylie Murray. My thanks to these colleagues and apologies for any errors in my interpretations of our personal correspondence.

2. A valuable history of the Fourth Estate is provided by Julianne Schultz (1998: 23–56).

3. U.S. Senator Bernie Sanders on Instagram at: https://www.instagram.com/p/CgXZOxSDnyi/?hl=en but also on Twitter at: https://twitter.com/BernieSanders/status/1550914666867589122.

4. Justice Brandeis in a dissenting opinion in *Myers v. United States*, 272 U.S. 52, 293 (1926) quoted by Stewart (1975: 634).

5. As he put his thesis, "The history of the world is but the biography of great men" (Carlyle 1841: 34).

6. See: Final Report of the Select Committee to Investigate the January 6th Attack on the United States Capitol, committed to the Whole House on the State of the Union. Washington DC: U.S. Government Printing Office, 2022. https://apps.npr.org/documents/document.html?id=23515535-jan-6-select-committee-final-r.

7. To paraphrase Andrew Keen (2008), after speaking at the Oxford Internet Institute, he half-jokingly said that the Institute was a Trojan Horse that brought internet studies into Oxford University.

8. https://www.theguardian.com/media/2009/nov/01/stephen-fry-twitter-quit-threat/.

9. https://vahidhoustonranjbar.medium.com/the-fetish-of-exaggerated-individualism-is-driving-us-to-extinction-209f8e83e471/.

10. Gaslighting is a strategy for fooling a person into questioning their own beliefs or perceptions about reality by feeding them false or misleading information.

11. Martin Moore, "Churnalism Exposed: A New Website Identifies Press Release Copy in the News," Columbia Journalism Review, March 3, 2011. https://archives.cjr.org/the_news_frontier/churnalism_exposed.php.

12. https://www.youtube.com/watch?v=8Zsf1JM2yLk/.

13. An overview of the project aimed at maintaining social cohesion rather than free speech is available at https://archives.cjr.org/the_news_frontier/churnalism_exposed.php.

14. Berkman Klein Center at Harvard University web page on the "herdict" project, launched by Jonathan Zittrain, at: https://cyber.harvard.edu/research/herdict.

Chapter 3

1. You can track Internet and social media use through Internet World Stats at https://www.internetworldstats.com/stats.htm/.

2. Quote Investigator at: https://quoteinvestigator.com/2014/07/13/truth/.
3. For example, see Peter Roesler, "8 of the Biggest Business Mistakes in History," Inc., no date: https://www.inc.com/peter-roesler/8-of-the-biggest-business-mistakes-in-history.html.

Chapter 4

1. Background on the Wiener Holocaust Library is available on their website at: https://wie nerholocaustlibrary.org/.
2. Julián Herber, "The Forgotten Massacre of Chinese Immigrants During the Mexican Revolution," Literary Hub, April 16, 2019: https://lithub.com/the-forgotten-massacre-of-chinese-immigrants-during-the-mexican-revolution/.
3. A collection of images the Southern Apache Museum documenting "Native American atrocities" is available on Pinterest at: https://www.pinterest.co.uk/apachemuseum/native-ameri can-atrocities/.
4. The U.S. Environmental Protection Agency, "Deepwater Horizon—BP Gulf of Mexico Oil Spill," last updated by the EPA in August 31, 2022: https://www.epa.gov/enforcement/deepwater-horizon-bp-gulf-mexico-oil-spill/.
5. Radoslav Chakarov, "How Many Blogs Are There? We Counted Them All!," *Web Tribunal,* April 6, 2022: https://hostingtribunal.com/blog/how-many-blogs/.
6. A website called ChartsBin tracks the number of newspapers by country. See: http://charts bin.com/view/34582.
7. The eight variables with ratings of 0, 1, or 2 were summed. Those with totals of 0–8 were rated spectators, 9–11 rated attentives, and 12 and over rated as potential Fifth Estate participants.
8. This relationship between the production of content and higher socioeconomic status is also clear in US surveys of internet use, such as Schradie's (2011) review of Pew surveys.
9. http://www.whatsinkenilworth.com/2012/06/martha-payne-and-story-of-neverseco nds.html.
10. A more detailed description of George Floyd's life that I've drawn from is provided by Bushey and Aladesuyi (2021).
11. Temporary interruption of these services resulted in serious problems for the Ukraine forces in the occupied regions of their nation (Holt 2022).
12. eyeWitness to Atrocities, created by LexisNexis in partnership with the International Bar Association in London, has an overview of the organization and its projects at: https://www.lexisnexisrolfoundation.org/projects/eyewitness.aspx?p=projects.
13. Levko Stek, "'They Killed People Systematically': Bucha Residents Allege War Crimes by Expelled Russian Forces," *Radio Free Europe/Radion Liberty,* April 4, 2022: https://www.rferl.org/a/ukraine-russia-bucha-massacre/31785407.html.
14. Alan Abrahamson and Miles Corwin, "Man Kills Self as City Watches," *Los Angeles Times,* May 1, 1998, https://www.latimes.com/archives/la-xpm-1998-may-01-mn-45260-story.html/.
15. The web desk at *The News,* "Christchurch Shooting: Horrifying Video of New Zealand Mosque Attack Live Streamed on Facebook," March 15, 2019: https://www.thenews.com.pk/latest/444349-christchurch-shooter-live-streamed-mosque-firing-on-facebook/.
16. Dipesh Gadher, "Don Taught Students from Wheel of His Car," *The Sunday Times,* November 29, 2020. https://www.thetimes.co.uk/article/don-taught-students-from-wheel-of-his-car-t807mtdzx/.
17. BBC News, "Woman who dumped cat in wheelie bin 'profoundly sorry'," August 25, 2010: https://www.bbc.co.uk/news/uk-england-coventry-warwickshire-11087061/.

Chapter 5

1. Madhumita Murgia, "WhatsApp shuts down Taliban helpline in Kabul," Financial Times, August 17, 2021: https://www.ft.com/content/d8e29de8-aebb-4f10-a91e-89d454d4a9f7.

2. Tanya Burke tells this story in her own words and how it inspired her to organize a social movement around MeToo: https://metoomvmt.org/get-to-know-us/history-inception/.

3. Jodi Kantor and Megan Twohey, "Harvey Harvey Weinstein Paid Off Sexual Harassment Accusers for Decades," *New York Times*, October 5, 2017: https://www.nytimes.com/2017/10/05/us/harvey-weinstein-harassment-allegations.html?hp&action=click&pgtype=Homepage&clickSource=story-heading&module=a-lede-package-region&region=top-news&WT.nav=top-news/.

4. David Ryder, "The hashtag #BlackLivesMatter first appears, sparking a movement," *History*, July 13 2013: https://www.history.com/this-day-in-history/blacklivesmatter-hashtag-first-appears-facebook-sparking-a-movement/.

5. This is the view of *Britannica* in an entry on Black Lives Matter: an international activist movement. See https://www.britannica.com/topic/Black-Lives-Matter/.

6. Lebron's (2017: xi–xii)) history of BLM also believes #BLM cannot be linked to any "single leader or small group of leaders" but is a "brand that can be picked up and deployed by any interested group of activists."

7. Black Lives Matter website at: https://blacklivesmatter.com/.

8. Interviews with Mike Richards, a historian and former faculty member at Sweet Briar College, were valuable in the interpretation of news and other coverage of this case.

9. A good timeline of the campaign to save the college is Appendix A of Leonard (2018: 202).

10. This revolved around whether the college was a corporation or a trust. If the former, it could be closed by the officials. If a trust, it could not.

11. William A. Jacobson, "Sweet Briar Saved as Settlement is Reached," College Insurrection (CI), June 22, 2015: http://collegeinsurrection.com/2015/06/sweet-briar-saved-as-settlement-is-reached/.

12. See "Saving Sweet Briar College Through Transformation Change Management," Changing Higher Ed Podcast 074 video of College President Meredith Woo interviewed by Dr. Drumm McNaughton: https://changinghighered.com/college-transformational-change-management/ and YouTube: https://www.youtube.com/watch?v=oPyNg1ZhQmY/.

13. Dana Poleski, "Virginia Center for the Creative Arts Purchases Mt. San Angelo Property from Sweet Briar College," Sweet Briar College News, July 1, 2020: https://sbc.edu/news/vcca-purchases-mt-san-angelo/.

14. Quote from the administrator of the Facebook page, "Flint Water Crisis," in May 2021.

15. Personal email from a participant on May 21, 2021.

16. Arthus Delaney, "Read a Whitleblower's Warnings About the Flint Water Crisis," *Huffington Post*, March 17, 2016, https://www.huffingtonpost.co.uk/entry/flint-water-epa_n_56e97a6be4b0860f99db2295?ri18n=true/.

17. This website continued to follow and post information important to address the water crisis until 2019: http://flintwaterstudy.org (last accessed May 2021).

18. Anna Clark, "How an Investigative Journalist Helped Prove a City Was Being Poisoned with Its Own Water," *Columbia Journalism Review*, November 3, 2015: https://www.cjr.org/united_states_project/flint_water_lead_curt_guyette_aclu_michigan.php/.

19. Eight-Year-Old Flint Girl Who Wrote Letter to Obama: "I Wanted Him to Know What Was Going On," see: Daniel White, "President Obama Plans to Visit Flint," *Time*, April 27, 2016: https://time.com/4309664/obama-flint-water-crisis-copeny-email/?iid=sr-link2/.

20. Daniel White, "President Obama Plans to Visit Flint", *Time*, April 27, 2016: https://time.com/4309664/obama-flint-water-crisis-copeny-email/?iid=sr-link2/.

21. Sophia Lotto Persio, "Who Is LeeAnne Walters?," *Newsweek*, April 23, 2018, https://www.newsweek.com/who-leeanne-walters-activist-who-helped-expose-flint-water-crisis-wins-top-897326.

22. Anna Clark, "How an Investigative Journalist Helped Prove a City Was Being Poisoned with Its Own Water," *Columbia Journalism Review*, November 3, 2015: https://www.cjr.org/united_states_project/flint_water_lead_curt_guyette_aclu_michigan.

23. One example is OWL that uses a 360-degree camera with microphones and speakers to bring all participants around a table into an online meeting or classroom. See the product website at: https://owllabs.co.uk/.
24. On Deman News, "Woman Throws Cat into Wheelie Bin," YouTube: https://www.youtube.com/watch?v=eYdUZdanSi8/.
25. ABC News, "American Dentist Accused of Killing Famous Lion," July 28, 2015: https://abcnews.go.com/WNT/video/american-dentist-accused-killing-famous-lion-cecil-safari-32746408/.
26. Josh Halliday, "Tory MP Louise Mensch Backs Social Network Blackouts During Civil Unrest," *The Guardian*, August 12, 2011: https://www.theguardian.com/uk/2011/aug/12/louise-mensch-social-network-blackouts/.

Chapter 6

1. Key ideas developed in this chapter originated as a policy brief prepared for the Occasional Paper Series in Science & Technology, Science and Technology Policy Institute (STPI) in Washington DC, later published (Dutton 2015). I thank David Bray, Michael Chui, Paul David, Jane Fountain, Brad Johnson, James Manyika, and Yorick Wilks.
2. The value of collaboration for the Fifth Estate examined in this chapter arose from a variety of case studies of distributed networks (Dutton 2008, 2015, Chui et al. 2009, and Richter et al. 2010), community networking initiatives (Zorina and Dutton 2014), and innovations in academic collaboration for research across disciplines, including experiments in citizen science (Dutton and Jeffreys 2010, Dutton 2011b). It is on this basis that there is ample evidence of the potential for networked individuals using the internet to provide a platform for building collaboration in support of the Fifth Estate.
3. http://www.iit.edu/~it/delphi.html/. Rand Corporation developed the Delphi method. Their website provides an overview at: https://www.rand.org/topics/delphi-method.html.
4. An overview of EMISARI is provided by OEP (1973) and is a core feature of an innovative book on computer conferencing (Hiltz and Turoff 1978).
5. Murray Turoff, Living Internet, in IRC History. See: http://www.livinginternet.com/r/ri_emisari.htm/.
6. A Swarm of Angels used the internet for international creator-led collaborative development in making a film. An excellent case study of the Swarm of Angels is available on the Creative Commons website at: https://wiki.creativecommons.org/wiki/Case_Studies/A_Swarm_of_Angels/.
7. Wikipedia guidelines and policies are online at https://en.wikipedia.org/wiki/Wikipedia:Policies_and_guidelines/.
8. Analysis of this hoax is covered on Wikipedia at https://en.wikipedia.org/wiki/Wikipedia_Seigenthaler_biography_incident/.
9. Updated figures on the size of Wikipedia are available on Wikipedia at: https://en.wikipedia.org/wiki/Wikipedia:Size_of_Wikipedia.
10. Ibid.
11. Hope Talbot, "Student Confusion over "Disappearance" of Rate My Teacher Reviews," *The New Trier News*, September 13, 2019: https://newtriernews.org/news/2019/09/13/student-confusion-over-disappearance-of-rate-my-teacher-reviews/.
12. See the ipaidabribe website at: https://www.janaagraha.org/i-paid-a-bribe/.
13. This description of IPAB is based on an interview and video with Venkatesh Kannaiah on July 20, 2015, when he was based in Bangalore, India, as a senior editor for Ipaidabribe.com. He was in the United States as a Knight International Journalism Fellow to build networks of journalists and "right to information" activists in south India.
14. This mission is part of a depiction of what Janaagraha seeks to accomplish is on their website, entitled "Transforming quality of life in India's cities and towns," at: https://www.janaagraha.org/home/.

15. India Risk Report, South Asia, on Gan Integrity at: https://www.ganintegrity.com/portal/country-profiles/india/.
16. Camilla Hodgson, "England Faces Ban on Single-use Plastic Cutlery, Plates and Cups," *Financial Times*, August 27, 2021: https://www.ft.com/content/163f4e08-bbac-40bb-972e-f9f46c198545/.
17. Lee Bock, "An Experiment in Crowscraping," *Story Maps*, undated, at: https://storymaps.arcgis.com/stories/dcbb5c9e009442b99944bd1ef6158bda/.
18. This example is based on an update of research conducted by me and three other researchers who were given client observer accounts, permitting us to log onto Sermo and see most posts and responses. In addition, interviews were conducted with the leadership of Sermo, and the internet was used to search for all journalistic coverage of Sermo, ranging from press releases by the company to blog posts by critics. The original case is available online in Bray et al. (2007) at https://papers.ssrn.com/sol3/papers.cfm?abstract_id=1016483/.
19. The Patients Like Me website is at: https://www.patientslikeme.com/.
20. See the about page of Patients Like Me at: https://www.patientslikeme.com/about/.
21. The Children with Diabetes website is at: https://childrenwithdiabetes.com/.
22. See the eyeWitness to Atrocities web site at: https://www.lexisnexisrolfoundation.org/projects/eyewitness.aspx?p=projects
23. This description of social intelligence is an update of a blog I posted based on an interview with Angus Cheong, who developed this initiative in Macau and Hong Kong. See billdutton.me/2022/10/05/social-intelligence/.
24. The tools and processes are those of uMax Data Technology Limited, uMax Data. They include xMiner, a platform for big data analysis; LawMiner, a platform for legal market insights; HK Plulse, a platform for social listening and analytics. But see https://www.umaxdata.com/ and https://www.divominer.com/en/ for information about the organization's tools and platforms.
25. Games with a purpose (GWAP) are human-based computational games that gamify problem solving such as by outsourcing steps in a computational process to human but in an entertaining way, as described in https://en.wikipedia.org/wiki/Human-based_computation_game#:~:text=A%20human%2Dbased%20computation%20game,an%20entertaining%20way%20(gamification).

Chapter 7

1. FBI, "Atom Spy Case/Rosenbergs," History, United States Government Website at: https://www.fbi.gov/history/famous-cases/atom-spy-caserosenbergs/.
2. Eddie Meadows (June 14, 1971), "Oval office meeting with Bob Haldelman, Nixon Presidential Materials Project, Oval-519, Cassette 747," audio tape.
3. A more detailed journalistic account of WikiLeaks, Chelsea Manning, Julian Assange, and the events outlined here is provided by Leigh and Harding (2011).
4. The overview of WikiLeaks on WikiLeaks is quite comprehensive and authoritative. See: https://wikileaks.org/What-is-WikiLeaks.html/.
5. Ibid. See: https://wikileaks.org/What-is-WikiLeaks.html/.
6. Reuters, "Assange Supporters Form Human Chain at UK Parliament," Reuters.com, October 8, 2022: https://www.reuters.com/world/uk/assange-supporters-form-human-chain-uk-parliament-2022-10-08/.
7. Jim Waterson, "Publishers Urge US to Drop Prosecution of Julian Assange for Cable Leaks," *The Guardian*, 29 November. In an open letter on November 28, 2022, on the Guardian website, the news organizations published the open letter: https://www.nytco.com/press/an-open-letter-from-editors-and-publishers-publishing-is-not-a-crime.
8. DW, "OpenLeaks," an interview with Daniel Domscheit-Berg, on the dw.com, December 14, 2010: https://www.dw.com/en/openleaks-aims-to-provide-a-more-transparent-alternative-to-wikileaks/a-6324646/.

9. SecureDrop is an "open-source whistleblower submission system that media organizations can install to securely accept documents from anonymous sources," see their website at: https://securedrop.org/.
10. A fuller and engaging account of OpenLeaks is provided by Greenberg (2012).
11. WikiLeaks has continued to operate as a "multi-national," founded by Julian Assange, and focused on "the analysis and publication of large datasets of censored or otherwise restricted official materials involving war, spying and corruption," as described in its website at: https://wikileaks.org/.
12. This section draws on details covered in multiple sources but relies most heavily on Glenn Greenwald's (2014) authoritative account of Edward Snowden and the leaks described here.
13. E.g., Democracy Now organized a conversation between whistleblowers Daniel Ellsberg and Edward Snowden, entitled "Truth, Dissent, & The Legacy of Daniel Ellsberg," marking the fiftieth anniversary of the release of the Pentagon Papers. Available at https://www.democracynow.org/2021/5/6/whistleblowers_daniel_ellsberg_edward_snowden_in/.
14. Programs exposed by Snowden's leaks are described online by COGIPAS, "Snowden Leaks: a Summary of the NSA Programs," at: https://www.cogipas.com/snowden-leaks-summary-of-nsa-programs/.
15. The Guardian, "Citizenship Decree for Snowden," September 27, 2022, p. 28.
16. A section of the Espionage Act was applied to obtain a search warrant for entering former President Donald Trump's Mar-a-Lago home to obtain classified documents kept there.
17. The documentary, produced by Sonia Kennebeck, entitled "United States vs. Reality Winner," sponsored by the International Documentary Association (IDA), is online at: https://www.documentary.org/project/united-states-vs-reality-winner

Chapter 8

1. An interview on UK Sky News, October 5, 2021.
2. The case for connecting Facebook use to the events is unconvincing but see LaFrance (2021).
3. See updated World Internet User Statistics that are available online at https://internetworldstats.com/stats.htm/.
4. See the vTaiwan project page online at: https://info.vtaiwan.tw/.
5. For example, controversy surrounded the denial of service and other cyber attacks on the FCC's consultation on net neutrality. An overview is provided by Devin Coldewey, "Deficiencies' that broke FCC commenting system in net neutrality fight detailed by GAO," TechCrunch, April 24, 2020: https://techcrunch.com/2020/04/24/deficiencies-that-broke-fcc-commenting-system-in-net-neutrality-fight-detailed-by-gao/?guccounter=1.
6. The founders were Colin Megill, founder & CEO, Michael Bjorkegren, founder & CTO, and Christopher Small, founder & lead data scientist. See the project's web page at: https://pol.is/company.html.
7. Statistics from The World Counts. You can search on their website for updated facts about plastic pollution at: https://www.theworldcounts.com/stories/interesting-facts-about-plastic-bags
8. Personal interview with Elizabeth Carr on October 7, 2021.

Chapter 9

1. Mark Townsend, "Facebook-Cambridge Analytica Data Breach Lawsuit Ends in 11th Hour Settlement," *The Observer*, August 27, 2022: https://www.theguardian.com/technology/2022/aug/27/facebook-cambridge-analytica-data-breach-lawsuit-ends-in-11th-hour-settlement/.

2. This section was anchored in news reports and by Alexandr Kogan's (2018) written testimony to a UK inquiry. See https://www.parliament.uk/business/committees/committees-a-z/commons-select/digital-culture-media-and-sport-committee/inquiries/parliament-2017/fake-news-17-19/.

3. Munsif Vengattil, "Cambridge Analytica and Parent SCL Elections Shutting Down," *Reuters*, May 2, 2018: https://www.aol.com/article/finance/2018/05/02/cambridge-analytica-and-parent-scl-elections-shutting-down/23425687/.

4. Noted in evidence Aleksandr Kogan submitted to the UK Parliament's Digital, Culture, Media and Sport Committee's Inquiry into Fake News, April 24, 2017.

5. Kogan conveyed this in a March 21, 2018, BBC radio interview: https://www.bbc.co.uk/news/av/uk-43487442/.

6. Paris Martineau, "Read the Full Email: Researcher Says Facebook is Scapegoating Him," *The Future*, March 22, 2018: https://theoutline.com/post/3838/read-the-full-kogan-email-researcher-says-facebook-is-scapegoating-him.

7. Josh Constine, "Facebook Announces Stricter Guidelines for Research And Experiments On Its Users," *TechCrunch*, October 2, 2014: https://techcrunch.com/2014/10/02/facebook-research-guidelines/.

8. David Ingram and Peter Henderson, "Trump Consultants Harvested Data from 50 Million Users," Technology News, *Reuters*, March 17, 2018: https://www.reuters.com/article/us-facebook-cambridge-analytica/trump-consultants-harvested-data-from-50-million-facebook-users-reports-idUSKCN1GT02Y.

9. Internet scholars continue to ask for access to Facebook data, often unaware of the reputational risks to Facebook and the research institutions (Gluckman 2018).

10. A March 9, 2022 version of Australia's "Harmful Digital Communications Act 2015" is available online at https://www.legislation.govt.nz/act/public/2015/0063/latest/whole.html.

11. Ofcom was "established by the Office of Communications Act 2002 and empowered under the Communications Act 2003." See https://www.politics.co.uk/reference/ofcom/.

12. A history of the work of the Internet Watch Foundation is on their website at https://www.iwf.org.uk/what-we-do/why-we-exist/our-history/.

13. The Online Safety Bill and its status can be tracked here at the UK Parliament website entitled Parliamentary Bills, at; https://bills.parliament.uk/bills/3137.

14. Based on a presentation of work on the Political and Health Information Seeking Project by Bianca C. Reisdorf, November 11, 2021. The project is a collaboration of the Quello Center at MSU, the OII at Oxford University, and the University of North Carolina, Charlotte.

15. China has begun regulating screentime for children, such as three hours of online gaming per week. See https://www.bloomberg.com/news/articles/2021-08-30/china-limits-minors-to-just-three-hours-of-online-gaming-a-week/.

16. Jane Wakefield, "Nearly a Third of Waking Hours Spent on TV and Streaming, Ofcom says," *BBC News*, August 5, 2021: https://www.bbc.co.uk/news/technology-58086629/.

17. Philippa Smith at Auckland University of Technology drew my attention to work being done via a New Zealand website, called Sticks n Stones for 8-to-18-year-olds at https://www.sticksnstones.co.nz/.

18. Jasmine Cameron-Chileshe and Ian Johanston, "MPs Seek Jail Terms for Tech Chiefs in Online Harms Bill," *Financial Times*, January 13, 2023, 3.

19. Jim Pickard and Ian Johnston, "MPs Press Donelan over Online Child Safety," *Financial Times*, January 14/15, 2003, 3.

20. See GlobalStats on statecounter, which tracks search engine market share worldwide, to gain a clear picture of the dominance of Google among its competitors, at: https://gs.statcounter.com/search-engine-market-share/.

21. The percentage of the global population using Facebook is available by region on Statista, at: https://www.statista.com/statistics/241552/share-of-global-population-using-facebook-by-region/.

22. Celso Martinho and tom Strickx, "Understanding How Facebook Disappeared from the Internet," Cloudfare Blog, April 10, 2021: https://blog.cloudflare.com/october-2021-facebook-outage/.
23. @elonmusk and see: The Economist, "Elon Musk buys Twitter at last", *The Economist*, October 28, 2022.
24. An analysis of the online Harms White Paper by Stefan Theil (2019) provides a comparison with German approaches to regulation.
25. The Online Safety Bill and its status can be tracked here at the UK Parliament website entitled Parliamentary Bills, at: https://bills.parliament.uk/bills/3137.
26. Facebook facts and statistics are provided online by wishpond at: https://blog.wishpond.com/post/115675435109/40-up-to-date-facebook-facts-and-stats#:~:text=There%20are%201%2C500%20average%20number,by%20Facebook%20users%20each%20day/.
27. See Jack Shepherd, "30 Essential Facebook Statistics You Need To Know In 2023," Social_Shepherd Blog, January 3, 2023, at: https://thesocialshepherd.com/blog/facebook-statistics#:~:text=1.62%20Billion%20users%20on%20average,population%20are%20daily%20active%20users!.
28. In the US, e.g., Section 230 of the Communication Decency Act recognizes that no provider of internet services should be treated as the publisher or speaker when information is provided by a user.
29. In China, an internet or social media company could lose its license overnight if it allowed users to cross red lines determined by the government and only guessed at by the private internet providers. This fear has led to overregulation of the internet and social media by these companies in China.

Chapter 10

1. This framing was even adopted by one of the pioneers of the internet David Clark (Clark and Claffy 2019).
2. See Joel Khalili, "The inventor of the World Wide Web says his creation has been abused for too long," *Techradar*, January 19, 2022: https://www.techradar.com/uk/news/the-inventor-of-the-world-wide-web-says-his-creation-has-been-abused-for-too-long/.
3. For instance, see Knake et al. (2021) who edited a special issue of an elementary school journal on the Fifth Estate and a review of this literature by Greenhow et al. (2020).
4. Emilia Askari used my early article on the Fifth Estate (Dutton 2009) along with a 2018 presentation of mine on Fifth Estate strategies to design her project for the class.
5. In the United States, this was enacted through Section 230 of the Communications Decency Act, which some have seen as the "most valuable tools for protecting freedom of expression and innovation on the Internet" (Electronic Frontier Foundation 2022). Ironically, the act was viewed by many as an infringement of free expression, but the provisions that were anti–free speech were ruled unconstitutional by the Supreme Court.
6. GCSCC, "Cybersecurity Capacity Maturity Model for Nations, 2021 Edition," Global Cyber Security Capacity Centre, Oxford Martin School, University of Oxford: https://gcscc.ox.ac.uk/cmm-2021-edition/.
7. Steve Jobs, "A Bicycle of the Mind—Steve Jobs on the Computer," *The Financial Review*, YouTube, interview conducted in 1990: https://www.youtube.com/watch?v=L40B08nWoMk/.
8. This section updates and builds on Dutton (2020), "The Fifth Estate: Canaries in the Institutions of Liberal Democracies," in Nagel et al. (2020), *Politische Komplexität, Governance von Innovationen und Policy-Netzwerke: Festschrift für Volker Schneider,* pp. 59–65.
9. Felix Richter, "Facebook Keeps on Growing," Facebook, February 4, 2021: https://www.statista.com/chart/10047/facebooks-monthly-active-users/.
10. Statistics on social media users are available at Wallaroo, "TikTok Statistics," Wallaroo Blog, January 12, 2023, at: https://wallaroomedia.com/blog/social-media/tiktok-statistics/.

Bibliography

Afifi-Sabet, K. (2020), "Cambridge Analytica Models Were Exaggerated and Ineffective, ICO Claims." *ITPro*, October 8, https://www.itpro.com/policy-legislation/data-protection/357 367/cambridge-analytica-project-was-ineffective-ico-claims.

Ahmed, M., Lewis, L., and Astrasheuskaya, N. (2021), "Belarus Olympic Sprinter Takes Refuge After Comments Spur Minsk Backlash." *Financial Times*, August 3, pp. 1, 4.

Alba, D. (2017), "The World May Be Headed for a Fragmented 'Splinternet.'" *Wired*, July 7, https://www.wired.com/story/splinternet-global-court-rulings-google-facebook/

Allen, A. (2022), "The EU's Opaque Policy-Making Has Never Been Clearer." *Financial Times*, April 29.

Amichai-Hamburger, Y., and Furnham, A. (2007), "The Positive Net." *Computers in Human Behavior*, 23: 1033–45.

Anderson, M. (2016), "The Hashtag #BlackLivesMatter Emerges: Social Activism on Twitter." Pew Research Center, August 15, https://www.pewresearch.org/internet/2016/08/15/the-hash tag-blacklivesmatter-emerges-social-activism-on-twitter/.

Anderson, M., Barthel, M., Perrin, A., and Vogels, E. A. (2020), "#BlackLivesMatter Surges on Twitter after George Floyd's Death." Pew Research Center, June 10, https://www.pewresearch.org/fact-tank/2020/06/10/blacklivesmatter-surges-on-twitter-after-george-floyds-death/.

Ang, Y. Y. (2014), "Authoritarian Restraints on Online Activism Revisited: Why 'I-Paid-a-Bribe' Worked in India but Failed in China." *Comparative Politics*, October, https://sites.lsa.umich.edu/yy-ang/wp-content/uploads/sites/427/2016/08/Ang-I-paid-a-bribe.pdf/.

Askari, E. (2022), "A Case Study Exploring How K-12 Students Learn to Use Social Media for Civic Good." PhD diss., Michigan State University.

Bachrach, P. (1967), *The Theory of Democratic Elitism: A Critique*. Boston: Little, Brown.

Ball, J. (2022), "Russia Is Risking the Creation of a 'Splinternet'—and It Could Be Irreversible." *MIT Technology Review*, March 17, https://www.technologyreview.com/2022/03/17/1047 352/russia-splinternet-risk/.

Barker, A. (2020), "TikTok More Popular Than TV Among Young Adults." *Financial Times*, August 17, p. 2.

Bartlett, Jamie (2018), *The People vs Tech: How the Internet Is Killing Democracy*. London: Ebury.

Bell, D. (1973), *The Coming of Post-Industrial Society: A Venture in Social Forecasting*. New York: Basic Books.

Bell, E. (2016), "The Unpredictable Course of Live Streaming Has Caught Us Unprepared." *The Guardian*, July 17, https://www.theguardian.com/media/2016/jul/17/live-streaming-viol ent-events-crisis-facebook/.

Benedictus, L. (2019), "I Know All Their Pet Peeves—Why Neighborhood Apps Are a Mixed Blessing." *The Guardian*, September 8, https://www.theguardian.com/media/2019/sep/08/i-know-all-their-pet-peeves-why-neighbourhood-apps-are-a-mixed-blessing/.

Benkler, Y. (2006), *The Wealth of Networks: How Social Production Transforms Markets and Freedom.* New Haven, CT: Yale University Press.

Benkler, Y. (2013), "WikiLeaks and the Networked Fourth Estate." In Benedetta B., Hintz, A., and McCurdy, P. (eds.), *Beyond WikiLeaks: Implications for the Future of Communications, Journalism and Society.* New York: Palgrave Macmillan, 11–34.

Benveniste, G. (1977), *The Politics of Expertise.* 2nd ed. San Francisco: Boyd & Fraser.

Berners-Lee, T., Hall, W., Hendler, J. A., O'Hara, K., Shadbolt, N., and Weitzner, D. J. (2006), "A Framework for Web Science." *Foundations and Trends in Web Science,* 1 (1): 1–134.

den Besten, M., and Loubser, M. (2008), "Resolving Simple and Contested Entries on Wikipedia." OII Working Paper, Oxford Internet Institute, University of Oxford.

Bevir, M. (2011), "Governance as Theory, Practice, and Dilemma." In Bevir, M., (ed.), *The SAGE Handbook of Governance.* London: SAGE, 1–16.

Bilefsky, D. (2015), "Foreign Poacher Extradited for Killing Lion." *New York Times,* August 1, p. A2.

Bispham, M., Creese, S., Dutton, W. H., Esteve-Gonzalez, P., and Goldsmith, M. (2022), "Cybersecurity in Working from Home: Problem or Enabler?" *Journal of Information Policy,* 12 (May): 353–86. https://doi.org/10.5325/jinfopoli.12.2022.0010.

Black, J. (2022), "Generation Z: How to Recruit and Retain Them." *The Financial Times,* July 31, https://www.ft.com/content/9eb9e9d2-6340-44e6-9d56-f2a140f7dee9

Blank, G., and Dutton, W. H. (2011), "Age and Trust in the Internet: The Centrality of Experience and Attitudes Toward Technology in Britain." *Social Science Computer Review,* 30 (2): 135–51. http://ssc.sagepub.com/content/early/2011/02/21/0894439310396186/.

Blank, G., Dutton, W. H., and Lefkowitz, J. (2019), "OxIS 2019: Dueling Perspectives on the Internet in Britain." November 26, SSRN:https://ssrn.com/abstract=3493763 or http://dx.doi.org/10.2139/ssrn.3493763/.

Blumer, H. (1954), "What Is Wrong with Social Theory?" *American Sociological Review,* 19 (February): 9.

Blumler, J. G., and Katz, E. (1974), *The Uses of Mass Communications.* Beverly Hills, CA: SAGE.

Bozorgmehr, N. (2022), "Iran Protestors Mourn Teenage 'Martyrs.'" *Financial Times,* October 15/16, p. 4.

Bradshaw, T. (2021), "Whistleblower Sparks Fresh Facebook Crisis." *Financial Times,* October 5, p. 10.

Bray, D., Croxson, K., Dutton, W., and Konsynski, B. (2007, revised 2015), "Sermo: An Authenticated, Community-Based, Knowledge Ecosystem." OII Working Paper, Oxford Internet Institute, University of Oxford, https://papers.ssrn.com/sol3/papers.cfm?abstract_id=1016483/.

Briassoulis, H. (2021), "Becoming E-Petition: An Assemblage-Based Framework for Analysis and Research." Sage Open (January–March), pp. 1–17, https://journals.sagepub.com/doi/10.1177/21582440211001354

Brin, D. (1998), *The Transparent Society: Will Technology Force Us to Choose Between Privacy and Freedom?* New York: Basic Books.

Brinkley, D., and Nichter, L. A. (eds.) (2014), *The Nixon Tapes: 1971–1972.* New York: Houghton Mifflin Harcourt.

Bruyn, S. T. (1966), *The Human Perspective in Sociology: The Methodology of Participant Observation.* Englewood Cliffs, NJ: Prentice-Hall.

Bushey, C., and Aladesuyi, O. (2021), "An Ordinary Man Who Became a Global Symbol." *Financial Times,* April 24/25, p. 13.

Cadwalladr, C. (2021), "The Latest Revelations Mark the Beginning of the End for the House of Zuckerberg." *The Observer,* October 10, p. 39.

Campbell, M. (2022), "Keeping Tabs on War Crimes from a Cul-de-Sac in Leicester." *The Sunday Times,* March 6, p. 23.

Capecchi, C., and Rogers, K. (2015), "Killer of Cecil the Lion Finds Out That He Is a Target Now of Internet Vigilantism." *New York Times,* July 30, p. A11.

Cardoso, G., Cheong, A., and Cole, J. (2009) (eds.), *World Wide Internet: Changing Societies, Economies, and Cultures.* Macau: University of Macau.

Cardoso, G., Liang, G., and Lapa, T. (2013), "Cross-National Comparative Perspectives from the World Internet Project." In Dutton, W. H. (ed.), *The Oxford Handbook of Internet Studies.* Oxford: Oxford University Press, 216–36.

Carlyle, T. (1841), *On Heroes, Hero-worship, & the Heroic in History.* New York: D. Appleton. Repr. of the Sterling Edition of Carlyle's Complete Works, 1905. Teddington, Middlesex: The Echo Library. www.gutenberg.org.etext/1091/.

Carrington, D. (2020), "Shell Accused of Gaslighting as Ocasio-Cortez Sends Tweet Viral." *The Guardian,* November 4, p. 13.

Cassarino, I., and A. Geuna, A. (2008), "Distributed Film Production: Artistic Experimentation or Feasible Alternative? The Case of a Swarm of Angels." OII Working Paper, Oxford Internet Institute, University of Oxford.

Castells, M. (1996), *The Rise of the Network Society: The Information Age.* Oxford: Blackwell.

Castells, M. (2001), *The Internet Galaxy.* Oxford: Oxford University Press.

Castells, M. (2009), *Communication Power.* Oxford: Oxford University Press.

Castells, M. (2012), *Networks of Outrage and Hope: Social Movements in the Internet Age.* Cambridge: Polity Press.

Cater, D. (1959), *The Fourth Branch of Government.* Boston: Houghton Mifflin.

Celeste, E. (2021), "Digital Constitutionalism: A New Systematic Theorisation." *International Review of Law, Computers & Technology,* 33: 1: pp. 76–99.

Celeste, E. (2022), *Digital Constitutionalism: The Role of Internet Bills of Rights.* London: Routledge.

Chadwick, A. (2011), "The Political Information Cycle in a Hybrid News System." *The International Journal of Press/Politics,* 16 (1): 3–29.

Chadwick, A. (2013), *The Hybrid Media System.* New York: Oxford University Press.

Chaffin, J., and Rogers, T. N. (2021), "Chauvin Verdict Is Milestone in Police Accountability." *Financial Times,* April 22, p. 7.

Clark, A. (2018), *The Poisoned City: Flint's Water and the American Urban Tragedy.* New York: Picador Metropolitan Books.

Clark, D., Berson, T., and Lin, H. S. (eds.) (2014), *At the Nexus of Cybersecurity and Public Policy.* Washington, DC: National Research Council, National Academies Press.

Clark, D. D., and Claffy, K. C. (2019), "Toward a Theory of Harms in the Internet Ecosystem." Paper presented at the TPRC47, https://papers.ssrn.com/sol3/papers.cfm?abstract_id=3443341/.

Clement, Jay (2020), "YouTube: Hours of Video Posted Every Minute 2019." *Statista,* 25 (August), https://www.statista.com/statistics/259477/hours-of-video-uploaded-to-youtube-every-minute/.

Cohen, M., and Ilyoushina, M. (2018), "Cambridge Analytica Researcher Touted Data-Mining in Russia Speech." CNN Business, March 3, http://money.cnn.com/2018/03/20/technology/aleksandr-kogan-video-facebook-cambridge-analytica/index.html/.

Cohen-Almagor, R. (2015), *Confronting the Internet's Dark Side: Moral and Social Responsibility on the Free Highway.* Cambridge: Cambridge University Press.

Coleman, S. (2004), "Connecting Parliament to the Public via the Internet." *Information, Communication and Society,* 7 (1): 1–22.

Coleman, S., and Blumler, J. G. (2009), *The Internet and Democratic Citizenship: Theory, Practice and Policy.* Cambridge: Cambridge University Press.

Condorcet, de, M. [1785] (1994), "Essai sur L'application de L'analyse a la Probabilité des Decisions Rendues à la Pluralité des Voix." Paris: l'Imprimerie Royale.

Cooper, S. D. (2006), *Watching the Watchdog: Bloggers as the Fifth Estate.* Spokane, WA: Marquette Books.

Corbyn, Z. (2012), "Facebook Experiment Boosts US Voter Turnout." *Nature,* September 12, https://www.nature.com/news/facebook-experiment-boosts-us-voter-turnout-1.11401/.

Costin, F., Greenough, W. T., and Menges, R. J. (1971), "Student Ratings of College Teaching: Reliability, Validity, and Usefulness." *Review of Educational Research,* 41 (5): 511–35.

Creese, S., Dutton, W. H., Esteve-Gonzáleza, P., and Shillair, R. (2021), "Cybersecurity Capacity Building: Cross-National Benefits and International Divides." *Journal of Cyber Policy,* 6 (2): 214–35, https://www.tandfonline.com/doi/full/10.1080/23738871.2021.1979617/.

Criddle, C., and Murgia, M. (2020), "Tech Groups Face Fines for Failure to Curb Abuse Material." *Financial Times*, July 6, p. 2.

Croft, J. (2022), "Patel Gives Green Light for Assange Extradition." *Financial Times*, June 18/19, p. 3.

Crouse, Timothy (1972), *The Boys on the Bus*. New York: Random House.

Crozier, M., and Friedberg, E. (1980), *Actors and Systems: The Politics of Collective Action*. Chicago: University of Chicago Press.

Cusick, J. (2013), "Prism, Privacy, and the Tragic Triumph of the Nixon Doctrine." *The Independent*, June 26, pp. 16–17.

Dahl, R. A. (1956), *A Preface to Democratic Theory*. Chicago: University of Chicago Press.

Dahl, R. A. (1961), *Who Governs? Democracy and Power in an American City*. New Haven, CT: Yale University Press.

Dahl, R. A. (1971), *Polyarchy: Participation and Opposition*. New Haven, CT and London: Yale University Press.

Dahlberg, L. (2001), "Extending the Public Sphere Through Cyberspace: The Case of Minnesota E-Democracy." *First Monday*, 6 (3), March 5, https://firstmonday.org/article/view/838/747/.

Dahlin, E. (2020), "Approaching Media as Socio-Technical Assemblages in a Datafied Age." *First Monday*, 25 (4-6), April, https://journals.uic.edu/ojs/index.php/fm/article/view/10341/9408.

Danziger, J., Dutton, W. H., Kling, R., and Kraemer, K. (1982), *Computers and Politics*. New York: Columbia University Press.

David, P. A. (2007), "Toward an Analytical Framework for the Study of Distributed Problem-Solving Networks." Working Paper, Oxford Internet Institute, University of Oxford.

Davidge, C. (1987), "America's Talk-Back Television Experiment: QUBE." In Dutton, W. H., Blumler, J. G., and Kraemer, K. L. (eds.), *Wired Cities: Shaping the Future of Communications*. Boston: G. K. Hall, 75–101.

Davidson, H. (2022), "Social Media Crackdown After Protest Against Xi in Beijing." *The Guardian*, October 15, p. 43.

Davidson, H., and Yu, V. (2022), "Street Protest Against Xi and Lockdowns Erupt in Beijing Before Crucial Party Meeting." *The Guardian*, October 14, p. 28.

Department for Digital, Culture, Media & Sport (DCMS). (2019), *Online Harms White Paper*. DCMS and Home Office, London, December 15, https://www.gov.uk/government/consultations/online-harms-white-paper/online-harms-white-paper/.

Department for Digital, Culture, Media & Sport (DCMS). (2021), *Draft Online Safety Bill*, CP 405. DCMS and Home Office, London, May 12, https://assets.publishing.service.gov.uk/government/uploads/system/uploads/attachment_data/file/985033/Draft_Online_Safety_Bill_Bookmarked.pdf/.

De Sola Pool, I. (1977) (ed.), *The Social Impact of the Telephone*. Cambridge, MA: MIT Press.

De Sola, Pool, I. (1983), *Technologies of Freedom*. Cambridge, MA: Harvard University Press, Belknap Press.

Deibert, R. J. (2021), *Reset: Reclaiming the Internet for Civil Society*. Tewkesbury, UK: September Publishing.

Deibert, R. J., Palfrey, J. Rohozinski, R., and Zittrain, J. (2008), *Access Denied: The Practice and Policy of Global Internet Filtering*. Cambridge, MA: MIT Press.

Deibert, R. J., Palfrey, J., Rohozinski, R., and Zittrain, J. (eds.). (2010), *Access Controlled*. Cambridge, MA: MIT Press.

Dickson, E. M. with Bowers, R. (1973), *The Video Telephone: Impact of a New Era in Telecommunications*. New York: Praeger.

Docter, S., Dutton, W. H., and Elberse, A. (1999), "An American Democracy Network: Factors Shaping the Future of On-line Political Campaigns." *Parliamentary Affairs*, 52 (3): 535–52.

Dove, T. (2015), "Anger and Activism Greet Plan to Shut Sweet Briar College." *New York Times*, March 22, https://www.nytimes.com/2015/03/23/education/sweet-briars-imminent-closing-stirs-small-uprising-in-a-college-idyll.html/.

Drezner, D. W. (2022), "The Perils of Pessimism." *Foreign Affairs*, July/August, pp. 34–43.

Dubois, E., and Dutton, W. H. (2012), "The Fifth Estate in Internet Governance: Collective Accountability of a Canadian Policy Initiative." *Revue française d'Etudes Américaines RFEA*, 143 (4): 81–97.

Dubois, E., and Dutton, W. H. (2014), "Empowering Citizens of the Digital Age: The Role of a Fifth Estate." In Graham, M., and Dutton, W. H. (eds.), *Society and the Internet*. Oxford: Oxford University Press, 238–53.

Dutton, B. (2019), Online Harms White Paper. Presentation at Ofcom, April, https://www.slideshare.net/WHDutton/online-harms-white-paper-april-2019-bill-dutton/.

Dutton, W. H. (1992), "The Ecology of Games Shaping Telecommunications Policy." *Communication Theory*, 2 (4): 303–28.

Dutton, W. H. (1996), "Network Rules of Order: Regulating Speech in Public Electronic Fora." *Media, Culture, and Society*, 18 (2): 269–90.

Dutton, W. H. (1999), "The Web of Technology and People: Challenges for Economic and Social Research." *Prometheus*, 17 (1): 5–20.

Dutton, W. H. (2005), "The Internet and Social Transformation: Reconfiguring Access." In Dutton, W. H., Kahin, B., O'Callaghan R., and Wyckoff, A. W. (eds.), *Transforming Enterprise*. Cambridge, MA: MIT Press, 375–97.

Dutton, W. H. (2007), "Through the Network (of Networks)—the Fifth Estate." Inaugural lecture, Examination Schools, University of Oxford, October 15, http://webcast.oii.ox.ac.uk/?view=Webcast&ID=20071015_208.

Dutton, W. H. (2008), "The Wisdom of Collaborative Network Organizations: Capturing the Value of Networked Individuals." *Prometheus*, 26 (3), September: 211–30.

Dutton, W. H. (2009), "The Fifth Estate Emerging Through the Network of Networks." *Prometheus*, 27 (1), March: 1–15.

Dutton, W. H. (2010), "The Fifth Estate: Democratic Social Accountability Through the Emerging Network of Networks," In Nixon, P. G., Koutrakou, V. N., and Rawal, R. (eds.), *Understanding E-Government in Europe: Issues and Challenges*. London: Routledge, 3–18.

Dutton, W. H. (2010c), "Networking Distributed Public Expertise: Strategies for Citizen Sourcing Advice to Government." Occasional Paper in Science and Technology Policy, Science and Technology Policy Institute, Institute for Defense Analyses, Washington DC, August, http://ssrn.com/abstract=1767870/.

Dutton, W. H. (2011a), "A Networked World Needs a Fifth Estate." *Wired Magazine*, October 22, www.wired.co.uk/magazine/archive/2011/11/ideas-bank/william-dutton.

Dutton, W. H. (2011b), "The Politics of Next Generation Research: Democratizing Research-Centred Computational Networks." *Journal of Information Technology*, 26: 109–19.

Dutton, W. H. (2012), "The Fifth Estate: A New Governance Challenge." In Levi-Faur, D. (ed.), *The Oxford Handbook of Governance*. Oxford: Oxford University Press, 39–55.

Dutton, W. H. (2013a), "The Fifth Estate: The Internet's Gift to Democratic Governance." *InterMEDIA*, 41, October: 20–24.

Dutton, W. H. (2013b), "The Internet and Democratic Accountability: The Rise of the Fifth Estate." In Lee, F. L. F., Leung, L., Qui, J. L., and Chu, D.S.C. (eds.), *Frontiers in New Media Research*. Abingdon, UK: Informa, Taylor and Francis/Routledge.

Dutton, W. H. (ed.) (2013c), *The Oxford Handbook of Internet Studies*. Oxford: Oxford University Press.

Dutton, W. H. (2015), "The Internet's Gift to Democratic Governance: The Fifth Estate." In in Coleman, S., Moss, G., and Parry, K. (eds.), *Can the Media Save Democracy? Essays in Honour of Jay G. Blumler*. London, Abington: Palgrave Macmillan, 164–73.

Dutton, W. H. (2015), "Lend Me Your Expertise: Citizen Sourcing Advice to Government." In Johnston, E. W. (ed.), *Governance in the Information Era: Theory and Practice of Policy Informatics*. Abingdon, UK: Taylor and Francis Routledge, 247–63.

Dutton, W. H. (2017), "Fostering a Cyber Security Mindset." *Internet Policy Review*, 6 (1), https://doi.org/10.14763/2017.1.443 and https://policyreview.info/node/443/pdf/.

Dutton, W. H. (2020), "The Fifth Estate: Canaries in the Institutions of Liberal Democracies." In Nagel, M., Kenis, P., Leifeld, P., and Schmedes, H-J (Hrsg.), *Politische Komplexität, Governance von Innovationen und Policy-Netzwerke: Festschrift für Volker Schneider*. Wiesbaden, Germany: Springer VS, 59–65. https://doi.org/10.1007/978-3-658-30914-5/.

Dutton, W. H., and Blank, G. (2011), *The Next Generation Users: The Internet in Britain*. Oxford: Oxford Internet Institute, University of Oxford.

Dutton, W. H., and Blank, G. (2013), *Cultures of the Internet: The Internet in Britain*. Oxford: Oxford Internet Institute, University of Oxford.

Dutton, W. H., Blank, G., and Karpauskaite, E. (2022), "A Digital Privacy Divide: How Privacy Concerns Reinforce Inequalities Online." Paper presented at TPRC, Washington College of Law, American University, Washington, DC, September 15–16.

Dutton, W. H., Blumler, J. G., and Kraemer, K. L. (eds.) (1987), *Wired Cities: Shaping the Future of Communications*. Boston: G. K. Hall.

Dutton, W. H., and Dubois, E. (2015), "The Fifth Estate: A Rising Force of Pluralistic Accountability." In Coleman, S., and Freelon, D. (eds.), *Handbook of Digital Politics*. Cheltenham, UK: Edward Elgar, 51–66.

Dutton, W. H., and Dubois, E. (2013), "The Fifth Estate of the Digital World." In Youngs, G. (ed.), *Digital World: Connectivity, Creativity and Rights*. London: Routledge, 131–43.

Dutton, W. H., and Dubois, E. (2023), "The Fifth Estate: A New Source of Democratic Accountability." In Coleman, S., and Sorenson, L. (eds), *Handbook of Digital Politics*. Cheltenham, UK: Edward Elgar, pp. forthcoming.

Dutton, W. H., and Fernandez, L. (2018/19), "How Susceptible Are Internet Users?" *InterMEDIA*, December/January, 46 (4): 36–40.

Dutton, W. H., and Guthrie, K. (1991), "An Ecology of Games: The Political Construction of Santa Monica's Public Electronic Network." *Informatization and the Public Sector*, 1 (4): 1–24.

Dutton, W. H., Helsper, E. J., and Gerber, M. M. (2009), *The Internet in Britain*. Oxford: Oxford Internet Institute, University of Oxford, https://oxis.oii.ox.ac.uk/reports/.

Dutton, W. H., and Jeffreys, P. (eds.) (2010), *World Wide Research: Reshaping the Sciences and Humanities*. Cambridge, MA: MIT Press.

Dutton, W. H., and Kraemer, K. L. (1978), "Management Utilization of Computers in American Local Governments." *Communications of the ACM*, 21 (3): 206–18.

Dutton, W. H., Law, G., Bolsover, G., and Dutta, S. (2013), *The Internet Trust Bubble: Global Values, Beliefs and Practices*. Geneva: World Economic Forum, http://www3.weforum.org/docs/WEF_InternetTrustBubble_Report2_2014.pdf/.

Dutton, W. H., and Loader, B. D. (eds.) (2002), *Digital Academe: New Media and Institutions in Higher Education and Learning*. London: Taylor & Francis/Routledge.

Dutton, W. H., and Meadow, R. G. (1987), "A Tolerance for Surveillance: American Public Opinion Concerning Privacy and Civil Liberties." In Levitan, K. B. (ed.), *Government Infostructures*. Westport, CT: Greenwood Press, 147–70.

Dutton, W. H., and Meyer, E. T. (2009), "Experience with New Tools and Infrastructures of Research: An Exploratory Study of Distance from, and Attitudes Toward, E-Research." *Prometheus*, 27 (3), September: 223–38.

Dutton, W. H., Reisdorf, B. C., Blank, G., Dubois, E., and Fernandez, L. (2019), "The Internet and Access to Information about Politics." In Graham and Dutton (2019), 228–47.

Dutton, W. H., Reisdorf, B. C., Dubois, E., and Blank, G. (2017), "Search and Politics: The Uses and Impacts of Search in Britain, France, Germany, Italy, Poland, Spain, and the United States." Quello Center Working Paper, Michigan State University, May 1, https://papers.ssrn.com/sol3/papers.cfm?abstract_id=2960697/.

Dutton, W. H., and Robertson, C. T. (2021), "Disentangling Polarization and Civic Empowerment in the Digital Age: The Role of Filter Bubbles and Echo Chambers in the Rise of Populism." In Tumber, H., and Waisbord, S. (eds.), *The Routledge Companion to Media Misinformation and Populism*. New York: Routledge, 420–34.

Dutton, W. H., Schneider, V., and Vedel, T. (2012), "Large Technical Systems as Ecologies of Games: Cases from Telecommunications to the Internet." In Bauer, J. M. et al. (eds.), *Innovation Policy and Governance in High-Tech Industries*. Berlin: Springer-Verlag, 49–75.

Dutton, W. H., and Shepherd, A. (2006), "Trust in the Internet as an Experience Technology." *Information, Communication and Society*, 9 (4): 433–51.

Dutton, W. H., Shepherd, A., and di Gennaro, C. (2007), "Digital Divides and Choices Reconfiguring Access: National and Cross-National Patterns of Internet Diffusion and Use." In Anderson, B., Brynin, M., Gershuny, J., and Raban, Y. (eds.), *Information and Communication Technologies in Society: E-Living in a Digital Europe*. London: Routledge, 31–45.

Dutton, W. H., Sun, H., and Shen, W. (2015), "China and the Fifth Estate: Net Delusion or Democratic Potential?" In Balcells, J., Battle, A., Padró-Solanet, A. (coord.), *The Impact of Social Media in Politics and Public Administrations* (online special issue). IDP. *Revista de Internet, Derecho y Política*. No. 20, 1–19, https://www.redalyc.org/articulo.oa?id=78840417007.

Dutton, W. H., and Zorina, A. (2021), "The Ecology of Games Reshaping Information Policy: Internet Access in Belarus to Cyber Harms in the United Kingdom." In Duff, A., (ed.), *Research Handbook on Information Policy*. Cheltenham, UK: Edward Elgar, 130–45.

Earl, M. (2005), "Wikipedia's Struggle to Govern a Knowledge Democracy." *Financial Times*, December 19, p. 19.

Ehrlich, B. (2020), "Ramsay Orta, Man Who Filmed Eric Garner's Arrest, Has Been Released from Prison." *Rolling Stone*, June 8, https://www.rollingstone.com/culture/culture-news/ramsey-orta-eric-garner-prison-release-1011646/.

Ellison, N. B., and Boyd, D. M. (2013), "Sociality Through Social Network Sites." In Dutton, W. H. (ed.), *The Oxford Handbook of Internet Studies*. Oxford: Oxford University Press, 151–72.

Ellsberg, D. (2014), "Daniel Ellsberg: Snowden Would Not Get a Fair Trial—and Kerry Is Wrong." *The Guardian*, May 30, https://www.theguardian.com/commentisfree/2014/may/30/daniel-ellsberg-snowden-fair-trial-kerry-espionage-act/.

Elstub, S., and Escobar, O. (2019), *Handbook of Democratic Innovation and Governance*. Cheltenham, UK: Edward Elgar.

Environmental Protection Agency (EPA) (2021), "Deepwater Horizon—BP Gulf of Mexico Oil Spill," https://www.epa.gov/enforcement/deepwater-horizon-bp-gulf-mexico-oil-spill/.

Espinoza, J. (2022), "Big Tech Backs Tougher EU Code on Fake News." *Financial Times*, June 14, p. 6.

Farrow, Ronan (2017), "From Aggressive Overtures to Sexual Assault: Harvey Weinstein's Accusers Tell Their Stories." *The New Yorker*, October 23, posted online October 10, https://www.newyorker.com/news/news-desk/from-aggressive-overtures-to-sexual-assault-harvey-weinsteins-accusers-tell-their-stories/.

Fazal, T. M. (2021), "The Case for Complacency: Does Washington Worry Too Much About Threats?" *Foreign Affairs*, September/October, 204–8.

Fileborn, B., and Loney-Howes, R. (eds.) (2019), *#MeToo and the Politics of Social Change*. Cham, Switzerland: Palgrave Macmillan.

Fisher, E. (2012), "E-Governance and E-Democracy." In Levi-Faur, D. (ed.), *The Oxford Handbook of Governance*. Oxford: Oxford University Press, 569–83.

Fitz-Gibbon, J. (2020), "Teen Who Shot Viral George Floyd Video to Get Human Rights Award." *New York Post*, October 28, https://nypost.com/2020/10/28/teen-who-shot-viral-george-floyd-video-to-get-human-rights-award/.

Foster, P., Barket, A., and Parker, G. (2020), "Tech Platforms Face Duty of Impartiality in Online Bill." *Financial Times*, November 13, p. 3.

Frier, S. (2020), *No Filter: The Inside Story of How Instagram Transformed Business, Celebrity and Our Culture*. London: Random House Business.

Ganesh, J. (2021), "Do Not Judge the US by Its Politics." *Financial Times*, June 2, p. 21.

Garnham, N. (1999), "Information Politics: The Study of Communicative Power." In W. H. Dutton (ed.), *Society on the Line*. Oxford and New York: Oxford University Press, 77–78.

Gibson, W. (1984), *Neuromancer*. New York: ACE.

Giles, J. (2005), "Internet Encyclopaedias Go Head to Head." *Nature*, 438: 900–901, https://www.nature.com/articles/438900a/.

Gluckman, N. (2018), "Why Internet Scholars Are Calling Out Facebook for Restricting Access to Its Data." *The Chronicle of Higher Education*, May 9, https://www.chronicle.com/article/why-internet-scholars-are-calling-out-facebook-for-restricting-access-to-its-data/

Goodwin, C. D. (1995), "The Fifth Estate Institutions for Extending Public Policy Debate in Emerging Democracies: Lessons from the American Experience." In Goodwin, C. D., and Nacht, M. (eds.), *Beyond Government: Extending the Public Policy Debate in Emerging Democracies*. Boulder, CO: Westview Press, 178.

Graham, M., and Dutton, W. H. (eds.) (2014), *Society & the Internet: How Networks of Information and Communication Are Changing Our Lives*. Oxford: Oxford University Press.

Graham, M., and Dutton, W. H. (eds.) (2019), *Society & the Internet: How Networks of Information and Communication Are Changing Our Lives*. 2nd ed. Oxford: Oxford University Press.

Greenberg, A. (2012), *This Machine Kills Secrets: How WikiLeakers, Hacktivists, and Cypherpunks Are Freeing the World's Information*. London: Random House, Virgin Books.

Greenberger, M. (ed.) (1985), *Electronic Publishing Plus*. White Plains, NY: Knowledge Industries.

Greengard, S. (2021), "Can a Free Internet Survive?" *Communications of the ACM*, November 23, https://cacm.acm.org/news/257005-can-a-free-internet-survive/fulltext/.

Greenhow, C., Galvin, S., Brandon, D., & Askari, E. (2020), "A Decade of Research on K-12 Teaching and Teacher Learning with Social Media: Insights on the State of the Field." *Teachers College Record*, 122 (6), https://www.tcrecord.org ID Number: 23303.

Greenwald, G. (2014), *No Place to Hide: Edward Snowden, the NSA and the Surveillance State*. New York: Penguin Books.

De Gregorio, G. (2021), "The Rise of Digital Constitutionalism in the European Union." *International Journal of Constitutional Law*, 19 (1): 41–70.

De Gregorio, G. (2022), *Digital Constitutionalism in Europe: Reframing Rights and Powers in the Algorithmic Society*. Cambridge: Cambridge University Press.

Fine, C. (2022), "Women Worldwide Cut Their Hair to Protest Death of Iranian Woman Who Violated Dress Code." *USA Today*, October 6, https://eu.usatoday.com/story/news/world/2022/10/06/mahsa-amini-protests-cutting-hair/8194746001/

Guthrie, K., and Dutton, W. H. (1992), "The Politics of Citizen Access Technology: The Development of Public Information Utilities in Four Cities." *Policy Studies Journal*, 20 (4): 574–97.

Habermas, J. (1991), *The Structural Transformation of the Public Sphere*. Cambridge, MA: MIT Press.

Hampton, K. N., and Shin, I. (2022), "Disconnection More Problematic for Adolescent Self-Esteem Than Heavy Social Media Use." *Social Science Computer Review*, August 5, https://doi.org/10.1177/08944393221117466.

Hampton, K., and Wellman, B. (2021), "All the Lonely People? The Continuity of Lament About the Loss of Community." In Leivrouw, L. A., and Loader, B. D. (eds.), *Routledge Handbook of Digital Media and Communication*. Abingdon, UK: Routledge, 281–96.

Hanna-Attisha, M. (2018), *What the Eyes Don't See: A Story of Crisis, Resistance, and Hope in an American City*. New York: One World, Penguin Random House.

Hanna-Attisha, M., LaChance, J., Sadler, R. C., Schnepp, A. C. (2016), "Elevated Blood Lead Levels in Children Associated with the Flint Drinking Water Crisis: A Spatial Analysis of Risk and Public Health Response." *American Journal of Public Health*, 106 (2), February 1: 283–90.

Hargittai, E., and Hsieh, Y. P. (2013), "Digital Inequality." In Dutton, W. H. (ed.), *The Oxford Handbook of Internet Studies*. Oxford: Oxford University Press, 129–50.

Hassid, J. (2012), "Safety Valve or Pressure Cooker? Blogs in Chinese Political Life." *Journal of Communication*, 62: 212–30, http://dx.doi.org/10.1111/j.1460-2466.2012.01634.x

Haugen, F. (2021), "Silicon Valley Foot Soldier Takes Whistleblowing to New Heights." *The Financial Times*, October 9/10, p. 14.

Helm, T. (2022), "Our Faith in Democracy Is Fading." *The Observer*, April 10, p. 14.

Higgins, E. (2021), *We Are Bellingcat: Global Crime, Online Sleuths, and the Bold Future of News*. London: Bloomsbury.

Hiltz, S. R., and Turoff, M. (1978), *The Network Nation: Human Communication via Computer.* Reading, MA: Addison-Wesley.

Hindman, M. (2009), *The Myth of Digital Democracy.* Princeton, NJ: Princeton University Press.

Hodgson, C. (2021), "Ban Proposed on Single-Use Plastic Cups and Cutlery." *Financial Times,* August 28/29, p. 3, https://www.ft.com/content/163f4e08-bbac-40bb-972e-f9f46c198545/.

Holt, K. (2022), "Frontline Ukraine Troops Are Reportedly Enduring Starlink Outages." *Engadget,* October 7, https://www.engadget.com/ukraine-starlink-outages-russia-elon-musk-173909699.html

Howard, P. N. (2011), *The Digital Origins of Dictatorship and Democracy: Information Technology and Political Islam.* Oxford: Oxford University Press.

Howell, W. G., and Moe, T. M. (2020), *Presidents, Populism, and the Crisis of Democracy.* Chicago: University of Chicago Press.

Huan, S., Dutton, W. H., and Shen, W. (2013), "The Semi-Sovereign Netizen: The Fifth Estate in China." In Nixon, P. G., Rawal, R., and Mercea, D. (eds.), *Politics and the Internet in Comparative Context: Views from the Cloud.* London: Routledge, 43–58.

Innis, H. (1950), *Empire and Communications.* Oxford: Oxford University Press. Rev. ed. Toronto: Toronto University Press, 1972.

Jackson, S. J., Bailey, M., and Welles, B. F. (2020), *#Hashtag Activism: Networks of Race and Gender Justice.* Cambridge, MA: MIT Press.

Jericho, G. (2012), *The Rise of the Fifth Estate: Social Media and Blogging in Australian Politics.* Brunswick, Victoria, Australia: Scribe.

Jie, Y. (2011), "'I-Paid-a-Bribe' Sites Put Payoffs Online." *China Daily,* June 14, p. 4.

Johansen, R. (1988), *Groupware: Computer Support for Business Teams.* New York: Free Press.

Johnson, D. R., Crawford, S. P., and Palfrey, J. G. (2004), "The Accountable Net: Peer Production of Internet Governance." *Virginia Journal of Law and Technology* 9 (9): 1–33, http://ssrn. com/abstract=529022/.

Jones, C. C. (2019), "Ramsey Orta Filmed the Killing of Eric Garner, so the Policy Punished Him." *The Verge,* March 3, https://www.theverge.com/2019/3/13/18253848/eric-garner-footage-ramsey-orta-police-brutality-killing-safety/.

Joutz, Marguerite (2018), "Sweet Briar College Almost Closed. What Will It Take to Thrive?" *New York Times,* May 17, https://www.nytimes.com/2018/05/17/opinion/sweet-briar-meredith-woo-interview.html/.

Judah, T. (2022), "Smartphones Play Vital Role in the Defence of Kyiv." *Financial Times,* April 11, p. 7.

Kan, M. (2013), "Beijing's Heavy Pollution a Boon for Air Quality Monitoring Apps." *Computer World,* January 31, https://www.computerworld.com/article/2827638/beijing-s-heavy-pollution-a-boon-for-air-quality-monitoring-apps.html/.

Karpf, D. (2012), "Online Political Mobilization from the Advocacy Group's Perspective: Looking Beyond Clicktivism." *Policy and Internet,* 2 (4), https://doi.org/10.2202/1944-2866.1098/.

Keen, A. (2008), *The Cult of the Amateur: How Blogs, MySpace, YouTube and the Rest of Today's User-Generated Media Are Killing Our Culture and Economy.* London: Nicholas Brealey.

Kerr, S. (2021), "Phones as Weapons in Palestinian Struggle." *Financial Times,* May 27, p. 8.

Kohli, A. (2022), "What to Know About the Iranian Protests Over Mahsa Amini's Death." *Time,* September 24, https://time.com/6216513/mahsa-amini-iran-protests-police/.

Knake, K. T., Daly, A. J., Frank, K. A., Rehm, M., and Greenhow, C. (2021), "Educators Meet the Fifth Estate: Social Media in Education." *The Elementary School Journal,* 122 (1), August: 2–7.

Kobie, N. (2020), "Facebook Exec Calls Cambridge Analytica Scandal a 'Non Event.'" *ITPro,* January 8, https://www.itpro.com/security/internet-security/354484/facebook-exec-calls-cambridge-analytica-scandal-a-non-event

Kornhauser, W. (1959), *The Politics of Mass Society.* New York: Free Press.

Kosinski, M., Stillwell, D., and Graepel, T. (2013), "Private Traits and Attributes Are Predictable from Digital Records of Human Behavior." *Proceedings of the National Academy of Sciences,* April 9, https://pubmed.ncbi.nlm.nih.gov/23479631/.

Kraemer, K. L., Dutton, W. H., and Northrop, A. (1981), *The Management of Information Systems*. New York: Columbia University Press.

Kranich, N. (2004), *The Information Commons: A Policy Report*. Democracy Program, Brennan Center For Justice, New York University School of Law, www.fepproject.org/policyreports/InformationCommons.pdf/.

Krishnappa, S. (2011), "Social Media Sites Like Twitter Deserve Nobel for Pro-Democracy Protest in Egypt, Libya & China?" *UK Financial News*, February 22. (No longer available online).

LaFrance, A. (2021), "Facebook Papers: History Will Not Judge Us Kindly." *The Atlantic*, October 25, https://www.theatlantic.com/ideas/archive/2021/10/facebook-papers-democracy-election-zuckerberg/620478/?utm_source=email&utm_medium=social&utm_campaign=share/.

Lakhani, K. R., Jeppesen, L. B., Lohse, P. A., and Panetta, J. A. (2007), "The Value of Openness in Scientific Problem-Solving." Working Paper Number 07-050, Harvard Business School.

Lambert, P. (2013), "What the Mandiant Report Reveals About the Future of Cyber Espionage." *TechRepublic*, February 25, http://www.techrepublic.com/blog/security/what-the-mandiant-report-reveals-about-the-future-of-cyber-espionage/9112/.

Lapowski, I. (2018), "Cambridge Analytica Took 50M Facebook Users' Data—and Both Companies Owe Answers." *Wired*, March 17, https://www.youtube.com/watch?v=Bbquf1hBBqQ/.

Laprise, J. (2013), "Reinventing the Wheel: US Information Security Policy from the Cold War to the War on Terror." Paper presented at the Annual Meeting of the International Communication Association, London, June 17–20.

Latour, B. (1987), *Science in Action: How to Follow Scientists and Engineers Through Society*. Cambridge, MA: Harvard University Press.

Latour, B. (2005), *Reassembling the Social: An Introduction to Actor-Network-Theory*. New York: Oxford University Press.

Laudon, K. C. (1977), *Communications Technology and Democratic Participation*. New York: Praeger.

Lebron, C. J. (2017), *The Making of Black Lives Matter: A Brief History of an Idea*. Oxford: Oxford University Press.

Leigh, D., and Harding, L. (2011), *WikiLeaks: Inside Julian Assange's War on Secrecy*. London: Guardian Books.

Leonard, L. W. (2018), "Dedicated, Tireless, Unafraid: A Case Study of the Effort That Saved Sweet Briar College in 2015." PhD diss., Frostburg State University, Maryland.

Leveson, The Right Honourable Lord Justice (2021), *An Inquiry into the Culture, Practices and Ethics of the Press*, Vols. 1–9. London: The Stationery Office.

Li, G. (2022), "China Tech Group Bank on Virtual Influencers." *Financial Times*, October 13, p. 13.

Lievrouw, L. A. (2011), *Alternative and Activist Media*. Malden, MA: Polity Press.

Lin, W.-Y., and Dutton, W. H. (2003), "The Net Effect in the 'Stop the Overlay' Campaign." *Party Politics*, 9 (1): 124–36.

Long, N. E. (1958), "The Local Community as an Ecology of Games." *American Journal of Sociology*, 64 (3): 251–61.

Macaulay, T. (1828), "Hallam's Constitutional History." *The Edinburgh Review*, 48, September: 165.

MacKenzie, D., and Wajcman, J. (1985) (eds.), *The Social Shaping of Technology: How a Refrigerator Got Its Hum*. Milton Keynes: Open University Press.

Mackinnon, A., and Standish, R. (2020), "Putin Fires His Puppet Master." *Foreign Policy*, February 21, https://foreignpolicy.com/2020/02/21/putin-fires-vladislav-surkov-puppet-master-russia-ukraine-rebels/

MacKinnon, R. (2012), *Consent of the Networked: The Worldwide Struggle for Internet Freedom*. New York: Basic Books.

MacKinnon, R., Hickok, E., Bar, A., and Lim, H-i. (2014), "Fostering Internet Freedom: The Role of Intermediaries." Report for UNESCO's Division of Freedom of Expression and Media Development. Paris.

Macknight, T. (1858), *History of the Life and Times of Edmund Burke, 1*. London: Hapman and Hall.

Malik, N. (2021), "For the Right, This Is Just a Brief Retreat in the Culture War." *The Guardian*, Journal, July 19, p. 1.

Malone, T. W., Laubacher, R., and Dellarocas, C. (2009), "Harnessing Crowds: Mapping the Genome of Collective Intelligence." MIT Sloan Research Paper No. 4732-09, February 3. Center for Collective Intelligence, Sloan School of Management, MIT. http://ssrn.com/abstract=1381502/.

Mao, F. (2022), "China's 'Bridge Man' Inspires Xi Jinping Protest Signs Around the World," *BBC News*, October 18. https://www.bbc.com/news/world-asia-china-63295749.

Marwick, A. E. (2013), *Status Update: Celebrity, Publicity & Branding in the Social Media Age*. New Haven, CT: Yale University Press.

Mayer-Schoenberger, V., and Cukier, K. (2013), *Big Data: A Revolution That Will Transform How We Live, Work and Think*. London: John Murray.

McDermott, L., Heard, L., Carr, E., Beecham, H., Wuikau, Y., and Stanton, T. (2021), *Extent of Single-Use Litter in the UK II: A Report by Planet Patrol*. UK: Planet Patrol.

McDougall, J. (2019), *Fake News vs Media Studies: Travels in a False Binary*. Cham, Switzerland: Palgrave Macmillan.

McGann, J. G. (2016), *The Fifth Estate: Think Tanks, Public Policy, and Governance*. Washington DC: Brookings Institution Press.

McLeod, D. M., and Detenber, B. H. (1999), "Framing Effects of Television News Coverage of Social Protest." *Journal of Communication*, 49 (3): 3–23.

McLuhan, M. (1964), *Understanding Media: The Extensions of Man*. London: Routledge.

McMorrow, R. (2022), "Censors Target Social Media Users After Beijing Protest." *Financial Times*, October 15/16, p. 8.

McNamara, M. (2018), *I'll Be Gone in the Dark: One Woman's Obsessive Search for the Golden State Killer*. New York: Faber & Faber, Harper Collins.

Mesthene, E. G. (1981), "The Role of Technology in Society." In Teich, A. H. (ed.), *Technology and Man's Future*, 3rd ed. New York: St Martin's Press, 99–129.

Meyer, E. T., and Schroeder, R. (2015), *Knowledge Machines: Digital Transformations of the Sciences and Humanities*. Cambridge, MA: MIT Press.

Michels, R. (1962), *Political Parties: A Sociological Study of the Oligarchic Tendencies of Modern Democracy*. New York: Free Press.

Mill, John Stuart (1860), *On Liberty*, 2 ed. London: John W. Parker & Son.

Miller, C. (2019), "Taiwan Is Making Democracy Work Again. It's Time We Paid Attention." *Wired*, November 26, https://www.wired.co.uk/article/taiwan-democracy-social-media.

Miller, C. (2020), "Taiwan's Crowdsourced Democracy Shows Us How to Fix Social Media." *The Guardian*, September 27, https://wearenotdivided.reasonstobecheerful.world/taiwan-g0v-hackers-technology-digital-democracy/.

Miller, M. L., and Vaccari, C. (2020), "Digital Threats to Democracy: Comparative Lessons and Possible Remedies." *The International Journal of Press/Politics*, 25 (3): 333–56.

Milmo, D. (2021a), "The Making of a Modern US Hero." *The Observer*, October 10, pp. 32–33.

Milmo, D. (2021b), "Tackle Harmful Algorithms or Face Threat of Criminal Charges, Dorries Warns Facebook." *The Guardian*, November 5, p. 15.

Mitchell, T. (2021), "Tennis Star Peng Denies She Was Assaulted." *Financial Times*, December 21, p. 8, https://www.ft.com/content/295ee5fa-b6e8-42f7-af8a-1d8abcd46713/.

Montesquieu, Charles de Secondat, Baron de (1748), *The Spirit of Laws*. N.p.

Morgan, M. (2012), *George Gerbner: A Critical Introduction to Media and Communication Theory*. New York: Peter Lang.

Morozov, E. (2011), *The Net Delusion: How Not to Liberate the World*. London: Penguin Books.

Morozov, E. (2013), *To Save Everything, Click Here*. London: Penguin Books.

Morozov, E. (2020), "The Internet, Politics, and the Politics of Internet Debate." In BBVA, *Change: How the Internet Is Changing Our Lives*, https://www.bbvaopenmind.com/en/artic les/the-internet-politics-and-the-politics-of-the-internet-debate/.

Mosco, V. (1982), *Pushbutton Fantasies: Critical Perspectives on Videotex and Information Technology.* Norwood, NJ: Ablex.

Mueller, J. (2021), *The Stupidity of War: American Foreign Policy and the Quest for Complacency.* Cambridge: Cambridge University Press.

Müller, M. (2015), "Assemblages and Actor-Networks." *Geography Compass*, 9 (1): 27–41.

Mueller, R. S. (2019), *Report on the Investigation into Russian Interference in the 2016 Presidential Election.* (Special Counsel Robert S. Mueller, III.) Washington, DC: Department of Justice.

Murphy, H. (2020), "Tech Chiefs Rapped in Senate over Content Moderation." *Financial Times*, October 29, p. 8.

Murphy, H. (2021), "Former UK Hedge Fund Partner Plots Return of Trump-Era Social Network Parler." *Financial Times*, September 14, https://www.ft.com/content/261fecd4-715f-4b90-a7fa-57d7d4013788/.

Murphy, H. (2022), "Twitter Reviews Policy on User Bans." *Financial Times*, October 13, p. 12.

Nagel, M., Kenis, P., Leifeld, P., and Schmedes, H.-J. (2020), *Politische Komplexität, Governance von Innovationen und Policy-Netzwerke: Festschrift für Volker Schneider.* Wiesbaden, Germany: Springer VS.

Napoli, P. M. (2019), *Social Media and the Public Interest: Media Regulation in the Disinformation Age.* New York: Columbia University Press.

Nash, V. (2014), "The Politics of Children's Internet Use." In Graham, M., and Dutton, W. H. (eds.), *Society & the Internet: How Networks of Information and Communication Are Changing Our Lives.* Oxford: Oxford University Press, 67–80.

National Telecommunications and Information Administration (NTIA) (2019), "More Than Half of American Households Used the Internet for Health-Related Activities in 2019, NTIA Data Show." December 7, https://www.ntia.doc.gov/blog/2020/more-half-american-households-used-internet-health-related-activities-2019-ntia-data-show/.

Nelson, T. E., and Oxley, Z. M. (1999), "Issue Framing on Belief Importance and Opinion." *The Journal of Politics*, 61 (4): 1040–67, https://doi.org/10.2307/2647553/.

Neustadt, R. E. (1960), *Presidential Power.* New York: John Wiley and Sons.

Newman, N., Dutton, W. H., and Blank, G. (2012), "Social Media in the Changing Ecology of News: The Fourth and Fifth Estates in Britain." *International Journal of Internet Science*, 7 (1): 6–22.

Nichols, T. (2017), *The Death of Expertise.* Oxford: Oxford University Press.

Nickerson, R. S. (1998), "Confirmation Bias: A Ubiquitous Phenomenon in Many Guises." *Review of General Psychology*, 2 (2), June: 175–220.

Nielson, M. (2011), *Reinventing Discovery: How Online Tools Are Transforming Science.* Princeton, NJ, and Oxford: Princeton University Press.

Nikolov, D., Oliveira, D. F. M., Flammini, A., and Menczer, F. (2015), "Measuring Online Social Bubbles." *PeerJ Computer Science* 1:e38, https://doi.org/10.7717/peerj-cs.38/.

Norris, P. (2001), *Digital Divide: Civic Engagement, Information Poverty, and the Internet Worldwide.* Cambridge: Cambridge University Press.

Noveck, B. S. (2009), *Wiki Government: How Technology Can Make Government Better, Democracy Stronger, and Citizens More Powerful.* Washington, DC: Brookings Institution Press.

Office of Communications (Ofcom) (2021), "Adults' Media Use and Attitudes Report 2020/21." London. April 28, https://www.ofcom.org.uk/__data/assets/pdf_file/0025/217834/adults-media-use-and-attitudes-report-2020-21.pdf/.

Office of Emergency Preparedness (OEP) (1973), "EMISARI: A Management Information System Designed to Aid and Involve People." Paper presented at the 4th International Symposium on Computers and Information Science, Miami Beach, Florida. (Assistant Director for Resource Analysis, Executive Office of the President.)

Ortega y Gasset, J. ([1932] 1957), *The Revolt of the Masses.* 25th ed. New York: W. W. Norton.

Page, S. E. (2007), *The Difference: How the Power of Diversity Creates Better Groups, Firms, Schools, and Societies.* Princeton, NJ: Princeton University Press.

Panicheva, P., Ivanov, V., Moskvichev, A., Bogolyubova, O., and Ledovaya, Y. (2015), "Towards a Linguistic Model of Stress, Well-being and Dark Traits in Russian Facebook Texts." Proceedings of the AINL-ISMW FRUCT Conference, Fruct Oy, November, pp. 186–88, https://www.researchgate.net/publication/301956502_Towards_a_Linguistic_Model_of_Stress_Well-Being_and_Dark_Traits_in_Russian_Facebook_Texts.

Papert, S. (1980), *Mind-Storms: Children, Computers, and Powerful Ideas*. New York: Basic Books.

Pariser, E. (2011), *The Filter Bubble: What the Internet Is Hiding from You*. New York: Penguin Press.

Parker, E. C. (1970), "Information Utilities and Mass Communication." In Sackman, H., and Nie, N. (eds.) (1970), *The Information Utility and Social Choice*. Montvale, NJ: AFIPS Press, 51–70.

Payne, M., and Payne, D. (2012), *NeverSeconds: The Incredible Story of Martha Payne*. London: Cargo.

Payne, S. (2021), "WhatsApp Is Where Real Political Power Lies in Britain." *Financial Times*, June 18, p. 22.

Perrigo, B. (2021), "Change Agent." *Time Magazine*, December 6/13, p. 27–32.

Piesing, M. (2020), "The Rise of Citizen Science: Can the Public Solve Our Biggest Problems?" *The Guardian*, December 21, https://www.theguardian.com/education/2020/nov/16/the-rise-of-citizen-science-can-the-public-help-solve-our-biggest-problems/.

Poleski, D. (2020), "Defining Leadership: Five Years After the Saving Sweet Briar Effort." *Sweet Briar College News*, March 3, https://sbc.edu/news/defining-leadership/.

Procter, R., Vis, F., and Voss, A. (2013), "Reading the Riots on Twitter: Methodological Innovation for the Analysis of Big Data." *International Journal of Social Research Methodology*, 16 (3): 197–214, https://doi.org/10.1080/13645579.2013.774172.

Putnam, R. D. (2000), *Bowling Alone: The Collapse and Revival of American Community*. New York: Simon & Schuster.

Rainie, L., and Wellman, B. (2012), *Networked: The New Social Operating System*. Cambridge: MIT Press.

Ratnam, G. (2019), "Mueller Report: Russia Hacked State Databases and Voting Machine Companies." *Roll Call*, April 22, https://rollcall.com/2019/04/22/mueller-report-russia-hacked-state-databases-and-voting-machine-companies/.

Reese, S. D. (2021), *The Crisis of the Institutional Press*. Cambridge: Polity.

Reinares, F. (2017), *Al-Qaeda's Revenge: The 2004 Madrid Train Bombings*. New York: Woodrow Wilson Center Press, Columbia University.

Reisdorf, B., Fernandez, L., Hampton, K. N., Shin, I., and Dutton, W. H. (2020), "Mobile Phones Will Not Eliminate Digital and Social Divides: How Variation in Internet Activities Mediates the Relationship Between Type of Internet Access and Local Social Capital in Detroit." *Social Science Computer Review*, March, https://doi.org/10.1177/0894439320909446.

Rhinegold, H. (1994), *The Virtual Community: Homesteading on the Electronic Frontier*. London: Secker & Warburg.

Rice, R. E., Shepherd, A., Dutton, W. H., and Katz, J. E. (2007), "Social Interaction and the Internet: A Comparative Analysis of Surveys in the US and Britain." In Joinson, A. N., McKenna, K. Y. A., Postmes, T., and Reips, U.-D. (eds.), *Oxford Handbook of Internet Psychology*. Oxford: Oxford University Press, 7–30.

Richardson, A. V. (2020), *Bearing Witness While Black: African Americans, Smartphones, & the New Protest #Journalism*. Oxford: Oxford University Press.

Richter, W. (2008), "Intellectual Property Law and the Performance of Distributed Problem-Solving Networks (DPSNs)." Working Paper, Oxford Internet Institute, Oxford University.

Richter, W. R., Bray, D. A., and Dutton, W. H. (2010), "Cultivating the Value of Networked Individuals." In Foster, J. (ed.), *Collaborative Information Behavior: User Engagement and Communication Sharing*. Hershey, PA: IGI Global, 1–15, https://www.igi-global.com/chapter/cultivating-value-networked-individuals/44478.

Rifkin, J. (2000), *The Age of Access: The New Culture of Hypercapitalism Where All of Life Is a Paid for Experience*. New York: Jeremy P. Tarcher/Putnam.

Robertson, A. (2021), "Reality Winner Has Been Released from Prison." *The Verge*, June 14, https://www.theverge.com/2021/6/14/22533366/reality-winner-prison-release-halfway-house-espionage-sentence.

Robertson, C., and Dutton, W. H. (2020), "The Fifth Estate Joins the Debate: The Political Roles of Live Commentary in the First Televised Presidential Debate of Hillary Clinton and Donald Trump." In Jones, J. M., and Trice, M. (eds), *Platforms, Protests, and the Challenge of Networked Democracy*. Basingstoke, UK: Palgrave Macmillan, 313–28.

Robertson, C. T., Dutton, W. H., Ackland, R., and Peng, T-Q. (2019), "The Democratic Role of Social Media in Political Debates: The Use of Twitter in the First Televised US Presidential Debate of 2016." *Journal of Information Technology & Politics*, https://doi.org/10.1080/19331681.2019.1590283.

Rogers, K. (2015), "U.S. and U.N. Respond to Killing of Lion in Zimbabwe." *New York Times*, July 31, p. A6.

Rogers, T. N. (2022), "Healing Remains Elusive Two Years After Floyd Murder." *Financial Times*, May 26, p. 4.

Rosenberg, M., Confessore, N., and Cadwalladr, C. (2018), "How Trump Consultants Exploited the Facebook Data of Millions." *New York Times*, March 20, https://www.nytimes.com/2018/03/17/us/politics/cambridge-analytica-trump-campaign.html/.

Runciman, D. (2018), *How Democracy Ends*. London: Profile Books.

Sackman, H., and Nie, N. (eds.) (1970), *The Information Utility and Social Choice*. Montvale, NJ: AFIPS Press.

Schattschneider, E. E. (1960), *The Semi-Sovereign People: A Realist's View of Democracy in America*. New York: Holt, Rinehart and Winston.

Schmidt, E., and Cohen, J. (2013), *The New Digital Age: Reshaping the Future of People, Nations and Business*. London: John Murray.

Schotz, M. (2018), "Cambridge Analytica Took 50M Facebook Users' Data—and Both Companies Owe Answers." *Wired*, May 17, https://www.wired.com/story/cambridge-analytica-50m-facebook-users-data/.

Schradie, J. (2011), "The Digital Production Gap." *Poetics*, 39: 145–68.

Schuler, D. (2001), "Cultivating Society's Civic Intelligence: Patterns for a New 'World Brain.'" *Information, Communication and Society*, 4 (2): 157–81. (An updated online version is titled "Towards Civic Intelligence: Building a New Socio-Technological Infrastructure.")

Seelye, K. Q. (2005), "Snared in the Web of a Wikipedia Liar." *New York Times*, December 4, https://archive.nytimes.com/www.nytimes.com/learning/teachers/featured_articles/20051205monday.html/.

Select Committee (2022), Select Committee to Investigate the January 6th Attack on the United States Capitol, "Introductory Material to the Final Report of the Select Committee." Washington D.C: U. S. Congress. https://int.nyt.com/data/documenttools/jan-6-committee-report-executive-summary/4d449a67cd79e131/full.pdf.

Shaker, Genevieve (2020), "At-Risk Colleges Should Do What's Best for Students, Alumnae, Donors, Employees—and Local Communities." *The Conversation*, February 4, https://theconversation.com/at-risk-colleges-should-do-whats-best-for-students-alumnae-donors-employees-and-local-communities-130276/.

Shandra, A., and Seely, R. (2019), "The Surkov Leaks: The Inner Workings of Russia's Hybrid War in Ukraine." RUSI Occasional Paper, July, Royal United Services Institute for Defense and Security Studies.

Shirk, S. L. (ed.) (2011), *Changing Media, Changing China*. Oxford: Oxford University Press.

Siddique, H. (2022), "War Crimes: Apps Captures 13,000 Pieces of Potential Evidence." *The Guardian*, July 26, p. 27.

Simons, B. (2004), "Electronic Voting Systems: The Good, the Bad, and the Stupid." *Queue*, October, https://dl.acm.org/doi/pdf/10.1145/1035594.1035606/.

Simons, B., and Jones, D. W. (2012), "Internet Voting in the U.S.." *Communications of the ACM*, 55 (10), October: 68–77.

Smith, D. (2021), "'I Should Have Revealed Truth of Vietnam War Sooner' Says Pentagon Papers Whistleblower." *The Observer*, June 13, 36–37.

Smith, G. (2019), "Reflections on the Theory and Practice of Democratic Innovations." In Elstub, S., and Escobar, O. (eds.), *Handbook of Democratic Innovation and Governance*. Cheltenham, UK: Edward Elgar, 572–81.

Snowden, E. (2019), *Permanent Record*. London: Macmillan.

Snowdon, P. (2020), *The People Are Not an Image: Vernacular Video After the Arab Spring*. Brooklyn, London, Paris: Verso Books.

Sormanen, N., and Dutton, W.H. (2015), "The Role of Social Media in Societal Change: Cases in Finland of Fifth Estate Activity on Facebook." *Social Media + Society*, July–December, pp. 1–16.

Stacey, K., and Bradshaw, T. (2021), "Testimony Deals Blow to Facebook." *Financial Times*, October 6, p. 10.

Stallman, R. M. (2015), *Free Software, Free Society: Selected Essays of Richard M. Stallman*. 3rd ed. Boston: Free Software Foundation.

Strossen, N. (2018), *Hate: Why We Should Resist It with Free Speech, Not Censorship*. Oxford: Oxford University Press.

Sunstein, C. R. (2004), *Infotopia: How Many Minds Produce Knowledge*. New York: Oxford University Press.

Sunstein, C. R. (2007), *Republic.com 2.0*. Princeton, NJ: Princeton University Press.

Sunstein, C. R. (2017), *#Republic: Divided Democracy in the Age of Social Media*. Princeton, NJ, Oxford: Princeton University Press.

Surowiecki, J. (2004), *The Wisdom of Crowds: Why the Many Are Smarter Than the Few and How Collective Wisdom Shapes Business, Economies, Societies and Nations*. New York: Doubleday.

Susca, M. (2017), "From the Pentagon Papers to Trump: How the Government Gained the Upper Hand against Leakers." *The Conversation*, June 15, https://theconversation.com/from-the-pentagon-papers-to-trump-how-the-government-gained-the-upper-hand-against-leakers-79159/.

Tambini, D. (2021), *Media Freedom*. Cambridge: Polity Press.

Tapscott, D., and Williams, A. D. (2006), *Wikinomics: How Mass Collaboration Changes Everything*. New York: Penguin.

Thompson, C. (2006), "Open-Source Spying." *New York Times Magazine*, December 3, http://www.nytimes.com/2006/12/03/magazine/03intelligence.html?pagewanted=print/.

Troianovski, A. (2022), "Russia Takes Censorship to New Extremes, Stifling War Coverage." *New York Times*, March 4, https://www.nytimes.com/2022/03/04/world/europe/russia-censorship-media-crackdown.html/.

Tsagarousianou, R., Tambini, D., and Bryan, C. (eds.) (1998), *Cyberdemocracy: Technology, Cities and Civic Networks*. London, New York: Routledge.

Tumber, H., and Waisbord, S. (eds.) (2021), *The Routledge Companion to Media Misinformation and Populism*. New York: Routledge.

Turculet, I. M., Achiricesei, R., and Mutu, M. (2017), "Meanings of the Expression Internet as Fifth Estate." *Logos Universality Mentality Education Novelty: Social Sciences*, 6 (1), 7–19, https://lumenpublishing.com/journals/index.php/lumenss/article/view/31.

Turk, V. (2019), *Digital Etiquette: The Future of Good Manners*. London: Ebury Press.

UN (2010), "United Nations E-Government Survey 2010." Department of Economic and Social Affairs, http://egovernments.wordpress.com/2010/04/15/united-nations-global-e-government-survey-2010/.

UN (2012,), "UN Report Exposes Mass Killings in Eastern DR Congo." Human Rights, Office of the High Commissioner, November 30, https://www.ohchr.org/en/stories/2012/11/un-report-exposes-mass-killings-eastern-dr-congo.

US Supreme Court (1887), *Western Union Tel. Co. v. Pendleton*, 122 US. 347, 7 S. Ct. 1126, 30 L.Ed. 1187, Legal Information Institute, Cornell University. https://www.law.cornell.edu/supremecourt/text/122/347/.

Van Dijk, J. (2019), *The Digital Divide*. Cambridge: Polity Press.

Verma, P. (2022), "The Online Guide Russians Use to Escape Putin's War." *Washington Post*, October 15, https://www.washingtonpost.com/technology/2022/10/15/russia-relocation-draft-guide/.

Voipicelli, G. (2019), "All That's Wrong with the UK's Crusade against Online Harms." *Wired*, April 9, Available at https://www.wired.co.uk/article/online-harms-white-paper-uk-analysis/.

Von Heppel, E. (2005), *Democratizing Innovation*. Cambridge, MA: Cambridge University Press.

Waters, R., and Murphy, H. (2021), "Who Is Facebook Whistleblower Frances Haugen?" *Financial Times*, October 9, p. 9.

Watt, L. (2014), "US Pollution Data on Beijing Blocked on Mobile App." APNews, Associated Press, November 11, https://apnews.com/article/68e3e918032042bc92e183f956b84582/.

Weaver, M. (2018), "Facebook Scandal." *The Guardian*, March 21, p.16, https://www.theguardian.com/education/cambridgeuniversity?/.

Webb, A. (2019), *The Big Nine*. New York: Public Affairs.

Weber, S. (2004), *The Success of Open Source*. Cambridge, MA: Harvard University Press.

Weinberg, A. M. (1981), "Can Technology Replace Social Engineering." In Teich, A. H. (ed.), *Technology and Man's Future*. 3rd ed. New York: St Martin's Press, 29–39.

Weizenbaum, J. (1976), *Computer Power and Human Reason: From Judgement to Calculation*. San Francisco: W. H. Freeman.

Wellman, B. (2001), "Physical Place and Cyberplace: The Rise of Personalized Networking." *International Journal of Urban and Regional Research*, 25 (2), June: 227–52.

White, E., and Germano, S. (2021), "Tennis Star Assault Claim Prompts West Rethink on China." *Financial Times*, November 25, p. 6.

Wilbanks, J., and Abelson, H. (2010), "Open Access Versus 'Open Viewing' for a Web of Science." In Dutton, W. H., and Jeffreys, P. (eds.), *World Wide Research: Reshaping the Sciences and Humanities*. Cambridge, MA: MIT Press, 322–24.

Williams, F. (1982), *The Communications Revolution*. Beverly Hills, CA: SAGE.

Williams, J. (2020), *Stand Out of Our Light: Freedom and Resistance in the Attention Economy*. Cambridge: Cambridge University Press.

World Internet Stats (WIS) (2021), "Usage and Population Statistics." https://internetworldstats.com/stats.htm/.

Wortham, J. (2011), "Google Praises Executive's Role in Egypt Revolt." *New York Times*, February 16, https://www.nytimes.com/2011/02/16/world/middleeast/16google.html/.

Wyatt, S., Thomas, G., and Terranova, T. (2002), "They Came, They Surfed, They Went Back to the Beach: Conceptualizing Use and Non-Use of the Internet." In Woolgar, S. (ed.), *Virtual Society? Technology, Cyberbole, Reality*. Oxford: Oxford University Press, 23–40.

Yeginsu, C., and Magra, I. (2017), "Chaotic Scramble as Fire Worries Force the Evacuation of 5 High Rises in London." *New York Times*, June 24, p. A8.

Yuan, Shawn. (2020), "Inside the Early Days of China's Coronavirus Coverup." *Wired*, May 1, https://www.wired.com/story/inside-the-early-days-of-chinas-coronavirus-coverup/.

Zegart, A. (2021), "Spies Like Us: The Promise and Peril of Crowdsourced Intelligence." *Foreign Affairs*, 100 (4), July/August: 168–73.

Zorina, A., and Dutton, W. H. (2014), "Building Broadband Infrastructure from the Grassroots: The Case of Home LANs in Belarus." *Journal of Community Informatics*, special issue on "The First Mile of Broadband Connectivity in Communities." 10 (2), http://ci-journal.net/index.php/ciej/article/view/949/.

Zuboff, S. (2019), *The Age of Surveillance Capitalism: The Fight for a Human Future at the New Frontier of Power*. London: Profile Books.

Zuckerman, E. (2017), "Mistrust, Efficacy and the New Civics." White Paper, Knight Foundation. Miami, Fl, https://dspace.mit.edu/handle/1721.1/110987?show=full.

Zuckerman, E. (2021), *Mistrust: Losing Faith in Institutions Provides the Tools to Transform Them*. New York: W. W. Norton.

Index

For the benefit of digital users, indexed terms that span two pages (e.g., 52–53) may, on occasion, appear on only one of those pages.

Tables, figures, and boxes are indicated by *t*, *f*, and *b* following the page number